Cloud
Enterprise
Architecture

Cloud
Enterprise
Architecture

Pethuru Raj

CRC Press
Taylor & Francis Group
Boca Raton   London   New York

CRC Press is an imprint of the
Taylor & Francis Group, an **Informa** business

AN AUERBACH BOOK

CRC Press
Taylor & Francis Group
6000 Broken Sound Parkway NW, Suite 300
Boca Raton, FL 33487-2742

© 2013 by Taylor & Francis Group, LLC
CRC Press is an imprint of Taylor & Francis Group, an Informa business

No claim to original U.S. Government works

Printed in the United States of America on acid-free paper
Version Date: 20120831

International Standard Book Number: 978-1-4665-0232-1 (Hardback)

Visit the Taylor & Francis Web site at
http://www.taylorandfrancis.com

and the CRC Press Web site at
http://www.crcpress.com

This book is dedicated to

my father, Chelliah (late) and my mother, Anna Marial

Contents

Foreword

Cloud computing is becoming a highly attractive paradigm, especially for business organizations, whether small, medium, or large. Reduction in capital and operating costs, agility of services development and deployment, as well as the ability of the cloud environment to allow scalability with respect to the highs and lows of demands of the enterprises' provisions are just some of the promises of this emerging trend. However, in order to achieve the benefits of cloud environments, organizations need to tread carefully and have the appropriate road map for migration to the cloud. Among other things, they need to have the enterprise applications developed in such a way that they are suitable for distributed environments as well as correct and appropriate data, information, and infrastructure architectures—collectively known as enterprise architecture (EA).

A well-established enterprise has a *strategic vision* that gives it future direction and provides guidance toward its *business strategy*. This, in turn, drives the *IT strategy* that helps to develop the EA. This presents an organizing principle that aligns the functional mission of the business with its IT strategy and execution plans. In this respect, there are a number of architectures that need to be taken into consideration, including *data and applications architectures, integration architecture, technology architecture,* and *management, security, and governance architectures*. All these need to be in place and correctly implemented.

The aim of this book on "Cloud Enterprise Architecture" is to develop a framework in terms of the aforementioned individual architectures and discuss these in detail in separate chapters. The objective is to align EA with the cloud technologies to provide a true value to the organizations' business strategy. The book presents some welcome "futuristic" ideas as well.

The book describes and presents suggestions as to how an EA can enable an enterprise to quickly adapt to the changing requirements as well as to address the new challenges. It talks about a number of well-accepted application-level architectures, such as those referred to as *service oriented, event driven, model driven, web oriented,* and so on. With respect to the data architectures, the book discusses topics such as parallel and distributed data crunching, as well as the issues of *big data*. IT infrastructures are discussed in detail with respect to partitioning, provisioning, deprovisioning, automation, and resource sharing. In a cloud environment, which is distributed, the IT infrastructure landscape is totally different and requires novel methodologies for networking and communication. There is a useful discussion about the integration technologies and methodologies in terms of connectivity (e.g., in case of *Cloud Bursting*), interoperability (which is an issue of concern), composition, collaboration, and brokerages. The book has three chapters on management, governance, and security, signifying the huge importance of these aspects in working with cloud environments. Reduced governance controls and security threats due to shared boundaries within the cloud environments (especially in the case of public clouds) are indeed some of the major issues for cloud consumers. This is in spite of the fact that cloud management solutions are being made available by reputable vendors and organizations such as NIST, CSA, and OASIS. These organizations are working toward developing open standards with respect to management, governance, networking, security, interoperability, and so on. The book discusses all the relevant core aspects in this context.

This book is a useful source of information for enterprise architects, managers, and directors of organizations, as well as students and researchers in the fields of cloud computing and EA. It provides a thorough and timely investigation of the convergence of cloud computing, on one hand, and enterprise data, applications, and infrastructure architectures, on the other. It is a welcome addition to the body of existing knowledge in these fields and emerging new technologies.

Zaigham Mahmood
University of Derby, UK

Dr. Zaigham Mahmood is a reader in applied computing and assistant head of Distributed and Intelligent Systems (DISYS) research group in the School of Computing and Mathematics, University of Derby, UK. He is also an Arcitura.com Certified Cloud Trainer. Dr. Mahmood has organized many conference tracks and workshops. He is an accomplished author with in excess of 75 presentations and articles. His latest book on *Cloud Computing for Enterprise Architectures* appeared in 2011. He is currently editing or authoring six books, including the two on *Cloud Computing: Concepts and Technology* and *Software Engineering frameworks for Cloud Computing Paradigm*.

Preface

The business landscape is in a continuously changing mode with a vast number of digitalization and globalization activities steadily springing forth and spreading. Information technology (IT) is being widely and wholeheartedly recognized as the greatest enabler of business. IT is penetrating deeper, and the dependence of business automation on IT is becoming stronger. There has to be a commendable coupling between business and IT. Markets are becoming extremely competitive and knowledge-driven; investors and executives demand more out of IT investments, and customers demand more pioneering and premium products from business organizations. The world economy is receding and is recessionary, and at best could achieve a rather muted recovery. Win–win partnerships are being established at a furious pace among enterprises to take on the brewing changes and challenges together, and smaller companies are consistently being usurped by larger conglomerates to gain more market and mind shares. Newer and nimbler avenues are being explored, experimented on, and expounded for fresh revenues.

IT budgets are silently being pruned, the innovation mindset is being insisted on among professionals to come out of the current constriction, and entrepreneurial spirits are being appreciated. Product vendors are releasing a plethora of path-breaking and people-centric solutions. Service organizations are proactively and preemptively conceiving and concretizing a battery of novel services to the market to sustain the edge earned. Acquisitions and mergers are being announced very frequently these days to retain the brand value gained. Factors such as productivity, flexibility, simplicity, adaptability, agility, openness, timeliness, and affordability are mandated these days on business operations, outlooks, and outputs. It is absolutely clear that business and IT ought to sail together to put up a unified face in order to decisively and distinctly take on the changing realities in the marketplace. The awareness, association, and alignment between business and IT are becoming stronger, deeper, and thicker.

In this very delicate and difficult scene, experts and evangelists insist on an integrated and insightful approach for tightly coupling business and IT. That is, business and IT alliance has become indispensable. Suppose a corporation wants to introduce a new product into its portfolio; there is, therefore, a need to define additional business processes, hire extra personnel, change the supporting applications, and augment the technical infrastructure to support the additional load. This new initiative could also lead to changes in the organizational structure. Fruitfully leveraging IT advancements to shape business automation, augmentation, and acceleration is a tedious and time-consuming task, and hence needs a lot of brainstorming, strategizing, and planning.

IT capabilities need to be weighed objectively, and the resulting knowledge has to be deposited safely for future access and articulation. Executives need to be in a position to quickly make informed and appropriate decisions. All these mandate that there has to be an integrated vision and mission in place to make business IT-aware and IT business-centric. Without such a synchronization mechanism in place, business may not profit from the series of innovations and improvisations happening in the hot IT domain and discipline. Business and IT strategies need to be intertwined in order to be relevant in the changing marketplace. This harmonization is able to pour out a stream of fresh possibilities and newer opportunities.

It is a widely recognized fact that enterprise architecture (EA) is the most efficient and effective way for perfectly attaining the business and IT alignment. EA has become the tool of choice for architects in order to establish the direct and decisive linkage between business and IT. EA is an enterprise-scale approach and instrument for accomplishing the beneficial integration between business and IT. Precisely speaking, EA is a coherent set of principles, methods, and models that is used in the design and realization of the enterprise's organizational structure, business processes, information systems, and infrastructures.

In recent years, a few business-driven technologies have emerged and evolved. Service oriented architecture (SOA) is the most notorious architectural pattern and is being projected as a promising and powerful design paradigm with a great potential for producing mission-critical, dynamic, adaptive, and enterprise-class applications. The much-published service thinking has the intrinsic capability of impacting the whole enterprise copiously. Not only service-based system engineering but also the goals of business integration, enterprise composition, and legacy modernization are being effortlessly fulfilled with the power of the service idea.

Another concept sweeping the entire IT industry is the cloud theme. While the service paradigm targets the arenas of software design and development, the much-debated, deliberated, and discoursed cloud idea assists exceedingly well in software deployment, delivery, and management. That is, the massive and mesmerizing adoption and adaptation of SOA and cloud computing greatly and gently could simplify and streamline the full-fledged and fail-safe implementation of the ideas and ideals of EA. In order words, SOA and cloud are the leading EA-enablement technologies. They are assisting and affecting the EA field immeasurably and incredibly. This book is all about articulating the distinctive, transformative, and augmentative capabilities of cloud computing on EA.

We write about the venerable mission of precisely and concisely presenting the impacts and implications of the evolving enigmatic cloud concepts on the EA. We have detailed the development of flexible and futuristic EA, how cloud meets, mingles with and molds EA, and how the convergence of cloud with EA is to bring bigger turnarounds and makeovers on small, medium, and large-scale enterprises. There are architectural frameworks such as TOGAF for facilitating the design of next-generation EA.

In this book, we have visualized all the noteworthy shifts due to the blending of cloud concepts with the traditional EA and written about the cloud-instigated enterprise integration, security, and management architectures. The first chapter is all about the salient and spectacular contributions of a number of powerful and potential technologies including the service and the cloud paradigms, for establishing smart enterprises. Leading IT players are extensively advertising and articulating smart enterprise technologies these days. Business intelligence, service orientation, mobility, machine-to-machine (M2M) integration, cloud, big data, and in-memory computing models are being prescribed as the fulfilling and failsafe mechanisms and methods for the forthcoming era of smart businesses.

The second and third chapters describe the transitions that the business and IT domains are going through with the stability and maturity of cloud concepts. The various limitations of IT and the glut of underutilized and unutilized IT infrastructures have laid the foundation for the breakthrough cloud idea, and this praiseworthy advancement in the IT field has resulted in a series of delectable and decisive ramifications on the business side. Several business models have been unearthed and published since then, and global enterprises (small, medium, and large) have instantly jumped on the cloud bandwagon in order to reap all the indicated and instinctive advantages of the cloud movement.

The fourth chapter describes what EA is, how EA enables enterprises to be adaptive to meet business changes and challenges, how EA guides the goal of attaining and retaining a tight alignment between business and IT, and so on. This chapter explains several promising and potential architectural frameworks, platforms, and tools for facilitating the design of EA in a systematic and simplified manner. With the seamless amalgamation of cloud concepts into an enterprise, the traditional EA is bound to be expansively modified to absorb and accommodate the cloud idea. We have named the resultant concept cloud enterprise architecture (CEA).

The fifth chapter is on cloud application architecture (CAA). Cloud business architecture (CBA) has to be taken toward its logical and physical conclusion using a suite of application, data, and technology architectures. In this chapter, we have talked about some of the prominent and dominant application-level architectures such as service-oriented architecture (SOA), event-driven architecture (EDA), model-driven architecture (MDA), service component architecture (SCA), mesh architecture, web-oriented architecture (WOA), and so on. There are processes, practices, patterns, products, and platforms for constructing service-oriented cloud applications (SOCAs) or cloud-based service applications (CBSAs).

In the sixth chapter, we describe cloud data architecture (CDA). Exquisite and elegant data models and schemas are very important for next-generation cloud enterprises. As clouds are being revitalized for accomplishing bigger and better things and requirements, such as for parallel and distributed data-crunching tasks to perform behavioral analytics, quick and cost-effective investigation of process and data-intensive applications, real-time business intelligence needs, and so on, the relevance of CDA is climbing sharply. Increasingly, nonrelational databases are built and posited in clouds to perform a plethora of emerging necessities. Clouds are being positioned for big data computing, which is being recognized as the futuristic computing model. New types of databases are emerging for cloud environments and cloud storage is a new shining domain. All of these clearly illustrate the power and value addition of CDA.

In the seventh chapter, we talk about cloud technology architecture (CTA). IT infrastructures are in transition phase. In fact, underutilized and unutilized computing machines are collected from different locations, consolidated and centralized in one place to provide optimal and managed resource provisioning, monitoring, and management services. IT infrastructures are steadily virtualized to be decomposed and composed as the situation warrants. Partitioning, provisioning, and deprovisioning are fully automated to enable resource sharing. With the addition of a series of novel mechanisms, resource availability is guaranteed in any circumstance. Elasticity is being ensured through the runtime creation of new cloud resources and once the job is over, all the resources can be put back. That is, runtime expansion and contraction is being realistically and readily provided to users. Self-service is one of the key differentiators of cloud infrastructures. A number of automated software solutions are introduced into any cloud environment in order to fulfill a number of manual operations that are becoming completely automated. Capacity planning is a vital research topic to achieve dynamic capacity planning. Load balancing, job scheduling, and so on are programmatically automated by competent software solutions. Cloud governance is another prospectus for cloud researchers.

In the eighth chapter, we discuss cloud integration architecture (CIA). As there are convincing reports from reputed and renowned market watchers and analysts on the huge market for cloud brokerages (CBs) with the increased migration, deployment, and delivery of services and applications by third-party clouds, the factors such as cloud connectivity, interoperability, integration, composition, and collaboration have gained immense traction. There is a range of broker software in order to establish linkage between different, distributed, and decentralized clouds (private, public, and hybrid). Cloud service aggregation, intermediation, arbitration, dissemination, mashups, and so on are some of the new-generation processes that ultimately lead to sophisticated and smart composite services, which in turn enable building and supplying cloud-based, people-centric services. Next-generation supply chain involves a kind of need-based integration of diverse and geographically distributed cloud services.

In the ninth chapter, we concentrate on the significance of cloud management architecture (CMA). With the unprecedented adoption of cloud computing, effective management, and governance of cloud resources (servers, virtual machines [VMs], applications, networks, services, and data) are paramount in order to readily get what was preached and pronounced earlier. Creation of new VMs and their optimized usage go a long way in realizing the stated business benefits out of the cloud idea. Every interaction happening in a cloud environment has to be closely monitored and acted upon. There are management platforms for cloud infrastructures emerging and evolving at a fast pace. Infrastructure software solutions providers, IT powerhouses, and behemoths are working overtime for producing standards-based cloud management software. Corporates and service organizations are buying, installing, and invoking an appropriate cloud management solution in their green and lean cloud centers to support and sustain business operations.

The tenth chapter is exclusively allocated to supply all the security information so that a well-intended security strategy is in place in order to ward off any kind of internal or external security threats, vulnerabilities, and risks. As widely reported, the security aspect is the main stumbling block for the glorified cloud movement. Providers and researchers are working in unison in order to arrive at and articulate wider kinds of security solutions (software as well as hardware). The cloud security architecture (CSA) leads to effective security strategy that in turn boosts the sliding and shrinking confidence of people.

The eleventh chapter explains the need for governance mechanisms for cloud environments wherein a variety of IT resources roam. We have supplied details regarding how policy comes handy in automatically enforcing only authorized interactions among cloud components.

The final chapter is about key onboarding services. This chapter explains all the mandatory requirements before adopting the cloud idea. The migration methodology is described in detail for the benefit of the reader. There is a set of best practices for arriving at a modernization and migration plan for any enterprise pondering the ways and means of switching over to the cloud infrastructures. There are innumerable legacy as well as modernized IT applications, platforms, and infrastructures. The main motto of this chapter lies in the pragmatic empowerment of them to be cloud-ready so that the target and task of cloud onboarding is smoothly nurtured and nourished.

Pethuru Raj, PhD
Enterprise Architecture (EA) Consultant
Wipro Consultation Services (WCS)
Wipro Technologies, Bangalore, India

Acknowledgments

First of all, I give all the glory and honor to our Lord and Savior Jesus Christ.

I express my sincere gratitude to John Wyzalek, Senior Acquisitions Editor, for immensely helping me from the conceptualization to the completion stage of this book. The publishing teams at CRC Press: Jennifer Stair, Project Editor and Full Service Coordinator and Leah Wohl-Pollack, Project Coordinator, diacriTech, USA, have been very prompt in this book project. Thanks a lot.

I need to remember my supervisors Prof. Ponnammal Natarajan, Anna University, Chennai, India; Prof. Priti Shankar (very recently passed away), CSA Department, Indian Institute of Science, Bangalore, India; Prof. Naohiro Ishii, Department of Intelligence and Computer Science, Nagoya Institute of Technology, Japan; and Prof. Kazuo Iwama, School of Informatics, Kyoto University, Japan, for shaping my research life. I express my sincere and heartfelt gratitude to Thomas Erl, the world's top-selling SOA author for granting me a number of memorable opportunities to write book chapters for his exemplary books.

From the bottom of my heart, I thank Yamini Ravishankar, MS student, Department of Electrical and Computer Engineering, George Mason University, Fairfax, Virginia, USA, for proofreading all the chapters very passionately. She came up with a number of valuable comments and corrections (syntax, structure, and semantics) for all the chapters.

I recognize the fruitful association with Prof. V. Vaidhyanathan, Prof. John Bosco Balaguru, Prof. Amirtharajan, and Prof. V. Venkatesh, the School of Computing, SASTRA University, Tamil Nadu, India, over the years. I also respect the close interactions with Prof. M. Nachamai, Prof. Ashok Immanuel, Prof. Sumitra Binu, and Prof. Peter Augustine, Department of Computer Science, Christ University, Bangalore, India.

I have to profoundly recognize Dr. Thandavan Settu (MD, Global Applied Materials, Ltd.) and his family for their unfailing love, affection, and care. I also extend my thanks to Daniel David, the Director, Celeste Engineering, Bangalore, India, for all the rewarding time spent together. I am extremely grateful to Mrs. Rani Robert from the United States for her weekly call, exhortations, and prayer. I recollect the unflinching support rendered by Dr. Mohanavadivu Periasamy, the CEO, Scientific Research Invision, Canada, and Dr. Devasia Kurian, the CEO, astTECS Solutions, Bangalore, India.

I would expressly like to thank my wife, Sweetlin Reena, and sons Darren Samuel and Darresh Bernie, for their perseverance as I have undertaken the tremendous and tedious challenge of putting this book together. I thank my brothers' and sisters' families for all their steadfast support extended to me during this long and arduous life journey. I thank Pastor George, Shalom Church, Naganathapura, Bangalore, for his earnest prayers.

I thank all the readers.

Author

Having obtained the competitive UGC research fellowship, I successfully obtained a PhD from Anna University, Chennai, India. Then, I obtained a CSIR fellowship to work as a postdoctoral researcher in the Department of Computer Science and Automation (CSA), Indian Institute of Science (IISc), Bangalore. Thereafter, I was granted a couple of international fellowships (JSPS and JST) to work as a research scientist for 3 years in two leading Japanese universities. I worked as a lead architect in the corporate research (CR) division of Robert Bosch, India, for 1.5 years.

I have gained more than 12 years of IT industry experience. Primarily, I have contributed as a technical architect for 8 years and as a software product architect for 4 years. Currently, I am working as an enterprise architecture (EA) consultant, focusing exclusively and extensively on EA-inspired business transformation capabilities. My ultimate aim here is to provide technology advisory services to worldwide organizations and business enterprises to enable a smooth transition to be smarter in their operations, offerings, and outputs, by articulating and empowering them to adopt, adapt, and apply proven, potential, and promising technologies, enabling and empowering architectural styles, infrastructure consolidation, and process optimization methods.

I have acquired good knowledge on some emerging technologies such as cloud computing, service-oriented architecture (SOA), event-driven architecture (EDA), and enterprise architecture (EA). Also, I have gleaned reusable knowledge in big data computing and Hadoop, real-time and real-world cloud analytics, machine-to-machine (M2M) integration/cyber physical systems (CPS), high-performance system design, and the development methods of smartphone applications. I have made use of the opportunities that came my way to focus on a few business domains, including telecommunication, retail, government, energy, and health care.

I have contributed book chapters for a number of technology books that were edited by internationally acclaimed professors and published by leading publishing houses.

CEA Book Audience and Key Takeaways

Enterprise architecture (EA) has been an important ingredient for any growing enterprise to support and sustain its ordained journey toward the envisioned target. EA's capabilities and contributions are paramount and pioneering for smoothening and streamlining the rough and tough route. EA brings out a holistic and shared view of the current business and IT landscapes. EA insightfully facilitates in unearthing the right and relevant nuances and niceties for effectively planning, controlling, strengthening, and innovating the business transition process and path toward its future and envisaged state. The other prominent advantage is to establish a tighter alignment and association between IT and business. That is, all kinds of business changes and challenges can be instantly and intelligently taken care of if the underlying IT resources, products, and processes are appropriately business aware and aligned. Precisely speaking, EA directly contributes to business agility, autonomy, and affordability. EA's success delightfully determines the success of a business.

Further, EA extracts and exposes business-critical and actionable information to business executives and visionaries to cognitively contemplate and justify tactical and strategic decisions. The decisions, being sound and sharp, enable and empower chief executives to plunge into the initiation and implementation mode straight away. The informed and timely analysis and actions will ultimately prove to be disruptive, inventive, and transformative for the whole enterprise to trek along to reach greater heights in less time. Further, EA participates in realizing an implementable road map for intelligently exploiting IT architectural building blocks, platforms, and infrastructures to achieve business augmentation and transformation with ease. There are several core and peripheral technologies emerging in order to realize the goals, methods, and processes of EA. Some have vanished with the speed they arrived and some are persisting with sheer power. Service orientation (SO) and cloud computing are the top two technologies showing immense potential and promise in tackling a variety of prickling and perpetual IT challenges. Also, these are very generic enterprise-scale technologies and hence are associated with EA. This extended technology ecosystem significantly elevates EA's role and responsibility in reaching the illuminated milestones of worldwide EA-adopted enterprises.

Cloud Computing—It is a well-received and recognized fact that the cloud paradigm has brought in a bevy of innovations for the IT discipline. The cloud technology, being a composite concept, has gained a lot of attention and drawn appreciable attraction from industry professionals and academicians these days. A number of pioneering and game-changing technologies (virtualization, consolidation, federation, service-oriented architecture [SOA], grid, utility, on-demand and autonomic computing models, dynamic resource provisioning, software as a service [SaaS], ambient communication, etc.) are intelligently combined, converged, and clustered together to lay the flexible and futuristic foundation for the forthcoming knowledge-driven and cloud-based service era. The much-discoursed and deliberated cloud technology has brought in a series of favorable and facilitating impacts on the enterprise IT.

Other prominent disciplines receiving effusive power and value from the pioneering and penetrating cloud idea are Web 2.0 (social computing) and Enterprise 2.0. Not only enterprises but also corporations, governments, and cities are keen to leverage the distinctive characteristics of the brewing cloud style to be highly automated, real time, and dynamic in their assignments. In a nutshell, the disruptive and transformative cloud paradigm promises sharp and significant increases in business dynamism, augmentation, and acceleration.

The Convergence of EA and Cloud Computing—In the past, we have moved from monolithic systems to multitiered architectures. As the service-orientation concepts become pervasive and popular, the enterprise IT is fully embracing them in order to be nimble and supple in their operations, offerings, and outlooks. Now, with the massive adoption of the path-breaking cloud idea, enterprises are steadily and smartly transforming themselves into on-demand, lean, instant-on, and adaptive organizations. The cloud, being an enterprise-class technology, can quite naturally merge and mingle with EA in preparing and providing advanced capabilities and capacities to global enterprises in precisely and perfectly anticipating volatile business needs and varying customer leanings. This acquired and extracted knowledge in turn leads to readying the underlying IT systems for proactively and preemptively conceiving, constructing, and delivering versatile and premium services. And this combination of EA and the cloud paradigm is definitely bound to result in a series of game-changing revolutions for enterprises. That is, the incredible cloud paradigm, in sync with EA, is collectively capable of producing remarkable results in taking business entities to the next level. It is overwhelmingly clear that with the right kind of cloud technologies, strategies, and methodologies, all kinds of nonfunctional (quality of service [QoS]) attributes can be effortlessly and speedily realized in cloud enterprises.

In this book, we discuss the great implications of the cloud paradigm on EA. We dig deeper to extract and elucidate the perceptible and positive changes that will affect EA design, governance, strategy, management, and sustenance. We envision and explain what kinds of desired transformations each of the architectural blocks of EA undergoes in the light of this strategically significant convergence.

The Audience—This is primarily for enterprise architects, cloud evangelists and enthusiasts, and cloud application and service architects. Further on, cloud center administrators, cloud business executives, managers, and analysts will find this book informative and inspiring while formulating appropriate mechanisms and schemes for sound modernization and migration of traditional applications to cloud infrastructures and platforms.

The EA tool vendors can benefit a lot from this book in identifying, understanding, and justifying the new cloud-induced features and functionalities to be attached in their products for the forthcoming cloud era. As there are several unique concerns and challenges (performance, scalability, dependability, availability, security, controllability, visibility, etc.) at the cusp of this distinct convergence, university students and scholars are set to gain a lot from this book.

The Key Takeaways—We give a modern overview of EA in the context of the surging popularity of cloud computing. We have reserved separate chapters for each of the contributing architectures (business, information, application, integration, security, and technology) of EA to vividly illustrate the current and impending implications of the cloud theme on each of them. We have included a full-fledged chapter on the enterprise cloud. In addition to these, the future is for federated clouds and the vision is to establish the intercloud. Considering these developments, we have incorporated a chapter on cloud integration and composition architecture. Also, a chapter on cloud security architecture has been added. A comprehensive strategy chapter is introduced for enterprise architects and business executives to ponder and plan for the cloud-inspired transformations.

1

Cloud-Enabled Smart Enterprises!

INTRODUCTION

Enterprises are steadily and strategically undergoing a number of note-worthy transformations due to constant and consistent shifts occurring in many of the business-related aspects. Enterprises are increasingly information technology (IT)-driven and solely and squarely depend on the IT improvisations and innovations to surge ahead in meeting the varying and vast needs of their customers, clients, and consumers. The association and alignment between business and IT is tending to be tighter. That means any shift in the IT domain and discipline has immediate and intrinsic impacts and bearings on business operations, outlooks, and offerings. Newer and nimbler technologies are emerging and evolving; business processes are being integrated and innovated; new products, platforms, patterns, practices, and procedures are being unearthed; and so on.

In the past, businesses were forced to leverage and manage with what-ever technologies were available at that point in time, but today the wide-spread scenario is quite contrary. That is, we come across a deluge of business-centric technologies these days. In other words, the gap between IT and business is being eliminated, and therefore IT is more tuned and turned toward business. Recent technologies are more business enabling and empowering. Any change or challenge within a business situation gets immediately noticed and attended to with the smart usage and leverage of these business-aware technologies.

Apart from these constructive and contributive technologies, flexible and futuristic architectures, epoch-making business models, facilitating frameworks, and proven methodologies are being frequently unfolded to prop up the envisaged business mission and subsequent strategy making, as well as their best-in-class realization. Business augmentation, acceleration, and

1

automation are being closely linked up with the simplicity, success, and sensitivity of information and communication technologies. Process engineering has become another active area of focus for IT professionals. Service orientation (SO) has become the most common architectural principle, paradigm, and pattern for designing and delivering enterprise-scale applications.

Composition is the most pragmatic and purposeful idea propelling the whole IT world today. Composites are emerging as the amenable, affable, and affordable building blocks for next-generation IT systems. Composite processes, interfaces, services, and applications are the ultimate result of the composition process. Composition containers, techniques, tools, languages, and standards are flourishing. IT infrastructures are going through a series of far-reaching transitions. We read and use the well-consolidated, centralized and converged, virtualized, automated, and sharable infrastructures very frequently. Standards-compliant and open platforms for application design, development, debugging, deployment, and delivery are hitting the market. Management and governance modules are increasingly produced and marketed in order to moderate the rising application complexity.

Multitenancy is a highly talked-about feature being inherently incorporated in IT servers, applications, platforms, databases, and services. Due to the extreme heterogeneity and multiplicity, the value and demand for multifaceted middleware backbones, containers, engines, hubs, buses, and fabrics is on the climb. That is, the reflective middleware is being made available for simplifying and streamlining the rough and tough integration, intermediation, aggregation, and arbitration requirements among application components in highly heterogeneous and complex IT environments. Other contributive components include software frameworks, design patterns and metrics, best practices based on experiences, and key guidelines out of expertise gained. These components individually as well as collectively are aiming to speed up and strengthen enterprise IT so that it can be furiously fast, supple, and sound in meeting next-generation business requirements.

THE BREWING IT TRENDS & TECHNOLOGIES

- **The Technology Space**—There is a cornucopia of disruptive, transformative, and innovative technologies (Computing, Connectivity, Miniaturization, Sensing, Actuation, Perception, Analyses, Knowledge Engineering, etc.).

- **The Process Space**—With new kinds of services, applications, data, infrastructures, and devices joining mainstream IT, fresh process consolidation, orchestration, governance, and management mechanisms are emerging. Process excellence is the ultimate aim.
- **Infrastructure Space**—Infrastructure consolidation, convergence, centralization, federation, and automation and sharing methods clearly indicate the infrastructure trends in computing and communication disciplines. Physical infrastructures become virtual infrastructures.
  - **System Infrastructure.**
  - **Application Infrastructure**—Integration Backbones, Broker Middleware.
- **Architecture Space**—Service-oriented architecture (SOA), event-driven architecture (EDA), model-driven architecture (MDA), and so on, are the leading architectural patterns.
- **The Device Space** is fast evolving (slim and sleek, handy and trendy, mobile, wearable, implantable, portable, etc.). Everyday machines are tied to one another as well as to the Web.

There are a number of spectacular shifts in the hot and happening IT space. Transformative, augmentative, and disruptive technologies are emerging and evolving steadily. In this section, we will discuss some of the pioneering and prominent technologies sweeping the IT discipline.

Miniaturization technologies are well received across the IT industry. Every hardware component is shrinking, whereas its power, usage, and value are on the climb. From the age-old mainframe era to today's personal and professional tablets, palmtops, and laptops, the aspect of miniaturization has been gaining a lot of traction and attraction. We read about invisible, disappearing, infinitesimal, and calm modules, tags, labels, stickers, chips, and pads collectively forming highly pervasive and persuasive computers, communicators, sensors, and actuators. Slim and sleek handy and trendy handhelds, wearables, implantables, portables, nomadic and wireless devices, industry machines, medical instruments, consumer electronics, web and information appliances, kitchen utensils, displays, gadgets, and gizmos are very dominant and prominent in our daily work and walk environments. Nanotechnology, system-on-a-chip (SoC), microelectromechanical systems (MEMS), and so on, are some of the eye-capturing and elegant miniaturization technologies.

Integration technologies are clearly occupying a top position. All kinds of siloed, legacy, closed, inflexible, and monolithic systems are accordingly modernized and made interoperable in order to create integrated IT environments. Business integration has been a challenging affair for IT service and solution providers due to the multiplicity of heterogeneity-induced complex systems. There are industry-strength and open standards being specified by agencies and consortiums. There are standards-compliant brokers, middleware, hubs (enterprise application integration [EAI]), fabrics, buses (enterprise service bus [ESB]), data services and composites, enterprise information integration (EII), and so on for simplifying and streamlining the diverse, distributed, and decentralized IT applications, services, and databases. Integration is the base for intermediation, aggregation, composition, collaboration, and so on among software components, networks, systems, and finally, environments.

Composition technologies are becoming popular due to the demand for creating business-aware and -aligned composites. In the recent past, mashups (business, information, and user interface) have been domineering. Orchestration and choreography are the popular mechanisms and schemes for ensuring real-world and real-time composites. In the sensor world, fusion is the buzzword; in short, composition technologies are penetrating into diverse fields. In a smart home environment, multiple sensors (heat, humidity, gas, fire, etc.) combine well to arrive at accurate and real-time information for remote, analytical, decision-enabling, and actuating IT systems to ponder about the next course of action in time.

Collaboration technologies are very popular with the heightened needs for several kinds of collaborative applications and services. Leading IT product vendors are showing extreme interest in producing and presenting a variety of collaboration suites for everyday use. E-mail, chat, and messaging are the well-known and ubiquitous types of collaboration software.

Recently, some of the underutilized technologies such as virtualization, federation, and automation have been gaining the upper hand in the IT space. In fact, the much-published Gartner report ranks virtualization as the leading technology. It is clear that virtual machines (VMs) have brought in drastic and desired changes on IT infrastructures. With the unprecedented usage of hypervisors, higher utilization, portability, interoperability, autonomy, and elasticity of IT infrastructural components are being easily ensured. Notably, there is a virtualization-sponsored segregation among software and hardware modules. That means any number and type of software could run on virtualized systems. Decomposition and composition are the main techniques empowering the value and power of virtualization. Considering the strategic significance, every kind of infrastructure is being meticulously virtualized in order to be shared across. There are hypervisors for large-scale systems and microvisors for resource-constrained devices. Creating and managing the scores of VMs out of physical servers is being simplified and presented as a viable and long-term solution for the ills confronting the expensive yet underutilized and unutilized IT infrastructures. In short, dependencies are being decimated toward a boundary-less information flow. Light coupling and decoupling are being insisted on for the future in order to bring in tightness between business and IT.

It is possible to run multiple applications sharing one physical machine or storage device to increase utilization rates, or to allocate multiple machines and storage devices to one application to increase its performance. In other words, the one-to-one dependencies between applications and their underlying platforms are removed. This hidden capability provides unprecedented flexibility in meeting service-level agreements (SLAs). IT optimization, resource utilization, and sharing are strongly growing with the materialization of virtualization and automated resource provisioning techniques. Other notable developments in the IT field include consolidation, centralization, and convergence. The combination and clustering of technologies scintillatingly induce newer and nimbler innovations and improvisations.

Connectivity technologies are the most pervasive and penetrating technologies these days. There are wireline as well as wireless communication technologies for networks of different sizes, scopes, and structures. There are generic as well as special-purpose networks such as body area networks (BANs), personal area networks (PANs), local area networks (LANs), metro area networks (MANs), and wide area networks (WANs). Worldwide consortiums and bodies are being formed to arrive at open and implementable communication standards that insist on specific protocols and technologies for certain scenes and situations. With embedded devices joining the mainstream IT space, there is a cornucopia of new communication protocols. The connectivity space is a very interesting and inspiring story for the globally as well as locally connected world. In the communication landscape, there are several buzzwords such as ambient, autonomic, and unified communication. The transition is from anywhere, anytime communication to everywhere, every-time communication. With the larger device space set to grow and glow exponentially, machine-to-machine (M2M) communication needs to thrive to facilitate the people-centric and premium services that must be delivered to the right users at the right time, in the right quantity, and at the right place.

Computing technologies are really inspirational and instrumental for the IT world. Leading IT players and pundits have brought out scores of computing paradigms with the ultimate objective of automating people's ubiquitous information and service access. Further on, with their maturity, financial transactions, commercial and business activities, and decision enablement are being greatly simplified and smoothened. That is, slowly yet steadily, personal as well as professional requirements, processes, and tasks are becoming fully automated with the embracement of computing technologies and infrastructures.

In the recent past, there has been a greater awareness and awakening on fulfilling the hard-to-crack nonfunctional requirements (quality of service [QoS] attributes) such as scalability, high performance and assurance, availability, security, dependability, affordability, amenability, consumability, and so on of the IT solutions, systems, networks, and environments. Since the beginning of the IT age, mainframe computers have been extremely powerful and capable of accomplishing billions of transactions per day without any slowdown and breakdown. Today's powerful and technologically advanced server machines cannot compete with the age-old mainframes in the QoS attributes. However, due to mainframes' rigidity and conservativeness, there came a host of delectable and dexterous transformations in the IT landscape.

Without an iota of doubt, the distributed computing model has definitely changed the structure and scope of enterprise IT. There is a myriad of flourishing distributed architectures and approaches such as the client-server and multitier methods. The indomitable web is the cool and catalytic paradigm fully subscribing to the distributed architecture. Through the redundancy of IT resources, high availability, accessibility, scalability, fault-tolerance, and other needs of IT applications are being realized quite easily and elegantly. Further on, peer-to-peer (P2P), cluster, and grid computing models could ensure high availability, performance, and scalability of various types of IT resources. Parallel, multicore, super, and petaflop computing models are fulfilling the high-throughput goals.

Mobile computing enables all kinds of wireless, nomadic, implantable portable, and mobile devices to achieve anywhere, anytime, computing. Besides, there are pervasive and ubiquitous computing concepts materializing for context-aware and cognition-enabled applications. Autonomic, on-demand, and utility computing styles are primarily to make computing a social utility. Real-time computing is for real-time applications.

For environmental sustainability, the idea of green computing is gaining widespread reception and recognition these days. Data centers and server farms comprising a deluge of varied and vast IT infrastructures and resources are drawing a huge amount of energy, which is unfortunately becoming scarce and expensive. The colossal IT centers are also dissipating a lot of heat into our living environment. Thus, it is absolutely clear that IT is one of the major culprits for environmental degradation. On the other hand, professionals and professors are overwhelmingly in unison on the overall view that IT-based technological advancements come in handy in effective energy preservation. That is, the emergence of IT-based energy harvesting and conservation technologies and methodologies is widely being given a warm welcome. For example, smart monitoring and metering of the electric grid and its subsystems (named as smart grid) is emerging as the frontrunner for energy efficiency in the energy-starved world. Thus, green computing is all about a bevy of computing techniques, tips, and tools for ensuring and enabling greener environments.

Biology-inspired computing models are fast emerging as a way out for solving computationally and intellectually challenging business, social, and scientific problems in our everyday lives. High-data and process-intensive applications are being tackled through a series of interdisciplinary efforts. DNA computing, quantum computing, optical computing, and so on are some of the maturing models creating waves and buzzes in the struggling IT industry.

Service computing is definitely a paradigm shift in the IT industry. Hordes of modernization, transformation, and optimization tasks are being readily achieved with the perfect and pragmatic usage of amazing service concepts. Every entity and element in IT is being expressed and exposed as a service. This clearly signals the vision of "IT as a Service" being established and sustained. In subsequent chapters, there will be detailed descriptions on this highly successful, sizzling, and succulent paradigm. This service enablement will ultimately land in the era of shared and virtual computing.

Smart computing is the latest in the annals of the expanding and enchanting computing world. Data-to-information transition is being sped up with a spate of path-breaking schemes and mechanisms. Subsequently, knowledge extraction and engineering disciplines are going through a slew of positive and progressive shifts with the rise of robust and resilient technologies in the fields of artificial intelligence, ambient intelligence (AmI), and swarm intelligence. There has been continuous empowerment of IT infrastructures, processes, and applications to be anticipative, adaptive, and articulate in their operations, offerings, and outlooks. The self-awareness and surroundings awareness go a long way in deriving and deploying next-generation IT solutions. The perfect and precise understanding of the changing needs of users enables advanced and adroit IT systems to be proactive, preemptive, and prompt to conceive and deliver multifaceted applications and services to users.

Situation awareness is zooming ahead with the voluminous production of miniaturized sensors and actuators. Mesh network technologies and topologies are substantially contributing to heterogeneous, wireless, and smart sensors to form ad hoc networks in order to gather, glean, and gain actionable and accurate insights about the users' movement, mood, and needs in a particular place. This extracted knowledge base enables cyber systems to fulfill both the mental as well as the physical needs in time with accuracy and alacrity. Thus, the noun "smartness" is pervasive, penetrative, and persuasive. Today, every tangible thing is being attached with this adjective "smart." For example, we come across advertisements such as smart hotel, home, hostel, hospital, and so on very frequently.

TREKKING TOWARD THE SMART WORLD

According to IT visionaries and luminaries, there will be a seamless and spontaneous merger of everyday technologies to create a kind of technology cluster and cloud to fulfill our personal as well as professional requirements insightfully, instantly, and instinctively. That is, there comes the possibility of merging our minds with machines. This shift is to enforce and empower a series of newer possibilities and opportunities. Learning will be an everywhere and all-time affair because we will have intimate and real-time access to the world's information assets and knowledge base using our accompanying electronic gizmos, and on the other side, we will also have an unfailing backup of our brains on massive-scale digital storages. Massive research endeavors and efforts are concertedly put into these seemingly magical and mesmerizing technology themes, which will let us beneficially connect our nervous systems to computers.

The next 20 years will see more influential innovations toward making our lives exciting, eerie, and exotic. Disruptive and transformative technologies with smart synchronization with a galaxy of precisely procuring, intelligently processing, perfectly perceiving, and instantaneously performing technologies will emerge to realize a wider variety of revolutionary and knowledge-driven applications and services that lead to making our daily environments insightful, interactive, and informative. Auto-identification tags digitally carrying our personal profile and preferences will map, mingle, mesh, and mash up with other contributing elements and entities in our personal as well as professional environments toward the realization of not only our information and transaction services but also our physical needs. The trickling trend is to enable seamless linkage between the physical and the cyber worlds. Sensors and actuators are the eyes and ears of next-generation IT.

Our daily articles, utensils, tools, and products can be transformed into smart objects and artifacts by attaching them with infinitesimal, invisible yet intelligent computers, communicators, codes, chips, controllers, sensors, tags, stickers, displays, and so on. That is, ordinary items become extraordinary. For example, our coffee cups, dinner plates, medicinal tablets, clothes, and other common, casual, and cheap things will be empowered to act smart in their interpretations and interactions with other entities in the vicinity, with remote IT systems, and with their owners. The overall process is highlighted here. First, all the tangible, worthy, and everyday things in our personal, professional, and social environments need to be quietly and quickly transitioned into sentient and digital artifacts. Secondly, they should be able to find and bind with one another seamlessly and spontaneously. In other words, the first is instrumentation and the second is service enablement. That is, every single entity becomes a service consuming, brokering, and/or providing element. The service enablement empowers them to talk through messaging. From there, the digitalized or smart objects and devices could compose and collaborate to be contributive and constructive for crafting sophisticated and situation-aware IT solutions. Service integration (direct or indirect) leads to adaptive and aware services. Outwardly, the service-exposing devices are strengthened to form resourceful and multipurpose device ensembles that are cognitive and context aware; ultimately, smart environments get formed and sustained.

This kind of fascinating, fabulous integration among all kinds of everyday things, such as implantable, mobile, wearable, handheld, portable, fixed and nomadic devices, kitchen vessels, medicine cabinets, manufacturing machines, vehicles on the move, robots, and consumer electronics at the ground level with local as well as distant IT applications (Web 1.0 [simple web], Web 2.0 [social web], Web 3.0 [semantic web], Web 4.0 [smart web], enterprise, and cloud-based software as a service [SaaS], etc.) will result in the Internet of Things (IoTs). Hence, there is no doubt that future generations will experience and realize complete and compact technology-sponsored and splurged living. The impacts and implications of information and communication technology (ICT) in our lives become bigger, deeper, brighter, yet calmer as days go by. The technology-inspired precision and perfection will be common, yet decisive and decision enabling. The disciplines such as

AmI, smart environments, ubiquitous computing, and cyber-physical systems (CPSs) are in one or another way related to the vision of IoT.

Today, everything is being given the adjective "smart." Leading IT players are brimming with confidence to make everything smart. Implementation technologies, methodologies, processes, infrastructures, middleware, best practices, key guidelines, evaluation metrics, and other enabling architectures, frameworks, utilities, widgets, and so on are being trimmed and tuned toward the goal of establishing the smart world. The stability, maturity, adaptability, affordability, and dependability of technologies are being critically reviewed and revisited through a host of transnational initiatives by IT professors, pundits, and professionals. Even enterprises are not left out, and there is a deluge of dissertations and deliberations on smart enterprises. In the ensuing sections, we will discuss the conspicuous contributions of cloud computing in designing, developing, and deploying smart enterprises.

REVISITING THE ENTERPRISE JOURNEY

Every enterprise is started with a clear-cut vision, realization strategy, implementation roadmap, constructive and contributive processes, people with sufficient education, experience and expertise, and so on. However, the ultimate success of all the endeavors and efforts solely and squarely depends on the underlying IT environment. In short, information technologies have a direct and distinct bearing on how enterprises are being run and managed in accordance with the varying expectations of their stakeholders. In the beginning, business was IT-driven, that is, businesses had been established and supported with the available technologies of those days. Therefore, the gap between IT realities and business sentiments was wider. However, today the scene is dramatically different. With the unearthing of business-aware and -aligned technologies, there is a closer and tighter alignment between business and IT. The distinct advantage due to this twist and turn is that any business change and challenge can be immediately taken care of in a positive manner by the enterprise IT. Precisely speaking, the strength and sustainability of technologies decides the success of enterprises.

Primarily, the nonfunctional attributes such as agility, sensitivity, responsiveness, autonomy, and adaptivity of enterprise computing are being strongly insisted upon by enterprise owners. Thus, the vision is to strategize, craft, and operate an optimal IT infrastructure that can support business agility, adaptivity, affordability, efficiency, and continuity. Visionaries and experts, through their illustrious and industrious experiences and expertise, have formulated the following traits and tenets for the next-generation IT ecosystem:

- Simplified, synchronized, and smart IT
- Sensitive, responsive, and real-time IT
- Converged, dynamic, on-demand, and autonomic IT

A few proprietary as well as standardized approaches to achieve the core objectives have been proposed by leading industry players as follows:

Dynamic Enterprises

Fujitsu's Triole (http://www.fujitsu.com/global/services/solutions/triole/index.html) is one such initiative for building and maintaining dynamic IT capability. Triole is a compelling architecture and product strategy to support and streamline complicated IT operations and management. It is a learned and refined process to create industrialized IT infrastructure. It is all about the optimal management of IT infrastructures and services through the two core technologies: virtualization and automation.

- Virtualization—As has been known for a long time, virtualization is all about flexibility. This is achieved by creating an additional layer for bringing in the desired flexibility among various IT resources in the stack. This new layer is for cleanly and clearly separating the prickling and perpetual concerns such as the inhibiting dependencies and deficiencies. In layman's terms, virtualization separates IT applications and data from their dedicated runtimes, which in turn leverage operating systems, processors, memory, and storage. The idea is to negate the traditional style of different applications running in different infrastructures. In other words, a single IT infrastructure can host, deliver, and manage a variety of diverse applications. Infrastructures are accordingly partitioned, provisioned, and even pooled to run different IT services and applications effectively. Virtualization enables IT infrastructures to adapt quickly to changing business requirements as software and hardware are elegantly segregated. Pooling encourages efficient utilization of resources; thereby, virtualization proves to be a highly impactful and insightful technology.

- Automation—Pundits and professionals encourage compact automation in place of manual operations as enunciated by IBM's autonomic computing concept. IT systems and platforms will be empowered to be autonomic in their diagnostics and decisions. This not only enhances the efficiency and affordability but also ensures continuity even in the midst of any unexpected outages and disasters.

Adaptive Enterprises

The white paper authored by Kerry Main, senior solutions architect, HP Canada, quotes the famous statement of Charles Darwin that "it is not the strongest of the species that survives nor the most intelligent, but the most responsive to change."

In an adaptive enterprise, business and IT are synchronized well to capitalize on all kinds of changes (business and technology). IT breaks away from the inflexible, closed, and silo-like systems of the past to create open and forward-looking systems that deliver more value and vigor to the business. The major gains being achieved by an adaptive enterprise include adding partners to supply chain system in hours rather than weeks or months, doubling the pace of product introduction without sacrificing the quality attributes, shifting IT investment from infrastructure maintenance to core competencies, and so on. The inherent capabilities of an adaptive enterprise include heightened business availability and continuity, enhanced IT consolidation and simplified services management, dynamic collaboration to maximize productivity through sharing and optimal utilization of IT resources, and so on.

According to SAP reports, this vision stands on business model innovations that can be pursued along three dimensions: customer-centric innovation, supply-chain-centric innovation, and organizational process innovation. It is argued that there is unmatched growth power based on business model innovation. It is difficult for competitors to reproduce the business model innovation. New business models are much harder for other companies and corporations to imitate since they are dependent on organization-specific competencies. The key gains include the facilitation of changes while retaining the successful business models, empowerment of people toward new realities, establishment of collaboration among all the constituents and participants, inspiration for cross-functional thinking in order to spur innovation, focused indulgence on process innovation, exploration and experimentation of newer avenues for fresh revenues, and so on.

On-Demand Enterprises

Businesses are bracing themselves for the on-demand era by improving efficiency and cutting costs, understanding and serving customers better, reducing risks, and improving agility in the marketplace through accelerating process integration and transformation. In the era of e-business on-demand, the ways in which technology changes business and business changes technology will continue to evolve. The technology environment needed to achieve on-demand business has to be integrated, open, virtualized, and automatic. Service-oriented architecture (SOA) is being touted as the best course of action as far as achieving on-demand business is concerned.

Globally Integrated Enterprises

With the copious advancements in globalization, connectivity, the Internet, distribution and service computing technologies, the time for globally integrated enterprises (GIEs) has arrived. The brewing business and IT trends are the key motivators for GIEs. Globalized supply chain, production optimization, and demands have blossomed and inspired the emergence of GIEs. GIEs are fast evolving as companies and corporations are consolidating their global processes and operating as a single and global-scale business entity to continue to grow and to reach more with rich services and solutions. Organizations have to evolve consistently by utilizing advanced technologies and proven methodologies to succeed in the years ahead. The benefits of this spreading include improved business management, greater visibility into processes, and standardized master data, as well as increased customer loyalty, real-time information for improved decision making, lower IT support costs, and so on.

A GIE fashions its strategy, management, and operations in pursuit of the worldwide integration of production and value. A GIE seeks to use the best resources from the best locations at the optimum time to gain a competitive advantage. Rather than leveraging only local resources and partners, GIEs position themselves to take advantage of resources and partners around the world. They thrive in a global economy by

- Securing specialized skills from a broad network of providers
- Leveraging infrastructures, applications, personnel, and other assets wherever they reside globally for the best, most economical results
- Enabling systems and platforms for an open, collaborative work environment and embracing opportunities for external collaboration

- Adopting the global values, skills, and processes needed to operate seamlessly across organizational, cultural, and geographic boundaries
- Managing the risks associated with doing business in an open ecosystem

Liquid Enterprises

BEA Systems Ltd., which was acquired by Oracle, introduced a new computing paradigm, "liquid computing," which builds upon SOA with the objective of aligning enterprise interactions with real-time business goals to help companies become service-driven enterprises, ultimately achieving enterprise compatibility, active adaptability, and breakthrough productivity. Today's enterprises are constrained by multiple application and data silos resulting in integration problems. Current integration approaches also lead to explosive costs and rigid infrastructures. As a way of alleviating these recurring issues, BEA had postulated this vision and had built a next-generation integration platform that promises to help enterprises to efficiently build, deploy, integrate, and manage applications and services. With BEA's takeover by Oracle, there is very little information available about the state of liquid computing concepts.

Proactive Enterprises

It is a well-known fact that IT is the real enabler of businesses. IT has become part and parcel of every enterprising initiative and implementation. The inventory of IT-supported business services and solutions is seeing rapid growth. Distribution has become the popular trend these days across the continents. Distributed services, applications, data, infrastructures, and workforce are set to grow noticeably in the years to come; hence, the challenges of provisioning and managing them become grimmer. M2M communication is going to replace user-to-machine interactions and transactions. Business processes are going through a number of path-breaking transformations. Process-based inter- and intraenterprise integration scenarios have taken solid ground. Communication-enabled business processes (CEBPs) are seeing a neat and nice reality. Analytics-attached business processes are another strategic trend. For enhanced agility and productivity, a robust, flexible information and communication infrastructure is the need of the hour.

The challenges for today's chief information officers (CIOs) are to manage the total cost of ownership (TCO), reduce operating costs, promote innovation through stable introduction of new services, and grow infrastructure in a timely fashion to remain competitive with the industry. Similarly, the aim is to shift the current IT system architectures and usage models from their current, mostly reactive and human-centered state toward one that is more proactive, integrated, and human supervised.

Connected Enterprises

Fresh network topologies and technologies are coming out of research labs and centers of excellence (COEs) frequently these days. Communication technologies, infrastructures and services besides standards-compliant and open connectivity solutions are being manufactured to make communication and collaboration pervasive. Communication is becoming ambient, autonomic, and unified. Enterprise Internet Protocol (IP) telephony and unified communication technologies have become popular. Multiservice networks combining enterprise voice, video, and data over a single IP-based infrastructure open up boundless possibilities to streamline enterprise communication processes.

IP telephony forms a unified communication network, and manages a set of available phone numbers, a set of specific services, and the availability of IP telephony service for users regardless of their current location (this goes beyond just a main office and may be at a corporate branch, at someone's home, or even when someone is on a trip). Corporate or regional branches are naturally integrated into an IP telephony network as soon as such a branch gets connected to a corporate IP network. Unified communications are a set of applications at the junction between the world of computers and the world of phones. The main purpose of unified communications is to speed up and functionally enrich interaction among company employees, the company, and its clients. The technological backbone of unified communications is IP telephony.

In summary, information technologies and infrastructures are the key for envisioning and enabling new capabilities and competencies to enterprise IT that in turn help in pondering about, prescribing, and promoting novel enterprise types to keep customers, consumers, and clients happy. All the leading technology creators and infrastructure providers have come out with new adjectives such as real time, connected, optimal, lean, extended, adaptive, proactive, on-demand, integrated, and so on through their historic and practical experiences and expertise for building responsive, resilient, and real-time IT infrastructures and enterprises.

SERVICE-ORIENTED ENTERPRISES

It is clear that the service paradigm has brought in scores of tectonic and trend-setting shifts in enterprise IT [1,3–5,9]. Predominantly, all the futuristic enterprises and their IT infrastructures are service driven and therefore self-driven. The prominent forces to be considered very deeply and diligently for the next-generation enterprises are

- Service-centric processes
- Service-enabled infrastructures and platforms
- Service-oriented practices and patterns

Service Thinking for Next-Generation Enterprises

For an illustrating and inspiring scene, we use an application from the car brokerage domain. We could quickly categorize the service-oriented enterprise (SOE) into two layers: service and business. The service layer consists of actual services, and the business layer represents the SOE business process.

Let us assume that an entrepreneur establishes a car agency, Enterprise Car (EC) (Figure 1.1). The business goal of this SOE is to provide a car brokerage package for perspective customers including searching cars,

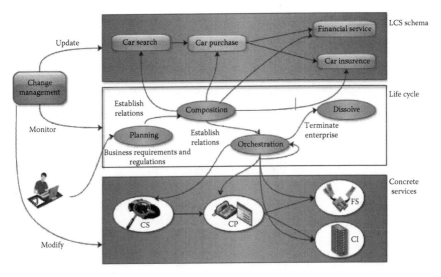

FIGURE 1.1
A car brokerage enterprise scenario.

purchasing cars, and applying for loans. During the planning phase, the following virtual services are identified: car search (CS), car purchase (CP), financial service (FS), and car insurance (CI). Second, the entrepreneur develops a specification for EC listing the services it will compose. The third step is the orchestration of EC, where it selects and invokes the member services that match the virtual service description. We assume the CS, CP, FS, and CI services are selected and orchestrated. Finally, EC may disband and gracefully terminate all partnerships, or wait for another orchestration request. This is the ideal sequence of events in EC's lifecycle. Thus, a service-centric business is flexible enough to accommodate business, market, process, and technology changes.

The Service Paradigm

The disruptive, transformative, and augmentative service idea is undergoing overwhelming and overriding adoption and adaptation across the globe. The service discipline has laid a sound and sustainable foundation for not only the enterprise IT but also for the embedded and cloud IT to grow and glow. Within a short span of time, there has been a widespread awareness and awakening among professionals about a stream of new opportunities and innumerable possibilities for individuals, innovators, and institutions to explore, experiment, and espouse new avenues for fresh revenues. SaaS is a direct derivative of the SO concept. Service enablement has become the sudden buzzword across the IT circle. Applications are being service enabled, whereas IT infrastructures, platforms, and middleware are being refactored and readied for the impending service era.

With the unprecedented maturity in the SO concepts, novel business, pricing, delivery, and consumption models are being widely conceived, concretized, and articulated. Services have implicitly and intently become the most sought-after abstraction unit for legacy modernization, software engineering, business integration, and service composition. These are all contributing immensely for establishing and sustaining service-centric organizations.

Service engineering is gaining steam and being supported by a variety of competent technologies, techniques, tips, and toolsets. A bevy of service and data middleware are hitting the market for forwarding service messages across the diverse, distributed, and decentralized application components. The hitherto unsuccessful goals such as application interoperability, service reusability, and composability are seeing the light at the end of the long tunnel. Versatile methods and mechanisms are being produced and prescribed for the simpler and spectacular service enablement of legacy as well as modern applications. Diverse business domains are very enthusiastic and optimistic about the grand success through service embracement. All these clearly indicate the emergence and sustenance of IT-sponsored on-demand, adaptive, real-time, and people-centric enterprises.

Service-Oriented Architecture

SOA is being portrayed as the resilient and rewarding architectural pattern, principle, and paradigm for enterprise IT. It is the mesmerizing buzzword in the IT industry and academic circles today. There is a palpable sense of anticipation and articulation about its potential and promise as SOA is consciously and consistently being unfolded and utilized by business behemoths as well as IT powerhouses. It is a hugely debated, discoursed, and deliberated, extensively written about, and widely presented design technique in worldwide forums. While white papers and weblogs on SOA are ceaselessly accumulating in the private and the public web, vendors of SOA infrastructures are merrily announcing the availability of a number of versatile platforms and products for enabling SOA design, development, debugging, deployment, and delivery. Researchers are painstakingly coming out with a growing array of best practices, patterns (design, modernization, integration, and composition), key guidelines, prototypes, proof of concepts, evaluation and measurement criteria and metrics, and so on.

SOA is proclaimed as the infallible and inspiring paradigm for enterprise modernization, integration, and composition. As far as legacy systems are concerned, it is the most practical renovation and rejuvenation mechanism. It is the first and true business-driven technology and is being projected as the foremost in comprehensively eliminating the widening gap between business realities and technological evolutions. It also brings relevant innovations to the domain of business processes, which are, of course, the central nervous system for any growing enterprise.

SOA promises a set of unique advantages and fresh ideas such as business agility and adaptivity, customer delight, productivity improvisations, new business and delivery models, real-time sense and respond (S & R), dynamic and real-time collaboration, complexity mitigation and moderation, and so on. In short, SOA is for business transformation, augmentation, and optimization. It is bound to play a very critical and crucial role in realizing a wider spectrum of next-generation, service- and people-centric businesses.

SOA is the first business technology that has the relevant wherewithal to bring the desired and demanded alignment between business and IT. This closer and tighter association between them leads to the easier realization of goals of present-day as well as future enterprises. Business agility, alacrity, availability, affordability, amenability, adaptivity, and so on can see the light with the smart and stringent adoption of SOA principles, practices, processes, platforms, and patterns. SOA brings a sort of semblance and orderliness for the prevailing business chaos. The much-proclaimed and -published service thinking facilitates a good grip on the business environment, and its journey, mission, and goals. Intra- and interenterprise integration, business-to-business (B2B) collaboration, and multienterprise processes will become smooth and gear up for high productivity.

Enterprise-Scale Architectural Approaches

On the other side, model-driven architecture (MDA) has emerged as the most crucial and critical nonlinear approach, which is distinctly varied from the age-old and conventional development paradigm. MDA is not only used for speeding up the developmental tasks but also for other essential functionalities such as application integration and modernization. Besides guaranteeing application productivity, portability, and openness, MDA enables a compact automation at higher layers of a typical enterprise software stack.

In a similar way, there are other significant architectural styles such as service component architecture (SCA), event-driven architecture (EDA), web-oriented architecture (WOA), resource-oriented architecture (ROA), composite-oriented architecture (COA), and so on. The real beauty is that SOA is such a generic approach that seamlessly and spontaneously interacts with these architectures in order to arrive at competent enterprise systems. SOA is capable of leveraging this brewing and bewildering synergy to help business giants maximize the competitiveness, productivity, agility, and adaptivity in their deliveries and interactions with their venerable suppliers, retailers, employees, customers, and other stakeholders.

Elucidating SOEs

Newer and nimbler business-centric technologies, business models, and enabling methodologies are being unearthed to prop up business goals and their realization [2]. Business augmentation and automation are being closely linked up with the simplicity, sensitivity, and sustainability of a stream of information technologies. Process engineering is another active and well-articulated field in the sense that composite, yet lean and flexible processes could see the light. And with the arrival of path-breaking and self-evolvable technologies and the maturity of existing technologies, there is a noteworthy and praiseworthy turnaround. That is, hordes of converged, virtualized, automated, and energy-efficient cloud infrastructures are fast emerging. Robust, reflective, and resilient platforms for development, mashup, execution, delivery, governance, and management purposes are being produced by leading software vendors. Especially with the disruptive and interruptive cloud paradigm undergoing overwhelming adoption, there have arisen a number of distinctive characteristics gaining widespread interest and imagination. For example, multitenancy is a highly talked-about attribute of present-day ICT platforms and products. Due to the extreme heterogeneity and multiplicity, the need for introspective middleware backbones is on the climb. Other contributive components include standards-based frameworks, design patterns and metrics, best practices based on experiences, and key guidelines based on the expertise gleaned and gained. These collaboratively speed up and streamline enterprise building, dynamism, openness, management, and sustenance.

With the unprecedented maturity in SO concepts, there is a renewed interest and inspiration in unfolding novel business, pricing, delivery, and consumption models. Services have implicitly and intently become the most sought-after abstraction unit and building block for efficient enterprise modernization, engineering, integration, and composition. Service engineering is growing fast and being supported by a variety of technologies, techniques, tips, and toolsets. In Chapter 5, we will dig down and dive deeper in order to extract and explain the key aspects of service orientation, service-oriented IT infrastructures, service-centric processes, the much-discussed closeness and coherence between services and processes, and how these sparkling advancements together extensively contribute toward the vision of engineering and establishing cloud-driven, process-centric, service-oriented, and smart enterprises.

CLOUD ENTERPRISES

As the cloud theme has brought in scores of enlightenment and empowerment to IT infrastructures, the enterprise IT is steadily moving toward the cloud IT by incorporating all the cloud concepts. Having understood the significance of cloud embarkation, enterprises are busy in cloud assessment, enablement, and on-boarding activities. We have extensively written about the reverberations of the cloud idea on business as well as the IT field in Chapters 2 and 3. Those who are new to cloud computing should read through Chapters 2 through 4.

As a widely discoursed, dissected, and deliberated concept across the world, cloud computing has brought in innumerable tectonic and trend-setting shifts for both IT as well as business. Though it is an evolutionary idea, it becomes extremely popular, penetrative, and pervasive because it implicitly represents a seamless cluster and the convergence of a dazzling array of proven, potential, and promising enterprise technologies. The implications of the much-hyped and -hoped cloud computing are majorly in two domains: business and IT.

On the business front, the cloud idea has enabled businesses to explore, experiment, and espouse fresh avenues for more revenues. That is, a cornucopia of newer and nimbler application deployment, delivery, usage, pricing, integration, collaboration, and management models have emerged nowadays, and they are doing exceedingly well with the faster stability of the cloud concepts and infrastructures. The traditional on-premise engagement model has been replaced and substituted with a delivery model that is efficient, centralized, monitored, managed, and maintained; innovation breeding; on-demand and off-premise; and affordable. That is, cloud-hosted and cared for applications and services are fast gaining the unshakeable confidence of corporations, governments, and organizations across the planet.

On the other hand, for IT, the irresistible cloud paradigm has ushered in a stream of spectacular and sparkling advancements and accomplishments especially in the discipline of IT infrastructures. That is, IT infrastructures have become a dynamic pool of consolidated, centralized, virtualized, automated, and shared entities. With these momentous transitions, IT infrastructures are becoming converged, optimized, dynamic, real time, on-demand, and autonomic. In other words, infrastructures are increasingly and incredibly service enabled, sharable, scalable, and sustainable and thus highly elastic, available, lean, and utilizable for ensuring business agility, autonomy, affordability, and continuity.

The cloud paradigm has greatly and graciously impacted every worthwhile enterprise these days. Enterprises are fast strategizing to absorb all the augmentative and transformative traits and tenets of the fast percolating and progressing cloud idea. The closer and tighter alignment and association between business and IT is becoming substantial and strong with the elegant embracement of cloud principles. The epoch-making business models initiated and ingrained with the smart leverage of cloud mechanisms have already started to bear fruits for companies. And the seismic shift from stagnant, inefficient, rigid, redundant, and silo-like infrastructures to business-aware, lean, self-provisioning, flexible, sharable, and virtual IT resources is bound to tactically as well as strategically empower enterprises to be people centric, instant-on, nimble, resilient, and versatile. In short, clinging to and capitalizing the cloud-induced transformational features, functionalities, and facilities takes any enterprising individual, innovator, and institution to greater heights in their outlooks and outcomes. Cloud enterprises are those that fully and firmly ingrain the pioneering principles, practices, procedures, and patterns of the cloud paradigm in order to be distinctively and decisively ahead of their competitors.

A raft of new cloud types (generic as well as specific) have originated and are doing well. We explain the potential and promising clouds in the following sections.

The Onset of Connected Clouds

It is absolutely clear that newer business and technical cases are fast emerging for manipulating and managing hybrid clouds appropriately. Significantly and strategically, clouds are becoming connected to reach greater and grander targets. There are grand initiatives by academics and corporations for achieving their unique needs leveraging the brewing ideas of the open cloud, intercloud, delta cloud, and so on. Ultimately, everything converges towards the roaring goal of the connected cloud. Standards-compliant and flexible connectivity solutions, orchestration patterns, and products are emerging; integration standards are being revisited and revitalized by consortiums for the impending cloud era; and so on. Service orchestration and choreography specifications are being refactored and refined toward programmatically composing services that are located in geographically distributed clouds. Crafting multifaceted (multidevice, multimedia, multimodal, and multichannel) data and service mashups out of remote and resilient cloud applications is gaining greater momentum these days with the unprecedented stability and scalability of clouds, which are touted and termed as dynamic, converged, on-demand, and autonomic deployment and delivery infrastructures for service-centric applications. In short, the much-published cloud horizon and ecosystem is on a growth trajectory. It is not an exaggeration to say that the future belongs to classic, catalytic, and connected clouds.

Autonomic Clouds

This is the probable output of the seamless convergence of autonomic and cloud computing models. As we all know, autonomic computing represents a paradigm shift. It is all about deeper empowerment and automation through embedding and embodying of right and relevant knowledge and wisdom into IT services, solutions, and systems to be self-monitoring, self-diagnosing, self-configuring, self-healing, self-defending, self-managing, self-organizing, self-optimizing, and so on. The instinctive and distinctive properties of biological systems are smartly being assimilated into IT systems so they are adaptive in their outlooks, offerings, and outputs. Next-generation IT products, platforms, and infrastructures are bound to be autonomous, self-describing, self-serving, and smart. Knowledge engineering, policy-based interaction, instantaneous transaction and behavioral analyses, event processing, semantics, real-time actuation, and so on are the major necessities for producing and shepherding autonomic systems.

With clouds being positioned as the futuristic and flexible IT infrastructure across the world, there will be revolutionary opportunities and fresh possibilities if these two computing styles (autonomic and cloud) combine well. A number of use cases are being prescribed and propagated for such a unique coexistence and coordination. Ad hoc, interoperable, and dynamic cloud environments can be quickly established for supporting emergency needs in war-ravaged, disaster-struck, and medical exigencies. Sensors, robots, and devices integrated with IT applications, and self-scaling clouds go a long way in accomplishing a bevy of people-centric and physical services.

Automation is highly prevalent in any cloud environment today. Resource and service provisioning and deprovisioning, workload and resource management, job scheduling, and so on are already automated in clouds.

However, with the synchronization of pioneering autonomic computing concepts, the power and productivity of clouds are bound to go up by several notches. That is, cloud administration and management becomes simpler. Self-service will be common and casual. Clouds could be dynamically configurable. That is, configuration should be completely automatable in any changing and unpredictable situations. Clouds could sharply enhance their performance and throughput in case of any emergencies. Clouds could come back to life quickly in case of any failure or malfunction. A hitch in a component should not spread to other components, and thereby any kind of slowdown or shutdown is fully avoided. Recoverability, continuity, reconfigurability, restorability, availability, and adaptivity are guaranteed with the maturity and stability of autonomic clouds. Security, sustainability, adjustability, and other QoS attributes are also ensured.

Federated Clouds

A federation is simply a union of its member entities. The members, while sharing their unique capabilities with one another, maintain their individuality and integrity. In other words, the members get the benefits accrued out of the union while retaining the unassailable control over their internal affairs. In the case of technology infrastructure federation, the key benefits of the union are the lower cost and the lesser risks associated with a pool of technology assets, which are available across a diversified set of independent networks. In the world of financial asset management, asset diversification is a common thing for mitigating and managing risks. In the case of application assets, a lower risk profile for any application could be achieved through the federation approach. By diversifying the production applications and data across multiple networks, the owner of the applications and data could significantly reduce the localized network performance problems that could lead to an unacceptable customer service. This is the very essence of good discovery practices. Yet with federation in place, disaster recovery can be smoothly accomplished with a fraction of the cost of a wholly owned disaster recovery mechanism.

Cloud service providers (CSPs) are instituting cloud centers in geographically distributed places across the continents to capture the ever-increasing cloud market. Business and IT services and applications are progressively finding their compact and cost-effective residence in local and remote clouds. Reusable and composable cloud services are being stocked in abundance for rapidly assembling people- and business-aligned services. That is, composite services are being programmatically crafted and served from competent cloud environments to worldwide subscribers. Today, there are many different CSPs available from industry icons Amazon, Google, Microsoft, and so on. However, these clouds vary hugely in a number of aspects such as technologies and platforms, and do not support the required mechanisms and policies for dynamically coordinating load distribution among different cloud centers in order to determine optimal location for hosting application services to achieve reasonable QoS levels.

Further, the cloud providers are unable to predict geographic distribution of users consuming their services; hence, the load coordination must happen automatically and distribution of services must change in response to changes in the load. In short, the lack of compatibility and interoperability among diverse cloud providers prevents providers and consumers from getting all the originally envisaged benefits of the cloud computing. There is a greater possibility of vendor lock-in issue creeping into the cloud domain. Collaboration is very limited in the cloud space today. As the business environment is predictably unpredictable, cloud resources and infrastructures need to be very open and trustworthy to mingle and mashup to ensure business agility and resiliency.

Importantly, clouds are greatly positioned as the new-generation infrastructure capable of elastically delivering extra capacity. That is, cloud resources can be automatically increased or decreased in order to cost-effectively fulfill agreed SLAs. Clouds could achieve more by subcontracting additional resources from collaborating clouds. This sort of interconnectivity for making use of internal as well as external cloud resources in times of specific need is the foundation for federated clouds.

In summary, cloud federation is quite a new concept of service aggregation characterized by interoperability features, which addresses the economic problems of vendor lock-in. Furthermore, it approaches challenges like performance and disaster recovery through methods such as co-location and geographic distribution. The concept of cloud federation enables further reduction of costs due to partial outsourcing to more cost-efficient regions, may satisfy security requirements through techniques like fragmentation, and provides new prospects in terms of legal aspects.

The Intercloud

This is the vision of the cloud paradigm. This, in a way, represents the cloud of clouds. The standards-based amalgamation and accumulation of cloud resources spread across the world goes a long way in fulfilling the unique idea behind the intercloud. All kinds of cloud environments (infrastructure, platform, software, etc.) dynamically link up with one another in order to share their functionalities, features, and facilities to accomplish superior and sophisticated things. Applications in one cloud can connect and access data in another cloud, which is situated in the vicinity or in other parts of the world. Applications can leverage a cheaper and more attuned infrastructure of different and distant clouds owned by someone else. A notification emanated out of a service hosted in a cloud can reach out to a host of applications that are in co-located and distributed clouds in real time. Thus, a kind of extreme connectivity and spontaneous integration among various cloud modules make the route toward the intercloud smooth.

The proposed intercloud is perfectly capable of facilitating just-in-time, opportunistic, and scalable provisioning of cloud services. All the internal cloud modules are equally empowered to provide and perform the goal of automated resource provisioning through competent software-based solutions. Further on, the uninhibited linkage with external cloud resources makes possible the process of provisioning toward the absolute fulfillment of desired and decided SLAs. That means every single criterion quoted in the SLAs and operation-level agreements (OLAs) can be fully met under any anticipated and unanticipated circumstances including variations in workload, user base, resource, and network conditions. The overall goal is to create a lean computing environment that intrinsically supports dynamic expansion or contraction of VM capabilities for handling unexpected variations in service demands and to make computing dependable and ubiquitous. Consortiums are working in unison in order to come out with a series of open and industry-strength standards for cloud infrastructure, platform, and application developers and providers so that all the semantic, syntactic, structural, and symbiotic differences among them can be minimal.

Ambient Cloud

Hybrid and community clouds are being recommended for certain scenarios. There are open and industry-strength standards being deliberated and decided by standard agencies and consortiums in order to realize the limitless possibilities of federated clouds. The seamless interactions facilitated among diverse and distributed cloud infrastructures and services go a long way in sharpening and shaping up the future of cloud computing. Today, high-end desktops, server machines, and storage appliances and networks are becoming interlinked to form cloud environments in order to revitalize and realize their innate capabilities and capacities.

However, recently, smartphones, tablets, and consumer electronics have become the handy and trendy computing and communication devices with a lot of memory and computing power. Also, the number of slim and sleek handhelds, portables, wearables, and fixed and nomadic devices is exponentially growing; hence, there is a big market and mind share for clouds formed out of everyday electronics. Similarly, smart sensors and actuators are increasingly tied up with one another as well as with remote cloud infrastructures and platforms in order to transmit, store, mine, and analyze the tremendous amount of man- and machine-generated data with the ultimate aim of knowledge discovery in real time. The vision of extracting and leveraging business and behavioral insights in real time is on the way toward reality.

Significantly, there are endeavors for creating and sustaining device and sensor clouds. The convergence of mobility and cloud computing models is also opening up a stream of fresh opportunities and possibilities for IT product vendors, service organizations, and mobile users. It is estimated that in the future, billions of devices and trillions of digitalized (smart) objects will be connected with one another as well as with remote clouds to realize the proclaimed use, business, and technical cases of the much-dreamt AmI theme. With such monumental connectivity and interactions brewing on the horizon, the computing power and the capacity of the resulting cloud will be simply enormous and envious.

Instant-On Enterprises

IT is consistently changing for good and is being prescribed as the far-reaching agent in business automation and transformation. Business behemoths are supposed to provide IT-enabled business services and solutions to their clients and customers whenever and wherever they need them. Business organizations have to deliver their services cost-effectively, securely, and quickly by operating their own IT divisions or by just establishing appropriate contracts with competitive IT services and solutions providers. Cloud computing has emerged as the next-generation IT optimization scheme through consolidation, centralization, virtualization, and automation. It has brought in a radically different service delivery method. The cloud concepts are reverberating as they could provide new levels of collaboration, agility, speed, and cost savings for business as well as IT enterprises of any size and type.

With the service era all set to blossom powerfully, IT is slated for a renaissance and is being visualized as a key service broker, mediator, and facilitator. Service-oriented IT enables business agility, whereas cloud-induced IT is creating a solid foundation for transitioning IT infrastructures to be more agile. If the underlying IT is nimble, then the business can easily attain the much-needed agility, autonomy, and affordability. Business operations, offerings, and outlooks are bound to change with the combined strength of service and cloud IT. The speed and quality of service delivery is set to see a considerable increase. HP goes further and farther to name cloud-enabled businesses as "instant-on" enterprises. Everything is becoming instantly planned, procured, produced, and provided. An "instant-on" enterprise is an enterprise that embeds technology into everything it does to better serve citizens, partners, employees, and clients. HP banks on the hybrid delivery model, which intrinsically leverages both conventional IT as well as cloud IT (comprising private, public, and hybrid clouds) to annihilate all the delivery blockades and blockages and speed up the service delivery mechanism.

Enterprise-Class Attributes for Successful Cloud Solutions

HP believes that a successful cloud solution for any enterprise must be

- *Secure*—guaranteeing delivery of agreed-upon security levels (e.g., threat protection, privacy, and compliance) and data and intellectual property protection
- *Open, not locked in*—comprising modular infrastructure and services that support heterogeneous environments
- *Automated*—incorporating policy-based automation and management that integrates cloud with legacy assets and services to provide integrated service catalogs and end-to-end service quality

- *Resilient*—providing sure delivery of agreed-upon availability, quality, and performance service levels
- *Seamless*—combining public and private cloud services with traditionally deployed services and outsourced services to deliver a seamless experience

Thus, cloud-initiated service delivery is set to completely revamp and revitalize how IT is used by businesses and people.

Extremely Integrated Enterprises

In the beginning, there were monolithic mainframes, but they are silos. Then, with the advent of personal computers and the Internet, we have computers connected locally as well as with the Internet. This is articulated as the Internet of computers. All kinds of manufacturing instruments, machines, toolsets, and electronics are being connected with one another and with the web and also signaling the reality of the Internet of devices. As everything is being exposed as a service, there are business, IT, and device services in plenty in any kind of enterprise environment. Now for the sake of creation of sophisticated applications, these services need to interact in order to craft composite services and processes fulfilling the vision behind the Internet of services. An extremely integrated enterprise (EIE) represents the seamless and spontaneous integration of all enterprise IT elements and ground-level entities via the service-level integration and aggregation methods.

In summary, the cloud idea is growing quickly and is being contemplated for greater things by IT divisions of all kinds of industries, IT service organizations, products and platforms vendors, infrastructure (software as well as hardware) providers, consulting companies, national governments, academic institutions, and so on. Today, all kinds of platforms ranging from development, deployment, execution, management, governance, and middleware are being modernized accordingly to be hosted in cloud infrastructures. Service delivery platforms (SDPs), cloud broker, cloud integration bus/cloud service broker, source, service, supply and support management systems, integration containers, database systems, and so on are the leading platforms to find a safe and scintillating residence in the cloud. Cloud enterprises are those that inculcate both the business and IT impacts of the cloud idea. Cloud enterprises are capable of incubating and sustaining an innovation culture and commitment, which collectively leads to a string of pearls in the form of newer processes and people-centric, premium solutions. A sample futuristic application scenario is pictorially explained in Figure 1.2.

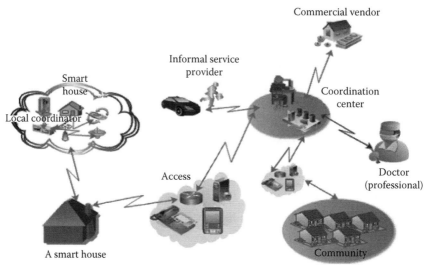

FIGURE 1.2
Smart enterprises will capitalize on the value of the cloud.

SMART ENTERPRISES

As we have indicated above, there is widespread interest in the smart planet vision (http://www-935.ibm.com/services/us/en/cloud-enterprise/). Many technologies have arrived, shone for some time, and then vanished into thin air. However, the cloud movement is something special that cannot be taken lightly. Its promise and potential are really outstanding. The cloud idea is breeding innovation in the enterprise space as pointed out earlier and is set to become the prominent and dominant technology for realizing the wide-ranging objectives and obligations behind smart enterprises. Already the cloud principle is being touted as the preferred method and means for enhancing the choice, care, convenience, and comfort of human lives. There are advertisements galore in print as well as digital media for instant transformation of an ordinary TV into a cloud-enabled smart Internet TV. There is not an iota of doubt that cloud enablement contributes substantially in making things smart, enterprises smarter, and people the smartest.

There are certain characteristics and criteria that stand out as the hallmarks for smart enterprises. The pervasive and path-breaking cloud concepts have brought in a series of improvisations and improvements that can be smartly leveraged toward the conceptualization and concretization of smart businesses. Ubiquitous information access (UIA) and instantaneous service delivery are definitely important parameters for smart enterprises. Other deciding factors include extreme connectivity and integration, awareness, and adaptation.

Today, we are bombarded with streams of novelty-packed, slim and sleek, trendy and handy, multichannel and multifaceted, and powerful computing, communication, sensing, vision, perception, and actuation devices in our hands, pockets, waists and wrists, rooms, roofs, homes, roads, expressways, work spots, gyms, and so on. The beauty here is that these heterogeneous devices are seamlessly interconnected with one another through standards-compliant protocols as well as linked up with the web. As laid out earlier, this trend is being termed the Internet of Devices.

The most-celebrated and calibrated service era has dawned on us. Services are being projected and promoted as the next-generation building block/ abstraction unit for IT solution engineering, business integration, legacy modernization, and application composition. Process-centric system building and sustenance has gained prominence with the unprecedented adoption and adaptation of SO principles, patterns, platforms, and practices. Without much ado, it is the Internet of services.

As indicated above, ordinary, casual, common, and everyday articles are being empowered with digitalization, distribution, and industrialization technologies to be computation and communication enabled and context aware so that they can partake purposefully in mainstream computing. Also, these digitalized entities and elements are being seamlessly tied up with the web and hence, the Internet of things (IoT) (alternatively called the web of objects) discipline and domain is calling upon enthusiastic people, engineers, and experts to focus more diligently and deeply on the augmentative, transformative, and articulative use/business/ technical cases of the IoT vision. That is, there is a seamless linkage between what is happening at the ground level to the centralized and remote monitoring, analytical, decision-facilitating, and control systems. The messages are being generated, transmitted, understood, and finally action-initiated among the various digital, physical, and cyber systems. Extreme connectivity and deeper integration are the keys for smart enterprises. Message-based interaction is the overwhelming overture for service and application-level integration. In other words, devices are connected, whereas applications are integrated.

Enterprises aiming for the next level ought to smartly utilize the data heap (operational, transactional, historical, real-time process data, etc.) to extract

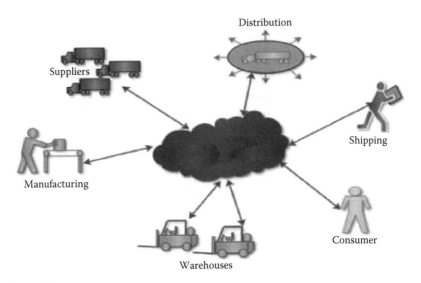

FIGURE 1.3
The necessity of connected clouds.

all kinds of beneficial trends, patterns, tips, associations, opportunities, risks, and rewards. This enables them to be information driven and insightful in their customer interactions, partner relationships, worker satisfaction, society responsibility, and ultimately people centricity. Other prominent improvements can be found in strategic planning, effective articulation, operational efficiency, environment sustainability, productivity, and adaptivity. With the IoT, the ground-level information gets mixed up with business data in real time to sharply increase the accuracy in forecasting, strategy formulation, action, and assurance. Precisely speaking, macrolevel monitoring, decision making, and governance will move up to microlevel management. With the surging popularity of cloud servers, all kinds of sensors, mobiles, tablets, laptops, and desktops are being integrated with private, public, and hybrid and community clouds. Figure 1.3 clearly describes how extremely connected and integrated enterprises could achieve next-generation applications.

THE ENABLING MECHANISMS OF SMART ENTERPRISES

Professionals are working at a furious and fabulous pace to identify and finalize the implementation technologies and methodologies for realizing next-generation smart enterprises. (http://www.infosys.com/building-tomorrows-enterprise/Documents/smarter-organizations.pdf).

The prominent computing styles, data crunching and knowledge engineering methods, and awareness and actuation mechanisms include

- Service computing
- Advanced analytics
- Cloud computing
- Big data computing
- In-memory computing

Service Computing

Service computing is all about creating, assembling, and running a raft of services for building service-centric web, mobile, social, enterprise, and cloud applications. Services are the central and core building block for futuristic software. Services are better in abstraction, encapsulation, and articulation of software applications. Extensively using and reusing third-party services goes a long way in shortening application development and maintenance. SOA, the associated architectural pattern, is the established means for classifying, connecting, and composing diverse and distributed services to construct adaptive, on-demand, enterprise-grade, and dynamic software systems.

Advanced Analytics

The quest for quicker and easier transition from data to information and then to knowledge has been gaining greater traction nowadays with the availability of competent technologies and methodologies (http://www.greenplum.com). Nowadays, data volume has been growing exponentially due to the surging popularity of social networking sites. With the unprecedented explosion of electronic devices, the size of data being generated, gathered, transmitted, and stocked is becoming massive. Most of the data are nonstructured and semistructured, and it is predicted that the data growth in the days ahead will be mammoth. Hence, it is mandatory for business establishments to invest their resources and energy into unearthing potential and promising processes for quickly extracting actionable insights out of data heaps in order to keep ahead of their competitors. Big data and in-memory computing paradigms are the leading models that help in mining and analyzing data in real time and also in extracting practical knowledge.

Event-Driven Architecture

EDA is emerging as the classic architectural style for building highly automated, dynamic, and real-time enterprise applications (http://msdn .microsoft.com/en-us/library/dd129913.aspx). The business landscape is going to greatly benefit from this distinctive architecture. Events are pervasive, high in scale and significance, and critical for insightful business automation. Millions of event messages are being generated and streamed from geographically distributed places. IT infrastructures and platforms are accordingly strengthened for receiving event messages, processing, analyzing, mining, and extracting any actionable intelligence in real time and subsequently alerting subscribers to ponder, decide, and activate the next course of action. Event-driven service-centric applications are, therefore, well received across the industry spectrum.

Next-generation enterprises should be able to glean actionable intelligence from different and distributed sources and resources. Not only gaining useful and usable insights but also acting on them quickly is the key differentiator in the knowledge-driven and cut-throat market. The IT infrastructures are empowered to make enterprises adept to all kinds of business changes and challenges such as market volatility and pressures; recessionary or recovering economy; mergers and acquisitions; and changing mindsets, business partnerships, and so on. Similarly, technological changes and technical challenges also come into the picture. Thus, correctly visualizing the prevailing as well as the looming situations and scenarios goes a long way in shaping up and strengthening enterprises to face any kind of uncertainties and threats and to capitalize on fresh opportunities.

Big Data Computing

Everyday environment sensors, cameras, computers, smartphones, satellites, industry machines, and scientific instruments are creating a huge collection of data (http://www.cra.org/ccc/docs/init/Big_Data.pdf). The data generated from geographically dispersed personal and professional applications, embedded devices, consumer electronics, process control systems, and so on, can be automatically transformed into actionable insights that can direct and dictate the right course of action. The web is being touted as the world's largest information superhighway. An assortment of professional and personal content in the form of audio, video, data, information, reusable services, and network-accessible applications is being aggregated and accumulated in the ever-expanding web. Due to a series of noteworthy advancements in the web world, a host of online, on-demand, off-premise, and managed commerce and business applications is being dynamically devised and delivered for all of humanity. Search engines such as Google, Yahoo, Microsoft Bing, and so on, by algorithmically collecting, painstakingly processing, and safely keeping a wider variety of data and information in their high-end storage networks and appliances, empower people to make informed decisions in their daily lives. These web-centric and web-scale companies collect trillions of bytes of data every day and continually add new premium services such as satellite images, street views, driving directions, and image retrieval. The societal benefits of these information-inspired services are immeasurable.

These larger volumes of data sets, often termed big data, are imposing newer challenges and opportunities around storage, analysis, and archival. The quest to solve the problems related to large-volume and semistructured data has led to the emergence of a class of newer types of database products. This new class of database products consists of column-oriented data stores, key/value pair databases, and document databases. There are nonrelational databases and software packages such as Hadoop in order to process data in a distributed and parallel manner using commodity systems. Big data computing will further revolutionize industries, governments, and knowledge workers. With clouds emerging and establishing cheaper and virtual supercomputers, distributed data crunching tasks are bound to be simpler and cheaper.

In-Memory Computing

IT is being consistently upgraded to transition from the age-old sentiment of a cost center to the elegant and exemplary business enabler (http://www.sap.com/solutions/technology/in-memory-computing-platform/index.epx). That is, IT infrastructures, processes, and people are being empowered accordingly to meet existing and emerging business requirements. Besides business efficiency, of late, cost-efficiency is being given more thrust by CIOs in order to augment the return of investment (ROI) and to lessen the TCO. With the rates of memory modules continuously failing down, the use of in-memory computing is growing substantially, especially for mission-critical and real-time applications. This price depreciation has led to a rethinking of how mass data should be stored and used. Instead of using mechanical disk drives, it is now possible to store the primary data copy of a database in silicon-based main memory resulting in heightened performance. This change in the way data is stored and manipulated will continue to bring paradigm shifts on enterprise applications and their nonfunctional (QoS attributes) needs. Having real-time information available at the speed of thought provides decision makers with game-changing insights that have, until now, not existed. That is, the speed with which data sets are accessed and utilized for building next-generation applications will matter in the days to come.

Cloud Computing

Cloud infrastructures are being prescribed as the best solution for all the ills of present-day stagnant, closed, inflexible, and costly infrastructures [8–10,12,14]. Cloud IT is stuffed with a number of unique capabilities. Virtualization is the leading one; job scheduling, workload management, and so on are automated; provisioning and deprovisioning of computing resources are smoothened; there are commercial-grade and open-source solutions for simplifying and streamlining the creation, configuration, and deleting VMs out of physical servers; cloud service and infrastructure management solutions are thriving; and security and governance aspects are being looked into sincerely and strenuously.

In short, cloud IT is opening up choices at cloud, physical server, and VM levels in order to fulfill changing computing requirements. Specifically, cloud infrastructures are renowned for effortlessly accomplishing non-functional requirements such as scalability, elasticity, high performance, availability, configurability, consumability, and so on. In short, the cloud is the convergence of mainframes and web infrastructures. The interconnectivity, integration, intermediation, aggregation, and arbitration capabilities of cloud IT clearly indicate and insist that in the future IT is in the safe, secure, and sustainable hands of the path-breaking and promising cloud paradigm. As mentioned above, the cloud breeds innovations. A growing array of computing models such as mobile, social, enterprise, and embedded computing is converging with cloud computing in order to visualize a bunch of newer and nimbler applications. We have described three distinct cloud-induced and people-centric systems as follows.

Smarter Homes

Homes are the liveliest and loveliest place for everyone to reflect and relax with their loved ones. There are home automation and integration technologies simplifying the establishment of smart homes. Micro- and nanoscale electronics are found in larger numbers in the houses of advanced countries. There is an explosion of devices for our personal and professional purposes. Our working, walking, and wandering environments are being steadily stuffed and sandwiched with a growing array of digital assistants. Home networking is another interesting topic of deeper study and research in order to dynamically enable home-bound devices, instruments, machines, utensils, appliances, gadgets, gizmos, and so on to find and network with one another using the pioneering mesh topology. That is, scores of ad hoc and opportunistic networks are being formed for conceiving and concretizing spatial, temporal, and people-centric applications and are disbanded once the purpose is well served.

Increasingly, all kinds of home devices and digitally empowered home artifacts are being interconnected via a centralized home gateway solution. In addition to that, they are being connected to the web via the gateway so that remote monitoring, activation, maintenance, and management of home-bound articles and assets are remarkably simplified. With the advent of converged, efficient, and adaptive cloud infrastructures, the common and reusable home services are being stocked up in a cloud-based home service repository. Also, home management software solutions are being developed and deployed in clouds in order to monitor and manage thousands of homes with a single software instance. In short, the cloud enables the establishment of smarter homes. Ambient-assisted living (AAL), energy optimization, remote management, enhanced care, choice, convenience and comfort for home users, and so on are the key applications of smarter homes. There is a post on a blogging site about the Android OS entering and empowering every tangible home device such as refrigerators, media players, TVs, and so on to facilitate greater and deeper automation. Figure 1.4 indicates the macrolevel integration of different spaces for the realization of a family of people-centric, aware, active, and articulate environments.

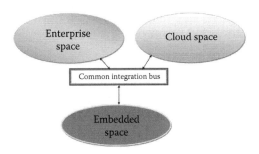

FIGURE 1.4
The seamless linkage of cloud, enterprise, and embedded spaces.

Smarter Cars

With the maturity and stability of a slew of implementation technologies, everything is becoming smart and every environment is slated to become smarter as the days unfold. People spend quality time inside cars for travel and leisure trips. Cars are being touted as the next-generation converged platform for enlightenment, edutainment, and entertainment. In-vehicle infotainment solutions are already decorating high-end cars. Connectivity has become the cool thing. Ubiquitous learning has become very common. Productivity is set to grow further. Car parking management, connectivity and device management, and driver assistance systems are some of the exclusive software solutions for cars. Now with clouds emerging as the centralized entity for hosting and delivering software, platform, and infrastructure as services, automobile experts and consultants are gradually plotting and planning for enabling seamless and spontaneous connectivity for car-bound devices with the distant service clouds. Cloud-based automobile service repositories and car management software will become critical and crucial for smart cars in the near future.

Smarter Environments

Our professional and personal environments are being filled up with a plethora of multipurpose and multichannel devices for alerting and assisting us in our daily routine assignments. Not only information and transaction services, but also sophisticated physical services are being delivered to us through smart interactions among devices in and around us. With the availability of ultra-high wireless broadband facilities and smartphones being the companion of humans everywhere, the goals of ambient and sentient computing, communication, sensing, perception, vision, and actuation are easily attainable. Devices are self-aware, surroundings-aware, and situation-aware and therefore our needs are being precisely and promptly understood and fulfilled through IT-enabled composite services unobtrusively in time. The latest smartphones are fitted with a number of smart sensors and further strengthened to interact with other devices in our surroundings to be true digital assistants in our daily dealings and decision-making activities. Device profiles for Web Services (DPWS) and the open service gateway initiative (OSGi) are the leading device integration standards for forming device ensembles. With the smartphone services repositories and service management solutions in clouds, smartphones are emerging as the core devices for realizing smarter environments around us.

CONCLUSION

Due to various compelling reasons, the phrase "more with less" has gained wider acceptance and has drawn broader attention. This narration and notion has gained considerable clout these days due to the economic slump, the subsequent slow recovery, and sliding into distress. Worldwide enterprises, down with the stuttering and sluggish economy, are hence keenly looking out for trend-setting and nonlinear methods to be competitively ahead in their service and solution offerings. Executives are frantically seeking out pioneering technology-based solutions. Technical managers and architects are on their toes in order to unearth out-of-the-box development approaches and state-of-the-art ICT infrastructures for faster software realization, integration, and modernization.

Service and cloud enablement is being prescribed as the best thing to improve IT efficiency, which in turn sharply improves the efficiency of business and people. In this chapter, we have exclusively focused on the unique selling points (USPs) of the inventive and inspiring cloud idea, which has laid the stimulating foundation for big data and in-memory computing models. How the adoption of the cloud paradigm shapes up and sustains the vision behind smart enterprises is also explained. With the massive adaption across the spectrum, the era of virtual computing will dawn on the world. Everything becomes virtualized so that all kinds of dependency-imposed hitches and hurdles get decimated; the vision of creative collaboration among all kinds of assets, articles, and artifacts in our environments becomes a reality. The cloud idea will be positioned as core and central to the future of virtual computing, which is very bright.

REFERENCES

1. Akram, S., A. Bouguettaya, X. Liu, A. Haller, F. Rosenberg, and X. Wu. 2010. "A Change Management Framework for Service Oriented Enterprises." *International Journal of Next-Generation Computing* 1 (1): 1–25.
2. Assmann, M., and G. Engels. 2008. *Transition to Service-Oriented Enterprise Architecture*. Berlin: Springer-Verlag.
3. Capgemini. 2005. "Service-Oriented Enterprise: How to Make Your Business, Fast, Flexible and Responsive: A Briefing for CxO-Level Executives," Capgemini, Bratislava, Slovakia, http://www.sk.capgemini.com/m/sk/tl/Service-Oriented_Enterprise__How_to_Make_Your_Business_Fast__Flexible_and_Responsive.pdf.
4. Chaari, S., K. Boukadi, C. B. Amar, F. Biennier, and J. Favrel. June 2008. "Developing Service Oriented Enterprise by Composing Web Services Based on Context." *International Journal of Computer Science and Network Security* 8 (6): 79–92.

5. Chang, H.-L. et al. 2009. "Assessing IT-Business Alignment in Service-Oriented Enterprises." *Pacific Asia Journal of the Association for Information Systems* 3 (1): 29–48.
6. Chang, M., J. He, and E. Castro-Leon. 2006. "Service-Orientation in the Computing Infrastructure." *Proceedings of the Second IEEE International Symposium on Service-Oriented System Engineering (SOSE'06)*, Santa Clara, California, October 2006.
7. Charri, S., F. Biennier, J. Favrel, and C. Benamar. 2006. *Towards a Service-Oriented Enterprise Based on Business Components Identification*. Berlin: Springer-Verlag.
8. Cisco. 2006. "Building an Infrastructure to Enable a Service-Oriented Architecture: A White Paper," http://www.cisco.com/cisco/web/UK/products/dc/pdfs/SOISOA Whitepaper_v4_finalpdf?c.
9. Facchini, C., F. Granelli, and N. L. S. da Fonseca. "Cognitive Service-Oriented Infrastructures." *Journal of Internet Engineering* 4 (1): 269–78.
10. IBM Global Technology Services. January 2008. "How Service-Oriented Architecture (SOA) Impacts Your IT Infrastructure: A White Paper," http://www-935.ibm.com/services/us/igs/pdf/wp_how-soa-impacts-your-it-infrastructure.pdf.
11. Luthria, H., and F. Rabhi. 2009. "Service Oriented Computing in Pctice—An Agenda for Research into the Factors Influencing the Organizational Adoption of Service Oriented Architectures." *Journal of Theoretical and Applied Electronic Commerce Research* 4 (1): 39–56.
12. Microsoft Services. 2010. "Service Oriented Architecture Infrastructure, Business Agility through Service Virtualization: A Dataervices," http://www.microsoft.com/microsoftservices/.
13. Skalle, H., S. Ramachandran, M. Schuster, V. Szaloky, and S. Antoun. 2009. "Aligning Business Process Management, Service Oriented Architecture and Lean Six Sigma for Real Business Results," IBM, http://www.redbooks.ibm.com/redpapers/pdfs/redp4447.pdf.
14. Zhao, Y. 2008. "Service Oriented Infrastructure Framework." *2008 IEEE Congress on Services*, Hawaii, July 8–11, 2008.

2

Cloud-Inspired Enterprise Transformations!

INTRODUCTION

Businesses are seriously and sincerely contemplating having a small IT center locally (on-site or on-premise) by smartly modernizing and migrating a large chunk of business and IT solutions to one or more infrastructures rented from one or more third-party and expertly managed public clouds (online, on-demand, hosted, remote, and off-premise). This kind of segregation accomplishes a lot for companies and corporations in various aspects of their business. One is to facilitate the realignment of companies so they can reset their priorities in order to focus more deeply on their core competencies. Also, there are other noteworthy benefits such as the transition from capital to operational expenditures (Opex). The richness and reach of cloud-based applications are definitely awesome. The objective of "more with less" will steadily see the light. The cloud idea is elegantly enabling and empowering scores of innovations and improvisations in IT. The maturity and maneuverability of the cloud paradigm is bound to confer more thrust on IT simplicity and sensitivity.

It is a known fact that, with the harvest and harmonization of myriad, multifaceted technologies, IT is becoming more powerful and poised. Cloud computing substantially expands the scope of IT and takes it to the next level. Notably, newer facets and fronts are being opened up for IT to close the gap between business and IT. The impacts and implications of cloud technology on IT are definitely overwhelming. As it is disseminated widely and wisely, cloud computing lays an invigorating foundation for a deluge of novel and strategic IT models that inspire next-generation business models. We have powerful, pragmatic, and cloud-inspired IT infrastructures. That is, cloud infrastructures are the seamless combination of

41

mainframe computers (familiar and famous for high performance and assurance) with modern-day servers (renowned for flexibility, openness, extensibility, etc.).

Frankly speaking, any promising enterprise-class technology will have a positive and progressive impact on enterprise architecture (EA), which must be minutely analyzed in order to embrace cloud concepts in any enterprise. In this book, we would like to understand cloud EA, which is the convergence of two major and mesmerizing disciplines: cloud and EA.

THE CLOUD SCHEME FOR ENTERPRISE SUCCESS

There are multiple factors determinedly deciding the success of any enterprise. As mentioned previously, the enterprise-wide architecture is one of the leading contributors. As widely accepted, IT is the most efficient and elegant enabler of business. Therefore, the key assignment of any enterprise architect is to roll out a series of proven mechanisms for enabling a tighter alignment between business and IT in order to reap the resulting business value. With this synchronization, enterprise-scale processes, practices, platforms, and metrics collectively lead to the enterprise success and sustenance.

IT has become the crucial cog for guaranteeing the long-standing aspirations (business agility, adaptability, and affordability) of executives and entrepreneurs. That is, the coupling between IT and business has to become stronger and deeper. The well-articulated vision of business and IT alignment and association is definitely bound to raise a storm of innovations and improvisations for establishing and sustaining people-centric, process-based, service-oriented, model- and event-driven, and cloud-enabled enterprises. These empowerments tend to make enterprises dynamic, on-demand, autonomic, and real-time. As IT and business are becoming intertwined and interlinked very tightly and tantalizingly these days, all kinds of advancements and accomplishments in IT are being easily and expediently replicated in business operations for much-needed business optimization, acceleration, and transformation. There are several empowering technologies, techniques, and tools emerging and evolving to tear down the inhibiting gap between IT and business.

On the IT infrastructure front, there are several important requirements [13] such as dynamic, virtualized, converged, automation-enabled, and shared infrastructures for structuring and sustaining next-generation enterprises [15]. Businesses are enthusiastic about capitalizing on modern methodologies and technologies for smoothly transforming their passive, stagnant, closed, inflexible, and silo infrastructures to open, modular, dynamic, adaptive, and lean ones.

Organizations are expected to extensively capitalize on proven and potential technology for their betterment. Corporations use technology to integrate and automate the value chain. Cloud enterprises adapt easily and innovate rapidly. They comply with policies and rules quickly, interact with stakeholders intelligently, and transact without losing integrity. They manage risk and environmental responsibilities effectively. The IT imperatives that define the success criteria for any enterprise are, therefore, flexibility, automation, insight, speed, and security.

The most visible, valuable, and vigorous IT innovation in the recent past is the cloud paradigm. Professionals and professors believe that the cloud is the inspiring, imaginative, and instinctive paradigm to fulfill this long-standing mission of business agility and adaptivity. Cloud computing has emerged with much promise and potential and is being positioned as the best strategic and sustainable IT paradigm to facilitate the much-desired harmonization between fast-changing business realities [10] and appreciable IT inventions. Business executives and entrepreneurs are highly optimistic about the unfolding concepts behind the cloud method, which is set to definitely and decisively deliver and guarantee the improvement of IT agility and autonomy in our extremely competitive and knowledge-driven society.

In summary, leading software and hardware providers are visualizing futuristic enterprises using their own technical competencies, focus areas, product offerings, and services, and articulating and advertising artistic phrases for public consumption. IBM trumpets around the vision of "On-Demand E-Business," HP is banking on "Instant-On Enterprise," Dell is promoting "Efficient Enterprise," and so on. Lately, terms such as service-oriented and cloud-enabled enterprises are going steadily and becoming popular. As enterprises need to grow in the midst of extreme globalization and digitalization, IT innovations are forced to catch up with the ferocious pace of business needs. In this chapter, we would like to explain the strategic advantages accrued from EA's seamless synchronization with the cloud idea. As the cloud is being promulgated as the next-generation enterprise-scale technology, it is logical to explore and expound the significant implications of the cloud on the EA domain. What are all the changes to be enacted on the existing EA [6]? How will the new-generation enterprise architects have to analyze and accommodate the ideals and impacts of cloud technology in order to keep up the yearned for and earned edge?

ELUCIDATING THE EVOLVING CLOUD IDEA

Business is booming in all aspects, and IT infrastructure is subsequently added to readily grasp all the incoming and impending business opportunities. However, the economy is tottering, and hence, IT expenditure is being pruned. The question is how to enable a lean yet anticipative, accommodative, articulate, and adaptive IT so that business can grow without any breakdown, slowdown, and even letdown. The most recent and resilient cloud concepts are being portrayed and prescribed as the savior and silver bullet for all the present and future needs of IT. Clouds in a way present an illusion of infinite computing and storage capacity. The hotly pursued and greatly pampered cloud paradigm is capable of decimating the age-old phrase "IT is a cost center" forever. That is the power and poise of the cloud idea, which is penetrating and permeating into every tangible domain these days.

Cloud computing is all about more with less. Fast-growing computing needs are being met by leveraging a dynamic pool of consolidated, virtualized, and service-enabled compute and storage servers in association with scores of automated tools that are mainly for effective virtual machine creation, monitoring, replacement, and management; dynamic load balancing; adaptive resource provisioning; and advanced job scheduling. A bevy of versatile technologies are smartly combined to realize the unique cloud idea and its massive adoption [4].

- SOA as the business enabler—In the recent past [14], SOA came along and laid the sound and stimulating foundation for achieving a host of complete and compact automation of tasks such as application composition, enterprise modernization, and business integration. That is, services, the most flexible and futuristic building block for adaptive, on-demand, and dynamic IT systems, can dynamically find one another, bind, and compose to generate smart and sophisticated services that in turn could lead to intelligent processes, novelty-packed mashups, and applications. Aspects like software building-blocks, such as components, classes, and services, and agents also contribute immeasurably for the much-anticipated self-adaptation in both personal and professional applications. MDA provides the distant yet distinct goal of developmental automation through standards-compliant code-generation cartridges, patterns, and tools. Generative programming, intentional programming, domain-specific languages, language-oriented programming (LOP), and so on are some of the MDA-related disciplines. Autonomic computing is a strategic initiative for bringing tangible and perceptible autonomy for enterprise IT, which is heading toward elastic IT. Thus, every noteworthy aspect in IT and business is becoming automated with competent, cognitive, and catalytic technologies.

- The cloud as an IT enabler—The most resilient and remarkable paradigm and platform for today and tomorrow's IT is nonetheless the cloud, which is being proclaimed as the prominent and dominant contributor and contender in the long-drawn battle toward IT autonomy and agility. The cloud paradigm brings several value-added qualities to IT: elasticity, scalability, performance, flexibility, consumability, modifiability, availability, and so on. The cloud model has certainly brought in scores of innovations and improvements to IT, which has been at the forefront in successfully fulfilling the fast-changing needs of the global business. The full cloud stack [12] is pictorially represented in Figure 2.1.

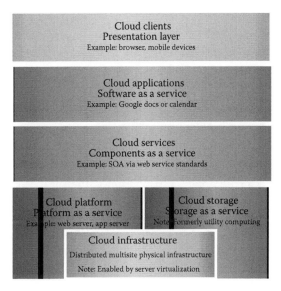

FIGURE 2.1
The cloud stack.

As the promised service era is about to dawn powerfully, the insistence on converged, dynamic, and on-demand service infrastructures is becoming intense. It is very clear that clouds are the most apt and advanced service infrastructures.

Several enterprise-scale technologies are being gelled well toward the creation and sustenance of the cloud paradigm, which has been turning out to be a strategically, systematically and significantly transformative and disruptive one for individuals, innovators, and institutions.

Cloud Technologies

The much-hyped concept of cloud computing is heading toward greater heights and insights due to the maturity of virtualization technology, which is mainly used for comprehensively decoupling hardware and software components. This loose coupling has done a lot of good for IT in bringing much-needed elasticity, exuberance, and elegance. That is, the inhibiting dependencies among various IT modules get decimated altogether to bring in fresh thoughts, possibilities, and opportunities in tackling all sorts of existing and emerging IT limitations and ills. Another differentiating factor is transparency. That is, location, technology, platform, and language transparencies are being easily achieved with cloud computing. There are other contributive technologies and tools such as

1. Cluster, grid, utility, on-demand, and autonomic computing
2. Consolidation, centralization, distribution, virtualization, orchestration, and federation technologies
3. Lean and green technologies
4. Service computing and SaaS
5. Techniques and tools for automated resource provisioning, clustering, decision management, capacity planning, load balancing, and job scheduling
6. Self-service technologies (VM creation, expansion, contraction, retirement, replacement, live-in migration, monitoring, and management)
7. Governance, security, monitoring, and billing

The cloud, being an enterprise-scale and energy-efficient technology, has to guarantee several quality attributes in its attempt to claim more market and mind share. As the cloud is being touted as a kind of sophisticated server infrastructure in the client/server realm, service- and operation-level agreements come into the picture. Incidentally, several enterprise-level and carrier-grade qualities are being realized with the adept leverage of cloud technologies. Newer deployment and delivery models are being unearthed, and hence, the lagging delivery system has systematically improved a lot. Thus, the cloud has become the new-generation rendering engine of late. Further on, the potential to cut down capital expenditure (Capex) and rein in operating costs is so compelling that CIOs have already started to push aggressively for cloud adoption. However, good managers understand that cost savings is not the only variable to consider when evaluating cloud enablement. The significance of cloud computing is that enterprises are eligible to take advantage of a tremendous amount of flexibility, affordability, and scalability by deploying and managing their IT services and applications on shared or dedicated cloud servers [3].

As far as the service providers are concerned, they always want to have highly optimized, dynamic, converged, and on-demand cloud infrastructures. To achieve the goal of an optimized cloud, they seek to optimize the use of resources and assets in their environment—from servers to storage to software licenses. Service providers are also held responsible for compliance to rules, regulations, and other conditions being imposed by their customers and citizens. For this reason, the final component in a mature and mellowed cloud infrastructure is cloud governance. With cloud governance in place, service providers not only will deliver superior value through cloud adoption but will also prove that the use of resources is reasonable, responsible, and aligned with the requirements of the business.

Cloud-Induced Innovations

Cloud computing lays the foundation for originating a number of momentous and memorable business and technical innovations described as follows:

- *Technology cluster*—Clouds represent the seamless convergence of proven and potential technologies, tools, and techniques (consolidation, virtualization, integration, federation, composition, provisioning, etc.).
- *Heterogeneity to homogeneity*—Clouds hide the multiplicity and heterogeneity-induced complexity of IT environments by leveraging a variety of optimized management platforms and containers, such as

a virtual machine monitor (VMM), and power, resource, and work-load management modules. A lot of internal deficiencies and discrepancies are smartly made transparent to the ultimate users. The cloud is being presented to end users as a single and simple instrument and interface for fulfilling vast and varied computational needs.

- *Service-oriented infrastructure (SOI)*—With the faster adoption of service orientation principles, newer interaction, orchestration, and consumption models have erupted and are evolving to meet the diverse needs of users. SaaS is the base that is laying the fertile foundation for encouraging an enormous growth of every IT resource being presented as a service to the general public via the web. The growing tendency is overwhelmingly moving toward the vision of IT as a Service (ITaaS). As the much-anticipated service era gradually and gracefully unfolds, the cloud's contribution as the elastic and epoch-making service infrastructure and platform is really tremendous and trendsetting for the forthcoming knowledge era. Clouds will become the indisputable and insightful infrastructure for next-generation service engineering, deployment, and delivery needs.

- *Business innovations*—The indomitable cloud idea has laid a strong and stimulating foundation for emitting newer business, service, licensing, and pricing models that are more tuned to changing business sentiments and customers' liking. There will be a paramount shift from the current Capex to Opex. Consumption-based metering and billing will become common. Ultimately, cloud enterprises will see the light with the beneficial synchronization between SOA, EA, and cloud infrastructures [7].

- *Green IT*—Due to the persistent calls from different quarters for energy efficiency and reduction of greenhouse gas emission for minimizing climatic changes, clouds are being established as a viable and valuable IT instrument for greener environments.

- *IT optimization*—Optimization of IT development and operations is gaining traction. Clouds contribute exceedingly well to this optimization goal. In short, clouds fulfill lean, elastic, catalytic, agile, and adaptive IT. Further on, clouds will enable computing to be the fifth utility. Finally, ITaaS is a foregone conclusion with the maturity of cloud standards, products, and technologies.

- *Extreme elasticity*—Capacity planning is a difficult exercise for IT as predicting exact usage, and acquiring just enough IT resources to avoid excessive under- or overprovisioning is a really tough call in this volatile world. Other internal as well as external factors contributing to this predicament are season-specific usage spikes that demand additional computational resources that otherwise remain idle. Elasticity of IT resources leads to application scalability. Clouds offer resources on-demand that can settle up or down with the changing demands of businesses.

- *Tending toward the on-demand era*—The vision of everything on-demand (computing, communication, intelligence, scalability, information, service, etc.) is set to see the light of day when cloud computing reaches a level of maturity and stability.

The specialty of cloud computing clearly lies in the realm of dynamically and decisively provisioning expensive computational assets (processors/cores, memory, and storage) to meet the fluctuating computing needs of users. This feature allows global users to acquire and release the resources on-demand and be accurately billed for the exact time or amount of usage. Cloud computing could mean different things to different sets of users. For business houses, it is dynamism, scalability on-demand, and customer satisfaction. Other attributes include efficiency, sensitivity, and flexibility to accurately meet unplanned business changes and emerging challenges. And for ordinary users, simplicity, ubiquity, security, consumption, and cost-effectiveness are the key criteria.

Why Cloud Enablement and Empowerment?

The ground-breaking idea of the cloud has silently yet solidly percolated into diverse domains. Cloud enablement has become the most articulated modernization mechanism these days. Every tangible space is undergoing the well-defined cloud-enablement procedure. Not only the enterprise space, but also the vast and untapped embedded space is toeing the same line. Besides the key motivators and drivers, the unprecedented growth being attained in the web domain is being quoted widely for the great and grand adoption of the metamorphic cloud concepts. There are four prominent trends happening in the Internet space.

1. *The information carrier*—The Internet has emerged as the cheapest and global-scale communication infrastructure. Both the wired and the wireless web contribute immensely.
2. *The digital repository*—The web is being stuffed with a wider variety of resources such as man- and machine-generated data. Further on, the

amazing growth in interlinked and metadata-attached web resources such as web pages, components, agents and services, and knowledge bases signals the web as the largest digital information superhighway/digital library. Services are catalogued and stocked in the web.

3. *The open platform*—There are web, application, database, commerce, integration, and directory servers in plenty in the fast-growing web. In short, the web is being positioned as the open, flexible, and affordable deployment, execution, and delivery platform for personal as well as professional applications and services.

4. *The collaboration environment*—Web 2.0 (the social web) technologies are positioning the web as the next-generation knowledge exchange and collaboration environment for specific as well as generic digital communities.

These advancements clearly vouch for employing the web beneficially for anything and everything. As clouds are the most agile, autonomous, and affordable web-based infrastructure, the push for properly utilizing the cloud concept has gained immense momentum these days.

Implementing Smarter Environments via Clouds

We need smart sensors and networks for smart spaces. All sorts of devices, appliances, machines, instruments, and other tangible objects in our daily environments are digitally enhanced to purposefully participate and contribute toward the success and sustenance of smart spaces. Extreme and deeper connectivity, service enablement, cloud infrastructure and platforms, and integration at the service level of all kinds of sensors and actuators are the major differentiators for creating and maintaining a bevy of intelligent environments.

- Integration of new features within devices (internal integration). Smartphones are the representative example.
- Attaching extra and external nanoscale modules (such as radio-frequency identification [RFID] tags, disappearing and diminutive sensors, actuators, etc.) onto devices (external integration).
- Device-to-device (D2D) integration (local).
- Device-to-cloud-device integration (global).

That is, instrumented, interconnected, and integrated systems pave the way for realizing active, aware, and adaptive environments.

Application Domains

Clouds will be an inseparable and insightful part of the hordes of automation initiatives that are being implemented across the spectrum of industries that include

- Manufacturing/process/factory/industrial automation
- Home and building automation
- Entertainment, education, and financial services
- Supply chain, energy, healthcare, retail, government, utilities, logistics and transports, physical security, homeland security, and so on.

The Future

Any powerful and impactful technology has to be adaptive and accommodative. The alluring cloud technology is not an exception and is converging seamlessly and spontaneously with other enterprise-class technologies to accomplish better and bigger things. The cloud idea has the innate power, provision, and potential in abundance to be an all-encompassing, elegant, and exceptional technology.

There are propositions and expositions abounding about a number of new concepts germinating from the cloud seed. There are write-ups, weblogs, and webinars on federated clouds. Companies are circulating this idea, which will encircle the IT industry soon. It is no exaggeration to write that the simultaneous adoption and adaptation of the cloud paradigm is on a fast track. This progressive and positive trend has clearly forced many to become CSPs. The result is that there are plenty of cloud infrastructures across the globe. The prickling and perpetual issue here with this turnaround is that providers are going for different locations and technologies. Businesses are swiftly modernizing and migrating their business services and applications onto cloud-based platforms. Thus, the cloud movement and moment has definitely arrived.

The Intercloud

There are both generic as well as specific cloud types. Public, private, hybrid, and community clouds are the common ones occupying a lot of space in print as well as electronic media. Then, for achieving specific purposes, there came a number of domain- and service-specific clouds such as science, knowledge, data, service, mobile, high performance, and government clouds. People are conceiving and concretizing their own clouds to achieve their goals.

Ultimately, the vision is to establish the intercloud. There are numerous challenges here. It is not as easy as the Internet, which is very common, casual, and cascading. In the web world, there are the easy-to-use and universally accepted protocol (http) and content markup language (html). There is a steady and steely evolution from the basic web contents to the web components and now to the web services. Replicating this openness and simplicity within the cloud landscape and ecosystem is beset with a series of problems. With the ubiquity of SOA, service-based integration within an enterprise or among contracted enterprises is quite manageable. However, the web- and cloud-based integration brings its own cup of challenges including security threats, risks, and vulnerabilities. The interoperability virtue is something that needs a lot of brainstorming and agreement. Professionals are quoting different names such as the open cloud, interoperable cloud, and so on.

In the recent past, in order to tightly couple myriad CSPs, cloud brokerage service (CBS) providers emerged to efficiently mediate between cloud consumers and providers. That is, cloud brokers and auditors are the new entrants into the cloud space. There are automated software solutions for cloud brokering. Thus connectivity, integration, composition, and finally collaboration in the cloud world are gaining momentum, and there are concerned parties working on competent solutions such as vendor-neutral, technology-agnostic, and location-transparent standards. Industry-strength consortiums, academic groups, and government agencies are collaborating together to ponder about and devise acceptable ways and means for the intercloud mission.

In a nutshell, the world of computing is undergoing a tectonic shift in order to guarantee extreme productivity and power to the users. Not only business behemoths and giants but also small and medium companies and even individuals are swiftly being hooked to massive and scalable server clusters and grids via the latest incarnation touted as cloud centers. Every IT infrastructural node individually and collectively is transitioning and being exposed as a usable, reusable, and composable service that is readily available for public discovery, usage, and leverage over any network. The dependency factor that kept IT resources as silos so far has been completely decimated and is gone forever, and henceforth, any software can run on any platform. Meshing and mashing up of heterogeneous

IT resources locally as well as globally will be very common, casual, and cheap. By seamlessly linking tens of thousands of servers and storage systems to power applications like search engines, social media, and online services, clouds represent the next evolution and revolution of computing. There is a new awakening in order to develop cloud-based services to support and streamline global-scale collaboration among cyber as well as physical entities and elements for the increasingly interlinked age. The cloud paradigm intrinsically represents Internet-scale efficiency and extensibility and allows the achievement of more with less with clean, lean, and green server farms.

IMPLICATIONS OF THE CLOUD ON ENTERPRISE STRATEGY

There are several enterprise constituents affected by adoption of the cloud. As we all know, EA is the aggregate of all the enterprise components. That is, EA directly and decisively deals with the enterprise as a whole and with its elements individually. EA has to efficiently and effectively manage the business side and the IT environment. Now, as the cloud is being offered as the most versatile technology, there are tremors amongst enterprise architects to quickly understand the implicit as well as the explicit transformation capabilities of cloud technology. Also, architects are expected to do the required cloud-induced twists and tweaks on already produced EA as well as on new EA. Enterprise architects are being increasingly tasked to tune their EA proposals to be meticulously cloud compliant. That is, whatever features and facilities are offered by cloud-stimulated business models as well as IT infrastructures need to be orchestrated into EA in order to capture and capitalize the impending opportunities in the cloud era.

Even enterprises are readying themselves to be termed as cloud enterprises through highly calculated and calibrated enhancements. This newly coined term "cloud enterprise" is zealously highlighted in the industry and media circles these days. That is, apart from the matured and modernized enterprise and web spaces, the cloud space is also emerging as the most promising landscape on the IT horizon. It is becoming clear that the evolving cloud space is really vast and very critical for future IT. Precisely speaking, cloud technology is very powerful and could shake and stun the entire enterprise and its architecture. Architects are bound to seriously and curiously enter, explore, and espouse the untapped potential of the cloud principles in order to arrive at highly sophisticated enterprise-wide architectures.

Architects have to take the cloud very sincerely before deciding, devising, depicting, and dictating a comprehensive, futuristic, flexible, and enterprise-wide architecture. A few visionaries across the world have argued that as companies trudge and move to cloud computing, the overall workload of enterprise architects goes down significantly. However, that is not the case as the boundary of IT is being extended with the inception and incorporation of the cloud story. There are more things to be taken into account, and to be probed and analyzed thoroughly, and hence the workload is always bound to go up. There are exhortations for the preference of private clouds over public clouds for some specific scenarios.

Shifting application and service portfolios to the cloud should make a lot of behind-the-scene headaches easier [2,5]. However, it does not eliminate the need for an effective enterprise strategy for putting together all the people, processes, and pieces in place in order to maintain business continuity and resiliency. Business has never really cared about what it was running on and just cares about its efficiency, versatility, and throughput. That means, even in cloud IT, the need for EA does not get diminished a bit. If anything, this cloud assimilation further complicates things. Not long ago, IT departments had the luxury of having full control of their entire landscape, which was built on top of matured and stable software packages. But, the emerging IT scene is presenting an altogether different picture. The unravelling and incubating cloud space brings forth a growing array of spectacular surprises and challenges alike for architects. In the sections to follow, we would like to focus on cloud-induced business shifts. In the ensuing chapter, we will see what sorts of changes are being enacted on IT environment by cloud technology.

ESTABLISHING A CLOUD-INCORPORATED BUSINESS STRATEGY

EA can be majorly segmented into two pieces: business and IT strategies. The business strategy mainly talks about the business objectives, processes, practices, models, illustrations, narratives, and so on. The current state and the ensuing state get clearly demarcated and highlighted so decision makers can ponder about the best course of action in order to journey toward the envisaged business vision with a missionary zeal. The details regarding business offerings, outlooks, operations, and outputs are to be duly and diligently dissected and discussed with the concerned authorities before arriving at an unquestionable business strategy.

A well-intended roadmap and implementation procedure has to be crafted and articulated by architects without any ambiguity to successfully and safely facilitate the strategy implementation.

New-Generation Business Models

Prominently and predominantly, there are two implications to be drawn out of the absorption of the cloud concepts. Entrepreneurs and out-of-the-box thinkers are coming out with newer and nimbler business models that reverberate and recognize people's expectations. The service-centric enterprise software design approach and the cloud as the efficient development, deployment, delivery, and management platform are collectively contributing to fresh opportunities. An array of quality models has emerged in the recent past and are performing well. Deployment, delivery, consumption, and pricing models are very hot in cloud environments.

As repeatedly mentioned previously, the powerful service paradigm is steadily permeating into every tangible domain and discipline these days. SaaS is the latest hit in the software industry. As per the leading market analysis and research reports, the SaaS market is going to be very huge. The cloud-based SaaS revenue will be approximately 150 billion dollars by the year 2015. Another noteworthy prediction is that around 75 percent of the worldwide enterprises by the year 2015 will have a presence in the service-enabled cloud environment.

Not only software modules but also the hardware infrastructures, software infrastructure solutions, and so on, are being exposed as services to be discovered remotely and leveraged purposefully over the open Internet anytime, anywhere, and on any device. Hence, there is a deluge of buzzwords such as hardware as a service (HaaS), platform as a service (PaaS), and so on. Besides these standard delivery models, there are deployment models such as private, public, and community clouds. All the conventional usage, IT licensing, and pricing models are being tossed aside. With many players in the ring, innovation and competitive pricing alone are going to decide and dictate the market as well as mind share in the impending cloud era. As postulated and prophesied a long time back, the vision that the network is the computer is set to see reality. Processing happens in consolidated, converged, and centralized servers, the cheap Internet has become the carrier and channel for transmitting messages, and results are compactly displayed in a variety of slim and sleek devices. The point is that these emerging business models have a lasting impact on a range of business elements.

The Business Process Journey

Business process is the core and central portion of any business today. As enterprise complexity is on the rise, process-level abstraction is being insisted upon for relieving complexity-induced difficulties. In short, the elasticity and elegance of business process gets reflected in the final software solution and its sustenance. The value of business process has gone up remarkably in the recent past with the service paradigm. There are fresh terminologies in the business process field such as business process innovation, orchestration, and governance.

Although centralization is the initial design criterion, distribution has, of late, caught up with the cloud idea. In view of the well-known and welcome fact that clouds are the next-generation infrastructure for service engineering, assembly, and delivery, SOA processes certainly have a telling effect on the cloud. On the other hand, cloud principles chip in with a number of influential improvements on enterprise processes.

Service-Oriented Processes

As the complexity and changes of enterprise IT are on the rise, technocrats are focusing on advancing the discipline of process engineering. Processes are the central nervous system for all kinds of IT systems and are being approached as the soothing artifacts. Processes facilitate modular application development, composition, and enhancement. With the widespread adoption of SOA, services are directly related to the processes and their subprocesses. A process model dictates which services are to be picked up and the order in which they have to be used for implementation. In other words, a process is composed by aggregating multiple services via orchestration and choreography methods. That is, composite services are used for completing a whole or partial business process or task. Due to surging popularity, plenty of process engineering, execution, and examination tools, engines, and containers are embedded in the standard SOA suite of leading SOA vendors. However, the traditional SOA processes face many challenges and concerns such as high performance, on-demand scalability, large payloads, memory constraints, real-time interactions, high availability, and reliability. In a distributed SOA environment, the real and root causes for more disturbances and deficiencies go up.

In most cases, the scalability bottlenecks across all these SOA parts (services, intermediary services, and service infrastructures) in a process occur when disk I/O, memory, or CPU saturation levels are reached. Moreover, the cluster technology, adopted by traditional SOA, can provide higher availability. However, it depends on static partitioning, where a single backup server is preassigned to serve requests from a failing server. The grid-enabled SOA provides a way to improve the performance, scalability, and availability of SOA processes in an economical manner [12,14]. Cloud computing shares the same goal as grid computing. While grid computing is mostly used for scientific research purposes, cloud computing is generally used for commercial purposes. Both allow service consumers to obtain computing resources on-demand and as much as they want. Self-service is another incredible aspect of cloud computing. Clouds are being recognized as elastic, green, shared, and virtual infrastructures for simplified service industrialization and delivery. SOA processes are the base for cloud processes to flower and flourish.

Cloud enablement spectacularly improves SOA process' capabilities such as scalability, performance, and availability. In summary, processes are the nucleus in any functional system. Process engineering is also going through a number of upgrades and updates today, as there are numerous hot topics that cater to process improvement, innovation, modeling, simulation, control, management, and so on. Besides, distributed and decentralized processes are being integrated seamlessly and smartly for multienterprise application engineering. Lean yet integrated and adaptive processes are much sought after these days.

Event-Driven Business Processes

Events are the latest entrant into the enterprise system domain and discipline. Enterprises are proactively remedying and readying their infrastructures and processes in order to quickly capture all sorts of incoming events, extract the actionable insights embedded in those event messages, and act upon them in real time. That is, any informed and timely action and reaction goes a long way in empowering dormant and dull enterprises to be at the forefront for conceiving and serving premium and pioneering services to their consumers, and customers. In short, events lay the foundation for real-time enterprises. Business event processing (BEP) is a new kind of method that allows businesses to be effective and efficient in creating and capitalizing newer opportunities.

There are containers capable of receiving millions of event messages from distributed sources and directing them to the appropriate recipients. Event-driven architecture (EDA) is an architectural style that is becoming very popular, and it is being attached with SOA in order to guarantee event-driven service-oriented enterprises. Processes are also accordingly strengthened to incorporate events and their passages. As clouds are the new vigorous and rigorous cyber systems and are centrally located and managed, EDA is bound to play a very important role in cloud-centric enterprises. Cloud processes are being strengthened to be dynamic, thoroughly automated, and real time with the incorporation of events and their inspiring value.

Communication-Enabled Business Processes

Communication is set to become unified and universal [8,10–11]. Wireless broadband standards and technologies on a fast track, and slim and sleek, handy and trendy devices are hitting the market very frequently. Devices are special purpose as well as generic in their functionality. In the recent past, we have come across scores of multifaceted smartphones and tablets with enhanced memory modules, multicore processors, and multitouch interfaces. In short, computing and communication have become ubiquitous. The unfailing trend is that computers are turning into communicators and vice versa.

For knowledge workers, sales and field teams, and executives on the move, personal devices are being integrated with central corporate servers remotely. This new connectivity method enables professionals to be precise, productive, and preemptive in their everyday operations and offerings. As there are many kinds [11] of input/output devices for receiving and sending information, enterprise processes are being attached with communication capabilities. That means users as well as systems can be notified in real time about the sequence of events and important messages. That is, all stakeholders, wherever they are and whatever they are doing, are very much in the loop. Not only macro-level management but also microlevel management facilities are being enabled.

Analytics-Attached Business Processes

Actionable insights in time are the most critical aspect for enterprises to keep ahead. Every industry is trying out various methods to extract and generate intelligence and to act on it proactively. Business intelligence, retail intelligence, supply chain intelligence, security intelligence, and so on are some of the widely used buzzwords. There are several techniques, tips, and tools for quickly arriving at useful intelligence such as integration, classification, clustering, composition and mining methods, predictive algorithms, analytic approaches, and presentation mechanisms such as dashboards, diverse charts, and so on. Due to the proximity and prominence of knowledge extraction and engineering with many business types, business processes are exquisitely emboldened with analytical capabilities.

Cloud-Impacted Business Processes

As indicated previously, the cloud principle has deftly impacted the subject of process. Processes are solidified so that achieving nonfunctional (QoS) attributes of any system becomes simpler and smarter. With new business models, process change is inescapable. The cloud enablement represents the epitome of all the process evolutions. Cloud process improvement is like the icing on the cake of technology-inspired process empowerments and excellence.

Ultimately, the target is to derive integrated and intelligent processes. Adaptivity happens profusely in an integrated space. Insights extracted by analytics are being fed for process excellence. Further on, optimization, efficiency, consolidation, and virtualization techniques being leveraged by the cloud paradigm can be used for sharply enhancing and sustaining process innovations. Besides the process-induced changes, there are several other noteworthy trends and tricks for the much-deliberated cloud enterprises.

In summary, the process discipline has been going through a swath of tectonic shifts due to seamless synchronization with pioneering advancements in the technology space. Now, the spectacular success of cloud computing imposes some solid and stunning transformations on the process domain. These transitions at the process level ultimately lead to the quicker and easier realization of the stated goals behind cloud enterprises. Process centricity and propensity go a long way in stabilizing and maintaining the ideas and ideals of cloud enterprises.

TRANSITIONING TO CLOUD-CENTRIC ENTERPRISES: THE TUNING METHODOLOGY

In today's knowledge-driven and globalized economy, the ability to be sensitive and responsive (S&R) to business and technology changes is more important than ever before. Information capturing, transmission, persistence, modeling, processing, mining, and analyzing in order to extract and engineer reusable and repeatable knowledge have become the key operational areas for most enterprises. Information is a vital asset to be taken care of in order to generate actionable insights for achieving several worthwhile and wonderful things such as shrinking cycle times; competitive offerings, and operations; and proactive, preemptive, and people-centric approaches. The market imperative to be in a nimble, receptive, and collaborative state have led to an increased interest in cloud-enabled production and provisioning of next-generation enterprise services. As per media reports, cloud adoption and adaption are shaping up well on the expected lines among global enterprises. Strategies are being decided, a roadmap is being created, and both primary and second resources are being put up in place. Here is a strategy for helping businesses to enter the cloud era.

This segment describes the key areas an enterprise needs to address during the transformation into a cloud enterprise. At the outset, EA professionals have a bigger role in setting right the tough-to-crack contract details. They have to engage fervently with various CSPs, infrastructure vendors, and other players in the cloud ecosystem to arrive at well-defined contract specifications. That is, apart from initiating the relevant process tasks in building an enterprise cloud, EAs have a greater and grander role in contacting and contracting with a few third-party CSPs and IT infrastructure vendors for enhanced enterprise value. EAs are supposed to draw and derive competitively defined and refined contractual obligations to execute efficient business transactions with others in a win-win mode. Having a broader as well as deeper understanding about the cloud theme comes in handy for EAs in arriving at sound SLA and OLA documents.

Service Categorization

As widely emphasized, service enablement is the first step toward cloud-centric enterprises. Services are the base and best unit for optimized business integration, application modernization, and enterprise engineering. Prominently, there are three types of services (software, platforms, and infrastructures) being offered by CSPs. In the recent past, with the unprecedented adoption of the cloud idea across the world, there have been innumerable innovators and individuals jumping on the cloud bandwagon in order to provide an increasing array of primary as well as peripheral services. Thus, there are CBSs, auditing services, procurement services, monitoring, profiling, security, carrier services, and so on.

Thus, any enterprise, before embarking on the long and laborious cloud journey, has to decide the major IT and business services to be subscribed from third-party cloud service providers. Thus, service cataloguing and classification has to happen in the first place. Some of the existing services can be remedied and readied for the cloud environment. Systematic planning and execution definitely smooths the road. Modernization and cloud migration are very important assignments that are of the utmost importance. For example, technology services such as storage, processing, and network can be availed on-demand from one or more infrastructure as a service (IaaS) providers. Similarly, "integration as a service" can be implemented internally or delegated to external service providers under certain circumstances.

The Selection Criteria of Services

As the value of cloud-inspired enterprise is consistently on the climb, newer cloud services and applications are hitting the market. However, which services need to be outsourced from external CSPs and which have to be sourced internally have to be decoded and decided very carefully based on the following criteria:

- Flexibility, visibility, dependability, and controllability
- Elasticity and availability
- Security, privacy, and time to market
- Business continuity via effective disaster recovery (DR)
- Standardized to avoid vendor lock-in
- SLA
- Financial implications and brand value
- Auditability and accountability
- User-friendly interfaces and automation tools for self-service and auto-scaling

After the selection of the service and the CSP, an important issue is to define the contract with the CSP to ensure superior business versatility, robustness, and resiliency. A simple strategy is to find, select, and start with those services that

- Do not have big interaction with other services and information bases
- Bring high value to the business
- Have lower security risks

The services that fulfill these attributes are the first candidates for transformation.

Leveraging EA Frameworks for an Enterprise-Wide and Long-Lasting Cloud Strategy

There are sound and solid EA frameworks in order to simplify and streamline EA development, management, and governance. Through collaboration with well-accomplished EA practitioners, The Open Group has crafted a comprehensive, compact and catalytic architecture framework known as "The Open Group Architecture Framework" (TOGAF). Leading business and infrastructure software solution providers such as IBM and Oracle have produced their own EA frameworks for their own purposes as well as for consulting. These architectural frameworks help immeasurably in arriving at a right cloud strategy that lends strategic value and leads to tighter business–IT alignment. There are proven EA development methodologies, fine-tuned knowledge bases, best practices and guidelines, mappings, matrices, and metrics to be taken into account while framing an easily implementable cloud strategy for growing enterprises. In addition to that, the integrated architecture framework (IAF) from Capgemini [1] helps to calculate the business value of services. Also, this EA framework [9] contains the relevant details of contract definition and management. These contribute immensely toward better strategy. Another observation is that it simplifies and streamlines the derivation of services across different areas ranging from business to technology.

Utilizing a Hybrid Cloud

Going straight to public clouds is full of risks and potentially injurious. Creating an enterprise cloud locally and on need basis, subscribing and accessing public clouds is a viable method. The private cloud stands as a cushion for any kind of deviation, deficiency, and disturbance in public clouds. Security, lack of transparency, visibility, and controllability, and so on are often quoted as the main barriers for third-party clouds. With these issues being attended to and addressed, there will be greater inclination toward public clouds at a later stage. Thus, going for hybridization is the reasonable and responsible choice. A community cloud should also be given due consideration as there are some specific circumstances that mandate it. Apart from these, there are domain- and purpose-specific clouds being built and sustained. Enabling cooperation among these distributed, diverse, and distinct clouds is critical.

Pondering Cloud Modernization and Migration

Every single enterprise is flooded with a growing collection of legacy as well as modern applications. Most of them might be monolithic, closed, and silo-like, whereas the remaining would be based on modular design approaches such as component-based and service-oriented paradigms. Other famous building blocks include formally defined models, agents, aspects, and, in the recent past, composites. Events are also contributing immensely to building event-driven applications that are very much relevant for fulfilling dynamic, adaptive, real-time, and S & R requirements. Event messages carry a deluge of actionable insights such as trends, tips, associations, alerts, patterns, risks, and so on to be captured and leveraged instantly and intelligently. Rules, policies, and ontologies are also enabling highly dynamic applications by sharply reducing the dependence on human interpretation, instruction, and intervention.

On the development front, a variety of building blocks are being astutely combined in order to create sophisticated applications. Component-based assembly, service-oriented orchestration, and mashups are the leading mechanisms. At the programming level, agile approaches are very hot compared to the traditional static programming processes. Of late, the agile principles are being smartly tied up with service- and model-centric approaches in order to speed up the tasks associated with application engineering and maintenance. That is, with this growing diversity and multiplicity of applications and their modules, the modernization of tasks becomes very complicated. Thus, there is a need for unearthing enabling methodologies and technology-sponsored solutions for modernization and migration.

Transitioning from Data Centers to Cloud Centers

With the stabilization and successful journey of the cloud paradigm, there is a vigorous and rigorous focus on wisely applying cloud technologies to transition present-day data centers into consolidated, virtualized, resource-provisioning, self-servicing, auto-optimizing, elastic, and shared data centers, which are termed cloud centers. There are competent technologies and tools emerging for facilitating this tectonic and seismic shift.

Creating Cloud-Centric Enterprise Policies

Policies are prevalent in any business IT environment. There are business, technical, operational, transaction, and security policies. When moving to assimilate the advantages of the cloud, policies play a critical role in shaping up the transition. All kinds of unwanted things get weeded out through appropriate policies.

Cloud migration is not easy. There are bigger challenges on the fronts of governance and management. There are automated solutions in order to minimize the management aspects. With more cloud providers, brokers, consumers, auditors and so on in the cloud space, cloud governance is emerging as a new domain of intense and intimate focus. However, professionals and proponents bring forth a deluge of cloud-centric strategies, mechanisms, guidelines, best practices, evaluation and measurement metrics, policy-enforcement monitors, and so on. In the following section, we would like to discuss in detail one prominent management topic: arriving at and agreeing to a contract with one or more external service providers.

CONTRACT MANAGEMENT IN THE CLOUD

There are several things being delivered from the cloud these days. That is, again, the concept of centralization gains much ground. Centralized hosting, transmission, distribution, and management of business as well as IT services are being given wider recognition. Not only software packages but also service-enabled IT infrastructures and platforms are being readied to be given to global users. In the recent past, there has been an intensive and interesting debate on buy versus build versus rent. That is, the days of commercial-of-the-shelf (COTS) products are ending.

Building is a time-consuming and risky affair. Thus, the trend is veering toward renting highly proficient IT solutions and services developed and managed by experts. Users need to pay for the amount or the time period of usage, although there other monitoring and billing options. Computing that is self-service, on-demand, and of high quality is becoming a reality.

The portfolio of cloud-based services is consistently on the rise. Innovations are being revealed and thriving. Companies need not bother about owning and managing an IT division in order to automate their business operations. That is, the total IT requirement of a corporation can be simply switched over to CSPs. This is the power of the enlarging and enigmatic cloud IT.

All kinds of IT applications are delivered via the Internet and consumed in real time by a growing array of client devices. Cloud services can interact with other local services within the cloud, with remote services that are in the enterprise space, or with services in other clouds. For example, considering the security implications, confidential and corporate information are still being stocked up in enterprise servers. However user-centric and client-facing business applications have already been moved to cloud environments. Thus, there is an intrinsic need for integration between cloud and enterprise servers in order to generate and give usable information to executives on time. In other words, enterprise and public clouds need to be seamlessly connected, and applications need to be integrated for information exchange.

Aspects such as cloud service integration, composition, and collaboration are increasingly relevant, and they are nearer to reality. The boundaryless flow of information is at the center of cloud computing. All these movements clearly indicate and insist that contract issues need to be handled very carefully as complexity is increasing. Experts need to be involved in signing contractual obligations as contracts are becoming murkier in the cloud space. Further on, there are myriads of regulatory environments in order to deliver service globally. Geographical, cultural, and legal issues abound as the world is becoming connected and synchronized via the cloud revolution.

It is all about open and beneficial interactions and how services can be delivered using the cloud in a reliable, efficient, and secured way. The evolving trend is that cloud interaction is becoming really global. It is being visualized that the fast emerging and merging embedded, enterprise, and cloud spaces will be the mainstream computing environment for the future. On the technical side, agencies and consortiums are being instituted in order to attend to the integration conundrum quickly through industry-strength standards.

Cloud Contract Characteristics

Liability and intellectual property are just a few of the issues that must be considered. Other contractual issues include the following:

- *End-of-service support (including reversibility clause)*—When the provider–customer relationship ends, customer assets, such as services, applications, and data, should be repackaged and delivered to the customer without any condition. And any remaining copies of customer data should be erased from the provider's infrastructure.
- *Provisioning and scalability*—Resource provisioning has to be made simpler and smarter. Additional resources can be quickly supplied by the provider with just a click. That is, auto-scaling has to be an inseparable part of infrastructure clouds. Also, unwanted resources can be immediately deleted to nip any kind of performance degradation in the bud. Supply and demand variance has to be very minimal.
- *SLA*—This includes defining the process of managing and monitoring capacity, data protection, data privacy, operational integrity, vulnerability management, business continuity, DR, identity management, and ownership of intellectual properties. Similarly, OLA requirements also have to be discussed threadbare and signed.
- *Payments and penalties models*—They define the payment contract between the providers of the service and the users. Some of the models can be pay per use and pay for capacity. What are the penalties for stopping the contract? Another challenge are the tracking and billing processes.
- *Availability*—The availability of cloud services has to be guaranteed by CSP in sync-up with the network service provider (NSP).
- *Issue resolution/escalation*—How and by whom are resolutions handled? When and to whom do issues need to be escalated? How are change requests being handled? Who has the rights?
- *Liability*—The CSP is responsible for ensuring that the provided services are compliant to relevant regulations and that subcontractors are also fully compliant. These result in a situation whereby the organization only needs to negotiate a contract with the main CSP.

Cloud Participants

Typically, there are CSPs and cloud service consumers (CSCs). However, with the considerable adoption of the pioneering and path-breaking cloud paradigm across the world, cloud service brokers (CSBs) are the new important entities in the burgeoning and bewildering cloud space. Cloud brokers are used for facilitating cloud integration, intermediation, and arbitration purposes. Cloud brokers are the abstraction of common middleware services from both cloud owners and users.

A cloud broker is an organization or entity that creates and maintains relationships with multiple CSPs across the globe. This makes it possible for cloud consumers to choose the best CSP (based on cost, location, QoS attributes, and so on) for particular service needs. Also, it is possible to simultaneously leverage diverse services provided by multiple providers for complex service requirements. That is, business-aware and business-aligned composite services can be crafted out of numerous CSPs via a cloud broker. CSPs are mandated to provide consistent and highly configurable user interfaces in order to enhance user experience.

Cloud brokers provide additional services such as intermediation, orchestration, and arbitration services. Client consumers and providers are linked up via cloud brokers. A cloud broker might provide consolidated billing, seamless switching between cloud computing services, or simultaneous connection to different cloud computing services, as well as federated identity management or other added services.

A cloud broker may also survey CSPs to understand their capabilities, liabilities, business models, and costs. This does away with the activation of multiple relationships and instead favors the forging of just one relationship with a trustworthy and competent cloud broker who would understand the client's IT service requirements completely. The cloud broker could, in turn, select the best cloud services for the client organization and expertly monitor those services on its behalf. A cloud broker will provide significant cost savings and enable every cloud user to better make use of the tactical and strategic cloud advantages. Cloud auditors are third-party CSPs exclusively for the public audit of CSPs.

Role of EA in Defining the Contracts with CSPs and CSBs

The EA has a key role in defining and maintaining effective contracts in order to facilitate communication and collaboration among providers, consumers, and brokers.

In summary, it is clear that the top-down, incremental roll-out strategy supported by business-led strategies will be more ideal and successful than IT-led initiatives for cloud enablement. Business goals, constraints, and cases are the main pillars and factors while chalking out a competent enterprise-wide strategy. At the same time, IT investments and services need to be considered along with the direct and indirect risks involved in cloud migration. In the end, it is all about business performance, competitiveness, and results that dictate technology adoption. In order to embark and embrace the sizzling cloud technology, there are two main things to do.

1. Set in place a team in order to define and govern the EA across the company and the cloud.
2. Define a strategy in order to accelerate the transformation, taking into account both the trends of the market and the value for the company.

There is a clarion call to evolve a company-specific accelerator framework that clearly helps in analyzing and articulating the capabilities and competencies of new technologies, the challenges and concerns related to their utilization, the internal as well as the external effects and factors of going for new technologies, the ultimate business outputs expected and elucidated, and so on.

CONCLUSION

In this chapter, we have discussed the distinct and decisive features of cloud computing and incorporated a brief discussion about the turnarounds that can be achieved out of any cloud-based EA initiative in any business organization. Also, we have explained how next-generation enterprises can leverage the stabilizing and sizzling concepts of the landmark cloud idea toward better-prepared enterprises to take on all kinds of business and technology-induced changes and challenges confidently. Going forward, soaring consumers' expectations can also be speedily, cleanly, and compactly incorporated into ICT systems. In short, the forthcoming cloud IT is more turned and tuned toward accomplishing people's demands quite naturally.

In the minds of many, there were some lingering doubts about the cloud paradigm as an assistive, assertive, and affective EA technology. This has ended with deeper understanding of cloud concepts. As we all know, the paradigm of EA has been prescribed for ages as the best instrument for building and enabling enterprises to be proactive and preemptive in accomplishing new realities and requirements. However, it has recently been found that the key principles of cloud computing contribute heavily in arriving and articulating at an extensible and elegant EA. Hence, professionals and pundits are competing with one another in bringing out the brewing, beneficial, and dynamic relationship between the cloud and EA. This chapter has done a bit in revealing the evolutionary as well as the revolutionary associations among them and in exhibiting and exhorting how this cool interdependence goes a long way in solidifying next-generation enterprises.

REFERENCES

1. Harrington, E. February 9, 2011. "Enterprise Architecture, Cloud Computing and the US Federal Government." The Open Group San Diego Conference, San Diego, CA, February 9, 2011, http://www.architecting-the-enterprise.com/pdf/presentations/enterprise_architecture_cloud_computing_and_the_us_federal_government.pdf.
2. Chahal, S. et al. June 2010. "An Enterprise Private Cloud Architecture and Implementation Roadmap," Intel Information Technology, Santa Clara, CA, http://www.intel.com/content/dam/doc/guide/intel-it-enterprise-cloud-architecture-roadmap-paper.pdf.
3. Cisco Systems. July 28, 2010. "Cloud Computing and the Economics of Enterprise IT," Cisco Systems, Inc., San Jose, CA.
4. Citrix Systems, Inc. 2010. "Is Your Load Balancer Cloud Ready? How NetScaler Helps Enterprises Achieve Cloud Computing Benefits," Citrix Systems, Inc., Fort Lauderdale, FL, https://images01.insight.com/media/pdf/0311Whitepaper2NetScalerIsYourLoadBalancerCloudReady.pdf.
5. Doddavula, S. K., and A. W. Gawande. 2009. "Adopting Cloud Computing: Enterprise Private Clouds." *SETLabs Briefings* 7 (7): 18.
6. Ebneter, D., S. G. Grivas, T. U. Kumar, and H. Wache. 2010. "Enterprise Architecture Frameworks for Enabling Cloud Computing." *IEEE 3rd International Conference on Cloud Computing*, Olten, Switzerland, July 5–10, 2010.
7. Grigoriu, A. 2009. "The Cloud Enterprise," BPTrends, Wokingham, http://www.bptrends.com/publicationfiles/TWO_04-09-ART-The_Cloud_Enterprise-Grigoriu_v1-final.pdf.
8. Herrell, E., R. Whiteley, and A. Crumb. 2010. "Enterprise Communications: The Next Decade," Forrester Research, Inc., Cambridge, MA.
9. Deloitte. 2010. "Deloitte Debates: Does Cloud Computing Make Enterprise Architecture Irrelevant?", Deloitte, New York, NY, http://www.deloitte.com/assets/Dcom-UnitedStates/Local%20Assets/Documents/us_consulting_CloudComputingDebate_092110.pdf.

10. NEC. 2009. "Enterprise Communications and Collaboration in a Fast Changing World," NEC, Irving, TX, http://www.nec.com/en/global/ad/itnw/pdf/fast_changing_wp.pdf.
11. NEC. 2010. "Converging Enterprise: Communications, IT and the Cloud (White Paper)," NEC, Irving, TX, http://www.nec-itsolutions.com.
12. Raines, G. October 2009. "Cloud Computing and SOA." 2009 MITRE Technical Papers, MITRE, Bedford, MA, http://www.mitre.org/work/tech_papers/index.html.
13. Somashekar, S. January 2010. "Opportunities for the Cloud in the Enterprise," CA, Inc., http://www.ca.com/~/media/Files/whitepapers/opp-cloud-enterprise_226125.pdf.
14. Tsai, W.-T., X. Sun, and J. Balasooriya. 2010. "Service-Oriented Cloud Computing Architecture." *New Generations (ITNG) Seventh International Conference on Information Technology*, Las Vegas, NV, April 12–14, 2010.
15. Verizon. 2010. "Solutions Briefs: Next-Generation Identity Management for Cloud-Enabled Ecosystems," Verizon, http://www.verizonbusiness.com/resources/solutionbriefs/sb_next-generation-identity-management-for-cloud-enabled-ecosystems_ en_xg.pdf.

3

Cloud-Instigated IT Transformations!

INTRODUCTION

Designing enterprise architecture (EA) presents a bigger challenge in the cloud era. With the gripping cloud idea, the business and IT landscapes are solidly expanding further and farther. Therefore, enterprise architects' roles and responsibilities are becoming diversified and complicated. To moderate the rising complexity, EA is increasingly being splintered into a bunch of smaller projects. That is, here too, the acts of decomposition and composition gain prominence. Toward the end, the aggregate of all of them is created and concluded. The impacts of the cloud in business goals, operations, service offerings, processes, and partnerships need to be fully understood in order to arrive at a comprehensive and convincing business strategy and architecture. Secondly, the IT improvements need to be taken into acute and astute consideration as it is being pronounced widely in world media that there are several incisive and decisive advancements out of embracing the cloud.

There are a series of promising and potential optimizations on IT infrastructure. Cloud infrastructures are being portrayed and presented as the next-generation service, on-demand, autonomic, elastic, and utility computing infrastructures. All kinds of development, deployment, testing, production, and management platforms for futuristic enterprise IT are also being incrementally laid on cloud infrastructures. Finally, all kinds of personal and professional services and applications are being sent to cloud platforms. Thus, with the aggressive adoption of the ever-shining cloud across the industry, there is a palpable and strategic shift in any IT environment. As discussed in Chapter 2, there are pioneering deployment, delivery, management, pricing, and consumption models emerging and evolving continuously. These business-centric models are being supported with the corresponding empowerment in IT infrastructures.

In short, the cloud idea bridges and blends the business and IT environments together to accomplish more and better things for humanity.

The domineering trend is that all sorts of IT products and solutions are becoming cloud-based services to be provisioned to millions of users simultaneously across the globe. In a nutshell, the stability of cloud facilitates the vision of "IT as a service." Cloud computing has become such a path-breaking and premium technology. All tangible modules of IT are being touched upon in an exemplary fashion. If there is not a well-intended and defined EA in place to spell out which cloud solution has to be used, what technologies are required, how they have to be approached and accomplished in the cloud context, and how it all fits into the big picture, eventually the enterprise is bound to suffer. The long-term perspective will be sorely missed.

The good news is that the shift to cloud services will actually simplify and sensitize IT to operate more systematically and successfully. Whether there is a different group of professionals responsible for managing and overseeing it, or it is built into the group's DNA, EA will be one of the prime enablers and exponents of IT in this modern world. From the cloud's ongoing journey, it can be inferred that the versatile idea of the cloud is to take enterprise architecture to the next level. That is, cloud architecture is all set to become an inseparable and indistinguishable part of EA. As cloud computing matures, it materially and mesmerizingly influences any organization that is hell-bent on leveraging the cloud's unique concepts and capabilities. Cloud adoption is bound to bring in a number of significant and delectable modifications in enterprise analysis, planning, strategy, execution, and enhancement. It is obligatory to seamlessly enable the smooth integration of enterprise procedures, processes, patterns, platforms, and practices into the cloud paradigm. Prominently, there will be several domains that get attracted and altered by the convergence of EA with the exploding and expanding cloud domain. Ultimately, the brewing IT trend is toward the realization of cloud-centric enterprises.

EXPLAINING CLOUD INFRASTRUCTURES

Cloud infrastructures can be segmented into a few major types: computing, communication, and storage infrastructures. Let us take a deeper and more detailed look at these in the following sections.

Cloud Computing Infrastructure

Apart from a series of groundbreaking innovations in introducing newer and nimbler business models, the doughty cloud idea has laid the stimulating and scintillating foundation for next-generation IT infrastructure, which is the most crucial and critical component for cloud-centric enterprises [1,4–7]. Cloud infrastructure is a dynamic pool of consolidated, virtualized, and automated server systems. With federated clouds emerging fast, federation has become a key enabler. These unique features, in association with the auto-provisioning and deprovisioning capabilities, enable and ensure unprecedented IT optimization. The utilization rate has gone up considerably. That is, several heterogeneous applications are being deployed, delivered, and managed in a single physical server through the partitioning and provisioning of multiple VMs.

IT portability and flexibility are on the rise with the clear separation of hardware and software components. That is, any software runs perfectly on any virtualized environment. As promoted by Sun Microsystems, Java technology has achieved platform portability whereas the .NET framework facilitates the language portability requirement. In a virtualized setup, any software coded using any language runs on any platform without any hitch. In a virtualized environment, all the IT resources are being controlled with better and deeper visibility. That is, memory, processing, and storage modules can be operated in a finely grained fashion. Allocation and deallocation of computing resources are being simplified using automated tools. Live-in migration of VMs is becoming a reality. Thus, in short, the virtualization seed has sprouted a number of fresh possibilities and opportunities as well. The end product is on-demand, lean, utility-like, green, affordable, and available IT infrastructure. The cloud technology has a stunning and soothing effect on power-hungry, mammoth, silo-like, closed, costly, and complicated data centers and server farms. Green activists are enthused by the lower electricity consumption and lesser heat dissipation from cloud centers. That is, the cloud idea has emerged as the most influential element for arresting climate change; thus, the goal of environmental sustainability through the reduced outpour of greenhouse gases will see the dazzling light at the end of the long tunnel.

There are several options such as public, private, hybrid, and community clouds. There are specific clouds such as science, knowledge, storage, government, information, service, and mobile clouds. However, the clouds of the future are federated clouds, which ultimately lead to the intercloud. As a first step, enterprises are building their own cloud. We are going to see how enterprise clouds are fully supporting various business operations and offerings of enterprises. Before that, a brief digression.

Cloud Communications Infrastructure

Enterprise architects focus not only on the computing front but also on the communication space in order to frame and formulate a comprehensive enterprise strategy [16–19]. There are both evolutionary and revolutionary movements in the hot communication field. Cutting-edge technologies and state-of-the-art infrastructures contribute immensely to making communication. Enterprise communication has also been through several remarkable and radical changes in the last decade, and the same is expected in the years to come. In the communication space, the often presented and pronounced buzzwords are ambient communication, autonomic communication, and unified communication (UC). The communication landscape is quite rewarding and pregnant with powerful technologies. Communication service providers; connectivity solution vendors; content, application, and service providers; standards consortiums; service integrators; and other important stakeholders are cognitively and collaboratively working tirelessly in producing new-generation and people-centric communication services to maintain revenue flows.

Now with the game-changing cloud technology sweeping the entire the ICT industry, there are more sophisticated, situation-aware, and premium services from cloud-enabled communication providers. Multifaceted mobile applications and services are increasingly stocked up and served from highly specific and smart cloud environments. For example, Apple has introduced a new mobile cloud "iCloud" for their iPhone and iPad users. The mobile space is already crowded with a wider variety of service providers and is buzzing with attractive and appealing services to keep mobile users happy. These mobile clouds decimate all sorts of media differences. Further on, all kinds of base services are seamlessly aggregated and composite services are produced on the fly to be made available according to users' locations and device capabilities via centralized cloud. The latest Forrester report [4] on enterprise communications insists on cloud-based multimodal services that directly provide much-needed multimodal communication and collaboration facilities.

Businesses have been asking for a bevy of deft and disruptive technologies to gain real-time connectivity and collaboration capabilities for their workers to sharply enhance their productivity while fulfilling real-time delivery within reasonable cost. The other critical segment is end users, who aspire for context-aware services. Technology advancements include innovative applications based on session initiation protocol (SIP), multimodal devices that displace landline phones, increased adoption of open source software, widespread video usage, and mobile business intelligence (BI) and UC for contextual collaboration. Social networking sites supply more relevant content and information for workers.

There is a rapid expansion of SIP for services and applications. Devices will provide greater functionality to replace or coexist with desktop phones. The growth of working remotely and telecommuting, which will create demand for secure mobile applications, will be facilitated by SIP. Video usage will become common and casual and promotes conversations and collaboration across enterprise. Video-based surveillance, security, and safety will get a strong boost in the days ahead. These changes will create and sustain an integrated workplace environment that facilitates real-time and purposeful collaboration to fulfill business goals and to assist in forming and firming up aware and aligned processes. Videoconferencing solutions will expand steadily and capture more market segments as they are inexpensive, and will open up a number of not-yet-envisioned options. Physical meetings will gradually become cyber as companies start to embrace hugely cost-effective video solutions for internal meetings and to engage with their customers over audio and video communication over the web. Video solutions will expand upward into large telepresence conference rooms and downward to individual desktops. The cost savings achieved on the reduction of travel costs often support the business case for video market expansion.

Other noteworthy trends include the much-maligned convergence in the mobile space. Computers are becoming communicators, whereas communicators tend to be computers. Cell phones are transitioning to smartphones with the smooth synchronization of mobile phones and personal digital assistant (PDA) functionalities. Miniaturization technologies superbly contribute for very large scale integration of multiple digital modules that work cohesively together within a phone. This terrific transformation helps mobile phones to be actively involved in business transactions. Professionals on the move benefit exceedingly from this great evolution. Wireless and mobile devices seamlessly bring together voice, the Internet, and video to support business communication. Integration with UC software allows workers to use their mobile devices for contextual and content-based collaboration and enables access to features that indicate a coworker's availability and location. Mobile BI and mobile-based commercial and financial transactions will flourish and proceed at a feverish pace. There will be a huge precipitation in mobile services. The mobile web will see a flurry of activity. Mobile governance, retail, banking, commerce, ticketing, games, and so on will become simpler and ubiquitous.

Virtualization for the Communication Industry

Of late, virtualization has become a highly impactful and insightful technology. Virtualization enables partitioning of any IT resource into a collection of independently composable and manageable modules. This makes the handling and usage of modules simpler, wastage of resources gets substantially reduced, energy costs crash down, complexity gets minimized, utilization goes up, innovation is facilitated, and so on. All communications activity needs to be capable of being virtualized, just like any other application. Communications servers and applications need to be virtualized and capable of being deployed over any thin clients including virtual desktops. The ultimate business benefit is not only to reduce costs but also to facilitate novel and flexible working models. With virtualization, enterprise managers and knowledge workers become less interested in where their platforms and applications are being hosted and run as long as their computing needs are being fulfilled in time and within the agreed cost. Centralized systems connected to remote locations using high-speed networks allow services to be produced and provided quickly. Centralization brings cost savings and effective management leading to new utility pricing and deployment models.

The Cloud Inspires the UC Paradigm

The emerging UC concept is definitely appealing and compelling. UC is all about the seamless and spontaneous convergence of all kinds of connectivity and communication methods between two or more people, from any application, using any device, at any location, via the most appropriate route, enabling effective and real-time collaboration with business-grade security.

With UC, IT departments can offer streamlined communication solutions and advanced productivity-enhancing applications throughout the network. Because of the facets it implicitly incorporates and combines, UC is a definite and decisive value-add for corporations focusing on communication-related services. UC is a powerful entity, capable of creating ample and accelerated business opportunities. Advanced UC applications, for example, provide the real-time status and availability of other staff, including preferred methods of contact and communication.

With this level of presence, employees can quickly determine who is accessible and where. Time and context will become critical deciding factors for crafting next-generation applications. Mobility solutions further extend the unprecedented capabilities of communications network beyond the confines of organization environments. Regardless of the location, mobility can provide presence and voice communications via smartphones as if the employee were physically in the office. Video communications and desktop collaboration have also emerged as promising UC solutions. Both can provide tremendous benefits. Around 90% of human communication is based on visual cues, so video serves as a logical extension of the UC network. With the addition of the brewing functionalities of desktop collaboration, such as the ability to share documents, presentations, and any stored media, UC is all set to become the dominant force in the days to come. That is, UC becomes not only completely versatile but increasingly indispensable in today's fast-expanding communication space.

Communication as a Service

The transformational cloud technology permeates into the money-spinning communication domain. Providing communication services from the cloud will turn the current communication landscape upside down. Communication as a service (CaaS), an offshoot of cloud enablement of communication services, is being projected as the next-generation communication method. Cloud empowerment brings the celebrated centralized service delivery into the communication landscape. Although currently an emerging market, CaaS offers greater accessibility for UC applications and services. Network service providers will offer communication and collaboration solutions to companies as a fee-based service offering, which incorporates the Web 2.0 technology stack with solutions from traditional premise-based providers.

CaaS eliminates the need for acquiring and operating on-premise telephone equipment and does away with the need for voice applications. Rather than overinvesting, companies can focus on their competencies such as adding novel communication applications. The adoption of integrated applications allows workers to use advanced applications. Integration will support a connected and well-knit workforce and reduce business delays due to existing limitations of current applications. Information workers can quickly launch conferencing and collaboration sessions with their peers, partners, and people, and accelerate decision making. It is all about efficiency and reducing waste.

In summary, it is very clear that cloud technology will have a deep impact on the communication industry. Communication will become pervasive, easily consumable, and affordable through a neat and nice integration and cooperation among computing and communication methods.

We all know that the impact of the cloud paradigm on IT infrastructures is really tremendous and trend setting. A number of strategic transformations are bound to occur and recur in the infrastructure domain and discipline with the exploitation of inventive cloud concepts. In the subsequent sections, we will discuss the futuristic cloud-based services and their refreshing features.

A BRIEFING ON NEXT-GENERATION SERVICES

All kinds of enterprise services and applications are being modernized and migrated to and managed in converged, cohesive, and highly automated cloud infrastructures and platforms [6,12–14]. Web-based services are being deployed in highly optimized cloud servers to be delivered and consumed via the public and open Internet. With the unmatched advancements in the device space (fixed, portable, nomadic, mobile, wireless, handheld, pocketable, implantable, wearable, etc.), the aura of device services performing and providing information, commercial, convenient, comforting, caring, financial, and even physical services is gaining ground.

In the recent past, device services are also being moved to clouds in order to reap the unique advantages being offered by the cloud paradigm. Sensors and devices-to-cloud integration frameworks middleware, services, and software packages are being given thrust in academic as well as in corporate circles in order to make the cloud the most natural choice not only for enterprise but also for embedded IT solutions. In short, future IT solutions will be mostly cloud centric. Traditional IT products will be methodically switched over to service-oriented and cloud-based methods.

There are several established as well as start-up companies offering lean, green, and special-purpose cloud infrastructures in order to capture and capitalize on the technology-sponsored and business-driven changes. Platform providers are also enthusiastically hyperactive in this growing space. Newer deployment and delivery models have erupted in the recent past and are being consciously supported to reach greater heights. In a nutshell, it is all about distributed and decentralized cloud centers taking care of the growing array of diverse services, applications, and data (personal as well as professional). This induces and inspires the need for reflective and introspective cloud brokers (a kind of software middleware for connecting, integrating, and composing people-centric and context-aware cloud services) and brokerage service firms. Primarily, brokerage services include discovery, negotiation, intermediation, and aggregation, arbitration, and collaboration services. Frankly speaking, cloud brokerage firms help cloud consumers in identifying and tying up with the best cloud providers. In this process, cloud providers also gain bigger market share.

As per Gartner's latest market research and analysis report on cloud computing, there is a huge market out there for cloud brokerage services. Novel services and applications can be built by professionals with the solitary goal of supplying them to the world from clouds. As the acceptability, accessibility, affordability, agility, adaptability, availability, and accountability of cloud services, platforms, and infrastructures are on the rise, there is a new group of companies and corporations emerging and establishing to act as viable and valuable mediators, auditors, procurers, arbitrators, and decision makers for the cloud era.

Emerging Cloud Types

We have a good understanding about public, private, hybrid, and community clouds. Besides these generic types, there are several domain- and purpose-specific clouds being unveiled. There are service, mobile, storage, knowledge, sensor, device, and high-performance clouds. Due to the diversity and multiplicity of infrastructure clouds, viable methods and mechanisms for federated clouds are being formulated. Ultimately, the intercloud is the vision.

Innovations are flourishing in the cloud space. The cloud-induced possibilities seem to be limitless, and there are a lot of refreshing opportunities available that are ready to be taken advantage of. These novel clouds enable visionaries and bright minds to visualize and articulate highly complicated and composite services that are multitenant, multipurpose, multidevice, multichannel, and even multienterprise. Self-, surroundings-, and situation-awareness and self-managing capabilities define new-generation services. Dynamism, modularity, openness, ubiquity, knowledge driven, transparency, utility, and so on are the preferred and profound qualities of services for the forthcoming knowledge era. In a nutshell, service orientation inculcates fresh air into the arena of software engineering in producing and preserving sophisticated and smart services. We need optimized and adaptive platforms and infrastructures to produce, deploy, and deliver these types of high-quality and state-of-the-art services. The cloud is the highly competent and efficient infrastructure for next-generation services.

Currently, server virtualization is being accomplished through the availability of multifaceted virtualization solutions (hypervisors) and hence server machines form the base and fulcrum for clouds. With the maturity and stability of desktop, embedded, and mobile virtualization technologies and solutions (microvisors), personal computers (PCs) and embedded devices will also ultimately join and jump on to the raging cloud bandwagon.

Ambient Cloud

This is the new buzzword in the cloud era. It is estimated that there will be two billion PCs in the year 2015. That is going to be a giant reservoir of unparalleled computing power as every new PC is being stuffed with powerful processer(s), gigabytes (GBs) of memory, and terabytes (TBs) of hard disk space. Each processor in turn comprises several cores (multicore computing). The prediction for smaller cousins such as laptops, tablets, and smartphones is still more fascinating. It is plausible to assume that the total number of mobile phones in use today will be roughly equivalent to the number of people on the earth. Smartphones are roughly half of that number at this point in time and are projected to grow faster than any other computational devices on the planet.

Typically, smartphones come out with 1 GHz processor, 512 MB RAM, and 32 GB storage capacities. As per the trend, smartphones will soon catch up with PCs. As days go by, smartphones will be powered with multicore processors. More cores means more computing power. Therein lies a lot of opportunity. Memory size will be truly stunning. Smartphones will become the universal and unified instrument for computing, communication, sensing the surroundings and situation, controlling all kinds of electronic devices in the vicinity, even remote monitoring and management of household items, delivering people-centric service unobtrusively, knowledge exchange, formation of digital communities, social networking, and so on. The possibilities are really staggering.

But all the exciting computing power in the world is of little use if the devices do not connect and collaborate with one another. Networking (wired as well as wireless) has to be seamless, and the data transfer has to occur at furious speeds. Zero latency has to be aimed at and achieved. We have 3G mobile connectivity these days and in the near future, and 4G communication based on Long Term Evolution (LTE) will become common. The research on 5G communication has already begun.

Within data centers using high bandwidth 1–100 Gbps interconnects, the latency is less than 1 ms within a rack and less than 5 ms across a data center. Between data centers, the bandwidth is far less at 10 Mbps–1 Gbps, and latency is in the hundreds of milliseconds realm. Current bandwidth rates and latencies for cell networks might not be sufficient to build and operate clouds. However, with faster evolution and the occasional revolution in the communication space, future clouds will definitely be based out of smartphones.

True high-performance computing (HPC) and low-latency-interconnect applications will not find a cell-based cloud attractive at all. But for applications that need to be highly parallel and manageable with short latencies, cell-based clouds present a very appealing phenomenon. Energy efficiency is another challenging arena for the device world. Besides device clouds, the sensor clouds will become ubiquitous. With these advancements, there will be mind-boggling real-world and real-time applications. The way we work, decide, interact, and so on will dramatically change.

In summary, as indicated in Chapter 1, firstly, the casual and common things in our everyday environments will become smart (scores of digitalization and implantation technologies will enable enhancements in computation, communication, sensing, and displays). Secondly, our working, walking, and wandering environments will become smarter, and our decision making will be the smartest. Ubiquitous computing (computing everywhere and every time) and AmI (intelligence everywhere) will become reality as the Internet of things (IoT) and cyber-physical system (CPS) technologies and solutions are quickly maturing. D2D, device-to-enterprise (D2E), and sensor-to-cloud integration and wireless machine-to-machine (M2M) interaction frameworks, platforms, and technologies are rapidly becoming stable. Thus, with technological convergence and clustering, the path for ambient clouds becomes smoother.

SERVICE INFRASTRUCTURES

We need robust, resilient, and reliable infrastructures and platforms for dependably hosting, delivering, monitoring, regulating, substituting, and retiring new-generation cloud services and applications. When the service paradigm was sweeping the entire IT industry, there was a push for switching over to SOI. That is, every tangible IT resource gets service enabled so that they can find one another dynamically, and interact toward business goals. Service enablement is the leading cause for achieving higher infrastructure flexibility, utility, usability, and visibility. Public discoverability, network accessibility, remote manageability and serviceability, and so on are the key business and technical cases for enterprises to join in the service bandwagon. Thus, a wider variety of service infrastructures and platforms have been conceived and brought out in plenty by open source communities as well as by leading IT vendors. In short, the service science, engineering, and management disciplines have been receiving a lot of attention.

There is informative and inspiring literature on service platforms and their features and functionalities. Recently, there is a new product category called the service delivery platform (SDP). The telecommunication industry first incorporated the SDP as the foremost infrastructural element for facilitating service delivery, and today there is a greater awareness and articulation across industries about the significance of SDPs.

There are competent software solutions for simplifying and streamlining service modeling, design, construction, inspection, performance, and so on. Services intrinsically support composition and choreography. Therefore, service orchestration engines, service collaboration platforms, service security and privacy solutions, and so on have become mandatory software packages in any generic service infrastructure. Today any reasonably established enterprise boasts about creative and compact solutions for event processing, rule/policy management, business process management, enterprise service bus (ESB), data services, portal, and so on.

With the additional complexity of enabling each service to find and communicate with one another, service virtualization has become an important topic. Thus, service registry repository, governance, and virtualization solutions are the other important constituents of the service infrastructure. Finally, for any organization with a growing array of business and technical services, service management becomes an essential ingredient for establishing a sort of interaction control and visibility in any service environment.

Further on, the network connectivity tier comprises routers, security solutions, load balancers, switches, gateways, proxies, and so on. As usual, enterprise services would run behind firewalls. Building a data center to support enterprise-class and -wide SOA is prohibitively expensive. It is nearly impossible for small to medium enterprises. For larger enterprises, the process of developing and sustaining data centers is beset with a number of practical difficulties, as the business processes are generally more diverse, distributed, and decentralised. Further, an enterprise has to connect data centers, since it has to connect and collaborate dynamically with its business partners, retailers, suppliers, customers, and other stakeholders. Moreover, many racks of servers in any large data center are sitting idle or passive, especially during the nonpeak hours, and resources are usually overprovisioned to meet any unexpected spike or surge in resource usage, resulting in huge cash losses.

Thus, expensive resources are terribly wasted, and a greater number of servers means more personnel are needed for manning and managing data centers. In short, higher energy consumption, heat dissipation and greenhouse gas emission, increased costs for operators, and so on insist on exploring, experimenting, and espousing alternative solutions. Also the present-day data centers are not enabling business alacrity and affordability. A typical service infrastructure for supporting a service-oriented organization is vividly illustrated in Figure 3.1.

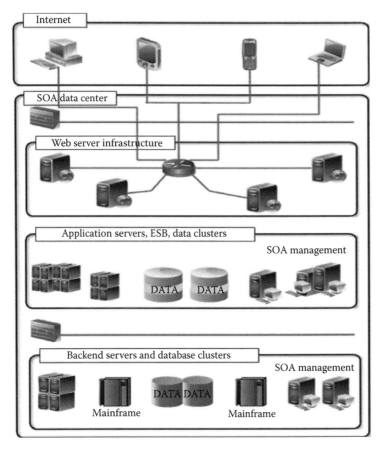

FIGURE 3.1
An enterprise-scale service infrastructure.

CLOUD INFRASTRUCTURES

Cloud computing is all about consolidation, centralization, optimization, higher utilization, smart delivery, and flexibility. In a way, sharing services, computation, and data from a highly modular server farm is the key differentiator. Services and data, made available in a cloud, can be more easily and ubiquitously found, bound, and accessed, often at a much lower cost. This shift solidly increases the monitored usage and leverage of IT resources as opportunities for enhanced collaboration, integration, and analysis on a shared common platform abound appreciably. A reference architecture for a cloud center is given in Figure 3.2.

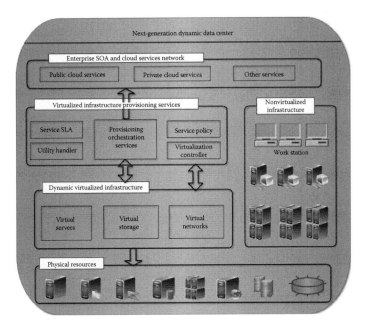

FIGURE 3.2
Next-generation dynamic data center.

Cloud Infrastructure Evaluation Parameters

Given the technological and organizational risks associated with the existing public cloud computing solutions, IT organizations evaluating these solutions need to determine the following:

- Whether the cloud infrastructure is standardized, consolidated, virtualized, and optimized
- Whether the infrastructure is modular, simplified, automated (automation of resource provisioning, VM creation, expansion, contraction, retirement, etc., job scheduling and load balancing, change and configuration management, service governance, fault diagnosis, patch management, etc.)
- Whether the cloud migration is made simpler and quicker
- Whether disaster recovery (DR), business continuity (BC), cloud center security, data integrity and confidentiality, and so on are facilitated by the cloud infrastructure providers
- Whether service integration, composition, and provisioning, flexible offerings, and so on are enabled

Cloud Infrastructure Capabilities

Given the technological [2] and organizational risks associated with public cloud offerings, organizations at the planning stage have to quiz CSPs to determine whether they are stringently providing the following facilities and features:

- The IaaS services advertised and articulated are fully compatible and competent to support their applications.
- The underlying cloud infrastructures are totally optimized and have reached a certain level of stability and maturity.
- The infrastructure should be strictly standards based. The infrastructural components such as servers, switches, gateways, appliances, storage networks, and so on have to be highly modular in order to support flexibility and modifiability. Also, the infrastructure has to be sensitive and simplified for configuration, customization, and consumption.
- CSPs have to have an extensive virtualization strategy as almost all the tangible IT resources such as server, storage, database, application, service, network, desktop, and so on are being virtualized. Lately, there are microvisors to enable virtualization of embedded devices.
- The CSPs must have automated as many data center processes as possible. This includes orchestration and provisioning; change and configuration management; resource reallocation; service monitoring; fault diagnosis; and software updates and maintenance.

There must be an appropriate level of redundancy throughout the infrastructure, coupled with a fast failover capability for secondary or backup resources. There must also be a multilayer security architecture that provides full isolation of virtual data centers and also provides the option of screening all host-to-host traffic within each tenant's virtual data center.

CLOUD INFRASTRUCTURE SOLUTIONS

As mentioned above, adept and assistive tools are very essential for the design and maintenance of a responsible cloud infrastructure. They enable quick identification of the environmental health status to facilitate effective capacity and environment planning, problem anticipation and instant resolution, and capacity expansion and contraction as needed to rapidly adjust to changing support requirements. Data center asset and configuration information is collected into a centralized repository that provides a holistic view of the cloud implementation. Not only does this provide a single point of access for viewing details about individual IT components, but it also provides insight into how those components interact.

Modeling solutions can provide easily digestible and actionable infrastructure intelligence, which is critical for enabling rapid cloud expansion to meet changing customer requirements. Intelligent modeling solutions go further to allow organizations to generate hypothetical scenarios so that quick and informed decisions can be made on infrastructure growth and improvement [5]. For instance, before adding a new server to an existing cluster, a modeling solution can identify if there is sufficient rack space, power, networking, and structural support for the new server. Since responsible cloud environments must rapidly adapt to support requirement changes without diminishing infrastructure reliability, a modeling solution can be an indispensable tool.

Automated tools go a long way in moderating the management complexity of IT infrastructures. Dashboards are very important in indicating the correct status in real time so that administrators and others involved in manning mission-critical infrastructures can contemplate tactical as well as strategic decisions.

Identity and Access Management Suite

Today's extended enterprises face the challenge of providing everywhere, every time, and every device access to business-critical applications and resources, not just to employees but also to field force, sales team, executives on the move, business partners/suppliers, distributors, wholesalers, retailers, and end users [15]. The current setup is that these resources are available via web-based applications or network applications accessed through a virtual private network (VPN). The task of managing which users can access which resources, both for security purposes and for compliance requirements necessitating documentation of access privileges and actual usage, is often costly and time-consuming. This challenge has become even greater in recent years for organizations moving to cloud-based software solutions, which can be deployed more quickly than on-premise solutions.

Increasingly, scores of business software, software infrastructure solutions, and enterprise applications are being deployed, managed, delivered, and billed in clouds. Salesforce.com is a highly successful customer relationship management (CRM) software in the cloud environment. Ramco Systems' enterprise resource planning (ERP) package is another popular one doing well. Corporations are delivering their software products as services from clouds. Every security solution is also being delivered from clouds these days. As clouds are being administered and managed by people with the right and relevant skills, many organizations have been moving their key business applications to public clouds. There are highly scalable directory services and identity management solutions in clouds. These cloud-based software modules offer compelling business efficiencies, less TCO, higher ROI, and so on. Centralized management is another main point in favor of overwhelmingly embracing clouds. Self-service is another favorable factor.

Now, with the opportunity to take advantage of hosted identity and access management (IAM), it is possible to deploy applications faster, control IAM operational and staffing costs, enjoy user-based and operational expense pricing benefits, and provide consistent, secure access to IT resources. Smaller organizations can now take advantage of security technology that may previously have been beyond their reach, and larger organizations can upgrade and extend access control to the applications that were not brought under their management due to resource constraints.

Cloud Infrastructure Management Solutions

In the past, the underpinning of any business service was limited to the IT resources that were wholly owned by the provider of that service. This had invited silo-based approaches to management of services in areas such as system, network, security, and IT governance. Now, with cloud computing, the business service architecture (BSA) crosses the organizational boundary and becomes a seamless composition of diverse and distributed resources which are separately manned and managed within different domains. Hence, the traditional IT management solutions do not work out well in this distributed and decentralized model. Cloud-centric IT management has to view the business service from a top-down perspective and provide capabilities in the following key areas.

Automated Management

Managing cloud infrastructure poses a number of unfathomable challenges due to consolidation, virtualization, and federation, which are the centrality of any cloud environment. The best way forward is to automate the configuration, administration, monitoring, management, and maintenance of cloud infrastructures that support a variety of business applications, services, and data through a host of sophisticated software solutions. This results in a more flexible and controllable environment that can support up-to-the-minute business requirements, with an eye toward maintaining SLAs.

Resource Provisioning

Self-service is the unique selling factor of cloud systems. That is, business users can decide, create, and leverage their computational requirements. If not needed anymore, they can let go of them right away. That is, new resources can be realized easily and released instantaneously. In other words, provisioning and deprovisioning of a variety of IT resources (applications, platforms, and infrastructures) is being significantly simplified in order to attract people and to retain them. In short, IT is becoming simpler and sensitive enough to be dictated by business managers and nontechnical people. Another point is that computing is all set to become the fifth social utility. Such a seismic shift is being made possible by cloud computing.

Cloud Performance and Scalability

With the increased complexity, performance and scalability requirements definitely present a tough time for CSPs. Performance and scalability are interlinked. That is, all of a sudden, there are more users or higher workloads, but the response time still has to be within the originally decided limit. Cloud infrastructures have to be designed to meet these server-specific needs. Capacity planning is the preferred approach. There are performance optimization best practices. Cloud modularity and visibility is the prominent characteristic for ensuring high-end performance and scalability.

End-to-End Cloud Service Visibility

The deeper visibility into the components of a composite application that may reside in multiple organizational domains optimizes resource management and utilization, streamlines IT processes, and reduces costs considerably.

Security Management and Federation

IAM is a critical component in cloud security management [3]. Policy-based access, control, empowerment, and management have become popular mechanisms in the enlarging cloud environment. Messages in transit and data in persistence are being encrypted in order to guarantee the utmost security in any open environment.

Cloud SDP

Cloud services deployment and execution containers, cloud service management platforms, cloud service security solutions, and so on are the leading software infrastructure solutions for cloud-based service applications (CBSAs). SDPs are gaining much ground these days as services are centrally placed and provided to global users with much clarity and without any performance degradation. Presentation, rendering, aggregation, transformation, and mediation engines are the chief modules of any standard SDP. Cloud service bus (CSB) is the introspective middleware being utilized to route (content as well as context based) service messages to their rightful owner(s), to broker among services with varying capabilities and contracts, and to aggregate outputs of participating services that are situated in different VMs, physical nodes, and clouds. SDP is the front end for all the backend resources including the CSB. A service portal is the UI part of any SDP. A mashup editor is a well-known module in the cloud service platform.

Responsible Cloud Infrastructure

Responsible clouds are another twist in the cloud paradigm. There are best practices and key guidelines galore for carefully designing responsible clouds, which are well managed to provide secure, compliant, and high-quality business services. Responsible cloud environments [10] deliver more secure, reliable, and flexible IT services to meet organizational requirements and reduce both capital and operational expenses. Whether building a responsible cloud infrastructure from existing computing resources or an entirely new infrastructure from the ground up, there are three design considerations: effectively size the infrastructure, ensure high availability, and minimize operating expenses.

The number of powerful servers in a cloud center has a direct and distinct impact on the cost (capital as well as operational). Additionally, the number of potential security and failure points is proportionally decreased, improving the overall reliability. Consolidated servers could be more easily pooled and could accommodate scores of shared resources. This allows new resources to be more rapidly added and provisioned to meet rising service demands. Capacity planning is essential for effective infrastructure sizing. Systems that consolidate a large number of resources, such as blade servers and mainframes, are physically larger and more powerful than standard servers. Automated tools should be employed as much as possible in order to make informed and instant decisions based on infrastructure usage, pilferage, performance, productivity, and so on. The information shared and knowledge gained help in quickly and cheaply accommodating newer services. The time taken to reach out to customers and consumers comes down sharply if the extracted and inferred insights are appropriately used.

Since cloud services are expected to be accessible all the time with high throughput, high availability is considered a mandatory infrastructure requirement. Clustered servers have the requisite ability to provide the much-desired capability of high availability. That is, if one server fails, the other servers in the cluster space take up users' requests so that the users do not feel any perceivable delay. That is, they can provide uninterrupted failover services in the event of an individual server experiencing a catastrophic failure or requiring downtime for maintenance. Load balancers are the primary module in understanding the workload of each participating server. Accordingly, service requests would be dispatched to those servers that are doing less work at any point in time. Thus, workloads are being equally segmented, failover and failback mechanisms are provided, job scheduling is being automated, resource provisioning and deprovisioning are being accomplished, and so on. All these portend a bright future for the cloud paradigm. Clustered environments are typically contained within a single physical location so that they can share storage systems and do not have any performance latency due to wide area network (WAN) traffic.

Large cloud implementations typically have multiple clustered environments at multiple facilities in different locations. This allows failover of a cloud service in the event of a site disaster due to a flood or fire. Individual cloud instances can be expanded to operate across multiple clustered environments, both local and remote, to create a "hub and spoke" architecture that ensures highly available and reliable computing services. Scores of automated tools should be employed to monitor the health of these systems as well as the availability of support services, such as power and network connectivity.

Professors and professionals are keenly watching and working on overcoming the chief cloud issues. Primarily, all the major nonfunctional requirements such as security, scalability, availability, adaptability, quick recovery, throughput, fault tolerance, and dependability are being attended to so that the adoption and adaption of cloud computing are bound to rise and ride on.

Cloud infrastructures must be technically advanced and are, in a way, a dynamic pool of modular and shared servers. Service centricity is the foundational and fundamental criterion for all kinds of cloud resources. Virtualization-induced sharing, optimization, and enhanced utilization of IT systems, services, and solutions are gaining significant ground these days.

CLOUDS FOR BUSINESS CONTINUITY

Disaster recovery, fault tolerance, and BC are the indisputable characteristics of any enterprise IT environment. Load balancing, fault prognosis, identification, self-healing, and clustering mechanisms are very much prevalent and prominent in mission-critical enterprise IT environments for ensuring high availability, dependability, and scalability. Due to the innate power of realizing substantial improvements in the enterprise space, enterprise IT steadily tends toward cloud IT. The pioneering contributions of cloud infrastructures to business continuity are twofold. That is, cloud systems are inherently highly available and also are utilized as an off-premise backup. For example, an enterprise may operate the whole system in a public cloud to achieve high availability, affordability, and disaster tolerance. A different enterprise may use a private cloud or a traditional in-house data center for their day-to-day business operations and offerings, while using a distant public cloud for backup. Thus, clouds bring cheers for CIOs and chief operating officers (COOs) by drastically reducing the backup and business continuity (BC) costs. Suppose that there is a need for seven or eight servers for an enterprise package to run smoothly. Then, there need to be another seven or eight servers at a DR site. Thus, there is a huge cost involved in guaranteeing BC. This is the reason that leveraging the cloud for BC is gaining considerable momentum these days.

THE RELEVANCE OF PRIVATE CLOUDS

The much-proclaimed cloud approach is definitely a trendsetter and clearly represents a bright spot for business transformations. The cloud paradigm is fast maturing and stabilizing toward a flexible and futuristic technology, not only for the service providers but also for service consumers, auditors, and brokers. The tactical and strategic implications are consistently on the rise. Data centers and server farms are being reimagined, rekindled, and recognized as cloud centers. Every single IT resource is being empowered and exposed as a virtual resource. A variety of automation and acceleration tools are being introduced for easier manipulation, monitoring, and management of all kinds of virtual resources.

A hybrid of bottom-up and top-down approaches is being recommended so both legacy as well as new applications can be in the cloud without a hitch. Business applications, services, and data are being accordingly modernized to be cloud ready and multitenant. It is not an exaggeration to say that the creation and sustenance of virtualized infrastructures and platforms are the tough and rough phases in the cloud journey. The cloud computing model brings together four dimensions of complexity:

1. Applications and services will further evolve from being monolithic and static toward being composite and dynamic. This in turn increases the reliance on network performance as well as the power of cloud center.
2. IT infrastructure will continue to shift from physical to virtual, complicating IT orchestration with more moving parts.
3. As infrastructure performance management becomes complicated, the operational domains of control will move from single to multiple entities.
4. Business models move from per-instance licensing to pay-as-you-go licensing, which will require better project financial management and exploration into chargeback methods.

The cloud style has brought forth a fresh set of ills and issues that cannot be taken lightly as their compact resolution leads to greater acceptance. As far as the third-party, external, commercial-grade, and public clouds are concerned, the major problem areas blocking the widespread adoption of the cloud style are listed as follows:

- Security and privacy
- Controllability and flexibility
- Visibility and availability
- Auditability and accountability
- Latency and performance/Throughput
- Compliance

Private clouds [4] are solving most of the problem areas of public clouds. However, the much-anticipated utility model gets missed out on in private clouds, which are catering to the needs of a limited set of users. For energy and cost efficiency, and for vertical applications, community clouds are being recommended. All kinds of underutilized and unutilized computing machines are being networked, clustered, and virtualized to act as community clouds that are capable of effortlessly tackling the specific needs of a particular community. Then, hybrid clouds are being suggested for enabling a seamless connectivity between private and public clouds through the cloud-bursting technique. This arrangement helps in times of greater needs of computing.

An overwhelming majority of users has voted and voiced that security is the main stumbling block; hence, CSPs and academic researchers are working overtime on minimizing the malevolent security threats and risks, thereby reversing the sagging and sluggish image of third-party clouds. Newer security holes via VMs have come to light. As the access for the public cloud is mainly through the Internet, all kinds of cloud sources and resources are very much liable for intensive and intimidating intrusion, hacking, and transgression. Therefore, myriad intercontinental initiatives are being expedited to unearth impenetrable and unbreakable security algorithms and solutions. There are security-specific best practices, key guidelines, and metrics. The currently used security mechanisms are also being strengthened for utilization with cloud systems. IaaS providers are lately open to providing more controllability, third-party auditability, flexibility, modifiability, and so on. Other drawbacks are also being attended to seriously. In summary, establishing private clouds is the logical step until there is a complete reliance on public clouds.

THE EMERGENCE OF ENTERPRISE CLOUDS

Every enterprise architect has to set his agenda and make his vision for instituting technology-sponsored private (internal) clouds clearly within his or her organization. Given the economic attractiveness of public clouds, it is logical to ask if there is a way to leverage the prime advantages of public clouds. The viable and value-added alternative for the looming cloud era would be to relate all the promising and proven cloud technologies into the organization's own data center. Clearly, if a commercial hosting entity is able to develop such an elastic and energy-efficient infrastructure, then it ought to be possible to create an "internal cloud" with equivalent performance and economics within the enterprise boundary.

Fortunately, there are competent and congenial solutions and technologies besides knowledge materials and know-how guides. These come in handy while revisiting and remodeling any existing data centers to function as an enterprise-wide private cloud. The high-level expectation is that the emerging and evolving cloud architecture should not adversely impact any existing assets and processes. On the other hand, the resulting private cloud has to smartly leverage the existing capabilities and capacities. The architectural stack of an enterprise cloud is given in Figure 3.3. The major requirements and constraints for typical internal cloud include

- Managing diverse compute, storage, and networking infrastructures
- Managing multiple and heterogeneous virtualized infrastructures
- Providing service-centric features for designing, measuring, and maintaining a growing catalogue of services and chargeback if necessary
- Not disrupting the existing security processes and procedures, application architectures, and application code bases or configurations
- Being compatible with tracking, logging, and compliance systems
- Providing per-user resource cost and usage metrics
- Ensuring utmost security for confidential as well as corporate information

With these operational requirements, an enterprise private cloud can generate the same value and verve as a public cloud. Essentially, the only difference is that the internal cloud is behind the firewall within our own facility and under our complete control. The private cloud is a completely

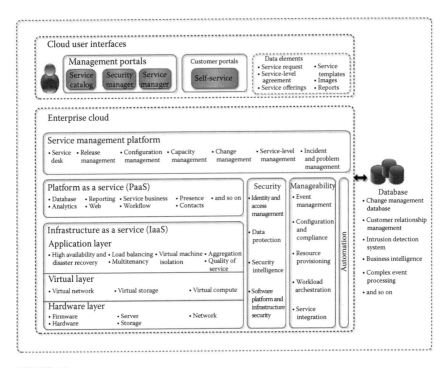

FIGURE 3.3

The architectural stack of an enterprise cloud.

shared and multitenant data center built on a highly efficient, automated, and virtualized infrastructure. Other key elements [1] of the cloud include standardized service, application, and database platforms provided as a service and a self-service portal that enables business analysts and managers to request and manage additional capacity for their applications. The short-term as well as long-term implications of cloud enablement and embarkation are manifold. All the deployment and delivery models are bound to instigate and inspire numerous improvisations and improvements in the current IT establishments and their operations. Above all, the traditional delivery mechanism will undergo a sharp turnaround toward synchronized and simplified service delivery. In this section, we will dig deeper in order to extract and enlighten all kinds of technical, business, and user-centric benefits. Enterprise clouds are for internal users only. Enterprise clouds [8] support

- Better visibility, traceability, flexibility, and controllability
- Resource elasticity and application scalability
- Auditability, accountability, and drillability
- Better capacity planning and management

- Unbreakable and impenetrable security
- Stricter privacy
- Fault tolerance and expandability
- High performance and workload predictability
- Improved infrastructure efficiency
- Real-time provisioning and higher resource utilization
- Agility, availability, adaptability, and autonomy
- Easy manageability, maneuverability, and malleability
- Consolidated, virtualized, dynamic, utility-like, and on-demand infrastructure
- Grid-enabled and optimized infrastructure
- Management console and automated job scheduling
- Compliant to SLAs, OLAs, government rules, and regulations

Affordability

There are expert ways and means to achieve huge cost reductions in setting up and sustaining enterprise clouds.

Resource Slicing, Pooling, and Sharing

Through the revolutionary virtualization technology, IT resources can be made, mapped, and managed as one or more configurable and composable pools of service-centric resources instead of islands/silos of independent elements. These pools can then be exposed in a granular manner for use by business applications and services. Fluctuations in the resource requirements of each application can be easily and quickly understood and met by using fewer technology resources. The economic benefits here are profound and paramount too. The risks of overprovisioning and underprovisioning are considerably reduced with this respectable advancement. The capital and operational expenses will come down as utilization rate goes up, and the number of data center devices and even data centers also slide down. In addition, the facility and overhead costs such as power, cooling, system administrators, and real estate expenses get remarkably decreased.

Clouds Are Lean and Green

Small and slim data centers ensure less energy consumption, heat dissipation, and CO_2 emissions. As the countries, counties, and cities across continents are consciously and cautiously formulating successful schemes for arresting the dreadful climate change and for fulfilling environmental sustainability goals, green hardware and software solutions besides IT solutions for green enablement are being given their due recognition. In this regard, the cloud is being elevated and exhibited as a promising technology for green IT.

Decoupling of Software from Hardware

Today, applications and services run on their specific platforms. Operating systems (OSs) depend on specific process architectures. All these constricting dependencies are to be decimated hereafter. Any number of OSs can run on a physical server. Every service and application becomes virtualized so that they can all run on any platform and infrastructure without any hitch or hurdle. There is a clear separation between applications and their runtime containers. The end result is that IT portability and modifiability will become easier and elegant. This light and loose coupling goes a long way toward increased utilization of IT resources and hence entails less capital, management, and operational costs.

Virtualized Data Storage and Management

By virtualizing storage, enterprise cloud computing allows the physical location of data to be abstracted from the underlying platform, making data vastly easier to migrate. Data can be housed on the platform that best meets particular cost or the security criteria at a given point of time according to a given policy.

Data and Disaster Recovery and Business Continuity

Implementing a common set of standardized and integrated system packages within a data center and across geographically distributed data centers makes workload migration and DR affordable and achievable for more applications and data.

Automated Tools

Use of a single-pane management console gives IT administrators a consistent and common view for each step in a technology life cycle: configuration, provisioning, compliance, management, and monitoring across platforms. These management tools let administrators set up and run automated utilization monitoring and workload-balancing policies. Load balancing, clustering, job scheduling, resource provisioning and deprovisioning, and workload management get completely automated.

The heightened resource utilization induced by virtualization and automation tools leads to a smaller team of IT administrators to manage a larger pool of resources. Capital expenditures to buy, install, and administer fresh infrastructures come down as existing resources can also be optimally used for new requirements. In other words, more with less is the goal in this uncertain economy, especially in advanced nations.

Multitenancy and Shared Environment

Shared resources, platforms, and infrastructures are the vision behind the cloud-emboldened and knowledge-driven service era. Multitenancy is the new buzzword with the uninhibited rise of the pioneering and path-breaking cloud idea.

In summary, a better understanding of the pros and cons of each contributive technology in the expanding cloud space is the first and foremost action point. Objective and unbiased analysis for precisely identifying all pain points and the probable areas of optimization in existing data centers is the second task. Capacity planning is a must to gain the decision-enabling details regarding the computing, communication, storage, and user-base requirements. The next activity is to incubate a new inclusive architecture with all the functional and nonfunctional information. Finally, refurbishing and reusing the existing investments to arrive at a vibrant cloud center is the reasonable and responsible mission.

CONCLUSION

Being an impactful technology, the cloud has brought forth a number of delectable innovations and renovations to both business and IT domains. Both business executives and IT professionals are equally ecstatic about the potential and promise of the cloud paradigm.

On the IT front, the major rejuvenation and restoration happens on IT infrastructures. Anytime, anywhere, and any device access of web-based content, components, services and data has been there. However, with the cloud eruption, application platforms and runtimes; service containers; integration backbones; orchestration and rule engines; management applications; software infrastructure solutions such as application servers, service buses, and so on; database systems; and integrated development environments (IDEs) are also centrally hosted and efficiently managed in cloud infrastructures. That is, these advanced and complicated software infrastructure modules are being expressed and exposed as services to the outside world. Software products are being delivered and consumed as services over the web. Consumers could access them as services and pay for their usage. The capital costs are phased out and the operational expenses come down. That is, the service idea has permeated into every nook and corner now.

Finally, IT hardware components such as processors, memory, storage, and networks are also being accessed as services, and customers pay for their usage. Thus, there is a total revolution in realizing the vision of "IT as a service." Cloud technology is the strategic and singular phenomenon in opening up a series of IT simplifications to make IT discoverable, accessible, consumable, and composable.

REFERENCES

1. Vishwanath, K.V., and N. Nagappan. 2010. "Characterizing Cloud Computing Hardware Reliability." *SoCC'10 Proceedings of the 1st ACM Symposium on Cloud Computing*, Indianapolis, IN, June 10–11, 2010, http://research.microsoft.com/pubs/120439/socc088-vishwanath.pdf.
2. SNIA, and Open Grid Forum. September 2009. "Cloud Storage for Cloud Computing," Storage Networking Industry Association, San Francisco, CA, and the Open Grid Forum, Muncie, IN, http://ogf.org/Resources/documents/CloudStorageForCloudComputing.pdf.
3. Demchenko, Y. July 16, 2011. "Defining InterCloud Architecture (for Cloud Based Infrastructure Services Provisioned On-Demand) and Cloud Security Infrastructure," *Cloud Federation Workshop at Open Grid Forum's OGF32*, Salt Lake City, UT, July 15–17, 2011, http://www.ogf.org/OGF32/materials/2314/ogf32-cloudfed-intercloud-security-v01.pdf.
4. VMware. 2012. "Cloud Infrastructure Architecture Case Study," VMware, Palo Alto, CA, http://www.vmware.com/files/pdf/techpaper/cloud-infrastructure-achitecture-case-study.pdf.
5. Harris, R. 2009. "Building a scalable shared file infrastructure," StorageMojo, http://www.cloudstoragestrategy.com/scalable_NFS_infrastructure.pdf.
6. CERN, and ESA. 2011. "Strategic Plan for a Scientific Cloud Computing Infrastructure for Europe," The European Organization for Nuclear Research (CERN), Geneva, Switzerland, and the European Space Agency, cdsweb.cern.ch/record/1374172/files/CERN-OPEN-2011-036.pdf.
7. Ashton, Metzler, & Associates. 2010. "Optimizing the Cloud Infrastructure for Enterprise Applications," Ashton, Metzler, & Associates, Sanibel, FL, http://www.navisite.com/Collateral/Documents/English-US/Ashton-Metzler-Associates-cloud-computing-white-paper.pdf.

8. Yee, T.-T., and Naing, T.T. 2011. "PC-Cluster Based Storage System Architecture for Cloud Storage." *International Journal on Cloud Computing: Services and Architectures* 1 (3), http://airccse.org/journal/ijccsa/papers/1311ccsa09.pdf.

9. Jones, T. November 30, 2010. "Anatomy of a cloud storage infrastructure: Models, features, and internals," IBM developerWorks, http://www.ibm.com/developerworks/cloud/library/cl-cloudstorage/cl-cloudstorage-pdf.pdf.

10. Brasen, S. August 3, 2010. "Designing a Responsible Cloud Infrastructure," Enterprise Management Associates, Boulder, CO, http://www.enterprisemanagement.com/research/asset.php/1810/Designing-a-Responsible-Cloud-Infrastructure.

11. U.S. GAO. 2010. "Organizational Transformation: A Framework for Assessing and Improving Enterprise Architecture Management (Version 2.0)," United States Government Accountability Office, http://www.gao.gov/assets/80/77233.pdf.

12. Sundara Rajan, S. November 19, 2010. "Cloud Enterprise Architecture and TOGAF–A Top-Down Approach to Building New Cloud Applications," SYS-CON Media, Inc, Woodcliff Lake, NJ.

13. Tang, L., J. Dong, Y. Zhao, and L.-J. Zhang. 2010. "Enterprise Cloud Service Architecture." *IEEE 3rd International Conference on Cloud Computing*, Richardson, TX, July 5–10, 2010.

14. Tsai, W.-T., X. Sun, and J. Balasooriya. 2010. "Service-Oriented Cloud Computing Architecture." *New Generations (ITNG) Seventh International Conference on Information Technology*, Las Vegas, NV, April 12–14, 2010.

15. Verizon, 2010. "Solutions Briefs: Next-Generation Identity Management for Cloud-Enabled Ecosystems," Verizon, http://www.verizonbusiness.com/resources/solutionbriefs/sb_next-generation-identity-management-for-cloud-enabled-ecosystems_en_xg.pdf.

16. Alcatel-Lucent and HP. 2011. "Cloud Ready Service Infrastructure for Communications Service Providers," Alcatel-Lucent and HP, http://www.telecoms.com/wp-content/blogs.dir/1/files/2011/10/HP_ALU_Cloud_WhitePaper110613-3 .pdf.

17. Cashman, G. 2012. "Impact of Cloud Computing on Communication Infrastructure and Service Providers.", *COMPTEL PLUS Convention & EXPO*, San Francisco, CA, April 15–18, 2012, http://www.comptelplus.org/Files/pastshows/2012Spring/GSC_Comptel_Presentation_2012%20CEO%20Breakfast.pdf.

18. Dialogic, Inc. 2011. "LTE Drives Opportunities for Cloud-Based Mobile Video Services, Operators, and Providers," Dialogic, Inc., Milpitas, CA, http://www.dialogic.com/en/solutions/cloud-communications/~/media/6211CCA1A34F4C109D84406F7F5C4BD6.pdf.

19. Siemens Enterprise Communications. 2011. "Competitive Advantage in the Cloud: Demonstrating the Value of Cloud Communications," Siemens Enterprise Communications, Reston, VA, http://www.siemens-enterprise.com/~/media/internet%202010/Documents/products/cloud-communication/06_Competitive_Advantage_in_the_Cloud_Siemens.pdf.

4

Cloud EA: Frameworks and Platforms

INTRODUCTION

Information technology is trekking and moving steadily toward much-promised agility, autonomy, and affordability. In business forums, media circles, and boardroom meetings, IT is being presented and pitched as the elegant, exclusive, and enviable enabler of business. The optimization, precision, speed, simplicity, and sensitivity power of IT is growing exponentially these days. In other words, IT is going to gain a strategically powerful affinity for and grip on every single business endeavor hereafter. Commoditization and industrialization of IT are on the upswing and digitalization is gripping every industry segment as never before.

However, businesses have outpaced and outclassed IT on several accounts and aspects and, hence, there is a noticeable gap between business and IT. Businesses are automated using available technologies, that is, IT-driven businesses are the reality today. Lately, however, there is a glimmer of hope for business-driven technologies such as SOA. Thereby, better alignment between business and IT can now be accomplished smoothly and swiftly. As IT and business are becoming intertwined very tightly these days, all kinds of advancements and accomplishments of IT are being expediently and easily replicated in business for much-needed business augmentation, transformation, and optimization. Several enabling technologies, techniques, and tools are emerging and evolving very fast in order to close down the inhibiting gap between IT and business.

Enterprise architecture (EA) is the proven architectural approach being overwhelmingly undertaken and applied for systematic, sustainable and strategic growth of enterprises. EA directly and decisively deals with all the relevant enterprise elements and provides a pragmatic and pioneering way to successfully steer the enterprise toward its drafted and defined vision. In other words, EA, if stringently acclimatized with ground realities, is highly capable of empowering executives and decision-makers to structure, simplify, and synchronize the enterprise strategy formulation, roadmap creation, smart execution, sagacious delivery, and sensible administration towards the envisaged glory. EA gives a holistic view and sensibly links the business automation and acceleration to the incredible advancements happening in the hot field of information technology (IT). That is, aligning IT structures with the organization's objectives and business processes is the only pragmatic way to achieve sustained improvements and a significant reduction in the cost of developing, maintaining, and upgrading IT systems.

The most incredible technologies sweeping and succeeding in the IT industry are, doubtlessly, the service and cloud paradigms. We often hear, read, and even feel service-oriented enterprises. As already highlighted in previous chapters, the cloud theme and trend also has a greater and deeper repercussions on enterprise and, notably, its architecture. In this chapter, we discuss the leading EA frameworks, architecture representation languages, and tools. These come in handy for enterprise architects in remarkably lessening the workload and the complexity of establishing flexible and futuristic enterprise architectures, as enterprises are fervently preparing to modernize and migrate to the service-based, process-centric, event-leveraging, model-driven and cloud-inspired IT environment.

Business-driven technologies: With the emergence of business-centric technologies such as SOA, the long-pending vision of business agility will soon see the light as SOA is inherently capable of tightly aligning business with IT. Now, with the unprecedented eruption of the cloud paradigm, IT agility is also set to be realized. As cloud infrastructure is being backed and billed as the most appropriate SOA infrastructure, the path to business agility is doubly smoothened. It is no exaggeration, therefore, to say that cloud is a solid foundation for the forthcoming knowledge-driven service era. As enterprises are embracing the salient and successful SOA concepts to empower their infrastructures and processes to become exceedingly service oriented, the days of SOIs and, ultimately, SOEs are not far away. With the cloud being positioned as the converged, dynamic, and adaptive SOA infrastructure, the IT journey is redirected toward cloud enterprises.

Professionals and professors are very optimistic that cloud computing is the most strategic and sustainable path to the much-desired synchronization and symbiosis between business and IT. Business executives, entrepreneurs, and engineers are highly optimistic that cloud computing will definitely and decisively deliver the envisioned success of businesses in the extremely competitive and cognitive market. The cloud revelation has an influential impact on EA, the correcting, common, and controlling blueprint for sustainable business growth.

Considering the prevailing and pulsating momentum, worldwide corporate houses and consortiums have turned to unearthing value-adding EA development frameworks and tools, guidelines, and so on. In this chapter, we discuss some of the highly visible and valuable architectural frameworks and tools that simplify the production of cloud EA (CEA).

SIMPLIFYING EA DEVELOPMENT

Why EA is the Preferred Approach

There is no doubt that the venerable and viable approach for establishing efficient enterprises is definitely a well-defined and designed EA implementation. The venerable approach for establishing efficient enterprises is the EA. For decades, corporate executives and project managers have been complaining about the frequent budget overruns and schedule delays of multifaceted and transformational IT projects. In many cases, projects initiated with much fanfare could not meet the envisaged business objectives and, thereby, there is a wide gap between expectation and supply. The most plausible causes include increasing complexities of modern organizations; the intricacy, multiplicity, heterogeneity, and size of applications; as well as the convoluted technology landscape. Further, it is being insisted that miscommunication between business, operational, and IT experts who each speak their own jargon is another underlying cause. Businesses and technologies are growing fast in different directions and paces, and there is a complicated mismatch between their growth stories. Embarking on the EA mission is being touted and termed the surest and purest way to suppress and surmount all these common obstacles. As a business-driven approach, this perspective encompasses broader relationships between business strategy and processes, as well as the supporting information systems, data, and IT infrastructure.

Leading IT vendors view EA as an enabling discipline that translates business vision and strategy into reality. By creating, communicating, and improving key principles, guidelines, techniques, and models that methodically describe a desired future state, EA sets the path straight and right for enterprises to meticulously journey toward the expressed state more quickly and easily. In a nutshell, EA is a collection of assets and "artifacts" such as processes, strategies, road maps, technology infrastructures, services and applications, best practices, metrics, and roles. The EA comprises a competent governance structure for monitoring how these constituents blend well to provide the promised business value.

If we are building a simple, single-user, and nondistributed system, we can probably manage without an architect. However, if we are plunging into building an enterprise-scale, mission-critical, and distributed system, then we need myriad architects for manning and managing the various modules (user interface, application modules, database access, software and hardware infrastructures, etc.) of the system. Architects are useful in effective planning, complexity mitigation, risk anticipation, opportunity visualization, course correction, and change management.

It is absolutely clear that for an enterprise to be successful, it has to weave an ingenious EA into its culture. The EA has to be embedded in every single and tangible activity in enterprise engineering and evolution. Typically, the life cycle of an organization includes capital planning, project management, asset management, resource allocation, and strategy formulation. The EA engineering process is a strenuous exercise and an arduous journey. It evolves over time and must have the intrinsic ability to adapt to changing market conditions; business diversification and expansion through acquisitions, mergers, and special partnerships; strategy shifts; exploration of new avenues for fresh revenue; and finally, accommodation of technological innovations. All along, the value of architecture goes up as the complexity of the business landscape continuously increases. We know that architecture facilitates business and IT communication using a common language, process, and structure. Similarly, inventive architectural frameworks for significantly moderating the complexity of EA building are required.

EA frameworks: Creating an EA from scratch can be a daunting task; hence, corporate houses and industry consortiums have come together in evolving, expressing and encouraging easy-to-use and effective EA frameworks. The idea is that EA frameworks come handy in guiding solution and enterprise architects in considerably simplifying the EA engineering tasks. Product vendors and experts have gelled well in creating and sustaining easy-to-use but effective EA frameworks that considerably simplify the EA engineering process and guide an architect in all areas of architectural engineering. Generally, an EA framework brings forth a collection of reusable assets and artifacts such as a knowledge base, methodology, processes, templates, best practices, guidelines, and metrics to assist in EA creation. The leading frameworks are as follows:

1. The Zachman framework for EAs, which is, although self-described as a framework, more accurately defined as a taxonomy
2. The Open Group Architectural Framework (TOGAF), which is, although called a framework, more accurately defined as a process
3. The federal EA (FEA), which can be viewed as an implemented EA or as a proscriptive methodology for creating EAs
4. The Oracle and International Business Machines (IBM) EA frameworks

Some EA tools: We have identified some outstanding tools and platforms that assist and even admonish enterprise architects to speed up the EA development process. The details are given in the section titled, "The EA Tools."

THE ZACHMAN FRAMEWORK

The Zachman framework is actually a well-defined taxonomy for organizing architectural artifacts such as design documents, specifications, and models, which takes into account both who the artifact targets are and what particular issue is being addressed. As John Zachman, the creator and author of this popular EA framework, retrospectively describes it, the EA framework, as it applies to enterprises, is simply a logical structure for classifying and organizing the descriptive representations of an enterprise that are significant to the effective management of the enterprise as well as the faster development of enterprise systems.

Zachman describes the process for house building as follows: In response to a future owner's initial and vague request to have a house built, an architect draws a planner view that roughly represents the main items that the house will include. This view serves as an initial agreement between the owner and the architect regarding what the owner wants. Next, the architect draws the owner's view of what the architect proposes to build. The architect draws his or her plans in a way that is understandable to the owner. The architect then draws the designer's view that constitutes the architect's plans in a form that is understood by the architect and generally not by the owner. The architect's plans serve as the basis for negotiation with the general contractor who will build the building. The general contractor draws his or her own plans, the contractor's view, for negotiating with subcontractors. Each subcontractor draws his or her own plans for their specific purpose. They are part of the subcontractor's view. The last view, the enterprise view, is the building itself.

These perspectives are complemented with types of description, that is, the kind of questions that can be asked about a given view. Zachman prescribes three types of description: (1) data, (2) function, and (3) network. These types of descriptions are answers to the questions what, how, and where. The orthogonal dimensions form a "six by three" information system architecture (ISA) matrix in which the rows represent the six perspectives and the columns represent the three types of description. Zachman and Sowa add three more types of descriptions: (1) people, (2) time, and (3) motivation. They correspond to the questions who, when, and why. The result is the complete "six by six" ISA matrix.

Despite the prominent position of the framework, there is little information publicly available to help designers create exact models that fit each other. Alain Wegmann and his team have proposed a conceptualization based on general systems theory (GST). The conceptualization provides concrete guidelines for creating models required by the framework and establishes a better understanding of the models and their relationships. This facilitates the creation and interpretation of models. It also improves the traceability between them.

THE OPEN GROUP ARCHITECTURE FRAMEWORK (TOGAF)

It is noted that TOGAF is simply an architecture framework. Precisely speaking, TOGAF has turned out to be an excellent tool in assisting the acceptance, production, use, and maintenance of different architectures. It is based on an iterative process model supported by best practices and a reusable set of existing architectural assets. Building on TOGAF has a number of advantages over creating an architectural framework from scratch:

- It avoids the initial panic and pandemonium that breaks out when the scale of a task becomes apparent.
- The use of TOGAF is systematic: It is "codified common sense."
- It captures what others have found to work in real life.
- There is a baseline set of resources for reuse in TOGAF.
- The framework defines two RAs in the enterprise continuum.

The unique selling point (USP) of TOGAF lies with its choice of four different yet interdependent architectural types for sharpening and streamlining EA engineering, that is, TOGAF primarily targets development of the four architectures presented in a tabular form here. It is widely recognized that these four architectures form the substantial portion in any EA and, therefore, the TOGAF brand value across industries is consistently on the rise:

Business architecture (BA)	Business strategy, business governance, business organization, and key business processes.
Data architecture	The structure of an organization's logical and physical data assets and data management resources.
Application architecture	A blueprint for individual application systems to be deployed, their interactions, and their relationships to the core business processes of the organization.
Technology architecture	The logical software and hardware capabilities required to support the deployment of business, data, and application services. This includes IT infrastructure, middleware, networks, communications, processing, and standards.

The TOGAF architecture views are as follows:

The "BA views" address the concerns of the users of a system and describe the flow of business information between people and business processes (e.g., people view, process view, function view, business information view, usability view, and performance view).

The "ISA views," comprising "data architecture views" and "applications architecture views," address the concerns of database designers and administrators, and system and software engineers of a system. They focus on how the system is implemented from the perspective of different types of engineers (security, software, data, computing components, communications) and how that affects its properties. Systems and software engineers are typically concerned with modifiability, reusability, and availability of services.

"Technology architecture views" address the concerns of the buyers, operators, communications engineers, administrators, and managers of the system.

"Composite views," such as enterprise manageability views, address the concerns of systems administrators, operators, and managers, and enterprise security view.

The major modules of TOGAF are as follows:

- The architecture development method (ADM) is the major module, and this architecture capability operates on a development method.
- The ADM is extensively supported and simplified by a wide variety of proven techniques, "deliverables," and guidelines.
- The whole TOGAF exercise is bound to produce veritable, reusable, and adaptable content to be stored in an enterprise-scale repository, which is classified according to the enterprise continuum. The repository is initially populated with TOGAF reference models.
- The TOGAF architecture capability framework.

All the terms related to TOGAF architecture are explained here:

The ADM, the major module of TOGAF, describes how to drive and derive organization-specific EAs that comprehensively address business requirements. The ADM, the pure and sure way to arrive at a well-defined EA, provides expert guidance for architects on a number of levels and layers:

- It provides multiple architecture development phases in a cycle as an overall process template for strengthening the architecture development activity.
- It provides a narrative of each architectural phase by describing the phase in terms of objectives, approach, inputs, steps, and outputs. The inputs and outputs deal with the architecture content structure and deliverables.
- It provides cross-phase summaries that fluently cover requirements management and supplies guidelines on enabling tools for architecture development.

The ADM consists of a number of phases (as mentioned earlier in this section) that cycle through a range of architecture domains that enable architects to ensure that a complex set of requirements is adequately addressed. The basic structure of an ADM is shown pictorially in Figure 4.1.

The ADM is applied iteratively throughout the entire process, as well as between the phases and within them. Throughout the ADM cycle, the validation of results against original requirements of the whole ADM as well as the particular phase of the process is mandated. Such a validation must reconsider scope, detail, schedules, and milestones. Each phase should help to reconsider assets produced from previous iterations of the process and external assets from the marketplace, such as other frameworks and models. There are finer details on each of the phases in the TOGAF 9 pocket guide that can be freely downloaded from the open group website. Without an iota of doubt, the gist and crux of TOGAF is the ADM, which efficiently directs and mediates the evolution of superior EAs.

The ADM techniques and deliverables provide sufficient descriptions, clarifications, tips, and techniques in order to effectively leverage an ADM

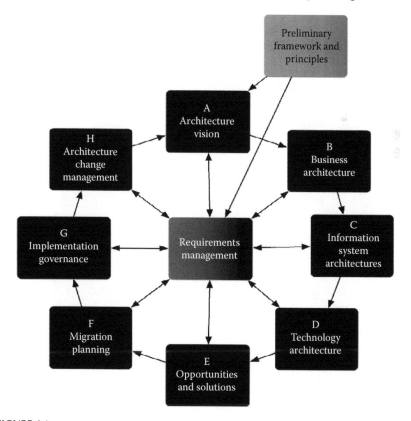

FIGURE 4.1
Architecture development method (ADM) life cycle.

to arrive at competent EAs. As vividly illustrated in the ADM cycle diagram (Figure 4.1), there are eight significant phases other than the preliminary phase.

The techniques, which are very informative, instructive, and inspiring, can significantly simplify the usage of ADM to deal elegantly with a number of usage scenarios, including different process styles and specific specialty architectures such as security. The techniques support specific tasks within an ADM such as defining principles, business scenarios, gap analysis, migration planning, and risk management. The authors of the TOGAF 9 pocket guide have taken pains to make everything so simple that enterprise architects could proceed smoothly and sensibly toward their vision of establishing flexible and futuristic EAs. Scenarios are copiously and carefully used in order to explain complex things. The key contents (deliverables) of each principle and technique are specified and explained in detail to considerably moderate all kinds of ambiguities and misunderstandings.

Guidelines for ADM usage: As mentioned earlier in this section, ADM has emerged as the unique, generic, and dependable method for crafting robust and resilient architectures for systems as well as organizations. However, enterprise requirements vary remarkably from one another and, hence, the need for fine-tuning an ADM to suit any specific need becomes critical. Therefore, EA experts rightfully insist on the necessity of doing a thorough and objective review of the entire process and its outputs to insightfully tailor it for its fearless usage and leverage. That is, gaps identified in the review and subsequent modifications lead to the creation of enterprise-specific ADMs. The pocket code enumerates and explains seven reasons why it is mandatory to go through this tailoring task. The ADM process can also be adapted to deal with a number of different usage scenarios including different process styles (e.g., the use of iteration) and also specific specialist architectures such as security.

All these are being recommended to ensure that the architecture development method is sufficiently value driven and multifaceted to accommodate other methods and frameworks. The TOGAF 9 framework recommends the consideration of organizational factors that influence the extent to which an ADM should be used in an iterative fashion, different styles of iteration, and a mapping of ADM phases to iteration cycles for architecture definition.

Architecture content framework (ACF): During the long ADM process, a number of valuable outputs are produced such as process flows, architectural requirements, project plans, and project compliance assessments. In order to collate and present these major work products in a consistent and structured manner, it is compulsory to have an ACF within which to place them. This allows easier reference and standard classification and also the structuring of relationships between various constituent work products that make up what is often referred to as an EA.

In order to assist the classification of new work products and because of the potential need to correlate with other content frameworks including any existing classified architecture work products, an ACF uses the following three categories to describe the type of architectural work products within its context of use:

1. A deliverable is a formal work product that is contractually specified and would normally be reviewed, agreed on, and signed off on by its stakeholders. Deliverables often represent the output of projects.
2. An artifact is a more granular architectural work product that describes the architecture from a specific viewpoint. It includes such things as a use-case specification, a list of architectural requirements, or a network diagram. Artifacts are generally classified as either catalogs (lists of things), matrices (showing relationships between things), or diagrams (pictures of things). An architectural deliverable may contain many artifacts.
3. A "building block" represents a (potentially reusable) component of business, IT, or architectural capability that can be combined with other building blocks to deliver architectures and solutions. Building blocks can be defined at various levels of detail and can relate to both architectures and solutions, with architecture building blocks (ABBs) typically describing the required capability in order to shape solution building blocks (SBBs), which represent the components to be used to implement a required capability.

A Content Model

The ACF is based on a standard content metamodel, which provides a definition for all types of building blocks that exist within the architecture. The metamodel illustrates how such building blocks can be described and how they relate to one another. When creating and managing architectures, it is necessary to consider various concerns such as business services, actors, applications, data entities, and technology. The content metamodel clearly highlights these concerns, shows their relationships, and identifies the artifacts that can be used to represent them in a consistent and structured manner.

The enterprise continuum provides a model for structuring a virtual repository and also methods for classifying architecture and solution artifacts, showing how different types of artifacts evolve and how they can be leveraged and reused. This is based on architectures and solutions (models, patterns, architecture descriptions, etc.) that exist within the enterprise and in the industry at large and that the enterprise has collected for use in the development of its architectures. A distinction is being made between architectures and their possible solutions. This provokes the creation of an architecture continuum and a solutions continuum.

The enterprise continuum supports reuse wherever possible, especially the avoidance of reinvention, and adroitly assists communication. The assets in both architecture and solutions continuums are structured from generic to specific in order to provide a consistent language to effectively communicate the differences between architectures. The appropriate usage of the enterprise continuum eliminates any ambiguities when discussing concepts and items among different departments within the same organization or even different organizations building EAs. Understanding the architecture helps to understand the solution better, and this in turn enables the avoidance of any possible contradiction or conflict at later stage.

Examples of assets within an enterprise are the deliverables of previous architecture work, and they need to be made available for reuse. The leading assets in the IT industry at large are the wide variety of industry reference models and architecture patterns. It is noted that TOGAF's technical reference model (TRM) is a generic and reusable asset. There are some specific assets such as the ARTS data model from the retail industry.

In ADM, there is a process of moving from the TOGAF foundation architecture to an organization-specific architecture. This foundation architecture is a highly general description of generic services and functions that provide a base on which specific architectures and ABBs can be built by adding relevant architecture assets, components, and building blocks from the enterprise continuum. Besides the TOGAF foundation architecture, TOGAF provides another reference model to be included in an organization's enterprise continuum: Integrated Information Infrastructure Reference Model (III-RM).

Architecture Repository

In a typical enterprise, multiple architectures would exist at any point in time. Some architectures would address specific needs, whereas others would be more general in application. Similarly, there would be many solutions in use or being prescribed to meet the emerging needs of the enterprise. Architectures that describe particular solution approaches, best practices, or patterns can be developed, or acquired and shared across the enterprise as reference models.

In this context, ADM can be regarded as describing a process life cycle that operates at multiple levels within an organization, operating within a holistic governance framework and producing aligned outputs that reside in an architecture repository (AR). The enterprise continuum provides a valuable context for understanding architectural models: It shows building blocks and their relationships to each other and the constraints and requirements on a cycle of architecture development. The major components within an AR are illustrated in Figure 4.2.

Supporting the enterprise continuum is the concept of an AR, which can be used to store different classes of architectural output at different levels of abstraction, created by an ADM. In this way, TOGAF facilitates

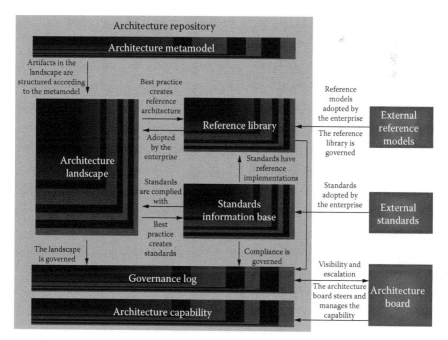

FIGURE 4.2
The TOGAF Architecture Repository Modules.

understanding and cooperation among stakeholders and practitioners at different levels. By means of the enterprise continuum and AR, architects are encouraged to leverage all other relevant architectural resources when developing an organization-specific architecture.

TOGAF Reference Models

As indicated in the last section, there are two reference models: TRM and III-RM. The TRM is universally applicable and can therefore be used to build any system architecture. The TRM is a model and taxonomy of generic platform services. The taxonomy defines the terminology and provides a coherent description of components of the TRM. Its purpose is to give a conceptual description of an information system. The TRM model is a graphical representation of the taxonomy that acts as an aid in understanding the model.

Whereas the foundation architecture describes a typical application platform environment, the III-RM focuses on the application software space. The III-RM is a "common systems architecture" in enterprise continuum terms. The III-RM is a subset of the TOGAF TRM in terms of its overall scope, but it also expands certain parts of the TRM, particularly in the business applications and infrastructure applications parts. The III-RM provides help in addressing one of the key challenges facing the enterprise architect today: the need to design an integrated information infrastructure to enable boundaryless information flow.

The architecture capability framework is a set of resources, guidelines, templates, background information, and so on, provided to help the architect establish an architecture practice within an organization. Implementing any capability within an organization requires the design of four domain architectures:

1. The BA of architecture practice, which highlights architecture governance, architecture processes, architecture organizational structure, architecture information requirements, architecture products, and so on.
2. Data architecture, which defines the structure of an organization's enterprise continuum and AR.
3. Application architecture, which specifies the functionality and/or application services required to enable the architecture practice.
4. Technology architecture, which specifies the architecture practice's infrastructure requirements in support of the architecture applications and enterprise continuum.

To keep an EA coherent during its full life cycle, frameworks alone are not sufficient. The relationships between the relevant types of domains, views, and layers of the architecture must remain clear and any change should be methodically carried out in all of them to ensure consistency. For this purpose, a number of methods and tools are available to assist architects in all the phases of the architecture life cycle. This is where TOGAF distinguishes itself from other frameworks in the industry today. Moreover, TOGAF is being supported by a large community of practitioners and is an open standard, unlike various vendor- and domain-specific EA frameworks.

In conclusion, TOGAF is the combined work of many dedicated, disciplined, and determined professionals and pundits across the globe under the direction, guidance, and governance of the Open Group. Based on their wide education, experience, and expertise, these professionals are collectively and collaboratively elucidating and empowering this architecture framework to meet existing and evolving concerns and challenges of worldwide business houses. This best-in-class framework has solidly captured and captivated architects to smartly utilize it in order to define and defend EAs as well as domain-specific architectures. Out-of-the-box thinking has been calmly and cognitively embedded into this tool. With the arrival and acceptance of cutting-edge technologies and state-of-the-art infrastructures, the future for TOGAF in establishing process-centric, service-oriented, cloud-based, model-driven, and event-driven enterprises is definitely great.

THE FEDERAL ENTERPRISE ARCHITECTURE

The FEA is the latest attempt by the federal government to unite its myriad agencies and functions under a single, common, and ubiquitous architecture. The FEA is the most complete of all enterprise methodologies. It has both a comprehensive taxonomy and an architectural process. The FEA can be viewed as either a methodology for creating EAs or the result of applying the EA development process to a particular enterprise, say, the U.S. government. Overall, the FEA comprises the following:

- An FEA perspective on how EAs should be viewed (the famous segment model)
- A set of reference models for describing different perspectives of an EA

- A process for creating EAs
- A transitional process for migrating from a pre-EA to a post-EA state
- A taxonomy for cataloging assets that fall in the purview of an EA
- An approach for measuring the success of using an EA to drive business value

The FEA perspective on EA is that an enterprise, typically comprising a number of distinct departments or divisions, is built of diverse segments. A segment is a major line-of-business functionality, such as human resources. There are two major types of segments: (1) core mission area segments and (2) business service segments. A core mission area segment is a segment central to the mission or purpose of a particular department within an enterprise. For example, for the health and human services agency of the federal government, health is the core mission area segment. A business service segment is one that is the foundation of most, if not all, departments. For example, financial management is a business service segment that is required by all federal agencies. Enterprise services are the other important assets of EAs. An enterprise service is a well-defined function that spans departments. For example, security service is the prominent enterprise service that works across the enterprise in a centralized fashion.

There are five FEA reference models that give standard terms and definitions for the domains of the EA, and they facilitate collaboration and sharing across the federal government:

1. The business reference model (BRM) gives a business view of the various functions of the federal government. For example, BRM defines a standard business capability called "water resource management," which is a subfunction of natural resources that is considered a line of business of the broader business area services for citizens.

2. The components reference model (CRM) gives a more IT-centric view of systems that can support business functionality. This is all about component-based system design and development. Reusability and composability of functional components from different departments go a long way in curtailing unwanted and unnecessary outlay. If there is a need for a customer analytics system to be built, the reasonable and right way to build one is to smartly aggregate the distributed components of the Internal Revenue Service (IRS)

and Government Printing Office (GPO) to arrive at a competent and compact customer analytics system.

3. The TRM defines the various prominent and dominant technologies, methodologies, tools, platforms, and standards that can be methodologically used for building IT systems.

4. The data reference model (DRM) defines standardized ways of describing data. The data and information architecture is the central point of this model.

5. The performance reference model (PRM) defines standard ways for describing the value delivered by EA. This is something related to the QoS/nonfunctional attributes of EA.

The FEA process is primarily focused on creating a segment architecture for a subset of the overall enterprise. The development process is as follows:

Architectural analysis: Define a simple and concise vision for the segment and relate it back to the organizational plan.

Architectural definition: Define the desired architectural state of the segment; document performance goals; consider design alternatives; and develop an EA for the segment including business, data, services, and technology architectures.

Investment and funding strategy: Consider how the project must be funded.

Program management plan and execution of projects: Create a plan for managing and executing the project, including milestones and performance measures that will assess project success.

The FEA success measurement: There is an FEA framework for measuring organizational success in using EA. Maturity levels of the following categories indicate success:

- Architectural completion
- Architectural use
- Architectural results

There are more relevant and refined details on each of these categories in FEA documents. In a nutshell, the best parts of previous EA frameworks are aggregated to derive this successful EA framework that quickens the process of building competent EAs for governments.

THE ORACLE EA FRAMEWORK

Typically, the EA frameworks include the following (http://www.oracle.com):

- Common vocabulary, models, and taxonomy
- Processes, principles, strategies, and tools
- Reference architectures (RAs) and models
- Prescriptive guidance (EA processes, architecture content, implementation road map, and governance)
- Catalog of architecture deliverables and artifacts
- The EA content metamodel
- Recommended set of products and configurations

There are a number of EA frameworks in the industry with the goal of addressing the basic challenge of assessing, aligning, and organizing business objectives with technical requirements and strategies. Examples include the Zachman enterprise framework, TOGAF, and FEA. Each framework possesses different strengths and weaknesses, which makes it difficult to find any one existing framework that is ideal for all situations. There are white papers comparing leading EA frameworks.

In a conciliatory and concerted effort to provide an efficient and business-driven framework to help customers align their IT and business strategies, Oracle has come out with a hybrid EA framework, which is influenced by TOGAF, FEA, and Gartner's EA. This simple yet practical and prescriptive framework is named the Oracle EA framework (OEAF). The OEAF is a simplified and stripped-down version of other established frameworks such as TOGAF. The original intent of building OEAF was to leverage the strengths of different industry frameworks and marry them with Oracle's long and lustrous experience in developing enterprise solutions for the world market.

The central theme of OEAF is to provide "just enough" structure, which can be created "just in time" to meet the varying business requirements of an organization. This best-of-breed approach overcomes many of the complexities, deficiencies, and unnecessary rigid structures associated with other frameworks. The OEAF is designed to provide quick and incremental results. Each process and artifact has been carefully analyzed to reduce waste and provide the appropriate level of detail required to meet the objectives of a business. The OEAF avoids time-consuming waterfall processes and allows multiple components to be developed in parallel.

To further increase the value of OEAF, Oracle has also tailored prebuilt RAs that define future state architectures. These proven RAs are drilled down from logical components (e.g., functional capabilities) to physical components (e.g., Oracle technologies and products) that complement a customer's existing environment and can be used to minimize implementation risks.

The major components of OEAF are illustrated in Figure 4.3.

The Business Architecture (BA)

The base for any EA is the BA that is supposed to align an organization's operating model, processes, functionalities, strategies, and objectives with the underlying IT. The BA has to provide a strong business case for IT transformations and a business-centric view of the enterprise from a functional perspective. The major components of BA are as follows:

Business strategy: Key business requirements, processes, goals, strategies, key performance indicators (KPIs), business risks, and the business-operating model

Business function: Key business services, processes, and capabilities that will be affected by the EA effort

Business organization: The high-level nature of organizational structures, business roles (internal audiences, external customers and partners), the decision-making process, and organizational budget information

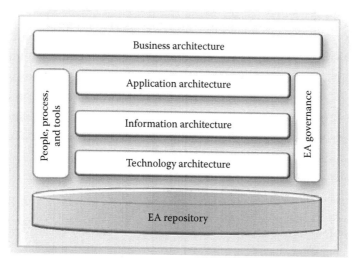

FIGURE 4.3
The Major Components of Oracle Enterprise Architecture Framework.

Application Architecture

This part of an EA provides an application- and service-centric view of an organization. Application architecture typically ties business functions to application processes and services to create or assemble application components in alignment with the application strategy. The application architecture's scope, strategy, and standards are a consequence of BA. The key components of application architecture are as follows:

Application strategy: The key application architecture principles (build vs. buy, hosted vs. in-house, open source vs. commercial grade, open standards vs. .NET, etc.), application governance, and portfolio management, and a set of reference application architectures relevant to the customer

Application services: An inventory of the key application services exposed to internal and external audiences who support the business services

Application processes: A series of application-specific processes that support the business processes in BA

Logical components: An inventory of relevant product-agnostic enterprise application systems that is relevant to stated business objectives

Physical components: Actual products that support the logical application components and their relationships to relevant components and services in information and technology architectures

Information Architecture

Information architecture provides information- and data-centric views of an organization, focusing on key information assets that are used to support critical business functions. It describes all the moving pieces and parts for managing information across the enterprise and sharing that information with the right people at the right time to realize the business objectives stated in the BA. The key components for describing information architecture are as follows:

Information strategy: Information architecture principles, information governance and compliance requirements, canonical data models, industry data model support strategy, and dissemination patterns and reference models

Information assets: A catalog of critical business data types and models (such as customer profile, purchase order, product data, and supply chain), relationships between such business data types, and all the services and processes that interact with these data

Technology Architecture

Technology architecture describes how the infrastructure underlying the business, application, and information architectures is organized. The principal components are as follows:

Technology strategy: It comprises technology architecture principles; technology asset governance methodology; portfolio management strategy; and technology standards, patterns, and RAs. These assets and artifacts go a long way in strengthening and sustaining technology-spurred business solutions.

Technology services: An inventory of specific technology services and their relationships, and the business services, application services, information assets, and logical or physical technology components that realize such services.

Logical components: The product-agnostic components that exist at the technology infrastructure tier to support each technology service.

Physical components: The set of technology products that exists behind each logical technology component to implement the technology service.

Technology architecture provides a TRM that is used to align technology purchases, infrastructure, and solution implementations with the enterprise IT strategies, architecture principles, standards, RAs, and governance model.

People, Process, and Tools

For crafting a working EA, a competent team of people, a pioneering process, and a set of tools are insisted upon:

People: Teams and individuals who are chartered with EA responsibilities from several perspectives such as architecture development, implementation, governance, and enhancement.

Process: Architectural development processes need to be chosen carefully and refined accordingly in order to guide the architecture design and development journey along a route that maximizes the chance of a successful implementation while minimizing resource expenditure.

Tools: Toolsets, tips, tricks, and technologies come in handy while authenticating, articulating, and accelerating the process of developing and managing an EA (micro as well as macro-level). Most of these tools fall under the category of modeling, portfolio management, and architecture asset repositories.

It is noted that EA governance provides the structure, scope, and processes for implementing an organization's businesses strategy and objectives through an EA. An EA governance body is used to guide each project and ensure its alignment with the EA during IT transformations and solution implementations. Successful EA governance includes the following:

- People: Teams, individuals, roles, and responsibilities of governance boards
- Processes and policies: Architecture life cycle management, change management, reviews of cycles, etc.
- Technology: Infrastructure for implementing the processes and policies of EA governance
- Financial aspect: IT cost allocation, project-funding models, business case tools to continuously monitor a positive return on investment (RoI), etc.

The EA repository is an internal repository for all the architecture artifacts and deliverables that are captured and developed throughout the life cycle of an EA. The objective of this repository is to provide information describing the current state of the architecture, and it contains a library of RAs, models, practices, procedures, and principles that describe the target desired state of the architecture.

In order to quickly create such EA-specific components, Oracle has developed a streamlined process named the Oracle Architecture Development Process (OADP). This validated process enables consultants to work collaboratively with corporate customers to align enterprise and solution architectures to defined business strategies and goals.

The OADP contains the following components:

Six high-level phases: The OADP comprises six phases, as illustrated in Figure 4.4. Oracle's approach enables many of these phases to run concurrently to reduce the time associated with creating architectures of various scopes. Also, OADP is meant to be a highly iterative process because architectures are developed and refined with feedback.

Tasks performed in each phase: The second component of the OADP is the list of tasks being performed in each phase. This component also prescribes expert guidance for successfully performing the tasks identified in a practical and efficient fashion, with the leverage of an Oracle EA repository of reusable architecture artifacts.

Deliverables created in each phase: Generally, one consumable Microsoft PowerPoint document that summarizes the results of each task and references all artifacts produced in each phase.

Artifacts created in each phase: Individual models and diagrams; a simplified documentation approach provides just enough detail without requiring excessive overhead associated with documentation.

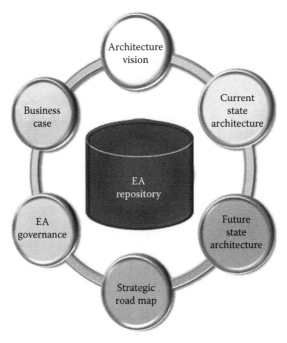

FIGURE 4.4
Oracle Architecture Development Process.

From the base OADP process, Oracle creates tailored OADP processes that target specific segments, domains, and/or solution architectures such as application portfolio rationalization and IT optimization. These tailored OADP processes use the basic structure and phases of the base OADP process. However, they are further streamlined by emphasizing the critical path for a given architecture engagement and by providing prescriptive guidance, case studies, sample artifacts, applicable reference models, and so on for executing the critical tasks and creating key artifacts.

In conclusion, the framework's practical approach allows architects to focus on the architecture and not be bogged down with excessive processes and artifacts or creating their own processes. The agile nature of OEAF enables continuous improvements to adjust to changing business conditions and new technologies. The OEAF uses industry EA concepts and terminology and leverages the best of other frameworks. Access to a set of best practices, tool sets, RAs, and tailored architecture processes around specific problems (applications rationalization, IT optimization, and more) will significantly reduce the time required to develop enterprise-wide and enterprise-grade architectures.

IBM'S ACTIONABLE EA

The IBM has come out with a rectified and refined EA framework (named "actionable EA") in order to significantly mitigate EA developmental complexity. There are four categories of reusable EA elements:

1. The strategy architecture details business vision, goals, objectives, and value propositions, as well as the strategies and tactics used to achieve them.
2. The BA includes but is not limited to capabilities, services, events, information, roles, locations, organization, and terminology.
3. The ISA comprises the business scenarios, processes, applications, services, components, data, personnel, and other elements that support or implement business functions.
4. The technology architecture incorporates specific hardware and software.

Actionable EA is a discipline that facilitates the execution of business goals by mapping strategies to the following:

- Business processes that carry out the enterprise mission
- Applications and information resources used to enable such business processes
- Technology infrastructure that drives such applications and information resources

This discipline fulfils three objectives: First, it provides a context in which to evaluate enterprise assets against business strategy—delivering the information needed to make quantifiable decisions for guiding enterprise planning and transformation. Second, it establishes a business analysis platform, communicating impact, risk, and an opportunity for change. Third, it encourages the development of new assets and business-driven technologies.

Actionable EA focuses on five solution areas:

1. Business efficiency: Executing a business transformation that eliminates organizational waste, resulting in maximum productivity
2. IT planning and optimization: Building an effective IT portfolio by identifying areas for consolidation and reuse, and unlocking operational budgets required for investment and growth
3. Enterprise governance: Attaining control of enterprise IT solutions deployments by standardizing components, data, and functions and understanding the dependencies of the organization
4. Systems of systems: Evaluating architectures across multiple systems to identify their gaps and redundancies, resulting in a qualitative analysis to maximize RoI
5. Service architecture: Constructing effective solutions out of enterprise and business elements that may in turn create new or updated elements that can be used in future projects

The inevitability of changing business conditions and emerging technologies demands an actionable approach to EA that helps organizations achieve quantifiable business goals by smartly leveraging the expanding technology, business process and application portfolio. The benefits of this approach include more rapid, productive, and effective implementations of new initiatives; faster response to marketplace changes; and lower costs of operations.

ENTERPRISE ARCHITECTURE TOOLS

Having understood the relevance of EA in bringing about a kind of clarity and competence, enterprises are showing much interest in assimilating and accommodating its unique capabilities. There are several facilitating frameworks. In this section, we discuss some of the key tools, languages, and platforms that are tightly or loosely coupled with frameworks in smoothening and strengthening the tedious, tough, and tardy process of developing workable and extensible enterprise-wide architectures.

There are hugely validated processes and knowledge bases comprising practices, techniques, tips, and guidelines for establishing pragmatic EAs. However, architecture description; communication and representation languages; and design, development, and management platforms and tools are very much in need to simplify the complexity-filled EA engineering tasks. Fortunately, the tool landscape for EA is quite vast and varied. There are generic and specific solutions from a variety of accomplished and acclaimed vendors for speedy and smart EA realization.

ArchiMate, the enterprise modeling language: Enterprise modeling is a very intimate and intricate affair. Modeling languages are very receptive to lessening the workload of enterprise-wide modeling. These enable unique representation and communication of architectural elements among a team distributed across the globe. Unified Modeling Language (UML) is the most prominent modeling language today. There are plenty of tools, editors, containers, and engines compliant with the latest UML standard specification. Modeling notations are the most critical components of modeling languages. Business process modeling notation (BPMN) is a specific modeling language for representing business process flows, elements, exceptions, and so on. Similarly, there are also several domain-specific languages.

Most languages provide concepts and notations to model specific domains such as business processes or software architectures. However, they are incapable of modeling the high-level relationships that exist between different domains. Such well-defined concepts are essential to tackle the problems of business–IT alignment and architecture optimization in a systematic way. Thus, in order to facilitate a service-oriented and model-driven approach to EA, a high-level modeling language is created and released. The uniqueness of this approach is that the different conceptual domains and their relationships can be captured and described at a sufficiently abstract level. The objective of the ArchiMate language is to provide well-defined relationships between concepts in different architectures, the detailed modeling of which may be done using standard or proprietary modeling languages. Concepts in the ArchiMate language currently cover the business, application, and technology layers of an enterprise. Services offered by one layer to another play an important role in relating the layers.

In a typical enterprise, there are different yet interdependent domains of interest, and existing tools and frameworks are capable of capturing the architecturally sound portions of the domains precisely and concisely. However, due to the heterogeneity of the methods and techniques used to document architectural concepts, these tools are unable to capture and capitalize the linkage details among the domains, that is, the dependencies, which are very prevalent, are not captured correctly. For example, the goal of the (primary) business processes of an organization is to realize their business services and solutions; there are innumerable software services and applications to implement these business processes; the technical infrastructure is in place to host, run, and manage the applications; information is used in the business processes and also processed by the applications; and so on. For optimal communication between domain architects and to compactly align the designs of domains, a clear picture of domain interdependencies is obligatory. Having perceived the need for a language-centric approach for modeling and capturing the intricacies and intimacies on interdomain relations, the authors have come up with this new language that empowers architects to model the global structure within each domain, show the main elements and their dependencies, and establish relationships between domains in a way that is easy to understand even by business analysts and managers.

ArchiMate distinctions and deliverables: In the paper titled "Enterprise Architecture Development and Modelling: Combining TOGAF and ArchiMate," which was authored by Marc Lankhorst and Hans van Drunen, a lot of fascinating details have been shared for public knowledge about the sterling roles of this architecture language. First, this language is easy to learn and understand as it has a limited set of concepts. It comprises a number of basic elements that are highly visible across the layers of the language. The creators have clearly distinguished between the structural or static aspect and the behavioral or dynamic aspect. Behavioral concepts are assigned to structural concepts to show who or what displays a behavior. In addition to active structural elements (the business actors, application components, and devices that display actual behavior, i.e., the subjects of activity), they have also recognized passive structural elements, that is, the objects on which the behavior is performed.

Second, the creators of the language have made a conscious distinction between an external view and an internal view on systems. As service centricity is being given prime importance, views and interfaces have gained prominence. Services are accessible through interfaces, which constitute the external view on the structural aspect.

Finally, ArchiMate defines more concrete concepts that are specific to a certain layer of the architecture. In this context, the three main layers are considered:

1. The "business layer" offers products and services to external customers, which are realized in the organization by business processes (performed by business actors or roles).
2. The "application layer" supports the business layer with application services, which are realized by (software) application components.
3. The "technology layer" offers infrastructural services (e.g., processing, storage, and communication services) needed to run applications, which are realized by computer and communication devices and system software.

The authors have thrown more light on each of these layers in their papers. Enterprise-wide modeling is a crucial cog in realizing adaptive EAs. Although modeling languages contribute lavishly to the realization of EAs, their main drawback lies in capturing the dependencies between different domains of an enterprise. ArchiMate is an artistic attempt at extracting and expressing the relationships concretely between domains.

The IBM Rational System Architect addresses EA enablement needs by providing a repository-based graphical modeling and analysis solution that facilitates the collection and analysis of information about enterprise elements. The use of shared enterprise element repositories provides a line of sight from strategic enterprise plans to the operations, information, applications, and infrastructure needed to implement these plans optimally. The powerful system architect business intelligence (BI) reports powered by an embedded IBM Cognos reporting engine expands EA visibility by providing business and IT decision makers the information they need to consolidate resources, implement successful projects, and propose new projects.

The ARIS EA solution enables companies to create, update, and optimize EAs based on architecture standards such as Zachman, TOGAF, and ArchiMate. The ARIS house acts as the basis for different EA frameworks. The fact that framework-specific methods are linked to the various ARIS method views, and to the central ARIS repository, gives companies a holistic view of their entire organization. Pivotal to the ARIS method is an object-oriented approach for reusing architecture artifacts across different views. This makes it possible to recognize how corporate strategy, business processes, and IT architectures interact and to build the necessary bridges.

This type of description highlights the impact of business process changes on the associated IT systems. Similarly, the business processes affected by system slowdowns and shutdowns and infrastructure changes can be easily identified, that is, standardizing business processes is very essential for arriving at a standardized IT environment. For this reason, the methods and integration tools used for IT architecture management must create a structure that is fully synchronized with process management. The ARIS value engineering for EA (AVE for EA) method provides the necessary models and procedures based on ARIS platform tools that enable corporate IT architectures to be aligned with business needs.

The ARIS Business Architect: The key functions of IT are implementing and continuously innovating corporate processes to confidently face newer challenges. Ultimately, any IT strategy has to reflect the corporate strategy. The IT architectures need to be documented, analyzed, and optimized from a business process perspective. Based on this insight, the aforementioned ARIS method begins by recording the corresponding corporate processes in the ARIS Business Architect, which is supported by a special process model. During the design phase, users can define core elements of the architecture such as organizational units, application systems, data, and IT system requirements. This can create organizational maps that show the relationship between corporate locations, business processes, and the underlying IT systems. A reporting mechanism allows data to be aggregated for further analysis and to generate overviews, that is, the map can be leveraged to create a road map for evolution of the IT environment.

Detailed analysis requires knowledge of the exact nature of processes taking place in the different parts of an organization and recognition of why they differ. The importance of this work lies in the fact that harmonizing processes is the key to harmonizing systems. Information system functions form the link between business processes and IT systems by describing a system in terms of its functionality. This allows these systems to be reused in business processes to document the IT system functionality required by a specific business function. An impact analysis then provides an easy way of establishing the extent to which an IT system is embedded in business processes and whether some IT systems duplicate the same functionality. Similarly, the ARIS EA solution serves as a helping hand in engineering other architectural styles (application, information, and infrastructure) and connecting them with business processes.

Benefits of the ARIS EA solution include the ability to identify which critical business processes at which locations are affected and will therefore need to be part of the migration project when replacing an IT system. Planners and IT managers can navigate the entire EA, following object relationships, and make informed decisions based on a holistic view of the company and a shared methodology. Users can compare the IT standards and target architectures defined in the repository with the actual situation and create a road map for future development. Importantly, ARIS Business Architect facilitates organization-wide EA management by supporting distributed teams. The resulting architecture information can be documented with the help of ARIS Business Publisher, a dynamic publishing tool, in a way that meets the needs of specific groups. The bringing together of business process design and IT architectures allows coordinated management of these two areas, enabling the kind of integrative approach that is particularly important for successful EA management given the interdependency of processes and IT structures.

In conclusion, by creating a seamless interconnection between IT and process architecture in a single repository from strategy level to infrastructure level, the ARIS EA solution makes it possible to fully align IT systems with business needs.

Sparx Systems' Enterprise Architect is a visual platform for designing and constructing software systems, for business process modeling, and for more generalized modeling purposes. The Enterprise Architect is a progressive tool that covers all aspects of the development cycle, providing full traceability from the initial design phase to deployment, maintenance, testing, and change control phases.

CONCLUSION

The essence of an EA initiative is to establish an organization-wide road map to achieve the organization's mission through optimal performance of its core business processes within an efficient and adaptive IT environment. Simply stated, EAs are the blueprints for systematically defining an organization's current (baseline) or desired (target) environment. The EAs are essential for evolving information systems and developing new systems that optimize their mission value. This is accomplished in logical or business terms (e.g., business goals, business functions, information flows, and systems environments) and technical terms (e.g., software, hardware, communications) and includes a validated and verified plan for transitioning from the baseline environment to the target environment. If defined, maintained, and implemented effectively, these blueprints assist in optimizing the interdependencies and interrelationships among the business operations of the enterprise and the underlying IT that automate such operations. In the absence of a sound EA program and an empowered department for diligently overseeing the EA road map, enterprises run the risk of buying and building systems that are duplicative, incompatible, and unnecessarily costly to maintain and interface.

In this chapter, we discussed the leading EA frameworks, tools, platforms, and languages that play a vital role in swift and successful EA development. Even with the emergence of the powerful cloud technology, the relevance of meticulously working toward EA initiative and implementation does not diminish a bit. Instead, enterprise architects are mandated to consider more possibilities, opportunities, and even risks to arrive at cloud-compliant EAs. As implementation of cloud technology ultimately leads to heightened IT resource utilization, the scope, visibility, and vivacity of cloud-mediated EAs grow sharply. Current EA tools and other utilities are accordingly modernized to work successfully in the imminent cloud era. Hopefully, EA frameworks will undergo a series of shifts to incorporate the features of cloud technology that will augment and accelerate IT processes.

REFERENCES

1. Zachman International, Inc. 2012. "Zachman Framework," http://www.zachman .com.
2. Sessions, R. 2007. "A Comparison of the Top Four Enterprise-Architecture Methodologies," ObjectWatch, http://msdn.microsoft.com/en-us/library/bb466232.aspx.

3. Singer, W. 2007. "The Origins and Purpose of the Zachman Enterprise Framework," Cambridge Technical Communicators, Cambridge, UK, http://www.tud.ttu.ee/material/enn/IDU0080_2011/12ProcessMeasurement/zachman_framework.pdf.
4. Covington, R., and H. Jahangir. 2009. "The Oracle Enterprise Architecture Framework," Oracle Corporation, Redwood Shores, CA, http://www.oracle.com/technetwork/topics/entarch/oea-framework-133702.pdf.
5. Sparx Systems. 2012. "Enterprise Architect," Sparx Systems Pty Ltd., Victoria, Australia, http://www.sparxsystems.com.
6. Visual Paradigm. 2011. "Enterprise Architecture (EA) Tools," Visual Paradigm, Hong Kong, China, http://www.visual-paradigm.com.
7. IFEAD. 2011. "Enterprise Architecture Tools Overview," Institute for Enterprise Architecture Developments, http://www.enterprise-architecture.info/EA_Tools.htm.
8. Troux Technologies, Inc. 2012. "Enterprise Portfolio Management (EPM) Solution," Troux Technologies, Inc., Austin, TX, http://www.troux.com.
9. Casewise Ltd. 2012. "Business Process Analysis (BPA), Business Process Management (BPM), Enterprise Architecture and Governance, Risk & Compliance," Casewise Ltd., Stamford, CT, http://www.casewise.com.
10. Innis, W., ed. "System Architect Information—The Enterprise Architecture Tool," IBM developerWorks, http://www.ibm.com/developerworks/rational/products/systemarchitect/enterprisearchitecturetips.html.
11. MEGA International. 2012. "EA Tools," MEGA International, London, UK, http://www.mega.com/en.
12. IFEAD. 2012. "Information Exchange Area of the Institute For Enterprise Architecture Developments," Institute for Enterprise Architecture Developments, http://www.enterprise-architecture.info.
13. Orbus. 2012. "Orbus website," Orbus Software, Washington, D.C., http://www.orbussoftware.com.
14. The Open Group. 2012. "Welcome to TOGAF® Version 9.1 'Enterprise Edition,'" The Open Group, Berkshire, UK, http://www.opengroup.org/togaf.
15. The Open Group. 2012. "ArchiMate®," The Open Group, Berkshire, UK, http://www3.opengroup.org/subjectareas/enterprise/archimate.
16. IFEAD. 2012. "Enterprise Architecture Tool Selection Guide," Institute for Enterprise Architecture Developments, http://www.enterprise-architecture.info.

5

Cloud Application Architecture

INTRODUCTION

"Any sufficiently sophisticated technology is nearly indistinguishable from magic" is a palatable and pampering quote made by many technocrats and industry icons. This is definitely a magical and mesmerizing world, and we are overwhelmingly surrounded and supported by a stream of people-centric technologies in all walks of our daily life. Technologies are indispensable for not only growing business enterprises but also the teeming population all over the world. The service oriented architecture (SOA) is certainly being established as a disruptive and transformative business technology for the booming ICT domain. The distinct and decisive factors and facets of SOA are that it is extremely simple, supple, extensible and, above all, aligned to business. Due to its extreme flexibility and adaptivity, several business behemoths and IT powerhouses create, demonstrate, and sustain their own service oriented architectures, frameworks, programming models, and tools. For example, Cisco Systems, Inc., San Jose, California, has successfully formulated service-oriented networking architecture (SONA) to closely and compactly acquaint and associate their products, skills, and services with the blooming service orientation (SO) concepts. For the device world it is service-oriented device architecture (SODA), whereas for enterprises it is SOE architecture (SOEA). For the cloud era, it can be service oriented cloud architecture (SOCA). However, there are some incredible gaps between what is expected out of SOA by business executives and what is being currently supplied by SOA; hence, there are focused efforts toward the empowerment of SOA in order to close the identified gaps between the enterprise IT landscape and the constantly evolving business realities.

Having grasped the tactical as well as strategic weaknesses of current SOA implementations, software infrastructure providers and market analysts have shown much interest in envisioning and elucidating next-generation SOA (succinctly referred to as NG-SOA) based on various parameters, profiles, and propositions. It is strongly believed that NG-SOA is capable of meeting the unique needs of new-generation enterprise IT. However, there is a perceptible lack of consistency in underlining and articulating the relevant facets and facts of NG-SOA. We envisage and highlight the most probable and profitable evolutions and revolutions taking place in this happening space and formalize them in a concise and precise manner in this chapter. We base our views on the following three perspectives:

1. Aligning newer technologies with the hot service paradigm
2. Achieving nonfunctional service capabilities
3. Accomplishing new-generation services

A number of pathbreaking service technologies are popping up in the enterprise space and are being passionately adjusted and advanced by incorporating the best-in-class features of other proven technologies. Service technologies are thus being made powerful through seamless convergence in order to effortlessly achieve more with less. With users' soaring expectations, embedding nonfunctional requirements (alternatively referred to as QoS) has become imperative at the technology level. With the stability of service platforms, containers, tool sets, and appliances, appealing and compelling services are being conceptualized and concretized. The vision is to equip and enable SOA through a sanguine and sagacious technology cluster. In other words, NG-SOA must be emboldened with a suite of compact and caring techniques so as to expound and espouse it as the most preferred design philosophy and paradigm for the futuristic cloud IT.

Cloud environments are flooded with scores of renovated as well as freshly developed applications and services. All the legacy and currently running web, enterprise, and mobile software packages are being methodically modified and moved to clouds in order to realize and reap all the stated and salient benefits of clouds. The much-published service orientation (SO) is being looked to as a refreshing and resilient architectural pattern, principle, and practice for designing, implementing, and sustaining enterprise applications. Enterprise IT heavily depends on a sturdy service paradigm for achieving flexible and reliable business automation, acceleration, and augmentation solutions. The pulsating service-oriented technologies, processes and infrastructures have laid a strong and stimulating foundation for the ensuing service era. That is, all sorts of enterprise-grade applications are being constructed or composed out of interoperable, reusable, adaptable, and configurable services.

The vision of "everything as a service" is all set to see the light soon with the sparkling synchronization between the much-taunted and trivialized service and cloud paradigms. Due to a series of trendsetting developments at multiple levels and layers, the cloud application landscape has grown remarkably. Business services and applications are finding their new and centralized homes in clouds. Service oriented architecture (SOA) is the principal design approach for building and hosting applications in clouds. These converged and congenial applications could be called service oriented cloud applications (SOCAs) or cloud-based service applications (CBSAs). Not only SOA, but other popular application-centric architectures, such as event driven architecture (EDA), service component architecture (SCA), model-driven architecture (MDA), composite oriented architecture (COA), web oriented architecture (WOA), and so on, can be used to construct cloud-based applications. We have discussed the next-generation SOA (SOA 2.0 or NG-SOA), which seamlessly combines these different yet enterprise-centric architectural patterns. In this chapter, we describe the power and value of SOA 2.0 that enables the production and sustenance of SOCAs to be easier and quicker.

CLOUD APPLICATION ARCHITECTURE

Application architecture is primarily concerned with creating a consolidated and consistent solution stack that fully meets the needs of a business. The key objective here is to align an organization's applications with business strategy. There are three major layers (presentation, business, and data layers) in a typical enterprise application. With the arrival of new kinds of input/output devices and new styles of inputting (multimodal) and outputting (multimedia), the presentation layer is becoming pretty complicated. Plenty of Web 1.0 and Web 2.0 technologies, platforms, and tools are emerging and evolving in order to ensure user-friendliness (consumability) and desktop experience (no latency) for web applications [6]. All these innovations lead to thin and thick clients. Presentation logic is therefore being shunted between client devices and application servers. The business layer generally comprises web and application servers for hosting and processing presentation logic, business logic, access logic (database, identity server, etc.), and integration logic modules. The data layer includes database servers for data persistence and management. On the data side, for realizing information visualization, data mining and analysis, actionable insights extraction, and decision-enablement, advancements such as BI servers and data marts, cubes, and warehouses are being accomplished .

With distribution and integration requirements going up, the complexity of the business layer is bound to climb further. Due to the deeper penetration of IT into every conceivable domain these days, a cornucopia of business automation, acceleration, and augmentation packages such as ERP, supply chain management (SCM), CRM, sales force automation (SFA), and knowledge management (KM) has come to the forefront. Due to the long-term advantages of indirect connectivity, a number of integration backbones, brokers, buses, hubs, and fabrics have also come up. Security management is another crucial requirement. In a nutshell, the business layer is an aggregation of several local as well as remote modules. As described in succeeding sections of this chapter, services are the key application building blocks and SOA is the next-generation application development method.

SERVICES AS ENTERPRISE BUILDING BLOCKS

We are bombarded with an array of abstraction entities such as procedure, data, object, component, agent, aspect, service, event, model, and now composite (Figure 5.1). Object orientation (OO), aspect-oriented programming (AOP), agent-based software development (ABSD), component-based assembly, service-oriented programming (SOP), and composite-oriented architecture are some of the prominent software engineering principles. It is noted that the service orientation (SO) paradigm has been on the rise for the past few years and services are uniquely positioned for seamlessly and spontaneously coexisting and collaborating with other building blocks in order to bridge the gap between business and IT domains.

Leveraging proven architectures, frameworks, reusable assets, tool sets, and engines, service developers and providers have embarked on producing multipurpose, multiplatform, and multichannel business and IT applications.

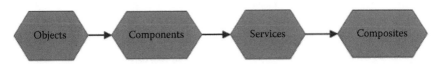

FIGURE 5.1
Evolution of software building blocks.

Service organizations are carefully and calculatingly heaping a variety of business and technical services so they can be easily found, accessed, and reused for quickening enterprise application development and maintenance activities. Another trend is that services are for not only enterprise applications but also embedded applications. Services run on personal gadgets; manufacturing and control machines; telecom equipment; medical instruments; security and storage appliances; kitchen utensils and vessels; infinitesimal sensors; an increasing range of actuators, robots, controllers, handhelds, and consumer electronics; an increasing array of personal as well as professional devices; and so on. The distinct nature of services is that they can be dynamically discovered, matched, extensively connected, and associated to empower applications to be distinct in their structural as well as behavioral traits.

Composites will soon become commonplace and service assemblage and usage will become pervasive. Services will be increasingly mated and meshed together to create sophisticated services; ensure business agility and alacrity; guarantee high elasticity, scalability, and availability; and to exhibit veritable smartness.

Services have the innate strength of quickly establishing a purposeful and congenial relationship with other prominent software building blocks. Further, services are capable of creating business-aware and -aligned composites that in turn automate full or partial business processes straightaway. Thus, service engineering, science, and management disciplines have absorbed and usurped a lot of IT space today. Internet of services (IoS) has become an intense and important subject of study and research for students and scholars across the world. Practitioners and professionals are proposing and propagating a deluge of service-centric application design and development technologies, methodologies, strategies, guidelines, best practices, patterns, and metrics. It is overwhelmingly clear that an enriched and empowered SOA is the clear-cut choice for next-generation IT. It has the innate strength to deliver the originally envisaged goals on both functional and nonfunctional application attributes such as scalability, availability, infallibility, performance, and dependability.

AMAZING DIFFERENTIATORS OF SOA

Industry leaders are very optimistic about the grand success of SOA in realizing adaptive, real-time, and on-demand enterprises. Services have emerged as the prime and proven construct for rapidly implementing, assembling, and sustaining mission-critical and enterprise-scale business systems. Services are the most efficient and energetic unit for realizing perfect abstraction and encapsulation of business realities and requirements. Services are publicly addressable, discoverable, accessible, and manageable. In addition, they are interoperable, reusable, and composable. Besides, services can be loosely coupled, highly cohesive, fine- or coarse-grained, virtualized, and sharable modules. Services are autonomous, self-contained, and self-describing. They inherently support and sustain automated resource sharing and collaboration, which are the much-desired and demanded features of next-generation IT. As they are infrastructure independent, services can be transmitted over any network and configured, deployed, executed, and administered on any standards-compliant platform or container. Services are extremely flexible for spotlessly converging with agents, aspects, formalized and digitalized models, POJOs, events, and composites. These remarkable characteristics have clearly elevated the value and verve of SOA in quickly and easily assimilating newer and nimbler concepts, modernizing languishing and sagging applications, integrating disparate and distributed systems, and realizing exciting and elegant composites. The near-term as well as the long-term implications are that complicated, closed, and costly business IT is definitely destined for a major overhaul and turnaround into affordable, adaptive, and agile IT.

The SOA, being the first and foremost business-driven technology, promises a closer and tighter alignment between business and IT as executives and managers are striving to find implementable and invigorating ways and means to do more with less. Significantly, service orientation is process-centric and this helps business and process consultants to revisit, refine, and realize resilient and robust business processes to achieve process excellence. The manipulation and management at the process level goes a long way in sharply minimizing enterprise complexity. There are methods and tools galore for effective process modeling, simulation, visibility, control, verification orchestration, and so on. In short, innovation at the process level is much desired. On the reverse side, service interactions also contribute toward cutting down the extra flab and crafting optimized processes.

Therefore, we are destined to get elastic, lean, and integrated processes that in turn lead to intelligent systems. In a nutshell, we are entering the era of exotic composites. In other words, SOA facilitates the quick generation of composite data, views, services, and processes that are predominantly user-friendly. These mashups facilitate rapid development of personal as well as professional applications. The origin and the growth story of SOA are incredibly and inspiringly phenomenal.

Finally, SOA has the wherewithal to provide unbelievably enormous amounts of assistance and assurance for cloud technology and, ultimately, for realizing the promised knowledge era. The service revelation is catching up and, as a striking consequence, the new subject of service science (SS) is spreading its wings wider. Service engineering is another intriguing discipline undergoing a meteoric rise in importance among students and scholars. The service orientation (SO) paradigm has brought in a dazzling array of innovations and improvisations in forming and formulating nimble business models especially in the areas of deployment, delivery, consumption, and pricing. The growing service community has unleashed an abundance of best practices, design metrics, key guidelines, proved methodologies, and tool sets to make the service idea more pragmatic and people centric. The fast-growing SaaS model (all varieties of software are centrally and remotely hosted, managed, and delivered as services to global users over any network), which is a direct derivative of SOA, rekindles a sense of hope and buoyancy among industry veterans and newcomers alike.

KEY DRIVERS FOR NG-SOA

The SOA, being the hot and promising architectural approach, still lacks some important aspects for achieving the distinct goals of next-generation enterprise IT. The SOA, as we know it today, mainly supports a kind of client–server (C-S) request and reply relationship among distributed services. However, not all business models, processes, and situations fit this prominent yet passive architectural model. Businesses today are mandated to be extremely proactive, on-demand, insightful, and very community centric. Business-centric events are turning out to be indispensable assets and artifacts for businesses to respond to customers and trade partners in real time. Similarly, formal, digitalized, and platform-independent models (PIMs) promise automation at higher levels, whereby system portability and higher productivity can be achieved. Another interesting aspect is the eruption of AOP, which enables dynamic adaptation of system components. Agents are magical and mysterious modules for empowering systems to act inspiringly and intelligently.

Due to the humble beginning and appreciable growth of IT in the last five decades, every enterprise is blessed yet barricaded by numerous application and data islands. It is a paramount challenge to renovate, integrate, and reuse them in order to preserve and increase their RoI and to keep TCO in check. This kind of transition helps to modernize monolithic and massive applications. This ultimately empowers such applications to coexist and coordinate with mainstream systems to present synchronized and real-time views, data, and services. Apart from modernization, integration, and composition technologies, there are semantic service technologies for fully automated discovery and for the leverage of services to craft sophisticated and self-managing services. When all these technologies fluently and fluidly converge with SOA, analysts, authors, architects, and administrators can contribute together in conceiving and constructing instant-on, collaborative, and knowledge-embedded e-business systems. Demands are constantly being made of researchers and experts to unearth cutting-edge technologies that are stringently adaptive, anticipative, and assistive in resolutely and resonantly equating software applications with business dynamics.

Apart from a growing family of promising technologies, we have standards-compliant and virtualized infrastructures lined up. We also frequently come across EA frameworks and enterprise-class architectural styles such as EDA, MDA, SCA, WOA, and mesh architectures. Reusable assets with strategic significance; constructive blocks such as services, agents, and PIMs; collated, correlated, and corroborated processes; internal and external knowledge bases (interaction log files, business rules and policies); design techniques and tips; and measurement metrics blend together and contribute to the steady and stimulating growth of SOA. The key drivers are classified as follows:

1. Eruption of service technologies and standards
2. Enhancements in process engineering and automation
3. Exciting service methodologies and derivatives
4. Erection of shared service infrastructures

The Growth Trajectory of the SOA

Changes are everywhere. Businesses are going through a host of scintillating shifts at different levels and layers; inventive technologies are emerging; process excellence is being mandated; virtualized and lean infrastructures and platforms are being readied; architecture centricity is being demanded; consumers' expectations are skyrocketing; stricter compliance to newer rules and guidelines is being insisted on for better governance and for risk-avoidance; interoperability standards are being formulated and circulated by worldwide agencies, consortiums, and groups; cool and creative ideas are being encouraged everywhere; operating procedures are being revisited to derive cost-effective operation models; policies and rules are being incorporated within enterprises to enable true dynamism; novel avenues are being searched for higher revenue and profiteering; service-oriented business simplification solutions are being designed, and deployed in cloud environments; and so on.

The SOA is currently going through an improvisational and transitional period and is on the verge of being proclaimed as the most comprehensive and complete business technology for future IT. There is a fervent appeal and aspiration for unfolding and incorporating an assortment of practical and pain-free improvements into the raging "service paradigm," which is silently yet strongly penetrating deeper into an ever-widening range of personal as well as professional domains. A series of concerted and corrective efforts are being made by professors and pundits to bring in a seamless convergence of SOA with an arsenal of business transformation and optimization technologies. In order to speed up and simplify complex service design, development, and delivery activities, a number of illuminating initiatives such as domain-specific modeling (DSM), intentional and generative programming, componentization, software product lines (SPLs), agile programming, model-driven engineering, and development on clouds are being contemplated. Further, a stream of enterprise-scale architectures has arrived on the scene and, above all, they are converging smoothly with SOA. It is expected that this flawless synchronization will ultimately empower and equip SOA to become the most sought after architectural style for all kinds of enterprise, cloud, and embedded systems engineering.

Apart from asset-based development, tool support is gaining immense momentum. Products and tools vendors are coming out with integrated environments, specialized execution containers and engines, widgets, wizards, utilities, and so on. We are inundated with a number of elegant and exquisite disciplines such as Web 2.0, Web 3.0, SaaS, dynamic business process management (BPM 2.0), operational BI (BI 2.0), and automated composition approaches. Further, there is renewed interest by commercial as well as open source communities in building and releasing a variety of slim SOA middleware and adaptors. There has been steady, steely, and spectacular growth for SOA among both solution and service providers in conceiving, constructing, and exposing a community of elementary as well as composite services for rapid realization and delivery of people-centric smart systems.

The service science is the most visible and viable research field today. Service engineering is a refined and resilient engineering field that is gaining unprecedented attention these days. All the remarkable advancements in service science promise futuristic enterprise systems that will be sensitive, adaptive, and responsive. Service computing is another grand offshoot of the service paradigm and is being simultaneously enhanced with cool contributions from several other mainstream computing disciplines such as cloud, grid, on-demand, mesh, utility, nature-inspired, and fabric computing. Other enterprise computing models such as mobile, autonomic, pervasive, embedded, and context-aware computing contribute immensely toward furthering and fulfilling the vision of strategic SOA empowerment (deeper enterprise visibility, sustainable vitality, and practicality). A positive and progressive trend continuously permeating into business IT is the service-enablement of a variety of IT assets and artifacts (legacy as well as modern). Agents, artificial intelligence (AI), and their allied technologies are being ceaselessly refined and readied for cognition-enablement of service-oriented business systems. A bevy of proven and potential mathematical mechanisms such as Petri nets, finite state automata (FSA), pi-calculus, and process algebras are being revitalized and realigned to contribute to process enrichment and elegance that will in turn make SOA a pathbreaking technology.

EXEMPLARY ENHANCEMENTS IN THE SERVICE PARADIGM

Since its inception, the service paradigm has been undergoing a number of notable corrections and incredible value additions. In the following subsections, we discuss the leading transformations that have occurred in this paradigm.

Process-Centric SOA for Flexibility, Agility, and Adaptivity

Analysts, industry gurus, and vendors have deliberated extensively about the distinct capabilities of SOA and have authored papers and articles on why it will become the most dominant and doughty enterprise-class architecture in the near future. In hindsight, SOA is used for producing sense and respond (S&R) systems. For that to fructify, patentable and process-level technological solutions need to be devised. The SOA inherently guarantees extreme flexibility by bringing in a number of indirection layers, and this way of thinking has clearly alleviated problems arising from unwanted dependencies. Precisely speaking, there is no tight coupling between different elements in the SOA stack. For example, process description, process flow, implementation logic, business rule, and so on, are cleanly segregated and they work together at runtime on a need basis. Separation of concerns is a mainstream software engineering technique, and the AOP paradigm has successfully adopted it in order to support inversion of control (IoC, alternatively termed dependency injection) concepts to neatly isolate repeated concerns. Services leverage aspects for some specific purposes. Another beauty of the SOA paradigm is that it enables perfect abstraction and encapsulation of business capabilities. Service virtualization is becoming very common.

One of the most distinguishable points of SOA is its process centricity, that is, there is a closer tie-up between processes and services in SOA. Business process modeling, control, engineering, and innovation are taking an altogether new perspective due to the massive adoption of SOA. First, process models are being made machine readable, persistent, and processable. Second, the process models are more open in the sense that they are even attached with details regarding implementing services, runtime platforms, and other interacting peripherals. Due to the astounding popularity of EDA, event-generating and event-consuming agents are also glued to process models (event-driven business processes). In short, process models are becoming formal, comprehensive, and consolidated so that they can be persisted, manipulated, and reused at a later point in time. In short, all kinds of next-generation requirements, such as alacrity, real-time response, adaptivity, and extensibility, can be attached to models at the process level itself. Another dimension is that business processes are made lean through optimizations. This process improvisation has a definite and direct impact on SOA.

Several important SOA attributes are highlighted in the literature. The foremost one is that in an SOA, business rules can be abstracted from the underlying implementation code. Traditional enterprise applications are monolithic, feeble, and tightly packaged. They try to be as all-encompassing as possible and to keep all the business and support functionalities together. The often-changing process details are embedded for delivering value to users. However, this containment makes it difficult to bring in desired changes. Embedded processes (tightly integrated logic and business rules) induce a sort of inflexibility in enterprise applications and they cannot be easily extended or amended to include new demands or to access services provided by other applications within or outside an organization. The SOA steps in and demolishes all this forever.

Thus, rules are being externalized in order to incorporate new requirements instantly. This separation brings in a situation in which business rules are developed independently and exposed as services (i.e., rules as a service [RaaS]) so that any service can access the rule service at any time to incorporate any authorized and relevant changes on service concretization and delivery. Further, SOA brings in a clear disconnection between process descriptions and their implementation modules (services) resulting in much-needed system fidelity and flexibility. Processes can be analyzed, modeled, validated, fine-tuned, and governed autonomously to create lean, nimble, and adaptive processes. Service composition promises process innovation. The overwhelming idea is to start the creativity aspect at the process level itself and SOA is the most apt style to do that.

Thus, principles such as process centricity, propensity toward formal processes, and SOA along with next-generation BPM suites are going to do wonders for application implementation and enhancement in the future. Clearly, worldwide service organizations are quick to assimilate these evolving and exuberant propositions in order to develop, host, or deliver service-oriented systems. In a nutshell, there is creative and constructive coupling and chaining between business processes and services and the resulting synergies are leveraged cognitively and completely to establish autonomic systems.

The process layer in any SOA ecosystem, a kind of indirection layer, brings in flexibility and productivity in the workings and offerings of enterprises. If there is any change in a company's objectives, strategies, and directions, newer, upgraded, or third-party services can be quickly substituted or leveraged in place of older services. Business rules can be suitably modified to painlessly accommodate new requirements. Organizational flexibility goes up sharply if externalized business process models are quick to embrace changes. In short, business goals become closely acquainted with the underlying IT. As processes form the central nervous system of any business application, process-driven SOA techniques and products will go a long way in sharpening and strengthening organizational agility and ability, enabling smoother collaboration with partners in lightening complexity and heightening customer satisfaction, operational efficiency, and system efficacy. Process excellence is the strategic and sustainable result of a stream of innovations in the SOA space.

Model-Driven SOA for Application Productivity and Portability

The MDA is a radical formation for realizing automation at high levels of the enterprise stack. Machine-readable models are being generated and exposed. Along those lines, process models have also become digitalized to be stored and processed electronically. The essence of MDA is to create platform independent models (PIMs), which do not comprise details about the underlying implementation technology, the runtime platform, and the communication protocol. Such overly generic models help in different situations and their usability, utility, and reusability factors go up drastically. Besides MDA, other automation-guaranteeing mechanisms include semantic SOA for dynamic discovery, matchmaking, and composition of services; and intelligent agents for task orientation and plan, policy, and goal awareness.

The MDA-based service development life cycle is as follows: From PIMs, MDA gadgets ensure automatic generation of platform-specific models and, from there, executable services in preferred programming languages can be generated through MDA-compliant tool kits, code generation cartridges, and a few specific patterns (transformation, technology, and implementation). The DSM languages (DSLs) are also being leveraged in order to create and craft process models that are then converted into deployable code using their code generators.

As businesses grow inorganically, often as a result of mergers and acquisitions, the need to integrate disjointed and dilapidated enterprise systems becomes a quintessential factor in the drive to remain steadily productive and strategically competitive. To this end, it is being widely recognized by experts that the decoupling of business requirements and implementation technologies provides the necessary leg space for enterprises to innovate consistently. By using MDA and architecture-driven modernization concepts spearheaded by the Object Management Group (OMG), it is possible to realize platform- and technology-agnostic business models that can be forward-engineered to executable modules. Reverse engineering and reengineering of software solutions are becoming realistic goals. The separation of business goals from underlying platforms goes a long way in guaranteeing the much-wanted application flexibility, portability, interoperability, composition, and modernization. These empower applications to absorb any kind of changes (business and technical) and ward off risks and vulnerabilities.

In service engineering, PIMs subsequently can be transitioned into platform-specific business services that can be registered in a registry and deposited and maintained in repositories. Today, there is better understanding of service concepts among business managers, process analysts, and application architects; as a result, generating loosely coupled services directly from validated and reformed models is the strategically correct move. In the future, even semantic services will be generated from PIMs and, thus, model and service concepts will go hand in hand in achieving rapidity and resiliency in system implementation.

The MDA is a full-fledged and proven automation strategy. It enables generation of services that can run not only on minicomputers and personal systems but also on futuristic devices such as handhelds, mobiles, and wearable and even implantable devices such as sensors and actuators. Model-driven systems development (MDSD) is a popular development methodology. Model-based SOA will become the most practical and preferred development practice for building service-oriented systems (SOSs) once more compact and compliant tool kits become available. Transforming models into executable services and vice versa go a long way in realizing faster growth in the stagnant domain of software engineering. Agile programming models also spotlessly merge with model- and service-driven development methodologies to result in agile SOA and MDA paradigms. Both forward and reverse engineering practices will get a new fillip and thereby software solutions and services can be made in minutes and not in days or months as is the practice nowadays.

Event-Driven SOA for Proactive and Real-Time Systems

Events are generally asynchronous and are expected to cognition-enable service interactions, which in turn lead to the dynamic realization of composite and parallel systems [2]. Precisely speaking, when something happens somewhere, this incident/activity (in other words, the state change) is compactly picked up, packaged, and passed as an event message to an event server, which in turn passes on the value-added messages to the right subscribers instantly to enable them to ponder the next move. This is a recursive operation. The following is a fitting example: Consider that we are ordering a book on SOA on http://www.amazon.com. There are a number of BI services (asynchronous event services on the server side) waiting to capture this order (initiating event). These knowledge services on the back-end server collaborate and corroborate to arrive at smart decisions, which ultimately lead to revenue generation opportunities for http://www.amazon .com. Enterprise systems such as e-commerce, CRM, sales force automation (SFA), and supply chain management (SCM) will become sensibly and spectacularly responsive with the leveraging of event-capturing and event-processing capabilities.

Events are turning out to be indispensable for businesses to thrive in this competitive and knowledge-based market environment in designing and delivering real-time and customer-centric services. In fact, there are thousands of enabling and enlivening events (happening inside as well as outside) in any growing enterprise these days. Therefore, enterprise IT is being aptly strengthened to receive, analyze, and mine such events proactively in order to arrive at a variety of hidden trends, tips, beneficial patterns, and insightful associations.

It is noteworthy that EDA is highly successful in establishing S & R applications. The interesting buzzword of complex event processing (CEP) is "event cloud," which is a huge repository of diverse events that flow through event-processing engines. Use of event clouds or heaps appropriately determines the success of enterprises in this market economy.

An EDA-compliant ESB is the most appropriate intermediary providing a decoupling layer among service consumers and publishers. Events are the best bet for dynamically implementing service composition. A composite service can be implemented using flowing events and event middleware, as illustrated in Figure 5.2. A service consumer sends the initiating event (a user pressing a submit button on a web form, an RFID reader reads a tag in a distant place, etc.). On receiving it, the central backbone (i.e., the ESB) routes it to a set of business services (service providers) that subscribe to this event.

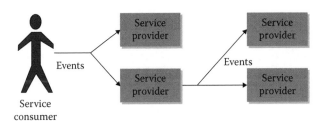

FIGURE 5.2

Implementing composite services using events. (From Boris Lublinsky, "Service Composition," Jul 26, 2007 an article on http://www.infoq.com.)

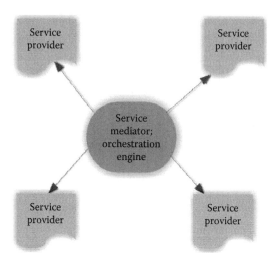

FIGURE 5.3
Implementing composite services using an orchestration engine.

On receiving the event message, one or more of these service providers formulate another message, which is again routed through the broker to another set of services. This sequencing of events effectively creates a composite service. This approach is significantly more flexible and easier as more of the low-level programming tasks get abstracted and encapsulated into the middleware. By changing the services subscribed to a particular topic, it is possible to completely change the structure and behavior of composites. Alternatively, the same can be achieved by changing the topic to which a consumer sends the original event. Experts believe that composite creation through orchestration engines (Figure 5.3) is a better approach for several reasons. Besides creating versatile and affable composites, event-driven SOA ensures real-time, service-based, and people-centric system design and development [3,8,10].

Service-Oriented BI

Information is power and the strategic asset for any corporation to predict the near future. Transitioning information into knowledge and wisdom is an imposing challenge for IT specialists. Data integration technologies and tools are hence very much in demand. In the beginning, data integration was handled by the well-known process of extract, transform, and load (ETL), which is a batch-driven process focused on integrating data during the nighttime. In today's connected marketplace, businesses do not have a quiet time for this process to occur. The corporate data pool is being constantly diversified with novel initiatives and this has resulted in a variety of new data files and types. Another trend is that there are millions of business events happening every day that encapsulate mission-critical data. Real-time data sharing and notification is expected by managers, sales teams, and end-users. Unfortunately, the current ETL process is not designed to handle such expectations, that is, there is a need for incorporating real-time data integration facility with the batch integration process. This has caused visionaries to focus on SOA for real-time data integration. Within a service solution, these events are readily routed, consumed, and integrated as part of an EDA process. For real-time data integration, researchers have come out with different options including the popular data mashup and EII-based information as a service. Enterprises are increasingly incorporating a data middleware (termed an enterprise data bus [EDB]), which is a collection of versatile and composite data services and adapters that seamlessly integrate dissimilar and distributed data sources in real time.

Data integration is the major contributor to the success of BI and corporate performance management (CPM). Therefore, industries are very optimistic about the much-trumpeted service-oriented, collaborative, semantic, real-time, dynamic, and operational BI (which is connoted as BI 2.0) [14]. As SOA is the intellectual fountainhead of technologies realizing BI 2.0, service-oriented BI (SOBI), the new jargon, has become very popular and BI services are being used to seamlessly connect and aggregate data for extraction and dissemination of actionable insights in real time.

The SCA for Simplified Construction and Composition

The SCA specification defines a fresh programming and assembly model along with a language-neutral syntax using extensible markup language (XML) for configuring and wiring disparate and distributed service components together to create business-aware composites [7]. The components provide the actual business logic, whereas the SCA assembly layer abstracts the configuration part of components and their dependencies on other services. The idea here is to achieve greater reusability of software components (local as well as remote, legacy as well as modern, etc.) through scenario-specific and need-based customization and wiring. Although individual components may be implemented in different languages, each component presents standard SCA metadata. A component presents the interfaces of both the offered service and the service reference it depends on. A composite creator (assembler) wires the component references to either services offered by other components or some external services.

Every functionality piece can be implemented in the language most suited to it and run in the best runtime. The idea is that all the pieces are integrated together in a simple and standardized way to build service-oriented applications. The promise given by SCA is that developers can use various languages running on different runtime engines to implement different parts of an application. For example, BPEL, Java, C++, another SCA composite application, a rule engine, a workflow engine, and technology adapters to interact with databases, queues, and file systems all work toward the ultimate goal of establishing a composite application and realizing its sustainability. Each such part of the application is called a service component. Each service component publishes a contract that describes its interface through a web service development language (WSDL) document. The developers just specify the functional link between different parts of the application and it is the prerogative of the SCA container or runtime engine to use the best communication protocol (native or binary) among the components.

The service components are loosely coupled and can work together without any knowledge about each other's implementation. This feature ensures flexibility and allows replacement of one service component with another. The SCA also specifies how the behavior of an application can be made configurable to allow administrators to apply respective changes in behavior without redeployment of the application. Service location can be changed at runtime without any impact on the availability of the application. The QoS aspects such as security and reliability can be configured accordingly, that is, configuration-centric implementation is realized. The SCA composite application can be assembled from a collection of SCA composites, which are then turned into deployable units.

In a nutshell, SCA is a service-based composition model for creating easily deployable and maintainable business solutions. The SCA provides special capabilities to noninvasively reengineer existing business functionalities into new, value-added, and process-centric solutions. It comes with a proven mechanism to build coarse-grained components as assemblies of fine-grained components. The SCA eventually relieves programmers from the drudgery of traditional middleware programming by abstracting the code for discovery, connectivity, and intermediation from business logic.

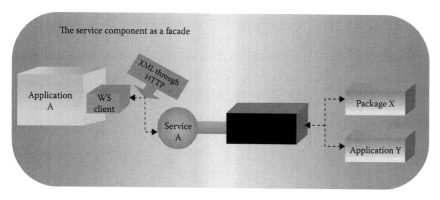

FIGURE 5.4

Composites generated from distributed service components and exposed to client applications and agents.

It allows developers to focus solely on writing business logic. In Figure 5.4, service A represents the interface for service component A, which is, incidentally, an implementation made by joining two smaller components extracted from two distributed packaged applications.

In conclusion, SCA facilitates portability of services between different infrastructures and the concept of service virtualization plays a stellar role here. Any programming language can be used for implementation, which is generally referred to as a servant of the business process. An implementation can provide a service, which is a set of operations defined by an interface that is used by other components. Implementations can also use service references to link other services (local or remote) referred by the service reference. An implementation may also have one or more configurable properties. A property is a data value that can be externally configured, and this activity affects the business function of the implementation. There are both commercial-grade and open source SCA containers for compactly assembling scattered and heterogeneous service components. Whereas SOA is a design approach, SCA shines as a development mechanism for the endearing services world.

When developers create an SOA composite application, what they are actually doing is working on XML files. What gets deployed in an SCA container is typically a collection of the following files:

- The WSDL and XSD files that describe the interfaces (contracts) of the application as a whole (the services it exposes), as well as the service components running inside the application.

- Files that are programs to run in BPEL and mediator engines or that define the human task to be performed by an end user.
- Files that describe how the SCA components are wired together to exchange XML messages to be processed at runtime.
- Definitions for how XML messages are to be transformed en route from one component to the next.
- Some XML files provide configuration details for adapters that can be used by the composite application to communicate with external technology platforms, such as databases, file systems, e-mail servers, and message queues.

Configuration plans apply environment-specific deployment details. Most of the XML files, by the way, are hidden from view by visual editors that present far prettier and easier-to-understand renditions of blocks of XML data. All the XML files are bundled together in archives—a Java archive (JAR) or a service assembly archive (SAR; aka SOA archive, a deployment unit that describes the SOA composite application)—that are deployed to the SOA suite container. The content in the preceeding paragraph is taken from the *Oracle SOA Suite 11g Handbook*.

Agent-Driven SOA for Awareness and Smartness

A software agent is a piece of software that acts autonomously to undertake tasks on behalf of users. The design of software agents is based on the idea that users need to specify only their high-level goals, constraints, and other relevant details instead of issuing explicit and formal instructions; this leaves the "how and when" decisions to the agents. An agent exhibits a number of extraordinary traits and tricks that make it different from other traditional software components. The distinguishing features are autonomy, goal orientation, ability to collaborate, extreme flexibility, self-starting ability, ability to perform disconnected operations, and mobility. Agent-like services are developed and deployed for specialized purposes today. A multiagent system (MAS) is found to be indispensable in establishing AmI environments.

Agents play a crucial role in dynamic service finding, binding, and composition. Composition can be intelligently achieved by deploying specialized agents. The standard life cycle of a composition process includes lookup for selection, matchmaking for compatible and conforming functionalities, and decision making to use the identified. Agents help in fully automating these subprocesses. Many times, reactive/late composition is imperative because of unpredictable and swinging business momentum. Also, new services are being added consistently into the global service reservoir by individual developers, the open source community, and even the IT units of worldwide organizations. The Internet is truly global and, hence, keeping the unique functionality of each service that is added and advertised in local/remote and private/public service inventories is a really tough job. All these push for dynamic service interaction and orchestration. Agents are critical in accomplishing this need. There are positive tidings, confidence-boosting prototypes, and products that guarantee the efficacy of software agents in fulfilling the seamless composition of services at runtime.

Semantic technologies contribute immeasurably in ensuring meaningful and dynamic composition of services. Agents can be duly empowered with blossoming semantic technologies toward completely automated composition. There are research papers proposing novel approaches for dynamic service selection and assemblage based on MAS. Agent technology offers excellent mechanisms to formally express and utilize richer semantic annotations. In short, agents add insight and buoyancy to the static service world. Human intervention, interpretation, and instruction required will lessen, and more automation will flower and flourish in the forthcoming service era with the ensuing association between SOA and agent concepts.

Semantic SOA for Automation and Dynamism

Attaching semantics to all kinds of IT resources (applications, services, data, etc.) to empower them to capture, process, and unambiguously understand users' preferences, prevailing situations, and impending needs to contact and connect all the right services for implementing the identified requirements is gaining momentum. In a nutshell, semantics-attached resources modules and models are pertinent and paramount for delegating more tasks to scores of automation devices. Technologies are being developed for enabling ICT systems to contemplate different options as per changing contexts and conditions, to choose the best answer, and remedy or route through a particular situation or scenario. Semantic technologies are much sought-after due to the tectonic shift they promise for the IT world.

The semantic web ultimately facilitates building and deploying semantic services and systems. It considers the sprawling web as a globally linked database in which web pages, applications, service components, and agents are marked with semantic annotations that make them machine processable and understandable. These annotations are assertions about the variety of web resources and their properties expressed in the resource description format (RDF). Along with RDF, one can use RDF schema to express classes, properties, ranges, and documentation for resources and the OWL-S ontology to represent deeper relationships and/or properties such as equivalences, lists, and data types. With semantic web infrastructures in place, applications that have profound impacts on efficiency can be written that use annotations and suitable inference engines, which automatically discover, corroborate, compose, and correlate services.

Now, with the faster proliferation and deeper penetration of SOA, the relevance and reliability of semantic methods are very much appreciated due to the unassailable fact that present-day services do not have any intrinsic support for empowering machines by themselves to make context-sensitive and cognitive decisions and actions. This hampers the initiation of applicable operations on services dynamically, that is, the automated checking of the service capabilities to deal with emerging business or technology scenarios is not yet in place. The goal is to minimize human intervention so that service collaboration can happen in a systematic, uninhibited, and task-driven way. To this end, experts are of the view that the seamless linking of semantic technologies to services would do wonders and would ensure expected results. This combination results in a stock of semantic services; the era of semantic SOA is fast approaching.

Semantic services are typically defined as self-contained, self-describing, and semantically empowered resources that can be published, discovered, choreographed, and executed in an automated fashion. The vision is to embolden both static and dynamic resources with semantics to facilitate meaning-based processing; thereby, next-generation systems can mimic human beings in their assignments. Semantic SOA gives a fillip toward the realization of fully automated business systems. For linking semantic services, the apt middleware is nonetheless the semantic ESB (S-ESB), which forms the key integration platform for connecting, mediating, transforming, routing, and securing distributed semantic services.

Service Virtualization for Simpler Service Plug and Play

It is noted that SOA sharply reduces the cost and complexity of constructing new and modular business systems through reusability. The point is that if the library of services in a company grows, so do the benefits of SOA. However, the complexity of service-based environments goes up when an increased number of services is being deployed and used. Generally, service-based applications are more complex than stand-alone applications as application modules (services) need to communicate with one another to fulfill business functionality. This communication factor, if more services are utilized in an IT environment, inherently induces performance degradation (as more code is needed for enabling services to communicate), deadlocks, security implications, and even mishaps. Application servers hosting several types of web components (beans, POJOs, aspects, etc.) provide a community of common services for threat management, thread and transaction management, security and session management, resource pooling, infrastructure support and access, and so on, so that developers can spend their time and talent in setting the flow and the functionality right. For services too, we need robust containers to abstract communication aspects and externalize them to be invoked and involved during runtime.

Any service-based application in a fast-growing environment typically involves an orchestration of services (Java, .NET, C++, or PHP services) and these services have to be configured, cared for, and made to communicate. Service virtualization is an emerging approach for effectively deploying and managing services by providing common plumbing functionality to the required services to communicate and collaborate. To do this, new services must be written to run as components in a service container, which has to provide the relevant features so that newly deployed services can be invoked and can invoke other services. The separation between service logic and its communication with other services determines the effectiveness of service virtualization.

Oracle Service Bus (OSB) is a high-performance, stateless ESB that provides service virtualization. The OSB can work with all types of data formats from XML to binary and structured text (SWIFT FIN or CSV for instance) or protocols, from SOAP to JMS and MQSeries.

The OSB can largely absorb all of the following:

1. Changes to the document format, say, due to XML schema changes or even changes to the version of structured binary data. Transformation can be done by Java code, XSLT, XQuery, or MFL to convert between structured binary and XML. The OSB supports any to any bridging between formats.
2. Changes to packaging, say, from SOAP 1.1 to SOAP 1.2 or even from REST to SOAP.
3. Changes to the routing or load-balancing logic.

4. Changes to the location of a service (change in address).
5. Changes to the security scheme, say, from HTTP basic authorization to web services security user name token.
6. Changes to the transport scheme, say, from HTTP to JMS. The OSB supports a large number of transports and you can also seamlessly plug in new custom transports. It supports any bridging between transports.
7. Changes to the invocation style, say, from one-way invocation to request/response. The OSB supports any to any bridging between supported invocation styles.
8. Changes to the data a message is enriched with. The OSB has a variety of ways to look up data. You can look up data in a database or invoke web services or Java code to do lookups.
9. Changes to the parallelization or sequence of requests. A service can be split into multiple services or operations to be invoked in sequence, in parallel, or in a mix of the two. Such parallelization can be used to greatly reduce response time.
10. Spikes in traffic. As service reuse increases, services might get overloaded during peak hours. The OSB can shape the traffic through throttling strategies.

EXCITING SERVICE CAPABILITIES

Services are very different from traditional building blocks. Developers and designers leverage these differentiators for the greater cause and killer value while crafting multifaceted business applications. The following subsections highlight the special qualities of services.

Service Composition

Services are endowed with several significant capabilities that can decimate most of the known constrictions of enterprise software engineering. Services are generally business-aligned, state-of-the-art, and modular functional units. The intrinsic interoperability feature guarantees smooth and studious integration of distributed and diverse service components that could have been carved out of legacy assets through modernization. Or the components could even be freshly crafted by utilizing the latest technologies.

Reusability, interoperability, and composability collectively lead to the unmatched success of services as the next-generation system building block. Services are aptly recognized as the most potent entity for modernization of legacy systems that dot most of the Fortune 1000 companies. However, the master stroke is none other than the much-vaunted and much-flaunted composition. Composition at design time helps build versatile composites that are coarser grained and more business oriented. At runtime, composition is also made possible using a number of adept technologies, that is, dynamic and semantic composition will become a reality. Further, old and obsolete services can be replaced and substituted with newly assembled and advanced services for greater technical as well as business efficiency. Dynamically composing software solutions out of a comity of generic and specific services is undoubtedly the best aspect of service computing.

Service composition or orchestration is not free from concerns and challenges. In many cases, multiple services need to be invoked to accomplish a task and all the relevant services need to respond to accomplish the task. If a service call fails due to some reason, the task may need to be undone or additional steps may be needed to overcome the problem. Multiple service calls can be made in parallel. Calls can be made to synchronous services, which send their reply as a return message to the request, and also asynchronous services, which call back at some later point in time to deliver their response. Clusters of service calls or composites represent a real business process or implement a composite service. Instances of such composites that perform service orchestration can run for long periods of time, for days or even months, when real business processes are implemented. Multiple instances of the same composite can be active at the same time.

There are intra- and intercomposition requirements. As per the Oracle SOA Suite, a mediator is a component that performs "intracomposite mediation" to connect components within a given composite. The OSB, on the other hand, is in charge of "intercomposite mediation," that is, it connects different composites together, and while doing that it can also carry out other fundamental tasks of a service bus such as service virtualization, protocol translation, service pooling, and so on.

Collaboration is the new trend gripping the resurgent ICT space. As we know, Web 2.0 sets the stage for greater collaboration among people in the web. When participation is high, productivity goes up and knowledge is exchanged without any inhibition. Specific digital communities are formed over the web for greater initiation and interaction. Rich Internet applications (RIAs) are being built for multifaceted environments. Hence, there is no doubt that services join in this web-sponsored collaboration toward greater and better service utility and usability.

Due to the unprecedented penetration of Internet infrastructures across continents, various phenomena such as global-scale distribution, resource sharing, electronic data interchange (EDI), and multisite enterprise applications have become buzzwords today. Another trend is that in order to significantly reduce complexity, systems are segmented and sliced into cooperative components (modularization). The interoperability of these modules enable business integration as the modules can proactively discover and discern other modules and conduct dialogs with one another (locally and remotely) at runtime in order to understand and accomplish situation-specific needs of users intelligently and resiliently. Stricter compliance to emerging open standards does bring in seamless interoperability that in turn leads to cool coordination, coexistence, and runtime substitution.

Collaboration enables effective resource sharing among various participants in any environment; the much-acclaimed shared model of computing resources and services is set to gain greater hold with the increasing availability of groupware along with connectivity, conferencing, and collaboration-enabling software. Device clusters, grids, and ensembles are fine examples of incredible resource collaboration and sharing. Services must be collaborative for them to be found, bound, and used at runtime. In short, collaboration and composition happens uninhibitedly and thrives in any integrated environment.

Modernization is the biggest challenge for Fortune 500 companies today as they have a lot of application and data silos loaded in monolithic and legacy mainframes, which are famous for their high TCO, high throughput, less flexibility, and deep complexity. However, rewriting or replacing legacy systems is not a viable option due to time, cost, and compatibility constraints and, hence, modernization is being touted as the best way out. Modernization not only joins such legacy systems to mainstream computing but also maintains the greatness and exactness of mainframe systems. Concepts such as web, service, grid, cluster, cloud, and mesh-enablement are being recommended to meet the goal of standardized migration and modernization. It is noted that SOA is all about service-enabling software artifacts and assets (in a noninvasive fashion) so that they can find each

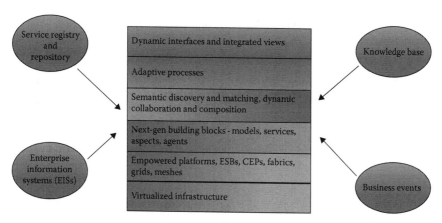

FIGURE 5.5
Reference architecture for SOA 2.0.

other and fuse with one another to construct and consolidate required business functionality and contribute to the quick evolution of business strategies.

These developments ease the realization of NG-SOA, which is policy based, goal aware, event driven, process centric, self-governed, applicable in real time, and adaptive. Figure 5.5 vividly illustrates the reference architecture for SOA 2.0.

Service Composites

With SOA set to become disruptive, enterprises have zeroed in on services and their emphatic derivatives such as composites. Composites will be the stylish and smart building blocks for next-generation business systems. As is widely known and understood, decomposition helps to mitigate the burgeoning complexity of software, whereas composition supports deriving sophisticated software libraries and packages rapidly and effortlessly through configuration and maneuvering of already implemented and sustained services. Composition is projected to occur at each layer of the SOA stack. That is, composite views, processes, applications, services, and data will be the pioneering faces of IT tomorrow. This phenomenon will definitely evolve further and a suite of implementation patterns, platforms, procedures, practices, and so on, will rise together to take the futuristic composite oriented architecture (COA) forward.

Services are very much conducive and constructive in realizing reso-nating and resilient composites, which frugally implement one or more business processes. Service composition is expected to facilitate the most elegant goal of process innovation. In short, composites are all set to play a compelling and mind-blowing role in shaping the emerging era of service-based systems.

Service Meshes

As experts all over the world are pondering the ways and means of achiev-ing the vision of IoS and IoT, several things are falling in place concur-rently and coincidently. The IoT idea is the most logical one for the future Internet. We already have the Internet of computers and, nowadays, we are experiencing the Internet of electronic devices, handhelds, smartphones, and so on. In other words, the web-enablement functionality has been a blessing and boon for people to have information and service access from any device, anytime, and anywhere. The next assignment is to empower our daily and tangible objects to become digital artifacts/smart objects (embedding computation, communication, sensing, and actuation capa-bilities on common and everyday articles and assets; wrapping such arti-cles with one or more standardized service interfaces to enable deep and extreme connectivity and integration with other smart objects in a net-work, etc.). Local as well as web integration of smart objects enables them to spontaneously participate in and contribute to the enhancement of comfort, convenience, choice, and care of human beings. In other words, every single artifact is cognition-enabled to know itself and to understand its whereabouts, surroundings, owners, users and historical interactions, transactions, and so on. Awareness of self, surroundings, and situations is the strategic goal.

The much-acclaimed integration supports establishing smart environ-ments (e.g., smart homes, hotels, hospitals, and offices) and realizing the vision of the glowing concept of AmI. Another twist is that all kinds of physical systems at our working and walking environments are becom-ing integrated (directly or indirectly) with remote cyber systems through a deluge of middleware packages. Thereby, the discipline of cyber physical systems (CPS) is receiving a lot of attention these days. Leading product companies give different terminologies for the paradigm of smart environ-ments. Cisco concentrates on connected cities, IBM focuses on the smart planet, HP insists on adaptive enterprises, university scholars do research on intelligent homes, and nations such as Japan are turning toward smart railway stations. In short, smart objects and service-oriented cloud infrastructures all team up and synergize to create and sustain generic as well as specific active, aware, and articulate spaces [18].

The gist of the service paradigm is the compact meshing of services as per the changing context in producing intelligent service meshes to produce and deliver people-centric services. Services are capable of mingling and meshing with one another in a network as semantics are being increasingly attached with services, policies are being incorporated at runtime, decision-making abilities are being supplied internally and externally through knowledge bases, and so on. It is noted that the service idea is tending toward making every single element a service-consuming, service-providing, or service-brokering entity. Thus, it is obvious that service meshing will be the primary key for future IT.

As articulated earlier in this section, the service paradigm brings in some delectable and desired changes for the total IT landscape. Every tangible thing (hardware as well as software) is being expressed and exposed as a service. In other words, not only high-end servers in data centers and server farms but also every wearable, portable, implantable, nomadic, mobile, fixed, and handheld device on the user side is becoming a service-emitting electronic gadget. With digitalization penetrating into ordinary articles, every commonly and casually found item in our surroundings becomes digitally empowered to participate and fructify the vision of AmI. In a nutshell, every tangible thing is viewed as a contributive object enabling the production of exotic services and applications for the ensuing knowledge era.

Services have come as viable virtualization elements for all kinds of IT resources. With the embedded virtualization field set to grow fast, virtual devices will be created on demand, using the disruptive service idea. That is, services could virtualize devices quite easily. In other words, devices hide behind service interfaces. This SOA-sponsored advancement plays a vital role in building highly competent and cognitive device ensembles and meshes that are the chief modules for setting up and sustaining smart environments.

Service meshes are very much constructive and contributive for not only the embedded space but also the enterprise space. The service model leads to on-demand and dynamic collaboration among a family of spatially distributed and decentralized services (atomic as well as composite) to result in cost-effective and QoS-compliant business services and solutions.

In other words, a service mesh enables services to find one another on an ad hoc basis, connect and coordinate with each other, and coexist together to achieve greater and better things.

Services, events, agents, models, widgets, aspects, and composites are increasingly mesh-enabled to create applications that are attentive, assistive, and adaptive. The SOA middleware including service bus, fabrics, connectors, drivers, adaptors, and mediators aids in runtime meshing. Figure 5.6 illustrates a kind of service mesh that connects three composite services.

Service Mashups

Mashup is a new buzzword in the Web 2.0 world. Key drivers that facilitated the growth of mashups are first, the zooming growth of the web as the world's largest digital library and cheapest business application platform, and second, the emergence of several key implementation technologies. Incidentally, Web 2.0 technologies have been nurtured decisively in order to guarantee enhanced user participation and collaboration within the web. With techniques for automated discovery, linking, synchronization, syndication, and presentation attaining marked maturity,

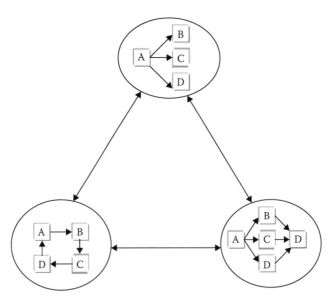

FIGURE 5.6
Meshing of composites.

the applicability rate for the raging mashup concept increases with the consistent unearthing of newer web contents such as widgets, services, agents, beans, and portlets. Mashup platforms find, corroborate, and correlate such web contents to form integrated and intelligent applications with dynamic and rich views.

A mashup literally represents a smart blending of different resources from distributed sources to create a new, purposeful, and integrated application. The most telling advantage is the ease of construction, deployment, and use of a mashup. Even subject-matter experts (SMEs) and business analysts can create business-aligned mashups. Primarily, there are data and service mashups. Service concepts have mingled nicely with the mashup paradigm, and this seamless union will accelerate generation and use of mashups in the days to come. Service mashup, a special kind of composite service, is defined as a design-time or run-time aggregate of heterogeneous services owned by different people. As the service era unfolds, we will definitely be bombarded with a growing array of services. Network services can be identified, matched up for their compatibilities and capabilities, and mashed up (Figure 5.7) to construct value-added and business-aligned composites. With the overwhelming acceptance of SaaS in IT, even mashup is empowered and exposed as a service (mashup as a service [MaaS]). Mashups, being business-aware composites, can be remotely found and linked to form business applications quickly.

FIGURE 5.7
Service mashups.

DYNAMIC AND CONVERGED SERVICE INFRASTRUCTURES

For the service paradigm to thrive, we need lean, elastic, and green platforms. Services are intrinsically intuitive and interactive. Going forward, services are discoverable, connectable, consumable and composable through messaging, verifiable against their functional as well as nonfunctional capabilities, and so on. Services are capable of accomplishing several other things if they are well-entrenched in appropriate platforms and infrastructures, for example, service engineering, testing, deployment, mediation, orchestration, execution, versioning, virtualization, management, governance, and delivery. We have standards-based, open source, and commercial-grade service middleware products. However, due to the growing complexity, heterogeneity, multiplicity, and distribution of middleware products, middleware solutions are transitioning to clusters, fabrics, and grids in order to guarantee QoS features such as high performance, assurance, availability, and scalability. Dependability, durability, manageability, usability, and modifiability are the other crucial needs for SOA infrastructures.

The ESB is the most commonly used backbone for service connectivity, compatibility, and composability. In addition, there are plug and play architecture-based integrated environments, workbenches, utilities, tool sets, compilers, etc., for performing service modeling, development, assembling, and testing. There are specialized solutions for service registry repository, management, and security purposes. Apart from the industry-strength service virtualization and governance solutions, there are a number of business rule management, business activity monitoring (BAM), BI, business performance management, CEP, dashboard and reporting, and corporate performance management (CPM) systems also.

Services that are deployed in heterogeneous and geographically distributed containers are elegantly mashed up to enhance user productivity. Extreme simplicity, sensitivity, and spontaneous connectivity features become the leading and indisputable service design principles. In ensuing paragraphs, we discuss the emerging infrastructural components in order to visualize the projected service era.

Service Grids

It is a well-known fact that ESB is the most prevalent and centralized integration platform for distributed services. In order to meet high-performance goals, clustered, federated, brokered, and hybrid service buses are conceived and recommended [17]. The next evolutionary model is nonetheless the service grid. Grid computing is the simplified model of distributed computing and a relatively cheaper option for supercomputing. Grids, classified as compute grids, data grids, business grids, and so on, are the most economic IT infrastructures in efficiently running enterprise-class and mission-critical systems that are becoming increasingly intertwined. Grids provide high-performance facilities at a very reasonable cost. Creating grids from connected, unutilized, and underutilized IT resources is the compelling scene for business behemoths and IT powerhouses in order to achieve more with less. A variety of horizontal as well as vertical grids are being formed and deployed in industries and defense organizations. In short, grids are the foundational infrastructures for establishing virtual organizations, and they will ultimately transform computing into a well-deserved social utility. In a service environment, message-oriented middleware (MOM) or service middleware is the mainstream intermediary for ensuring service collaboration.

Thus, grid-aware service middleware (service grid) has emerged as a viable option for efficient service message filtering, routing, transformation, and adaption. Grid-based middleware also empowers a spectrum of services to be instantly deployed, readily reused, easily shared, and smoothly composed. A service grid is a kind of resilient, fault-tolerant, load-balancing, and introspective middleware platform for beneficially linking dispersed and disparate services. In short, value-added and business-linked composites can be created using service grids. Figure 5.8 depicts how service grids intelligently link distributed complex services. As systems and devices are virtualized by services, service grids virtualize distributed services.

SOA Fabrics

Fabric architecture is a resilient method in several scenarios. Products complying with fabric structure and behavior are therefore definitely popular. This is the primary motivation for constructing fabric-compliant SOA products to achieve affordability and affability. When SOA received much attention and coverage in the press and amongst other interested parties, most of the EAI vendors quickly jumped on the SOA bandwagon and upgraded their products to be compatible with SOA principles. Basically, ESB is an extended messaging infrastructure leveraging bus

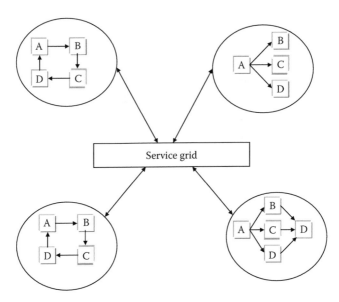

FIGURE 5.8
Centrality of the service grid in next-generation service systems.

topology. Although ESB is doing well in service integration, it is found wanting in several other aspects that are crucial to the success of the originally specified service principles.

Several product vendors including IBM have proceeded in realizing a standards-compliant fabric server. The most remarkable aspect of a server fabric is that it is a smart combination of several accomplished infrastructural modules. According to an IBM press release, WebSphere Business Services Fabric is an end-to-end SOA platform to model, assemble, deploy, manage, and govern composite business services. It provides design-time tooling, runtime environment, industry reference models, and prebuilt SOA assets to enable rapid development of loosely coupled composite services. WebSphere Business Services Fabric includes WebSphere Process Server, WebSphere Services Registry and Repository, and WebSphere Integration Developer. It is used for composition, deployment, and governance of flexible and service-oriented business processes. In short, fabric is a hot-pluggable and comprehensive infrastructure providing a variety of functionalities and features.

Traditional ESB empowers collaboration among distributed systems through message passing. But as we saw in earlier sections, there have been strategic value additions in the form of process flexibility, system malleability, real-time composites, architectural convergence, dynamic view, etc. That is, proven building blocks and enterprise-grade architectures have seamlessly and surprisingly mingled and merged with service concepts recommending a far bigger role for SOA in future enterprises. For an empowered SOA, we need equally competent and sophisticated SOA suites. This is why we see frenzied activities going on among solution providers in conceptualizing and releasing blueprints for the next-generation service fabric, which is capable of assimilating additional complexities that are imposed by newer internal as well as external systems. In other words, the present-day service bus must evolve from just an integration tool to a versatile integration backbone.

As discussed earlier in this section, service fabric is a comprehensive server that must discover, direct, mediate, and secure service messages flowing among distributed enterprise systems. SOA fabric must have all the Java Enterprise Edition (JEE)-compliant application server features for executing services and enabling seamless service collaboration. It is noted that SOA fabrics enable formation of business-aligned, robust, and reusable composites (data, service, view, process, etc.), meshes, and ensembles because of its masterful capabilities such as automated discovery, semantic matching, dynamic collaboration, and composition. They encompass the CEP engine, business rule management system (BRMS), BPM/business process execution language (BPEL) manager, business activity monitoring (BAM) product, etc. Other dominant modules include a directory service, data services for real-time integration, BI and performance management tools, an SCA, a composition, a mashup, agent and aspect containers, and a bridge for model-driven integration.

Further, NG-SOA fabrics include an autonomic manager, enterprise knowledge repository, sensor and RFID platform for context awareness, actuation and robotics framework for delivering physical services on-demand, migration and modernization utility for transitioning from legacy to modern blocks, and semantic and mesh engine. In short, an SOA fabric is a clustered and modular platform for smoothly interlinking a variety of enterprise building blocks in order to empower them to be intensely and instinctively interactive and distinctively collaborative.

The "SOA virtualization and governance solution" is of high importance in the unfolding era of services. It is noted that ESBs provide mediation functionality, which is the most basic form of service virtualization. However, management of services is not addressed by ESBs because ESBs only address communication between services and do not provide a container to host a service. Thus, a standardized SOA fabric must have a service virtualization container, which provides more advanced governance features for effective monitoring and control, deeper design and runtime visibility, etc.

Cloud-Hosted Service Middleware

Clouds are emerging as very powerful IT infrastructures in which software assets, applications, and agents are stocked and served cheaply through the Internet infrastructure. The cloud paradigm has attained unprecedented popularity due to its unique property of combining a variety of trendsetting and trustworthy technologies such as dynamic provisioning; virtualization; multitenancy; SOA-induced agility; grid-based resource linkage and sharing; cluster-based error tolerance and high availability; and the utility-based delivery, metering, and billing model. Clouds guarantee extreme elasticity, high throughput and flexibility, and affordability. Clouds have brought in a number of novel trends such as IaaS, PaaS, SaaS, and integration as a service. There are data as well as service clouds that follow the famous private, public, community, and hybrid cloud models.

Product vendors and service organizations are hosting service development platforms, middleware, and SOA fabrics in clouds in order to reap the benefits of the salient and scintillating features of cloud infrastructures. Cloud integration bus or Internet service bus (ISB)/cloud broker suites will become very popular for enabling cloud-hosted services and on-premise business data to talk to each other seamlessly in order to create all-inclusive business insight and an integrated view for executives and engineers. This is able to facilitate the realization of integrated, composite, and modern business systems. A group of support services (cloud services) is being built for simplified configuration, administration, accessibility, availability, modifiability, and sustainability of business services in clouds. Clouds started as centralized infrastructures, but later on the sound and successful distribution mechanism has caught up with clouds also. Today, there are initiatives for standards and proven mechanisms for federated clouds and the intercloud. In short, delivering clouds as a service will soon become a reality.

Middleware for Embedded SOA

The SOA has already captivated the enterprise space and is now moving toward the much larger embedded space. There are billions of embedded devices around us at this point in time and it is forecast that trillions of highly miniaturized, invisible, disappearing, and calm embedded systems will be manufactured in the coming decades. Our varied environments (homes, offices, cars, manufacturing plants, etc.) are becoming increasingly saturated with scores of generic as well as specific embedded devices.

The goal is to transition our passive and lifeless surroundings into lively, lovely, and smart places. For this to happen, there must be a deep connectivity among all physical and ground-level devices. Further, such devices have to interact with remote and centralized IT systems such as ERP systems, BI systems, dashboards, data warehouses, and data mining systems. In other words, ground-level devices at a location that are in sync with IT systems are capable of understanding our needs at that place and time precisely, conceiving and concretizing these requirements as services, and delivering them to us unobtrusively. In other words, device-to-device as well as device-to-IT integration must happen without any inhibition in real time. Standards-based service middleware is being overwhelmingly recommended in order to speed up and simplify discovery, connectivity, and integration tasks.

The key point here is that every embedded system hides behind a service interface and this enables every participating device to be viewed as a service. This segregation of interface and implementation brings in a spectacular shift. In other words, all the device heterogeneities are transparent to the outside world. Thus, service-enabled appliances, sensors, electronics, instruments, networks, infrastructures, and machines become capable of finding and sharing their unique capabilities with one another. Embedded devices play the roles of service consumer, provider, broker, gateway, and proxy for other devices. Research scholars and scientists have come up with introspective middleware for affecting potential linkages among such disintegrated, distributed, decentralized, and dissimilar devices. Device services will soon become very common with the surging popularity of the SODA concept and the service-oriented device integration standards such as DPWS. The OSGi provides another prominent means for device integration. Further on, the exquisite characteristics of RESTful services come in handy for seamlessly and spontaneously integrating deeply embedded and resource-constrained devices.

In conclusion, there are a number of diverse infrastructural elements for supporting service-oriented applications. In this section, we discuss only a few of them. There are innumerable books focusing more decisively and incisively on the various service platforms and tool sets used in service-oriented applications.

DIRECT AND DISTINCT IMPACTS OF NG-SOA

Visionaries are united in envisioning and eulogizing the radical shifts promised by enriched SOA. Next-generation SOA will soon become the mainstream enterprise-grade architecture; the current rigid, monolithic, and closed enterprise IT will exit and a kind of elastic, responsive, and adaptive IT will emerge in its wake. Business houses and end users will be the prime beneficiaries of these silent yet sparkling transformations.

The Service Oriented Enterprises (SOEs)

It is of interest that IT managers are ceaselessly exploring and devising a slew of measures to achieve business competency, resiliency, and versatility. The IT infrastructures are compactly consolidated to be presented as a pool of centrally placed and effectively managed compute machines, which are made easily maneuverable, approachable, and usable using virtualization technologies; automated using a string of automation solutions; presented as large-scale sharable resources; leveraged for solving high-performance problems using matured grid concepts; etc.

Without an iota of doubt, it has been proved that service is the sublime and subtle abstraction unit for engineering, integrating, and modernizing enterprise systems. Since the service paradigm ensures business agility and continuity, executives, entrepreneurs, and engineers are overwhelmingly assimilating, accentuating, and accelerating the much acclaimed SO concepts. Not only software but also hardware components are being neatly abstracted as services and, hence, both software and hardware infrastructures are being service enriched. Every single gizmo or gadget is being projected as a service-enabled device so that it can energetically participate in the fast-evolving service environments.

Smart Hospital

Creating and sustaining smart environments and enterprises is the ultimate vision of next-generation IT [12]. Researchers are unfolding a suite of

- Implementation technologies (pervasive computing; ambient communication; M2M communication; ubiquitous sensing, vision, perception, and actuation technologies)
- Lean, integrated, and open processes

- Consolidated, virtualized, automated, sharable, and dynamic cloud infrastructures
- Connected devices (robots, appliances, machines, kitchen utensils, gizmos, gadgets, media players, consumer electronics, and instruments)
- Everyday and ordinary articles and assets that are digitalized and made smart (digitalized cots, chairs, windows, doors, tables, wardrobes, and so on, by attaching invisible RFID tags, light-emitting diode [LED] displays, sensors, actuators, controllers, chips, stickers, smart dust, motes, etc., to them)
- The SODA standards such as DPWS and OSGi
- The RESTful services for virtualizing embedded and resource-constrained devices

In a nutshell, the mandatory features of any smart environment are dynamism, ubiquity, transparency, resiliency, versatility, openness, utility, and autonomy. Besides these, nonfunctional requirements (scalability, availability, security, sustainability, malleability, consumability, etc.) of the enabling ICT systems are also demanded. Tentori and Favela introduced the concept of activity-based computing (ABC) in order to realize the elusive smart health care. The service paradigm has evolved to a workable and winning concept for producing and maintaining smart systems. Services are essential for the seamless integration of diverse and distributed devices in order to realize connected systems. The D2E, D2D, and device-to-cloud (D2C) interactions are simplified and streamlined by the service paradigm. Semantic and smart services are being developed for various horizontal and vertical requirements. In particular, aware services (self-, situation-, and surroundings-aware services) are able to find one another by conceiving imaginative service clusters. Decision-enabling and knowledge services find prominence in smart spaces.

Actuation services are also possible with the involvement of a collection of networked robots, sensors, and actuators for helping disabled, disadvantaged, and debilitated patients. Special electronic modules (microscale and nanoscale modules) are generated and glued to all kinds of tangible articles in order to transform them into digital and intelligent artifacts. Medical devices, instruments, and gadgets are being subjected to external as well as internal enablement to be smart, sensitive, and simple in their operations and outlooks. Health-care software packages are remodeled and redesigned as libraries of interoperable services. Based on service and process-centricity capabilities, novel clinical procedures are being developed; hospital IT actors and assets are tagged and remedied to make them service-enabled; and medical processes are relooked at and revised in order to make them mean, green, and clean. Services can be meshed and mashed up dynamically to form activity-aware composites that in turn enable health-care ICT systems to behave insightfully based on changing situations.

With NG-SOA, bloated enterprises can happily move to lean and agile SOEs. Composites, which are the enticing building blocks in enterprise IT, are expected to facilitate a variety of rich and dynamic service-based systems. It is noted that SOIs will be the crucial contributors of futuristic cloud enterprises [1].

Rich Enterprise Applications

With the massive adoption of the web, thin clients (browsers) have become the norm for users to interact with remote web services and applications, that is, UI is the dominant consumer layer through which users interact with service systems to fulfill their needs. This layer enables any organization to expose its valuable business capability and data to subscribers judiciously and securely. With the arrival of Web 2.0 technologies, the UI domain is silently and strategically undergoing a number of drastic changes. It is noted that AJAX, the leading Web 2.0 technology, promises a desktop experience for usually slow web applications. There is an enhanced richness in the presentation and a higher reach is accomplished. Real-time connectivity and collaboration are possible as AJAX internally supports asynchronous interactions.

Web 2.0 technologies go a long way in forming digital communities and realizing enhanced user participation through the web platform. Another trend is to have visually charming and functionally rich UIs that are resonating, eye-catching, and refreshing. Mature Web 2.0 technologies convert the passive web systems into fertile, lively, and people-centric systems. End users are entitled to receive content and services in real time. Enterprise mashups play a key role in creating orchestrated services and composite views. Thus, web-oriented architecture (WOA) and Web 2.0 standards, products, and tool sets are all set to unleash a number of RIAs.

Web 2.0 technologies maximize user productivity and application flexibility by decoupling presentation logic from application code. The synergy of RIA technologies with loosely coupled business services deepens the value proposition of these technologies. As depicted in Figure 5.9, the

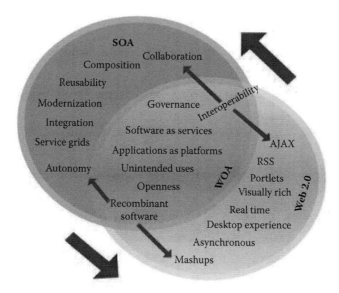

FIGURE 5.9

Convergence of Web 2.0 and SOA for realizing WOA.

combination of Web 2.0 technologies and SOA leads to the era of rich enterprise applications (REAs). Synchronization, richness, dynamic composition, real-time interaction, and so on will become the norm.

Service-Oriented Business Applications

Services are discrete units of application logic conceived and capitalized for exemplary modularity, composability, and reusability of systems. They can be adroitly combined to create multipurpose, multichannel, and feature-rich services that fully automate business processes. When provided as a collection of services in the context of a particular business domain, these services could lead to service-oriented business applications (SOBAs). In other words, sophisticated business systems can be dynamically derived by adaptively linking a variety of business and infrastructure services at runtime. Although BPMN, Petri net, SOA, WOA, and EDA guarantee the conceptual and design style/structure for the resulting system [4], there are promising assembling and execution techniques, programming tools, and models in the forms of SCA, MDA, BPEL, and so on, which ensure the success of robust and resilient SOBAs. For example, customer and content management, asset and field service management, inventory, shipping, and other related management services collectively and collaboratively lead to a complete and composite SOBA. In addition, changes can be easily incorporated into the relevant service or at the process level and, as a result, the total system will be incredibly lean and appreciably adaptive and agile.

Mashups are closely related to SOBAs because SOBAs also combine functionality from a myriad of services to create an integrated and insightful experience. What mashups have and SOBAs lack is a rich interface. Further, SOBAs implement business processes in a systematic and governed manner, whereas mashups do not. By combining the two, business applications rich in features with visually appealing interfaces can be quickly established. This grand unification enables SOBAs to create and configure themselves accordingly. Mashups significantly enhance business value and applicability of composites in diverse domains. Businesses are solidly augmented to be fiercely competitive, ideally adaptive, and sensitive in their offerings and outlook. In short, SOBAs, which form a kind of dynamic, enterprise-scale, and mission-critical business application, are capable of quickly absorbing and adapting to all kinds of known and unknown changes (market, organization, government, technology, etc.). The cloud is the unified hosting and delivery platform for SOBAs.

Dynamic Business Applications

Dynamism is turning out to be the most-wanted feature of any IT system, as change is pronounced the only constant thing in this knowledge-driven society. Unfortunately, today's enterprise packages are inimical for any unplanned, forced, and perpetual change. Enterprise systems need to be extremely amenable to change, as they must readily accommodate market-driven and customer-desired changes in order to guarantee business agility.

For achieving the goal of dynamism, business systems are structured as an array of loosely coupled and highly cohesive components. Events that are, in general, asynchronous and decoupled are greatly associated with the real-time characteristic of enterprises. Further, the business logic portion is separated from business rules (instead of embedded processes, open processes are recommended), process descriptions are segregated from process implementations, PIMs (without embedding technology, protocol, language, and infrastructure details) are created and persisted, cross-cutting concerns such as software building blocks, like services, events, agents, composites, models, and so on, are externalized and injected on a need basis, policy- and goal-aware agents are introduced to empower applications to be smart in their operations, etc.

Thus, a sort of loose interdependence is prescribed as the correct medicine for the ills affecting software engineering. This separation of concerns paves the way for the various system modules (process model and logic; rule, configuration, and policy files) to be open to absorbing all kinds of shocks and shifts. The leading market research group Forrester has identified business rules platforms as a key enabler for dynamic business applications (DBAs) because they allow applications to be built for incorporating changes in minutes rather than months. Rules are the indispensable underpinnings of enterprise IT today. Policies and operational procedures are used to make decisions, determine workflow, establish prices, facilitate choices, enforce constraints, and comply with regulations. In addition, many rules of businesses change fast and quickly become archaic. It is noted that BRMSs provide a suite of special capabilities for readily and regally integrating and injecting rules/policies onto application modules at runtime. Apart from making and managing business rules independent of applications, business people (nontechnical persons) can tinker with business rules. Further, business rules can be constructed, construed, and advertised as a service (RaaS) for any local or remote business application to leverage it in runtime to embed relevant information and required changes in application structure as well as behavior. Precisely speaking, BRMS, BPM, SOA, and clouds collectively play an elegant and essential role in establishing DBAs [5].

Multienterprise Business Applications

Due to the unprecedented globalization being realized by the deeper penetration and pervasiveness of the Internet infrastructure, businesses of all sizes, structures, and scopes are fast expanding their operations, deliveries, and sales to all parts of the globe. Every worthwhile business establishment today boasts of an army of trading partners, suppliers, retailers, employees, shareholders, and customers from every nook and corner of this increasingly connected world. The much-vaunted supply chain has become integrated and, hence, any change in one part or aspect gets immediately reflected across the globe.

The resulting reality is that businesses are mandated to interact with several business partners at the same time. In other words, multibusiness collaboration has become a mandatory mode for survival and success in today's multipolar world. Thereby, persistent demands for sophisticated and smart approaches, platforms, processes, practices, and tools are being made to empower businesses to be seamlessly sensitive and compactly collaborative with their partners, peers, and people alike. This is the basis for the quick unfolding of next-generation B2B e-business (multienterprise) software solutions.

Now with the heightened awareness of SOA as the most promising and prominent business integration and transformation mechanism, SOA is being prepared and pampered for designing, developing, and maintaining multienterprise business systems. Multienterprise business applications (MEBAs) are a new class of applications that can be used to support business processes that span enterprise and organizational boundaries. The SOA principles, patterns, products, and so on generate a kind of hope in realizing and managing an assortment of 24/7 MEBAs. With the emergence of cloud infrastructures, the process of implementing and hosting high-performing and scalable MEBAs has picked up.

The MEBAs also have some differentiating requirements. As scenarios may include participants distributed all over the world and MEBAs are mission-critical applications, there is a need to have a robust architecture and infrastructure in place that can ensure high availability and performance of MEBAs, besides having features such as auditing, reporting, and regulatory compliance. Unlike traditional SOA applications that are more focused on functional capabilities within a single enterprise, MEBAs extend the SOA concepts and technologies to business processes that span multiple enterprises. Because MEBAs operate between organizations, their primary concerns are also different—including community and identity management, process execution management, and multienterprise governance—from those of traditional SOA. Moreover, MEBA architecture encompasses a proven composition suite for orchestrating, choreographing, and executing composite services derived from a library of common and foundational services so that it is proactive in understanding and fulfilling changing business sentiments. In a nutshell, empowered SOA is critical and crucial in making MEBAs that are elegant, elastic, and evolvable. The cloud as the centralized entity with powerful and enormous processing and storage capacities enhances the future of MEBAs.

Real-Time and Dynamic Enterprises

Businesses are expected to adhere to real time in their operations and obligations besides being adeptly responsive. In this unparalleled transition, business events and their skilful collection, utilization, and manipulation are anticipated to play a very influential role in shaping next-generation enterprise IT. There is a constant push and rush for accomplishing real-time IT. This unique capability empowers and elevates enterprises to be categorized as "zero latency enterprises" (ZLEs) or "real-time enterprises" (RTEs). On the one hand, many business applications can be integrated in a near real-time fashion (e.g., important events can be instantly propagated throughout an enterprise). Although SOA has captured much attention and market shares for many IT organizations, it has been materializing as a simplified style of request/response (R/R) and C-S computing. Generally, services are connected in a linear and predetermined order to create business-aware services. This is clearly not enough if one wants to manage a universe of asynchronous events effectively.

It is noted that EDA can capture a stream of complex, less predictable, and asynchronous events happening in parallel and process them as per business strategies and policies in order to trigger intelligent and real-time responses. A business event is any notable activity or event that happens inside or outside a business. Events have a heavy impact on and can decide the strength, direction, and even the fate of enterprises. Depending on the size of a business, there can be hundreds to millions of notable events that occur on a daily basis. A network device emitting a warning message that the temperature is too high, a snowstorm occurring in one region of the country causing employees to be late to duty, and a pallet of goods passing through an RFID reader in another part of the globe are all significant business events. It is no exaggeration when one says that all businesses are interestingly and intrinsically driven by events. Hence, enterprise IT needs to be in a position to glean, grasp, analyze, mine, and extract action-oriented insights and to predict the correct course of actions to be taken when an event occurs so that customer delight is ensured and enhanced.

Thus, businesses spend most of their time, resources, and energy on optimally dealing with events from different and distributed resources. Business processes are made creative enough to act and react simultaneously on events within a stipulated time. Misdirected resources, upset customers, delayed responses, frauds and deviations, sudden spikes in sales, and every other kind of situation imaginable clearly demonstrate why events and their effective management are critical for the continued success of businesses. Hence, the event-processing capability of businesses enable them to track, trace, coordinate, corroborate, and correlate events; analyze events for any positive trends and tips, favorable associations, insights, and patterns; and finally predict any measurable impacts of identified situations. Rapid action can be contemplated and taken to prevent or minimize any kind of negative consequences. Thus, SOA, EDA, and cloud infrastructures and engines for event processing are the most important modules incorporated into enterprise IT to realize the move toward dynamic enterprises.

Integrated, Adaptive, and Modernized Enterprises

With the amalgamation of multiple, heterogeneous, underutilized, and closed assets in the IT division of any growing organization, the need for IT consolidation, federation, automation, and utilization picks up fast. In other words, the unwanted factors such as multiplicity, heterogeneity, and proprietary ownership contribute for IT silos in companies these days and hence, there is a clarion call for the acceleration of developing competent, calm, and configurable technologies for seamless linking, sharing, and interaction to guarantee the growth of lean, integrated, and nimble enterprises. With the multiplicity of technologies, tools, products, platforms, and devices used, clustering, grid-enabling, concurrency, and configurability needs increase correspondingly. The SOA is, without a doubt, the overwhelming choice for realizing these requirements.

Services endorse and enable composition at design time as well as at runtime. Composition in the midst of a library of distinctly capable services results in adaptive systems. Finally, due to the large amount of legacy, inflexible, closed, monolithic, and bloated systems in Fortune 500 companies, there is a rush for modernization technologies, methodologies, tools, tips, and best practices. Here too, SOA empowered by cloud infrastructures shows a lot of potential and gives a lot of promise in effortlessly renovating, reengineering, rearchitecting, refactoring, and rehosting old business applications.

CONCLUSION

Every incredible and distinguishable technology, process, and product is invariably given adjectives such as next generation, futuristic, and smart these days. Some have even gone to the extent of adjoining numerical adjectives such as 2.0 for marking and marketing new-generation evolving technologies. We are stepping into the era of Computer Science 2.0, which is an adept combi-nation describing new buzzwords such as Web 2.0, Enterprise 2.0, BI 2.0, BPM 2.0, and Internet 2.0. Value addition through seamless synchronization, consolidation, clustering, feature incorpora-tion, and cross-fertilization of technologies is an ongoing process in any field. The service paradigm also goes through the same route in order to simplistically and sensitively fulfill evolving business scenarios and demands. There is a convergence on the view that NG-SOA is a fascinating and futuristic subject worthy of deeper study, research, and application for solving a host of real-world problems. With enterprise IT being slated for a major and overdue overhaul, the relevance and reality of NG-SOA as an engineering methodology and mechanism is gaining the upper hand and garnering widespread attention. With an enhanced knowledge of this pioneering paradigm of service engineering, including its short-term and long-term impacts on enterprise IT and the debilitating issues currently faced by it, IT professionals are collaboratively visualizing and validating the subject of NG-SOA.

REFERENCES

1. Andy, M., R. Daniels, and T. Hall. 2008. "The Cloud and SOA—Creating an Architecture for Today and for the Future," Capgemini and HP, http://www.hp.com/hpinfo/analystrelations/wp_cloudcomputing_soa_capgemini_hp.pdf.
2. IBM Corporation. November 2007. "Smart SOA: Best practices for agile innovation and optimization," IBM Corporation, ftp://ftp.software.ibm.com/software/solutions/soa/pdfs/WSW14001-USEN-00_smart_soa_FINAL.pdf.
3. Ter Beck, M. H., A. Bucchiarone, and S. Gnesi. 2007. "Web Service Composition Approaches: From Industrial Standards to Formal Methods." *Second International Conference on Internet and Web Applications and Services (ICIW'07)*, Mauritius, May 13–14, 2007, http://fmt.isti.cnr.it/WEBPAPER/final-ICIW07.pdf.
4. van Hoof, J. February 2007. "SOA and EDA: Using Events to Bridge Decoupled Service Boundaries." *SOA Magazine*, Issue IV.
5. Bajwa, I. S., R. Kazmi, S. Mumtaz, M. A. Choudhary, and M. S. Naweed. 2008. "SOA and BPM Partnership: A Paradigm for Dynamic and Flexible Process and I.T. Management," *World Academy of Science, Engineering and Technology* 45, http://www.waset.org/journals/waset/v45/v45-4.pdf.
6. Wikes, L., and R. Veryard. 2007. "Extending SOA with Web 2.0," Everware-CBDI, Inc., ftp://public.dhe.ibm.com/software/solutions/soa/pdfs/CBDI_IBM_SOA_and_Web_20.pdf.
7. OASIS. 2012. "SCA: Support for Composing Existing Applications in an SOA Solution," OASIS Open CSA, http://www.osoa.org.
8. Leutenmayr, S. 2007. "Selected Languages for Web Services Composition: Survey, Chal-lenges, Outlook." PhD Thesis, http://www.pms.ifi.lmu.de/publikationen/diplomarbeiten/Stephan.Leutenmayr/Diplomarbeit%20Stephan%20Leutenmayr.pdf.

9. Wang, W., W. Yu, Q. Li, W. Wang, and X. Liu. 2008. "Service-Oriented High Level Architecture," Simulation Interoperability Standards Organization, Edinburgh, Scotland, http://arxiv.org/ftp/arxiv/papers/0907/0907.3983.pdf.

10. Lublinsky, B. July 26, 2007. "Service Composition," http://www.infoq.com/articles/lublinsky-soa-composition.

11. Arcitura Education, Inc. 2012. "Service Technology Magazine", Arcitura Education, Inc., http://www.soamag.com.

12. Trifa, V. M., C. M. Cianci, and D. Guinard. 2008. "Dynamic Control of a Robotic Swarm Using a Service-Oriented Architecture," http://www.im.ethz.ch/publications/180__Trifa_paper.pdf.

13. TIBCO. 2012. Service-Oriented Architecture (SOA) Resource Center, TIBCO Software, http://www.tibco.com/solutions/soa/default.jsp.

14. Anicic, D., M. Brodie, J. de Bruijn, D. Fensel et al. 2006. "A Semantically Enabled Service Oriented Architecture," http://www.heppnetz.de/files/wimbi2006.pdf.

15. "Service Oriented Architecture—SOA," IBM, http://www-306.ibm.com/software/solutions/soa.

16. Raj, P. "Information Technology Portal," http://www.peterindia.net.

17. Karimi, O., and N. Modiri. September 2011. "Enterprise Integration Using Service Oriented Architecture." *Advanced Computing: An International Journal* 2 (5): 41–7.

18. IBM Global Technology Services. 2008. "How Service-Oriented Architecture (SOA) Impacts Your IT Infrastructure: Satisfying the Demands of Dynamic Business Processes," IBM Global Technology Services, http://www.majorcities.eu/generaldocuments/pdf/ibm_soa_satisfying_the_demands_of_dynamic_business_processes.pdf.

6

Cloud Data Architecture

INTRODUCTION

Business and IT environments are becoming very dynamic as there are incredible changes taking place and challenges rising up in the marketplace as a result of the tottering economy, ever-changing government rules and regulations, and ever-increasing expectations and specific preferences of customers. Promising technologies with much potential; production of standards-compliant IT infrastructures; mass availability of slim and sleek devices; speedy evolution of the pervasive web; purpose-specific handy and trendy appliances; infinitesimal and invisible tags, labels, and stickers; productivity-enhancing solutions; and connectivity products are completely redefining the IT landscape. In such a constantly changing environment, executives need to take insightful yet timely decisions to steer their enterprises in the right direction on the chosen paths. In other words, delivering actionable insights to decision makers goes a long way in arriving at the right decision at the right time. It is very clear that every aspiring industry is therefore leaning toward agile and adaptive BI systems, which are in place to precisely and perfectly anticipate, augment, and advance its journey. Next-generation BI systems are concisely descriptive, creatively prescriptive, and cognitively predictive in establishing smart enterprises.

The pressure on IT to deliver the right information at the right time is on the rise. This is achieved by using a combination of historical data found in data warehouses and data marts, low-latency data found in operational data stores, and real-time data obtained from operational systems. In other words, there is a strong need for elegant and exemplary data integration platforms, practices, and procedures in order to provide an integrated and insightful view of data to various stakeholders.

In this chapter, we incorporate a sizeable description of data integration techniques, technologies, and tips. The database field is getting ready for radical and rapid innovations, which will be made in the days to come with the availability and speedier acceptance of converged, elastic, optimized, and dynamic IT infrastructures that are highly scalable and increasingly autonomic, client aware, federated, and shared.

Elasticity, the pay-per-use feature, low up-front investment, less time to software deployment and delivery, self-service, and delegation of risks are some of the major enabling features that make cloud computing a path-breaking paradigm for deploying and delivering novel applications that are not economically feasible in a traditional enterprise infrastructure. This has also led to the proliferation of applications (enterprise, embedded, social, and cloud), resulting in a remarkable increase in the scale and variety of data generated, aggregated, processed, disseminated, as well as consumed by such applications. The pressure on data size and diversity forces many to ponder and prescribe out-of-the-box proposals toward new types of data infrastructures and platforms such as databases, data management systems, query languages, data integration hubs, and adapters for transactional as well as analytical purposes. Cloud analytics is a well-groomed and futuristic proposition that is highly recommended these days all over the world for its powerful implications and improvisations.

The cloud movement is expectantly and expediently thriving and trend-setting a host of delectable novelties. A number of distinct disruptions and tectonic transformations on the business front are being activated and accentuated with the faster and easier adaptability of the cloud IT principles. The cloud concepts have opened up a deluge of fresh possibilities and opportunities for innovators, individuals, and institutions to conceive, conceptualize, concretize, and carry forward new-generation business services and solutions. As we saw in earlier chapters, a dazzling array of path-breaking and mission-critical business augmentation models and mechanisms have emerged, and they are consistently and convincingly evolving toward perfection as the cloud technology grows and glows relentlessly in conjunction with other enterprise-class technologies.

On the IT side, too, there have been some exhilarating and extraordinary transitions. Apart from highly acclaimed IT simplicity, sustainability, and sensitivity, the goal of self-servicing IT resources in order to enable business managers and consultants to play around is seeing becoming a reality. A growing set of systems are finding their new residence in the clouds. Especially on the data level, there are plenty of cloud-based databases, master data management (MDM) systems, predictive analytics modules, data marts, cubes and warehouses, decision making systems, business intelligence (BI) tools, database management systems, data integration containers, engines, platforms, brokers, buses, fabrics, and so on. Aside from remedied and rejuvenated techniques and tips, practices, processes, and patterns are being experimented with and explained in order to simplify and streamline cloud analytics. In this chapter, we discuss and detail all the data-related systems and how they interrelate to perfectly accomplish what was originally intended as the cloud vision.

A PERSPECTIVE ON BIG-DATA COMPUTING

A series of evolutions and revolutions taking place in the web and the device ecosystem have resulted in the production of large volumes of multistructured (unstructured, semistructured, and structured) data, which are gathered and transmitted over the Internet communication infrastructure from distant, distributed, and decentralized sources; subjected to processing, filtering, cleansing, transformation, and prioritization through a slew of computing and data-intensive processes; and stocked in high-end storage appliances and networks. For decades, companies have been making business-critical decisions based on transactional (structured) data stored in relational databases. Today, the scene is quite different. Data sources are distributed and increasing in number, data come in different formats, and data volume is on a consistent climb. This mandates highly competitive technologies, tools, and methodologies to capture, process, and extract actionable insights in real time. Primarily, there are two groups of data: (1) human-generated and (2) machine-generated data. Weblogs, microblogs, video songs, e-mail messages, PDF files, Microsoft Word documents, presentations, Microsoft Excel sheets, data from sensors and actuators, and photographs from cameras form the latest semistructured data types. These can be appropriately mined for extracting useful and usable information in the forms of tips, trends, hidden associations, alerts, reusable and responsible patterns, insights, and other hitherto unexplored facts.

Data are flowing in torrents into every area of the global economy. Companies churn out a burgeoning volume of transactional data, capturing trillions of bytes of information on their customers, suppliers, and operations; millions of networked sensors are being embedded in the physical world in devices such as mobile phones, smart energy meters, automobiles, and industrial machines that sense, create, and communicate data in this age of IoT. Indeed, as companies and organizations go about their business and interact with individuals, they generate tremendous amounts of digital "exhaust data," that is, data created as a byproduct of other activities. Social media sites, smartphones, and other consumer devices including PCs and laptops have allowed billions of individuals around the world to contribute to the amount of big data available. The growing volume of multimedia content plays a major role in the exponential growth of the amount of big data. Each second of high-definition video, for example, generates more than 2000 times the number of bytes required to store a single page of text. In a digitized world, consumers in their day-to-day life—communicating, browsing, buying, sharing, searching—create their own enormous trails of data.

The McKinsey Global Institute (2011) Report on Big Data.

Big-data computing involves a bevy of powerful procedures, products, and practices that comprehensively and computationally analyze multistructured and massive data heaps in order to create and sustain fresh business value. Sharp reductions in the cost of both storage and computing power have made it feasible to collect and capitalize this new-generation data proactively and preemptively with much enthusiasm. Companies are looking for ways and means to include nontraditional yet potentially valuable data along with their traditional enterprise data in predictive analysis. The McKinsey Global Institute (MGI) estimates that data volume is growing at a rate of 40% per year. There are four important characteristics that define the ensuing era of big-data computing:

1. Volume: Machine-generated data is growing exponentially in volume compared to human-generated data. For instance, digital cameras produce high-volume images and video files to be shipped and

succinctly stored; they are also subjected to a wide variety of tasks including video surveillance and security. Smart energy meters and heavy industrial equipments and machineries such as oil refineries and drilling rigs generate huge volumes of data.

2. Velocity: Social networking and microblogging sites create a large amount of information. Every day, millions of people use Web 2.0 (social web) platforms to read and write their views and reviews on all subjects under the sun; to list their complaints, comments, and clarifications on personal as well as professional services and solutions; to share their well-merited knowledge with a wider community; to form user communities for generic as well as specific purposes; to advertise and promote new ideas and products; and to communicate and collaborate with each other to enhance productivity. Although the size of information created and shared in this manner is comparatively small, the number of users is huge and hence the frequency is on the higher side resulting in a massive collection of data. Even at 140 characters per tweet, the extremely large number of tweets results in a huge volume of data (over 8 TB per day).

3. Variety: Newer data formats are entering the scene every day, compounding the problem further. As enterprise IT is continuously strengthened with the incorporation of nimble embedded systems and versatile cloud services to produce and provide premium and people-centric applications to the growing population, new data types and formats are continuously emerging and evolving.

4. Value: Data is an asset and it has to be purposefully processed, prioritized, protected, mined, and analyzed utilizing a group of advanced technologies and tools in order to bring out hidden knowledge that enables individuals and institutions to carry forward their future course of action.

Why Big-Data Computing?

The main mandate of IT is to capture, store, and process a large amount of data to output useful information in a preferred format. Lately, a stream of competent technologies has come up to derive usable and reusable knowledge from information bases. The much-wanted transition of data to information and then to knowledge is simplified by smartly leveraging IT solutions. Thus, data has been the main source of value creation for the past five decades. Now, with the eruption of big data and its enabling platforms, corporate houses and consumers are yearning for better and bigger value derivation. Indeed, big-data computing breeds innovations that realize robust and resilient productivity-enhancing methods, means, and models for sustaining business value. The hidden treasures of big data are being technologically exploited to the fullest extent by businesses in order to zoom ahead of their competitors. Big data–inspired technology clusters facilitate new business acceleration and automation mechanisms. In a nutshell, the scale and scope of big data is to bring forth numerous noteworthy transformations.

For governments, the big-data journey ensures a bright and blissful opportunity to boost their efficiency in delivering citizen services. With the use of big data, IT spending comes down while IT-based automation is enhanced. There are research results enforcing the view that the public sector can boost its productivity significantly through the effective use of big data.

When big data is dissected, distilled, and analyzed in combination with traditional enterprise data, corporate IT can gain a more comprehensive and insightful understanding of its business, which can lead to enhanced productivity, a stronger competitive position in the marketplace, and an enabling atmosphere for greater and grandiose innovations. All these will have a momentous impact on the bottom line.

For people, big data delivers a growing array of incredible benefits. For example, the use of in-home and in-body monitoring devices such as implantable sensors, wearables, fixed and portable actuators, robots, computing devices, LED displays, and smartphones having ad hoc networking capabilities to accurately measure vital body parameters and monitor progress continuously is a futuristic way to drastically improve the health of patients. In other words, sensors act as the eyes and ears of new-generation IT and their contribution spans from environmental monitoring to body-health monitoring. These kinds of creative and catalytic advancements happen to be a breeding ground for crafting elegant and exotic services.

Sellers and shoppers can gain much from communication devices and information appliances. The proliferation of smartphones and other global positioning system (GPS) devices offers advertisers an opportunity to target consumers when they are in close proximity to a store, coffee shop, or restaurant. This opens up uncharted avenues of fresh revenue for service providers and businesses. The market share and mind share of such proactive businesses is bound to grow by leaps and bounds. Retailers can make use of social computing sites to understand people's preferences and preoccupations to smartly spread out their reach. The hidden facts and patterns elicited in this manner can enable them to execute much more effective microcustomer segmentation and targeted marketing campaigns. Further, they come in handy when one is eliminating supply chain disturbances and deficiencies.

A LOOK AT BIG-DATA INFRASTRUCTURE

Data diversity is one of the most formidable challenges faced by BI today. This is because most BI platforms and products are designed for operating on relational data and other forms of structured data. Many organizations struggle to extract BI value from the wide range of unstructured and semistructured data types, including text, clickstreams, log files, social media, documents, location data, and sensor data. Hadoop and its allied and associated technologies are renowned for making sense of big data [6,23]. For example, developers can push files containing a wide range of unstructured data into Hadoop Distributed File System (HDFS) without needing to define data types or structures at load time. Instead, data is structured at query or analysis time. This is a good match for analytic methods that are open-ended for discovery purposes. For BI/data warehousing (DW) tools and platforms that demand structured data, Hadoop Hive and MapReduce can output records and tables as needed. In this way, HDFS can be an effective source of unstructured data, although it generates structured output for BI/DW purposes.

Hadoop products show much promise as viable and valuable platforms for advanced analytics, thus complementing the average report-oriented data warehouse with new analytic capabilities, especially for analytics with unstructured data. Outside BI and DW, Hadoop products also show promise for online archiving, content management, and staging multistructured data for a variety of applications. This puts pressure on vendors to offer products having good integration with Hadoop and to provide tools that reduce the manual coding required today. There are numerous scenarios for big-data computing in which Hadoop can contribute immensely to mainstream analytics [20,22].

In the trend toward advanced analytics, users are looking for platforms that enable analytics as an open-ended discovery or exploratory mission. Discovering new facts and relationships typically results from tapping big data that were previously inaccessible to BI. Discovery also comes from mixing data of various types from various sources. HDFS and MapReduce together enable exploration of this eclectic mix of big data. There are several infrastructural components being released and recommended to this end. The most dominant and prominent ones are NoSQL databases, NewSQL databases, and the MapReduce-compliant Hadoop software suite.

NoSQL Databases

There are some serious flaws on the part of relational databases that come in the way of meeting the unique requirements of modern-day social applications, which are gradually moving to reside in cloud infrastructures [1,3–5,7–9]. Another noteworthy fact is that data analysis for BI is increasingly happening in clouds. In other words, cloud analytics is emerging as a hot topic worthy of diligent and deep study and investigation. There are some interested groups in academic as well as industry circles that are stretching further and striving hard to achieve the necessary advancements in order to support and sustain traditional databases to cope with the evolving requirements of social networking applications. However, new breeds of versatile, vivacious, and venerable database solutions such as NoSQL and NewSQL are coming up, capturing the imagination of many.

The business need to leverage complex and connected data is driving the adoption of scalable and high-performance NoSQL databases. This new entrant to the market evokes and sharply enhances data management strategies of various businesses. Several variants of NoSQL databases have emerged over the past decade in order to handsomely handle the terabytes and petabytes of data generated by enterprises and consumers. They are specifically capable of processing multiple data types. In other words, NoSQL databases contain different data types such as text, audio, video, social network feeds, weblogs, and many more that cannot be handled by traditional databases. These data types are highly complex and deeply interrelated. Therefore, the demand is to unravel the truth hidden behind these huge yet diverse data assets. Understanding insights and acting on them enable businesses to plan ahead.

Having understood the changing scenario, web-based businesses have been crafting their own custom NoSQL databases to elegantly manage the ever-increasing data volume and diversity. Amazon's Dynamo and Google's BigTable are the shining examples of homegrown databases that can store lots of data. These NoSQL databases were designed for handling highly complex and heterogeneous data. The key differentiation here is that they are built not for high-end transactions but for analytic purposes.

Why NoSQL Databases?

Business-to-consumer (B2C) e-commerce and B2B e-business applications are highly transactional, and leading enterprise application frameworks and platforms such as JEE directly and distinctly support a number of transaction types (simple, distributed, nested, etc.). A trivial example is as follows: A flight reservation application must be rigidly transactional; otherwise, everything is bound to collapse. As enterprise systems become increasingly distributed, ease of transaction is being pronounced as a mandatory feature.

Social applications have been growing rapidly recently. Youth are especially fascinated by them and utilize a stream of social websites. Hence, such sites are undergoing astronomical growth. It is no secret that the popularity, ubiquity, and utility of Facebook, LinkedIn, Twitter, and other blogging sites, are increasing incessantly. There is a steady convergence of enterprise and social applications. In other words, enterprise applications are being empowered with additional competencies and capabilities through this cool synchronization. For example, online sellers understand and utilize customers' choices, leanings, historical transactions, and so on in order to do more business. In other words, businesses are more receptive, open, and inclined toward customers' participation to garner and glean their views to reach out more across the globe and to produce business-aligned and aware REAs. Specialized protocols and Web 2.0 technologies (Atom, RSS, AJAX, mashup, etc.) are available to programmatically tag information about people, place, and proclivity to dynamically conceive, conceptualize, and concretize more and more people-centric premium services.

The point here is that the generally dormant and dumb database technology must evolve faster in order to accomplish the aforementioned new-generation IT capacities and capabilities. As data today are more complicated and connected, NoSQL databases need to have the implicit and innate strength to handle them. A NoSQL database should enable high-performance queries on these data. Users should be able to ask the following questions: "Who are all my contacts in Europe?" and "Which of my contacts ordered from this catalog?" A white paper titled "NoSQL for the Enterprise" by Neo Technology (2011) lists the uniqueness of NoSQL databases for enterprises. I have reproduced the essential concepts from that paper in the following paragraphs.

Simplified Data Representation

A NoSQL database should be able to easily represent the complex and connected data that make up today's enterprise applications. Unlike traditional databases, a flexible schema that allows multiple data types also enables developers to easily change applications without disrupting live systems. Databases must be flexible, extensible, and adaptable. With the massive adoption of clouds, NoSQL databases ought to be more suitable for clouds.

End-to-End Transactions

Traditional databases are famous for "all or nothing" transactions, whereas NoSQL databases are given a kind of leeway on this crucial property. This is because the prime reason for the emergence and evolution of NoSQL databases was that they can process massive volumes of data quickly to produce actionable inputs. In other words, traditional databases are for enterprise applications, whereas NoSQL databases are for social applications. Specifically, the consistency aspect of ACID transactions is not rigidly insisted upon in NoSQL databases. It does not matter much when one operation fails here and there in a social application. For instance, there are billions of short messages being tweeted every day and Twitter will survive if a single tweet is lost. But online banking applications relying on traditional databases have to ensure very tight consistency in order to be meaningful. This does not mean that NoSQL databases are off the ACID hook. Instead, they are supposed to support ACID transactions including XA-compliant distributed two-phase commit protocol. The connections between data should be stored on a disk in a structure designed for high-performance retrieval of connected data sets while enforcing strict transaction management. This design delivers significantly better performance for connected data than that offered by relational databases.

Enterprise-Grade Durability

Every NoSQL database for an enterprise needs to have the enterprise-class quality of durability. In other words, a transaction committed to the database will not be lost at any cost under any circumstance. If a flight ticket is reserved and the system crashes due to an internal or external problem, the allotted seat must be there even after the system is retrieved. The durability feature is predominantly ensured through the use of database backups and transaction logs that facilitate the restoration of committed transactions, despite the occurrence of any software or hardware hitch. Relational databases have successfully used the replication method for years to guarantee enterprise-class durability.

Classification of NoSQL Databases

There are four major categories of NoSQL databases available today: (1) key-value stores, (2) column family databases, (3) document databases, and (4) graph databases [4–5,7]. Each database is designed to accommodate huge volumes of data with enough room for future data types. The choice of NoSQL database depends on the type of data you need to store, its size, and its complexity.

Key-Value Stores

A key-value data model is quiet simple. It stores data in key and value pairs where each key maps to a value. It can scale across many machines but cannot support other data types. Key-value data stores use a data model similar to the popular memcached distributed in-memory cache, with a single key-value index for all the data. Unlike memcached, these systems generally provide a persistence mechanism and additional functionalities, such as replication, versioning, locking, transactions, sorting, and other features. The client interface provides options for data insertions, deletions, and index lookups. Similar to memcached, none of these systems offer secondary indices or keys. A key-value store is ideal for applications that require storage of massive amounts of simple data, such as sensor data, or for data that change rapidly, such as stock quotes. Key-value stores support massive data sets of very primitive data. Amazon's Dynamo was built as a key-value store.

Column Family Databases

A column family database can handle semistructured data because in theory every row can have its own schema. It has a few mandatory attributes and a few optional attributes. It is a powerful way to capture semistructured data but often sacrifices the consistency attribute for ensuring the availability attribute. Column family databases can accommodate huge amounts of data and they help to sift through the data very fast. Database writes are much faster than reads, so one natural niche is real-time data analysis. Logging real-time events is a perfect use case. Another use case is random and real-time read/write access to big data. Google's BigTable was built on a column family database. Apache Cassandra, the Facebook database, is another example that was developed to store billions of columns per row. However, it is unable to support unstructured data types or query end-to-end transactions.

Document Databases

A document database contains a collection of key-value pairs stored in documents. Document databases support more complex data than key-value stores. Although it is good at storing documents, it was not originally designed with enterprise-class transactions and durability in mind. Document databases are the most flexible of key-value-style stores; they are perfect for storing a large collection of unrelated and discrete documents. Unlike the key-value stores, these systems generally support secondary indices, multiple types of documents (objects) per database, and nested documents or lists. A good application is a product catalog, which can display individual items but not related items. You can see what is available for purchase, but you cannot connect it to other products bought by customers with similar tastes after they viewed the catalog. MongoDB and CouchDB are examples of document databases.

Graph Databases

A graph database uses nodes, relationships between nodes, and key-value properties instead of tables to represent information. Typically, this model is substantially faster for associative data sets and uses a schema-less and bottom-up model that is ideal for capturing ad hoc and rapidly changing data. Much of today's complex and connected data can be easily stored in a graph database in which there is great value in the relationships among data sets. A graph database accesses data using traversals. A traversal is how you query a graph: You navigate from starting nodes to related nodes according to an algorithm and find answers to questions such as "What music do my friends like that I do not yet own?" or "If this power supply goes down, what web services are affected?" and thereby query the graph. Using traversals, you can easily conduct end-to-end transactions that represent real user actions.

Cloud Databases

Relational database management systems (DBMSs) are integral and indispensable components of enterprise IT and their importance is set to grow with time [11–12,15]. However, with the advent of cloud-hosted and -managed computing and storage infrastructures, the opportunity to offer a DBMS as an off-loaded and outsourced service is gaining momentum. Carlo Curino and his team members introduced a new transactional "database as a service" (DBaaS) approach. The DBaaS promises to move much of the operational burden of provisioning, configuration, scaling, performance tuning, taking backups, privacy, and access control from database users to the service operator, offering lower overall costs to users [13]. The DBaaS provided by leading cloud service providers does not address three important challenges: (1) efficient multitenancy, (2) elastic scalability, and (3) database privacy. The authors argue that before outsourcing database software and management to cloud environments, these three challenges need to be suppressed and surmounted. The key technical features of DBaaS include a workload-aware approach to multitenancy that identifies the workloads that can be colocated on a database server, achieving higher consolidation and better performance than existing approaches; the use of a graph-based data partitioning algorithm to achieve near-linear elastic scale-out even for complex transactional workloads; and an adjustable security scheme that enables SQL queries to run over encrypted data, such as ordering operations, aggregates, and joins. An underlying theme in the design of components of DBaaS is workload awareness: By monitoring query patterns and data accesses, the system obtains information that is useful for various optimization and security functions, reducing the configuration effort for users and operators. By centralizing and automating many database management tasks, a DBaaS can substantially reduce operational costs and perform well.

There are myriad advantages of using cloud databases [16–18]:

- Fast and automated recovery from failures to ensure business continuity
- Cheap backups, archival, and restoration

- Automated on-the-go scaling with the ability to simply define scaling rules or manually adjust them
- Potentially low cost; ensures device independence and better performance
- Scalability and automatic failover/high availability
- Discoverable, accessible, and usable anytime and anywhere by any device, any media, and any network
- Less capital expenditure and usage-based payment
- Automated provisioning of physical as well as virtual servers in the cloud

Some of the disadvantages include the following:

- Security and privacy issues
- Requires a constant Internet connection (consider bandwidth costs)
- Loss of control over resources
- Loss of visibility on database transactions
- Vendor lock-in

THE HADOOP SOFTWARE FAMILY

Despite all the hubbub and hype surrounding Hadoop, very few IT professionals know its key drivers, differentiators, and killer applications. Because of the newness and complexity of Hadoop, there are several areas in which confusion reigns and restrains the full-fledged assimilation and adoption of Hadoop. The Apache Hadoop product family includes HDFS, MapReduce, Hive, HBase, Pig, Zookeeper, Flume, Sqoop, Oozie, Hue, and so on. HDFS and MapReduce together constitute core Hadoop, which is the foundation of all Hadoop-based applications. For business intelligence, data warehousing, and big data analytics applications, core Hadoop is usually augmented with Hive and HBase, and sometimes Pig. The Hadoop file system excels with file-based big data, including files that contain non-structured data. Hadoop is excellent for storing and searching multistructured big data, although advanced analytics is possible only with certain combinations of Hadoop products, third-party products, or extensions of Hadoop technologies. The Hadoop family has its own query and database technologies. These are similar to standard SQL and relational databases so that BI/DW professionals can learn them quickly.

HDFS is a distributed file system designed to run on clusters of commodity hardware. It is highly fault-tolerant because it automatically replicates file blocks across multiple machine nodes and is designed to be deployed on low-cost hardware. The HDFS provides high-throughput access to application data and is suitable for applications with large data sets. As a file system, HDFS manages files. Because it is file based, HDFS itself does not offer random access to data and has limited metadata capabilities when compared to any traditional DBMS. Similarly, HDFS is strongly batch oriented, and has limited real-time data access functions. To overcome these challenges, one can layer HBase over HDFS to gain some DBMS capabilities. The HBase is one of the many products from the Apache Hadoop product family. It is modeled after Google's BigTable; hence, HBase excels with random and real-time access to very large tables containing billions of rows and millions of columns, just like BigTable. HBase is limited to straightforward tables and records with little support for more complex data structures. The Hive metastore gives Hadoop some DBMS-like metadata capabilities.

When HDFS and MapReduce are combined, Hadoop easily parses and indexes the full range of data types. Furthermore, HDFS, as a distributed system, scales well and has a certain amount of fault tolerance based on data replication even when deployed atop commodity hardware. For these reasons, HDFS and MapReduce can complement existing BI/DW systems that focus on structured and relational data. MapReduce is a general-purpose execution engine that works with a variety of storage technologies, including HDFS, other file systems, and some DBMSs.

As an execution engine, MapReduce and its underlying data platform handle the complexities of network communication, parallel programming, and fault tolerance. MapReduce controls hand-coded programs and automatically provides multithreading processes so that the programs can execute in parallel for massive scalability. The controlled parallelization property of MapReduce can be applied to multiple types of distributed applications, not just the analytic ones. In a nutshell, Hadoop MapReduce is a software programming framework for easily writing massive parallel applications that process vast amounts of data in parallel on large clusters (thousands of nodes) of commodity hardware in a reliable and fault-tolerant manner. A MapReduce job usually splits the input data set into independent chunks, which are processed by the map tasks in a completely parallel manner. The framework sorts the outputs of the maps, which are then supplied as inputs for the reduce tasks (which in turn assemble one or more result sets).

Hadoop is not just for new analytic applications; it can revamp old ones, too. For example, analytics for risk and fraud that are based on statistical analysis or data mining benefit from the much larger data samples that HDFS and MapReduce can extract from diverse big data. Further, most 360° customer views include hundreds of customer attributes. Hadoop can provide insight and data to bump that up to thousands of attributes, which in turn provide greater detail and precision for customer-base segmentation and other customer analytics.

In summary, Hadoop is a futuristic technology that allows large data volumes to be organized and processed while keeping the data on the original data storage cluster. HDFS is the associated file system.

Functional Features of Big-Data Infrastructures

As for DW, data marts, and online stores, an infrastructure for big data also has some unique requirements. The ultimate goal is to easily integrate big data with enterprise data to conduct deeper and influential analysis on the combined data set. As per the white paper titled "Oracle: Big Data for the Enterprise" (2011), there are three prominent requirements (data acquisition, organization, and analysis) for a typical big-data infrastructure. It is noted that NoSQL satisfies all three requirements intrinsically.

Acquisition of Big Data

The infrastructure required to support the acquisition of big data must deliver low and predictable latency in both capturing data and executing short and simple queries. It should be able to handle very high transaction volumes often in a distributed environment and also support flexible and dynamic data structures. The NoSQL databases are the leading infrastructure for acquiring and storing big data. They are well-suited for dynamic data structures and are highly scalable. A NoSQL database typically stores a wide variety of data, because the systems are intended to simply capture all kinds of data without categorizing and parsing them. For example, NoSQL databases are often used to collect and store social media data. Although the customers facing the applications change frequently, the underlying storage structures are kept simple. Instead of designing a schema with relationships between the entities, these simple structures often contain just a major key to identify the data point and a content container to hold the relevant data. This extremely simple and nimble structure allows changes to take place without any costly reorganization at the storage layer.

Organizing Big Data

In classic data warehousing terms, the act of organizing data is called data integration. Because there is such a huge volume of data, a trend that is gathering momentum is to organize data at their original storage location. This saves a lot of time and money as there is no data movement. The current need is for a robust infrastructure that is innately able to organize big data and process and manipulate the data at the original storage location. It has to support very high throughputs (often in batch) to deal with large data-processing steps and handle a large variety of data formats.

Analyzing Big Data

Data analysis can also happen in a distributed environment. In other words, data stored in diverse locations can be accessed from a data warehouse to accomplish the intended analysis. The appropriate infrastructure required for analyzing big data must be able to support deeper analytics such as statistical analysis and data mining on a wide variety of data types stored in diverse systems, scale extreme data volumes, deliver fast response times driven by changes in behavior, and automate decisions based on analytical models. Most importantly, the infrastructure must be able to integrate analysis on a combination of big data and traditional enterprise data to produce exemplary insights for realizing fresh opportunities and possibilities. For example, analyzing inventory data from a smart vending machine along with the events calendar for the venue in which the vending machine is located will dictate the optimal product mix and replenishment schedule for the vending machine.

It is widely reported that big-data computing is gaining a foothold in the IT market. Product vendors are advertising and articulating a number of products for enabling big-data computing. Use, business, and technical cases are being published and presented to a larger community of users and executives.

INFORMATION-ORIENTED ARCHITECTURE FOR CLOUD ENVIRONMENTS

There is a comprehensive report on information-oriented architecture (IOA) authored by Robin Bloor (2011) [24]. This document discusses the significance of information architecture for cloud enterprises, describes the best practices on crafting well-defined information architectures, and specifies the role and responsibility of IOA in shaping futuristic enterprise-scale BI applications.

Software architects tend to adhere to one of two distinctive views of software: (1) process-centric view and (2) data-centric view. The data-centric view visualizes a useful collection of well-defined simple and compound data items that are transformed by various processes into usable forms for the greater good of the data consumer. The relational database movement is fundamentally data centric, and software applications orbit around a database. The applications built using relational databases are very often data centric. Indeed, with referential integrity, cascade deletions, database constraints, and stored procedures, the database does its best to subsume processes.

The process-centric view is the opposite of data-centric view. In other words, software applications are a set of complex transformations that are carried out in order to fulfill user needs and, to this end, are fed with the appropriate data. The object-oriented (OO) movement was actually process oriented. Objects were collections of processes to which data could be assigned. Data was something that either persisted, if it were to be used again, or could be disposed of once used. Both component-based assembly and service-oriented programming (SOP) are process centric. As per the service-oriented paradigm, services are the building blocks for enterprise-class applications and the abstraction unit for application integration and modernization. For service mashup and composition, services are the appropriate encapsulation entity. In the cloud era, services are the delivery unit. Further, services are the implementation and orchestration unit of business processes, that is, process tasks are programmatically implemented by services. Services can be discovered, compared, and combined differently in order to embark on not only process implementation but also innovation. Precisely speaking, the newer concept of service orientation (SO) establishes a flexible and futuristic linkage among distributed and dissimilar IT resources for optimal process integration, as a result of which service-based applications and data integration techniques are subtly and succinctly subsumed. In other words, SOA innately leverages IOA, which enables the integration of all contributing data sources that comprise an enterprise information landscape.

While finalizing information architecture for cloud environments, numerous factors have to be taken into consideration. The primary purpose of creating an IOA is to provide a reference architecture (RA) for any organization that can make use of it. The IOA will be used for the following purposes:

- As an inventory of components to think about and capabilities to consider when designing or augmenting software architecture in the BI area
- As a reference point when planning to build or enhance data services within an organization, as an adjunct to investigating and selecting technology products for enabling such services
- As a map for implementing corporate data policy and corporate data governance
- As a reference model, or starting point, for building and implementing a true IOA

Characteristics of IOA

A well-intended information architecture is necessary to establish a truly agile BI for any enterprise or cloud environment (Figure 6.1). The first and foremost quality required for an IOA is that it must be complete. The information architecture must accommodate every kind of BI application used by organizations and every kind of available data store. It must deliver any information service that any user or program might require.

The IOA Ecosystem

The information architecture typically comprises the following three constructive and contributive components:

1. The BI applications
2. The BI application infrastructures including BI middleware

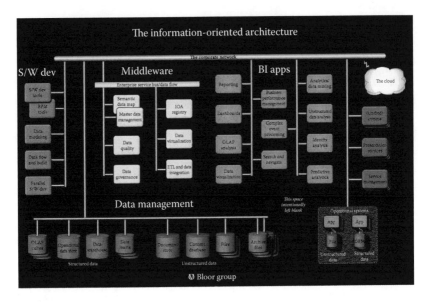

FIGURE 6.1

The information-oriented architecture.

Leading BI Applications

There are several kinds of BI applications leveraged by small-, medium-, and large-scale enterprises:

Reporting: This is a common BI application used extensively for report generation, polishing, and presentation to all sorts of decision makers who ponder the next course of action. Actionable insights can be formulated in a report format to be given to C-level executives.

Dashboards: This is another typical BI application commonly found in enterprise arenas. This is used mainly for giving graphical and visual presentation and notification of key business performance indicators. Any state change, noteworthy incident, threshold breach, and decision-enabling change for any given department or even the whole organization can be quickly captured and promptly delivered to authorized people. Fed with relatively up-to-the-minute data, these applications tend to live on desktops or in portals; staff can peruse these applications when they feel the need.

Online analytical processing analysis: This is the pervasive drill-down form of reporting, in which users access multidimensional tables in various ways to get detailed summaries of information or even individual items. Slicing, dicing, aggregation, and dissemination of data are facilitated by this application. This often depends on a dedicated OLAP-specific database. The reporting capability and the data it accesses are closely linked.

Data visualization: One way of analyzing large heaps of data is to present various two-dimensional (2D) and three-dimensional (3D) representations of the whole data set or parts of it. This allows users to identify and observe useful trends or discover anomalies.

Business/corporate performance management: This constitutes a set of management and analytic processes that use data from operational systems to enable micro- as well as macrolevel management of corporations by objectives. This facilitates companies to meet their performance goals and if there is any indication of any hitch or hurdle on that aspect, this tool helps managers to formulate appropriate measures proactively. Performance management (PM) is prescribed as a more sophisticated BI package compared to dashboards.

Search and navigation: This is a very basic BI application for identifying specific data or exploration of enterprise data resources. For example, there are search engines such as Google that target unstructured data and engines that have hybrid capabilities that target the investigation of both structured and unstructured data.

The business event processing (BEP): Event processing is a critical element in BI as events individually and collectively contain right and relevant information that must be squeezed out, understood, and utilized cognitively for business optimization. Simple and complex event processing algorithms and platforms are currently emerging and evolving for aptly and artistically using incoming events comprising multistructured data. Simple events can be aggregated dynamically to form complex events, which in turn are capable of supplying highly accurate and accountable information. Streams of business events from distributed and decentralized sources can be fed to business event processing applications and they can be processed quickly to extract knowledge. Real-time data analysis out of massive data treasure troves is possible through the numerous advancements in the BI field. The analysis derives instant and insightful feedback on various functions of the divisions/departments of an enterprise or on the enterprise as a whole.

Analytics and data mining: Data mining is one part of data analysis, and it identifies trendsetting and trustworthy patterns in data heaps using scores of proven techniques such as statistical analysis and neural networks.

Analysis of unstructured data: Data formats are becoming increasingly diverse; with the eruption of social computing applications, the volume and value of unstructured data have gone up significantly. Text analysis and mining are currently the dominant activities. Audio, video, and speech analytics will also come up in due course with the solidification of competent technologies.

Identity analysis: This is an emerging field for analyzing multiple data sources simultaneously to pinpoint any kind of identity fraud. This analysis helps to avoid data duplication and eliminate the possibility of an individual providing two separate identities.

Predictive analytics: There are a wide variety of BI applications that rely on an organization's information assets to generate value, but this category of applications is a deviation from mainstream BI applications. For enterprises to plan strategically, there is a need for pioneering and powerful algorithms and best-of-breed implementations that can project and predict the future. A variety of techniques are drawn from statistics, pattern matching algorithms, and gaming theory that analyze data in order to make predictions about the future.

The BI Application Infrastructures

Robust and resilient application infrastructures are forthcoming to guarantee BI success. The choice of BI application infrastructures and the deployment architecture is crucial to success as there are several inherent complications and contradictions associated with BI. There are situations that insist on real-time BI applications. The timeliness of these applications is critical to their usefulness. There are BI applications that do not insist on immediate response. Further, there are different network and database loads associated with each BI application. Some may pose queries that require considerable IT resources to answer, whereas others need little effort. Some BI applications may finish quickly, whereas others may take minutes, hours, or even days to complete.

Another important factor to be taken into consideration is that data can be stored local to the application or in remote servers. If data is stored locally, there might be a need to refresh data individually; the data can be refreshed at varying time intervals. These processes can be automated, but they remain complex. As far as storage is concerned, BI applications follow multiple ways to cache data. Data warehouses and marts are the prominent infrastructures used for holding and querying data. It is also possible to cache data in desktops. Due to the continuing rise of memory capacity of personal computers and communicators, data cache and processing will happen in personal devices in the near future. In-memory databases and hardware storage appliances are enlarging the BI scope. The BI applications may be running on personal devices such as laptops, tablets, and smartphones or in remote data centers accessed by browsers; they can also run in the cloud infrastructure.

All these boil down to the fact that how BI applications and their data caches are associated with each other determines BI success. Query simplicity and complexity also play an influential role in shaping the BI industry. We should expect all kinds of internally as well as externally imposed variations while formulating amenable and adept information architectures. Thus, timeliness is an important ingredient in BI applications, and latencies imposed by networks and workloads cannot just be brushed aside in such applications.

Data Storage Infrastructures

There is a need for new kinds of data stores because the existing relational databases do not cater well to multidimensional tables. As far as structured data are concerned, there are four types of storage infrastructures: (1) the OLAP cubes, (2) data marts, (3) data warehouses, and (4) operational data stores (ODSs). These are all data stores that are populated with data from different sources with the use of extensive ETL and data-cleansing processes. Originally, data warehouses were envisioned to act as comprehensive corporate data stores to be used by BI applications so that corporate data could be made available to everyone at the click of a button. However, there was a huge amount of traffic to data warehouses and, hence, data warehouses were slow, with latencies ranging from days to weeks. Professionals and specialists explored and expounded two other viable and valuable options: One is a data mart, which is specific for a business division; as a result of this, traffic is comparatively less and there is quick rendering of answers.

The second one is none other than the ODS. Practically, ODS does not hold all corporate structured data and excludes some time-consuming processes such as data-cleansing activities in order to provide data that are almost current. All the data that were fed in the last 15–30 minutes are made available through the ODS. The event processing applications provide the most recent data; they normally manage their own data feeds

206 • *Cloud Enterprise Architecture*

but may retain the data in a data mart for subsequent use. The OLAP cubes are very specific ways of storing structured data so that they meet the requirements of the OLAP BI applications that touch them. Structured data have metadata that simplify the understanding of what they mean. There is no equivalent mechanism for unstructured data. Consequently, analyzing it is more difficult. These necessities have resulted in a stream of versatile solutions. In other words, there are a lot of positive and progressive advancements such as NoSQL and NewSQL databases, the Hadoop software that is the implementation of the popular MapReduce algorithm, and so on, for effortlessly tackling unstructured data as enumerated in the beginning of this chapter. In short, big-data computing is emerging as a hot computing paradigm with the collection, classification, and commingling of social and enterprise data.

The BI Middleware

In the recent past, several new types of data formats emerged with the fast proliferation of social applications and personal devices. This forced many vendors to come up with new kinds of databases. Software infrastructure vendors and business software providers have kept pace by delivering competent database management solutions. Further, groundbreaking BI data stores are being unearthed and sustained as BI applications are becoming increasingly complex and contributive in a number of ways, including complexities in querying, performance requirements, client devices, and the type of data being analyzed. The ultimate goal is to empower BI applications to connect any data store (physical and virtual, local and remote, homogeneous and heterogeneous, etc.) without inhibitions to extract and supply relevant information which in turn produce actionable insights. However, this target is beset with numerous challenges (business, technology, process, etc.). In other words, we need standardized software solutions that do much more than just facilitate connectivity. A layer of indirection has to be incorporated. Although the addition of new layers affects performance, flexibility is a much more important trade-off in a distributed, divergent, and decentralized environment. All kinds of middleware operations such as connectivity, discovery, extraction, mediation, aggregation, dissemination, and delivery must be performed by BI middleware solutions. The three prominent activities of BI middleware are as follows:

1. Mapping
2. Doing performance management (PM)
3. Data integration

Mapping

Ultimately, a map of some kind describing the available data resources in a useful way must be made available to IT users and applications. There are three prominent components of a map:

1. The IOA registry is like an SOA registry in that it openly declares and describes the available data services. It is a catalog of all the registered data services for public consumption. The registry can be easily discovered and accessed for any BI tool.
2. Master data management (MDM) is a recent phenomenon in enterprise IT. The main goal of MDM is to achieve data consistency as MDM ultimately facilitates knowledge extraction and engineering for BI. The MDM tries to arrive at a single, consistent, and unambiguous definition of the data of an organization. Usually, multiple potentially damaging definitions of data likely remain in use in operational systems. There may be no single version of the truth in some areas. The MDM is the best way forward since new data stores and data records are being defined all the time. For some organizations, mergers and acquisitions are more prevalent and can be rather disruptive to any MDM effort that is in progress. Certainly, an effective IOA requires a reliable and usable map of corporate data and MDM is the best hope for creating such a map. This in turn offers additional value in BPM.
3. A semantic data map is used to complement an MDM map. The MDM mostly targets structured data. Structured data has metadata, which describes the meaning of structured data to some degree, although without a great deal of sophistication. Above and beyond such metadata, there is a kind of business vocabulary that expresses some basic truths about an organization. As a simple example, a data record that describes an insurance policy will list many of the important attributes of the policy—objects insured, the term of the policy, and so on—but it will not tell what insurance actually is. Also, it is not easy to deduce the full range of valid insurance claims that might be made from the simple data record. In other words, the systems either do not hold this information at all or do not hold it in a convenient

form. For this reason, an MDM map can be usefully complemented with a semantic map of corporate data, which embodies a kind of business vocabulary. Such semantic information can be useful in the analysis of unstructured data and in setting governance policies.

Doing Performance Management

Two components that focus specifically on managing the performance of requests for data are data virtualization and the ESB/data flow component. Data virtualization is an intelligent software component that automatically builds caches of data to satisfy demand. Data virtualization federates data from multiple sources, ODSs, data warehouses, and operational systems and learns where to place data for optimum performance by analyzing the query traffic to determine which data is commonly queried. It then caches that data in a place that is as local as possible to the querying BI applications. Exactly where this place should be can be determined by several factors, including available server resources, network speeds, and the need for resilience. Such a capability is central to an information architecture.

A second aspect of PM is the management of data flows within an information architecture whether they are caused by individual queries or by batch loads of data from one database to another. Some data flows, such as query responses, have a higher priority than others. So there is a need to balance competing workloads over available resources. This is the kind of task to which an ESB is suited. It is all about getting data flows to happen when they need to, at a required speed and with a guaranteed service.

Data Integration

Data integration is attracting a lot of attention in the BI community. In the following section, there is an in-depth explanation of existing and emerging data integration trends, techniques, technologies, and tips.

A DETAILED LOOK AT DATA INTEGRATION

Data integration is the leading contributor to the much-acclaimed goal of business integration, and it is an increasingly strategic endeavor. Business integration brings in a number of distinct business as well as technical benefits. Precisely speaking, business integration ultimately leads to on-demand, responsive, sensitive, cost-effective, competitive, and smart enterprises. As corporate data volume increases, its value also shoots up if it is leveraged pro-actively and positively through time-tested processes and tools. Information derived from the data being generated, extracted, created, buffered, and mined is potentially powerful and, hence, companies are going that extra mile to entice and enable customers, partners, and decision makers to derive maximum value from all their corporate data. Due to the significance of data integration in business transformation, several vendors have entered the scene to produce new-generation and high-performing data integration technologies, products, and platforms. Data integration is a critical piece of work for adaptive, on-demand, and real-time BI infrastructure.

With the deeper penetration and pervasiveness of messaging middle-ware, SOA-aware ESB, CEP engines, EII, EAI, composite data services, and mashup server infrastructures, "near-real-time" and real-time data integration services and solutions are being realized these days. The term near real time is used to describe target data that has a low latency of a few minutes or maybe a few hours. Data with zero latency is known as real-time data. Notification has to be given in real time and only then can businesses initiate countermeasures quickly. End users also demand real-time response for their queries and requests. Hence, IT pundits and pupils are sincerely plotting ways and means for realizing real-time IT technologies, processes, and infrastructures. Batch data integration is the prominent technique at this point in time and will continue to be in the future, according to industry stal-warts and visionaries, due to the surging popularity of real-time data integra-tion. Data integration techniques (Figure 6.2) are technology-independent approaches for performing data integration. A wide range of technologies are available for implementing data integration techniques.

"Data consolidation" processes capture data from multiple sources and integrate them into a single persistent data store. With data consolidation, there is usually a delay, or latency, between the time at which updates occur in source systems and the time at which these updates appear in the target store. Depending on business needs, this latency may be a few seconds (low latency), several hours, or many days (high latency). Target data stores that contain high-latency data are built using batch data integration applications that pull data from sources at scheduled intervals. Low-latency target data stores are updated by online data integration applications that continuously capture and push data changes to the target store from source systems. This push approach requires the data consolidation application to identify the changed/updated or newly inserted data. In other words, the changed-data capture (CDC) technique is essential for data consolidation applications to

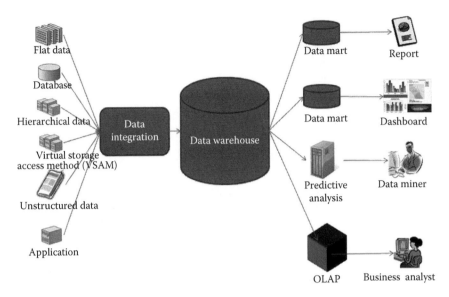

FIGURE 6.2
Physical data integration architecture.

be successful. Pull and push consolidation modes can be leveraged together: An online push application can accumulate data changes in a staging area, which is queried at scheduled intervals by a batch pull application. It is required that the push mode is event driven and the pull mode is demand driven. Interfaces used for this purpose include de facto standards such as Open Database Connectivity (ODBC), Java Database Connectivity (JDBA), Java Message Service (JMS), and native database and application interfaces.

The advantage of data consolidation is that it allows large volumes of data to be retrofitted, reformatted, reconciled, scrubbed, and remedied as they flow from the source to the destination. It is noted that ETL is being heralded as the backbone technology for data consolidation, and it is being utilized for creating physical data warehouses and data marts. In short, it is fully responsible for the heavy-lifting processes that capture operational data, invoke data quality processes, perform the integration and transformation procedures, and finally load the data into a data warehouse or data mart for analysis and reporting and mining purposes. Another data consolidation technology is enterprise content management (ECM), which mainly focuses on consolidating and managing unstructured data such as documents, reports, e-mails, and web pages.

The ETL solutions are able to run batch jobs at scheduled intervals to capture data from flat files, relational databases, legacy systems, application packages, XML files, weblogs, EAI sources, web services, and unstructured data and consolidate them into a data warehouse. Similarly, ETL tools can consolidate data into EAI targets and web services. The most recent ETL solutions are empowered with distinct capabilities such as metadata management, error recovery, job scheduling and tracking, data profiling, user-defined exits, data quality management, and support for standard programming languages. Finally, improved usability, better performance (parallel processing, load balancing, caching, support for native DBMS application, and data load interfaces), and enhanced security extend the use of ETL products beyond consolidation of data for DW to realize a wide range of other enterprise data integration projects.

"Data federation" provides a virtual view of one or more source data files. When a business application issues a query against this virtual view, a data federation engine retrieves data from appropriate data sources, integrates it to match the virtual view and query definition, and sends the results to the client application. Data federation pulls data from disparate and distributed sources on demand. Any required transformation is done on the data as it is being plucked out of source files. One of the key elements of a federated system is the metadata used by a federation engine to access the source data. In some cases, this metadata may consist solely of a virtual view definition that is mapped to the source files. In more advanced solutions, the metadata may also contain detailed information about the amount of data that exists in the source systems and the access paths that can be used to access it. This more extensive information helps the federated solution to optimize access to source systems.

The main advantages of a federated approach are that it provides access to current data and removes the need to consolidate source data into another intermediate data store. Data federation is not well-suited to retrieving and reconciling large amounts of data or for applications in which there are significant data quality problems in the source data. Another consideration is the potential performance impact and overhead of accessing multiple data sources at runtime. Data federation is an excellent fit if the cost of data consolidation is huge. Operational query and reporting is an example. Data federation can be beneficial when data security policies and license restrictions prevent the copying of source data. Syndicated data usually falls into this category. Data federation is a good option for a short-term data integration solution following a company merger or acquisition.

EII supports the data federation technique for data integration. The objective of EII is to enable applications to see dispersed data as though it resides in a single database. EII shields applications from the complexities of retrieving data from multiple locations where the data may differ in semantics and formats and may use different data interfaces. In its basic form, EII access to dispersed data involves breaking down a query issued against a virtual view into subcomponents and sending each subcomponent for processing to the location where the required data resides. The EII engine then aggregates the retrieved result and sends the final result to the application that issued the query. More advanced EII products contain sophisticated performance facilities that tune this process for optimal performance.

The most recent EII platforms support SQL (ODBC and JDBC) and XML (XQuery and XPath) data interfaces. Most EII solutions provide read-only access to heterogeneous data; some solutions incorporate update capabilities also. The EII products are able to cache results and allow administrators to define rules that determine when the data in the cache is valid or needs to be refreshed. Finally, the distinguishing features for production selection include the data sources and targets supported (web services, unstructured data, etc.), transformation capabilities, metadata management, source-data update capabilities, authentication and security options, and performance.

Critical data and analytical logic are spread across multiple databases and applications in various parts of an organization. A federated architecture knits these disparate environments together virtually rather than physically. It is neither centralized nor decentralized but a hybrid of the two options, maximizing the benefits of both options while minimizing their downsides. Moreover, a federated architecture is fluid, that is, it changes shape as an organization reinvents itself to respond to new market realities.

Types of Data Integration

There are certainly various types of data integration. At the macrolevel, there are two approaches: (1) physical data integration and (2) virtual data integration.

Physical Data Integration

This technique uses processes that capture, cleanse, integrate, transform, and load data into a target data store. Data is typically consolidated using ETL technologies, which obtain data from operational data sources, transform it to the corporate standard, and load it into physical data stores.

Virtual Data Integration

This technique uses processes that provide a real-time integrated view of disparate data types from multiple sources, thereby providing a universal data access layer. Data federation uses EII technologies to create virtual stores of data from data warehouses, data marts, operational data stores, and operational systems.

Comparison of EII versus ETL

A fully federated data warehouse is not recommended because of performance and data consistency issues. However, EII must be leveraged to extend and enhance a DW environment to address specific business needs. One issue is that federated queries may need access to an operational business transaction system. Complex EII queries against such a business-critical system can affect the performance of the applications running on that system. Similar to ETL processes, detailed profiling and analysis of the data sources and their relationships with the targets is required for EII also.

"Data propagation" applications copy data from one location to another. These applications usually operate online and push data to the target location (event-driven applications). Updates to a source system may be propagated asynchronously or synchronously to the target system. Synchronous propagation requires that updates to both source and target systems occur in the physical transaction. In the case of asynchronous propagation, the business transaction may be broken down into multiple physical transactions. An example is a travel request that is segmented into separate but coordinated airline, hotel, and car reservations. Propagation guarantees the delivery of data to the target, and this aspect is a key distinguishing feature of data propagation. It is noted that EAI and enterprise data replication (EDR) are data propagation technologies.

The EAI technologies use a strategy or a framework by which an organization centralizes and optimizes its application integration or process automation processes, usually through some form of data replication or message brokering mechanisms. In other words, EAI integrates applications by allowing them to communicate and exchange transactions, messages, and data with each other using standard interfaces. The EAI is usually used for real-time operational business transaction processing. It is noted that EAI technology, through remote procedure call (RPC), remote method invocation (RMI), CORBA, or a standard messaging infrastructure (hub, bus, fabric, etc.), helps to extend integration to heterogeneous sources, for example, mainframe legacy environments, cross-platform operational applications, and BI environments. It also enables corporations and governmental agencies to move all sorts of data efficiently and effortlessly. Due to the surging popularity of SOA, interest in data propagation techniques and EAI technology has risen sharply.

The advantage of data propagation techniques is that they emerge as the favorite for real-time or near-real-time movement of data. Data propagation is also used for workload balancing, taking backups, and disaster recovery. The EAI can be used to transport data between applications and to route real-time event data to other data integration applications such as an ETL process. Access to application sources and targets is done through web services (WSDL), .NET/JEE interfaces and adapters, and so on.

Comparison of EAI versus ETL

It must be noted that EAI and ETL are not competing technologies and there are circumstances in which both cohabitate and cooperate with each other. Whereas EAI can act as an input source for ETL, ETL can act as a service for EAI. One of the main objectives of EAI is to provide transparent access to the wide range of applications existing in an organization. An EAI-to-ETL interface could therefore be used to give an ETL product access to this application data. This interconnection could be built using a web service or a message queue. Such an interface eliminates the need for ETL vendors to develop point-to-point adapters for these application data sources. Also, given that EAI focuses on real-time processing, the EAI-to-ETL interface can act as a real-time event source for ETL applications that require low-latency data. The interface can further be used as a data target by an ETL application. Many organizations, instead of using a dynamic EAI-to-ETL interface, utilize EAI products to create data files, which are then inputted to ETL applications. In the reverse direction, EAI applications can use ETL as a service. The ETL vendors allow their developers to define ETL tasks as web services that are in turn invoked by EAI applications.

In conclusion, data integration is a critical and fundamental element of a variety of technologies, including data warehouses, BI, SOA, MDM, customer data integration (CDI) applications, and data-centric architectures.

Generic Criteria for Selecting a Data Integration Tool

In order to guarantee unified and ubiquitous information access, it is imperative to integrate data from a wide variety of disparate and distributed sources. However, businesses view data integration as being very expensive and hard to implement. A recent study has revealed that data integration is ranked in importance second only to BI in organizations' information/data management strategy. Business executives therefore insist on cost-effective tools that fully meet all the existing and emerging data integration requirements with reduced TCO and enhanced ROI. The data integration tools market is comprised of vendors who offer software products to enable the construction and implementation of data access and delivery infrastructure for a variety of data integration scenarios, including the following:

- Data acquisition for BI and DW
- Creation of integrated master data stores
- Data migrations and conversions
- Synchronization of data between operational applications
- Creation of federated views of data from multiple data sources
- Delivery of data services in an SOA context
- Unification of structured and unstructured data

Gartner defines several classes of functional capabilities that vendors of data integration tools must possess in order to deliver optimal value to organizations in support of a full range of data integration scenarios:

- Connectors/drivers/adapters
- Data transformation and delivery
- Data transformation
- Metadata and data modeling
- Design and development environments
- Data governance (data quality, profiling, and mining)
- Runtime platform
- Operations and administration
- Architecture and integration
- Compliance to SOA
- Interaction with message queues
- Data services, EII, and CDC capabilities
- Security and performance features

Business Drivers for Data Integration

A number of differently capable data integration tools are available in the market. Market analysts have come out with benchmarking results on their varied capabilities, market share, adoption rate, ease of use, sophisticated features, standardization, growth continuity, cost, and so on. Without a doubt, ETL technologies and tools for constructing data warehouses dominate the data integration scene today. Unfortunately, simply "making my data warehouse work" is not a business driver for companies anymore. Enterprise architects, together with line-of-business managers, are looking for reasons to justify the IT expenses and organizational changes associated with integrating and leveraging data. They recognize the role played by information management in high-profile initiatives such as MDM, BI 2.0, CDI, and SOA. Drivers for data integration stem from the need to eliminate stumbling blocks associated with turning data into agile information and actionable insights in these high-profile initiatives. According to an Oracle survey on the data integration market, three things most likely dominate as the principal business drivers of data integration: (1) improved agility, (2) customer intimacy, and (3) cost cutting. They are described as follows:

Improved agility: Accurate, manageable, and transparent data allows organizations to identify and respond to internal and external events more quickly. Data integration solutions foster this type of agility by uniting heterogeneous data sources across an enterprise. However, these solutions must be governed well to ensure that data is incorporated into business processes and that data integration is a part of the change management process. Data quality, data profiling, and data governance components are essential to establish and maintain the improved flexibility provided by complex data-centric architectures.

Customer intimacy: Improving the customer experience is one of the leading drivers for data-centric architecture initiatives. Data integration is one of the key enablers of improved customer intimacy. When customer data is clean, consistent, and up-to-date, it dramatically improves the ability of a company to deliver high-quality and seamless customer experience.

Cost cutting: The cost of data integration is directly related to the volume of data. More storage space, CPU cycles, and time are needed to manage more amounts of data. Because data volume is continually increasing, managing cost becomes increasingly important. Hence, cost cutting continues to be a key driver for data integration. Some of the measures are eliminating risks associated with inaccurate and inconsistent data; suppressing the increasing complexity; simplifying data architectures; optimizing data integration processes; consolidating data structures, marts, and management systems; extensively leveraging data tools, utilities, wizards, and widgets; and obliterating redundancies in data flows.

Top Five Functional Capabilities of Any Data Integration Solution

In the previous subsection, we list several functional capabilities of a data integration solution. The top five capabilities without any room for disagreement are as follows: (1) data movement, (2) data synchronization, (3) data quality, (4) data management, and (5) data governance.

Data Movement with Core ETL

ETL can transform not only data from different departments but also data from different sources. For example, order details from an ERP system and service history from a CRM application can be consolidated into a central data hub for a single view of the customer. Although ETL technology is still heavily used for DW and BI initiatives, data and knowledge management professionals are increasingly demanding additional data integration capabilities from their ETL vendors to support complex data integration challenges.

Data Movement with Next-Generation Extract, Load, and Transform (ELT)

A new and optimized data movement technique is ELT. Transformations occur on either the source or the target. This also allows greater flexibility, improved scalability, and greater performance. The ELT approaches can also reduce IT infrastructure costs. The following factors should be considered when evaluating an ELT solution:

- Performance optimizations for set-based transformations.
- Heterogeneous relational databases.
- Optimizations for database appliances.
- No hardware requirements. Runtime agents should be deployed on the databases themselves.
- Data that always goes from source to target through optimized database pathways. Data should never move through the intermediary.

- Extensible support for standard Java and SOA environments.
- Design tools that support out-of-the-box optimizations. There must be no need for users to write special scripts or custom code to enable optimized performance.

Data Synchronization

There are many ways to extract data from a DBMS, including queries, replication, table dumps, storage snapshots, and calls to application programming interfaces (APIs) of an application that sits over the database. The CDC technique is an emerging data extraction method; it enables data integration to operate closer to real time. The CDC can be applied to most database brands, including relational, legacy, mainframe, and file-based DBMSs. A simple example of CDC is as follows: Two separate data sources for a web storefront (one for customer data and one for order data) are consolidated into a single data warehouse. To simply update order details in real time, only the delta (or set of orders and new customer information) needs to be propagated across to the data warehouse. This does not require moving all the data for both systems.

Data replication is another key component of synchronization technology that is required in any effective core data integration offering. It is a distinct requirement of CDC in that it is often needed in deployment considerations for mirroring or maintaining identical data across data centers. The CDC is required for synchronizing data across heterogeneous data sources, whereas data replication technology is often embedded in database tools or DW tools.

Data Quality

The demand for trusted data continues to increase due to the emergence of a bunch of new-generation enterprise applications such as corporate performance management and actionable BI. Strategic IT initiatives such as MDM and CDI also add to the pressure. Further complicating the matter, regulatory compliance initiatives require one to trace the source of data used in financial reports, as well as examine, track (through snapshots), and certify the state and quality of business data. Data profiling is a data investigation and data quality–monitoring mechanism that allows business users to evaluate data quality using metrics, discover or infer rules based on this data, and monitor the evolution of data quality over time.

Data Management

Any data management solution consists of metadata management, MDM, and data modeling facilities. Metadata management improves data visibility toward enhanced understanding of how data is used and how it relates to other data within a global data-centric system. Metadata management and data relationship management are cornerstones for MDM-based solutions that reveal data relationships within a single source of truth. Data lineage is a key example of metadata management often used by BI utilities to allow business users to independently track data sources. If the data lineage falls short of the actual source and is not integrated properly to the data integration solution, it is very difficult for business users to identify gaps in the data. Data modeling is a key element of the design aspect of creating and describing information architectures.

Data Governance

Data trustworthiness, integrity, and confidentiality are vital to enterprises as data leads to information, which in turn paves the way for knowledge creation. In addition, information managers need to define what data means to their organizations through data governance. Governance is a series of serious activities associated with influencing the actions and behavior of an environment. The concepts of SOA governance, data governance, process governance, and application governance are all interrelated. In other words, activities associated with each concept should work fluently in conjunction with the rest of the governance discipline. Data governance helps in defining not only data quality rules but also processes in which the rules are maintained, approved, and iterated. As companies increase in scale and grow, these established processes become critical in managing the life cycle of enterprise data-centric architectures. Data governance must include multiple data quality and data management capabilities, as well as allow for the human element in implementing a governed data-centric environment. For example, a company might define certain data off-limits to a set of roles that is integrated across multiple data hubs. This type of governance can be implemented by combining identity management and data access services or through an entitlement policy that is executed at runtime. In other cases, data quality might require a complex set of business logic to be specified as a business rule or business processes might automate a workflow of data exception management. In each example, governance processes are the key to successful enterprise implementations.

DATA SERVICES

Data services have transformational influence and effect on enterprise data-centric architectures. Data services are the foundation of many SOA deployments and are needed to bridge gaps between processes and the core application infrastructure. Data access services are the most common data service, and there are three important scenarios in which data can be exposed as reusable access services:

1. Single data access
2. Data hub access
3. Data federation services for multisource data access

Single data access is a base functionality that is provided by most of the tools today. Consolidating data into a hub using ETL and CDC and then building real-time access points as services is another viable option. However, virtually aggregating data access services from multiple heterogeneous sources is more challenging. Data federation leaves data at the source and consolidates information virtually. Data federation allows companies to aggregate data across multiple sources into a real-time view that can be reused as a service. When there are restrictions for accessing data at the origin rather than at the data hub, this technique, when synchronized with data consolidation approaches, is especially useful.

The SOA-Aware Data Services

Data integration is becoming tightly embedded in the SOA style. As a result, data services will likely follow the mainstream adoption and successful momentum of SOAs. It is believed that data services will solidify the data abstraction layer and evolve into multiple types, facilitating enterprise search, reporting, and a single view of the truth. Data services will move ahead of simple data federation to multisource data access services. As federation becomes useful for BI and MDM applications, the value of data services is bound to rise sharply. When enterprises begin to build hybrid data-centric environments that include both data hubs and data aggregates, they will turn to new types of data governance offerings for data services. In the long term, data services will most likely be a part of overall data integration and data management strategies.

ENTERPRISE DATA MASHUPS

Principles that are now defining the modern trends in data integration are as follows:

1. Allow loose coupling between data and sources through service orientation.
2. Benefit from data virtualization for lighter integration architectures.
3. Meet the growing demand for real-time data services.
4. Leverage the web as the fundamental enterprise repository to automatically query, browse, or search for data and enable business applications.
5. Unify both structured and unstructured data.

The essence of data integration is an abstraction process that generates new executable data structures from dispersed heterogeneous sources. This fundamental promise is extraordinarily important when data integration moves from internal corporate data stores and core enterprise applications into the arena of the web and unstructured content.

ORACLE'S BIG-DATA SOLUTION

After a shaky start, Oracle could firmly catch up with the cloud paradigm. Today, it embraces cloud technology in different layers and levels of its enterprise stack. Oracle database and fusion middleware are already hosted in public clouds. Oracle is also betting on cloud-based DW services and solutions. Oracle Exadata provides outstanding performance in hosting data warehouses and transaction-processing databases. Oracle Exalytics can be used to derive and deliver a wealth of information to different stakeholders, especially business analysts and managers.

Oracle Exalytics is an engineered system providing speed-of-thought data access for the business community. It is optimized to run Oracle Business Intelligence Enterprise Edition with in-memory aggregation capabilities built into the system.

Oracle offers a complete and integrated solution to address the full spectrum of enterprise big-data requirements. Oracle Big Data Appliance is an engineered system that combines optimized hardware with the most comprehensive software stack featuring specialized solutions to deliver a complete and easy-to-deploy solution for acquiring, organizing, and loading big data into Oracle Database 11g. It is designed to deliver extreme analytics on all kinds of data types, with enterprise-class performance, availability, supportability, and security. It is also tightly integrated with Oracle Exadata and Oracle Database. This grandly integrated system empowers businesses to complete data analysis with excellent performance. Figure 6.3 shows how Oracle Big Data Appliance fits into the entire ecosystem of Oracle-engineered systems for big data. Oracle Big Data Appliance addresses the data acquisition and organization requirements for data stored in NoSQL solutions.

Hardware Components

Oracle Big Data Appliance comes in a full rack configuration with 18 Sun servers for a total storage capacity of 432 TB. Every server in the rack has 2 CPUs, each with 6 cores for a total of 216 cores per full rack. Each server has 48-GB memory for a total of 864 GB of memory for a full rack.

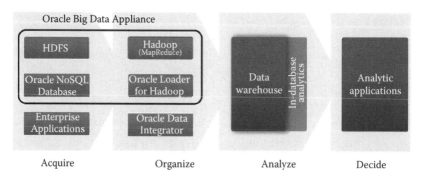

FIGURE 6.3
The big data analytic methodology.

Software Components

Oracle NoSQL database is a distributed, highly scalable key-value database delivering a general-purpose, enterprise-class key-value store by incorporating an intelligent driver on top of a distributed Berkeley DB. This intelligent driver keeps track of the underlying storage topology, shards the data, and knows where data can be placed with the lowest latency. The primary use cases for Oracle NoSQL database are low-latency-data capture and fast querying of this data, typically by key lookup.

The communication between Oracle Big Data Appliance and Oracle Exadata happens via InfiniBand, enabling high-speed data transfer for batch as well as query workloads. Oracle Big Data Appliance, in conjunction with Oracle Exadata Database Machine and the new Oracle Exalytics Business Intelligence Machine, delivers everything that customers need to acquire, organize, analyze, and maximize the value of big data within their enterprises.

CLOUD ANALYTICS

Cloud technology is widely touted the next big thing in IT. It ensures extremely high flexibility for organizations in adapting to their changing needs. Cloud computing extensively relies on virtualization, which includes virtualization of physical servers into virtual servers; virtualization of storage and networking; and virtualization of applications, services, and data. Virtual desktop infrastructure (VDI) is attracting a lot of attention these days as desktop virtualization technologies are flourishing. Further, embedded virtualization is picking up steam. In particular, mobile virtualization is empowering the trendy and handy smartphones to use all operating systems, including Google Android, Apple iOS, BlackBerry OS, and Windows Phone OS. In short, virtualization is turning out to be immeasurably impactful in making every tangible IT resource virtual, and the stage is set for virtual computing.

The surging popularity of cloud technology is due to the fact that it makes IT infrastructures globally available to individuals and businesses for a small fee as a service over the pervasive Internet. This transformation is more efficient than transformations based on fixed infrastructure, which is expensive, rigid, insensitive, and so on. Through service enablement of all IT resources (applications, data, platforms, and infrastructures), the

the vision of IT simplicity and sensitivity will see a neat and nice reality. Self-service is the key mission in the era of making computing a social utility. In other words, clouds are being positioned and presented as a converged, dynamic, and optimized service infrastructure. What does this mean? In the near future, analytics will be perceived as a service first and then provided from connected and federated clouds.

Without an iota of doubt, BI occupies the top spot in any data management strategy that causes enterprises to grow and glow. Businesses are spending a sizeable amount of money in maintaining their BI systems and services to meet the varying requirements and expectations of consumers and clients. With the exponential growth of data and data formats, BI as a field of study and research must evolve in order to sustain its lead position in data management strategies as gaps between BI offerings and business expectations are widening. Hence, next-generation BI must include real-time, dynamic, service-oriented, cloud-based, and event-driven technologies and must supply actionable insights in order to make real-time informed decisions. In short, BI systems must be sophisticated, smart, and mission-critical systems for the survival and sustenance of enterprises in this recessionary and reactive period. Clouds are emerging as a compact, cheap, and catalytic environment for BI systems, and current opportunities for performing cloud analytics are definitely and decisively manifold.

SUMMARY

Enterprises depend solely on a variety of data for their day-to-day functioning. Both historical and operational data have to be religiously gleaned from different and disparate sources, cleaned, synchronized, and analyzed in totality to derive actionable insights that in turn empower enterprises to stay ahead of their competitors. In the recent past, social computing applications have brought out a cornucopia of people's data. The current need is for enterprise data to seamlessly and spontaneously link with social data in order to make organizations more proactive, preemptive, and people centric in their decisions, discretions, and dealings. Data stores, bases, warehouses, marts, cubes, and so on are flourishing; they congregate and compactly store different data. There are several standardized and simplified tools and platforms for meeting data analysis needs. There are also dashboards, visual report generators, business activity monitoring (BAM) systems, and PM modules to deliver information and knowledge to authorized persons on request.

Data integration is an indispensable part of the long and complex process of transitioning data into information and knowledge. However, data integration is not always easy and rosy. There are patterns, products, processes, platforms, and practices galore that help in meeting the data integration goal. In this chapter, we describe the importance of information architecture in realizing next-generation cloud applications.

REFERENCES

1. Orend, K. 2010. "Analysis and Classification of NoSQL Databases and Evaluation of their Ability to Replace an Object-Relational Persistence Layer," Master Thesis, Technische Universität München, Munich, Germany.
2. Sasirekha, R. 2010. "NoSQL: The Database for the Cloud," Tata Consultancy Services, http://www.tcs.com/SiteCollectionDocuments/White%20Papers/Consulting_Whitepaper_No-SQL-Database-For-The-Cloud_04_2011.pdf.
3. Oracle. September 2011. "Oracle NoSQL Database," Oracle, http://www.oracle.com/technetwork/database/nosqldb/learnmore/nosql-database-498041.pdf.
4. Harrison, G. August 26, 2010. "10 Things You Should Know about NoSQL Databases," TechRepublic, http://i.techrepublic.com.com/downloads/Gilbert/dl_10_things_nosql.pdf.
5. Tweed, R., and G. James. 2010. "A Universal NoSQL Engine, Using a Tried and Tested Technology," M/Gateway Developments Ltd, http://www.mgateway.com/docs/universalNoSQL.pdf.
6. Oracle. February 2011. "Hadoop and NoSQL Technologies and the Oracle Database," Oracle, http://www.oracle.com/technetwork/database/hadoop-nosql-oracle-twp-398488.pdf.
7. Burd, G. 2011. "NoSQL." *;login:* 36 (5): 5–12, http://static.usenix.org/publications/login/2011-10/openpdfs/Burd.pdf.
8. Weber, S. 2011. "NoSQL Databases," http://wiki.hsr.ch/Datenbanken/files/Weber_NoSQL_Paper.pdf.
9. Pokorny, J. 2011. "NoSQL Databases: A Step to Database Scalability in Web Environment," *The 13th International Conference on Information Integration and Web-based Applications & Services (iiWAS2011)*, Ho Chi Minh City, Vietnam, December 5–7, 2011.
10. Hogan, M. 2009. "Database Virtualization and the Cloud: How Database Virtualization, Cloud Computing and Other Advances Will Reshape the Database Landscape," Scale DB Inc., http://www.scaledb.com/pdfs/Cloud_Databases_WhitePaper2.pdf.
11. Brantner, M., D. D. Florescu, D. Graf, D. Kossmann, and T. Kraska. 2009. "Building a Database in the Cloud," http://www.dbis.ethz.ch/research/publications/dbs3.pdf.

12. Michel, D. 2010. "Databases in the Cloud," HSR University of Applied Science Rapperswil, http://wiki.hsr.ch/Datenbanken/files/CloudDatabases.pdf.

13. Curino, C., E. P. C. Jones, R. A. Popa, N. Malviya et al. 2011. "Relational Cloud: A Database-as-a-Service for the Cloud," *5th Biennial Conference on Innovative Data Systems Research (CIDR 2011)*, Asilomar, CA, January 9–12, 2011. http://www.cidrdb.org/cidr2011/Papers/CIDR11_Paper33.pdf.

14. Abounlnaga, A., K. Salem, A. A. Soror, U. F. Minhas, P. Kokosielis, and S. Kamath. 2009. "Deploying Database Appliances in the Cloud," *Bulletin of the IEEE Computer Society Technical Committee on Data Engineering*, http://sites.computer.org/debull/A09mar/aboulnaga.pdf.

15. Ion, M., G. Russello, and B. Crispo. 2011. "Enforcing Multi-user Access Policies to Encrypted Cloud Databases," *2011 IEEE International Symposium on Policies for Distributed Systems and Networks*, Piza, Italy, June 6–8, 2011. http://www.computer.org/csdl/proceedings/policy/2011/4330/00/4330a175-abs.html.

16. Dory, T. 2011. "Study and Comparison of Elastic Cloud Databases: Myth or Reality?", Master Thesis, Computer Engineering Department, Université Catholique de Louvain, http://www.info.ucl.ac.be/~pvr/MemoireThibaultDory.pdf.

17. Tiwari, A. 2011. "Distributed Aggregation in Cloud Databases," Indiana University Bloomington, IN, http://salsahpc.indiana.edu/b534projects/sites/default/files/public/5_Distributed%20Aggregation%20in%20Cloud%20Databases_Tiwari,%20Aparna.pdf.

18. Mathur, A., M. Mathur, and P. Upadhyay. June 2011. "Cloud Based Distributed Databases: The Future Ahead." *International Journal on Computer Science and Engineering* 3 (6): 2477–81, http://www.enggjournals.com/ijcse/doc/IJCSE11-03-06-115.pdf.

19. Dory, T., B. Mejías, P. V. Roy, and N.-T. Tran. 2011. "Comparative Elasticity and Scalability Measurements of Cloud Databases," http://www.nosqlbenchmarking.com/wp-content/uploads/2011/05/paper.pdf.

20. Manyika, J., M. Chui, B. Brown, J. Bughin, R. Dobbs, C. Roxburgh, and A. H. Byers. May 2011. "Big Data: The Next Frontier for Innovation, Competition, and Productivity," McKinsey Global Institute.

21. Neo Technology. November 2011. "NoSQL for the Enterprise," Neo Technology.

22. 2011. "Big Data for the Enterprise," Oracle.

23. Russom, P. 2011. "Hadoop: Revealing Its True Value for Business Intelligence," TDWI International, http://www.tdwi.org.

24. Bloor, R. 2011. "Enabling the Agile Business with an Information-Oriented Architecture," The Bloor Group, http://www.insideanalysis.com/wp-content/uploads/2012/04/TheIOA-WP-Final-0419.pdf.

7

Cloud Technology Architecture

INTRODUCTION

Transition is an inseparable factor and force of the expanding IT land-scape. Once in a while, transformational and trendsetting technolo-gies erupt and energize IT service organizations, product vendors, and consultants to provide technology-sponsored business simplification, augmentation, and optimization solutions. Cloud technology is not an exception to this predominant and perpetual trend. Enterprises are in the thick of actions with the largesse of improvements, improvisations, and innovations being supplied and sustained by the indomitable spirit of the cloud paradigm. The elegant and exciting history of IT goes back to the era of monolithic and centralized mainframes. They were followed by client-server (CS) programming and multitier distributed comput-ing, which are dominating the IT scene these days. Tiered and layered approaches are making it easier for designers, architects, and developers to build a bank of business services and applications and, hence, they are still in the limelight. Simplicity and sensitivity are the gist and crux of these paradigms. In short, as IT has been drifting toward distribu-tion and decentralization methods, the much-maligned centralization has come to the forefront again with the unprecedented adoption of cloud concepts and ultrahigh broadband communication technologies. Enterprise IT is bound to leverage scores of consolidated, virtualized, and shared servers. This centralization concept simplifies centralized monitoring, management, and maintenance. It is noteworthy that this tectonic shift is being enunciated and edified by the lively cloud concept. In a nutshell, one can think of IT as a pendulum that swings between two extremes, centralization and distribution. As the Internet is being utilized as the most affordable, pervasive, and open communication infrastructure, the long-abandoned and -aborted centralization technique is springing back to long and glorious life.

Initially, the shift to server-based computing was supported using a highly siloed architectural approach. In this approach, every single application gets its own dedicated stack and a single server hosts and runs the application. But as the stack gets subdivided into multiple layers and as these layers become standardized, applications get distributed across multiple servers that reside in different geographical locations. In other words, both logical separation and physical separation are prevalent. A single application typically has exclusive ownership of these servers in a multitier architecture. But the real issue is that it is still very much a siloed architecture with low utilization rate. The worrying aspects of this architecture, such as the underutilization and the growing management complexity of servers, have led to the development of a string of complexity-moderation and -mitigation techniques. Server sprawl is a key driver for cloud computing. Separation of concerns has been a beneficial software engineering technique for a long time. Decomposition of applications into smaller, manageable components (beyond the traditional macrolevel tiers such as web/UI tier, application/business logic tier, and database tier) comes in handy in the complex field of software engineering. It is noted that SOA is the leading scheme that takes this decomposition method very seriously and uses it successfully. In other words, applications are systematically decomposed into a dynamic pool of reusable and composable services in an SOA. On the other hand, SOA facilitates the composition of decomposed, distributed, and diverse service components into business-aligned and -aware composites that collectively implement one or more business processes.

Although virtualization is an old technology, its technical and business values have shot up with the realization that portability is the need of the hour; hence, it is a recurring and resilient theme in the IT industry today. Virtualization technology has matured a lot and there are companies producing software solutions for creating and controlling virtual machines (VMs) out of physical servers. Decoupling software from specific and dedicated hardware is the key goal of virtualization technology. In other words, all the inhibiting dependencies of software on the underlying hardware are decimated by virtualization technology; thereby, any software can run on any machine. Not only consolidation, federation, and virtualization concepts, but also grid, cluster, utility, and on-demand computing paradigms have contributed immeasurably to the unprecedented success of cloud computing. Automation of resource provisioning and management, job scheduling, workload management, capacity planning and management, VM creation and elimination, and so on go a long way in taking the cloud concept to greater heights.

Both centralization and distribution have significant and strategic merits for enterprise IT. Centralization of control and management enables consistency, economies of scale, and efficient rollout of innovations that are applicable across the enterprise. Distribution of control makes departments agile, allowing them to flexibly respond to needs and imperatives specific to their roles within an organization. A perfect balance between centralization and distribution is definitely beneficial for enterprises.

It is not the ownership of high-end IT infrastructures and platforms, but their optimal administration and management that happen to be the real differentiators and cost-savers for any enterprise. Many times, organizations do fail to recognize an effective operational model. Armed with smart operational and delivery mechanisms, administrators could deploy, configure, and run services and applications effectively to reap the promised results. Generally, an efficient deployment method is a crucial criterion that is extensively encouraged and used to calculate the return on investment (RoI) and the total cost of ownership (TCO). There are options galore as far as the deployment, consumption, and management infrastructures and platforms for software are concerned.

Now, with the powerful emergence of clouds as the greatly optimized, centralized, easily extensible, elastic, and autonomic service infrastructures, professors and professionals are working overtime on a range of cloud deployment strategies, frameworks, tools, tips, and techniques. In this chapter, we exclusively discuss the various cloud infrastructures (generic as well as specific). Further, we focus on the prominent delivery and consumption methods. Cloud integration bus (CIS), cloud broker, and cloud middleware represent the latest entrants into the cloud ecosystem. The market researchers, watchers, and analysts are unhesitatingly articulating that there is a huge market scope for cloud brokerage services, and there is a separate section allotted for different deployment scenarios and schemes for cloud middleware. With the cloud landscape steadily expanding, cloud management schemes and suites are being leveraged to optimally control virtual machines (VMs), services, applications and their performance, scalability, accessibility, and so on. Finally, we discuss how various cloud infrastructures and platforms need to be deployed to reap better outputs for enterprises that are different in size, scope, and structure.

GENERIC CLOUD TYPES

In the beginning, monolithic, inflexible, closed, and packaged applications were run on mainframes and workstations. Recently, services entered the scene as key building blocks of adaptive, on-demand, and open enterprise systems, and they are increasingly being leveraged for constructing new-generation business applications. Old systems are reconstructed as a collection of services. Thus, services facilitate application engineering and composition through reuse and orchestration. Legacy modernization and enterprise integration are the other two prominent tasks being simplified and streamlined by the use of services. Finally, service-centric applications are deployed on and delivered through competent service infrastructures. Messaging brokers, application servers, service buses and runtimes, transaction-processing monitors (TPMs), service delivery platforms (SDPs), integration hubs and containers, service governance solutions, event-processing engines, rule management systems, business process modeling systems, management and execution solutions, BI systems, business activity monitoring systems and dashboards, and so on, simplify and streamline service hosting, management, maintenance, and consumption.

The cloud paradigm is in the fast lane. Organizations across the world are jumping on the cloud model bandwagon with great optimism. There are generic as well as specific clouds that meet different requirements. The cloud paradigm has already laid a strong foundation for newer and nimbler business and consumption models. The cloud model is breeding a bevy of innovative models that facilitate business efficiency, resiliency, and success one way or the other. Another noteworthy factor is the widespread applicability and easy adoptability of the disruptive and transformative cloud paradigm. The cloud principle brings in a number of optimizations, transformations, and augmentations to the IT space and, hence, it easily captivates and captures the minds and hearts of engineers, executives, and entrepreneurs worldwide. The outlook for the cloud is definitely bright. Scores of classic and catalytic use and business cases for fast-growing cloud concepts are being thrown around for public review, blogging, and musings. Professors also show much interest in communicating and articulating the special capabilities of the exploding cloud concept to their students and scholars. Market watchers, analysts, researchers, and visionaries are united in projecting and presenting the unique abilities of clouds in automating a number of complicated business operations in a different manner. Models, measurements, and metrics are being unearthed and published as viable mechanisms for bringing more clarity and confidence on the nonfunctional requirements of clouds.

In cloud infrastructures, VMs are used for hosting and running a variety of software suites. The VMs are created and managed by a virtual machine monitor (VMM), which is a layer of software between the operating system (OS) and the physical machine. The VMMs (predominantly called hypervisors) can supply and manage multiple VMs that share the physical machine's resources adaptively. Each VM has its own stack including an OS for hosting and running its applications. The VMM creatively isolates each VM so that a VM runs independently and uses physical resources as per emerging needs. The VMM saves and restores the image of a running VM, and the live migration of VMs from one physical machine to another is very much possible due to this elegant isolation. The typical problems arising from dependencies or tight coupling of software and/or hardware modules are fully eliminated in a virtual environment. Decomposing physical servers into a number of VMs has clearly brought in several interesting propositions and provisions for providers as well as users. On-demand creation, addition, and elimination of VMs take care of fluctuating user bases and workloads. The VMs not only enhance resource utilization sharply but also guarantee software portability. With a dynamic pool of VMs at hand, software scalability and capability will soar.

Public Cloud

A public cloud is a massive server infrastructure (consolidated, centralized, virtualized, and automated) for remotely providing compute, storage, and other specialized infrastructures and instruments to global users over the Internet communication infrastructure. This is the modernized version of the huge data centers and server farms of yesterday. In other words, cloud-inspired standardization, augmentation, and optimization techniques are applied liberally across all the computing, network, and storage systems to achieve affordability, greenness, leanness, manageability, and sustainability; that is, a cloud center is a dynamic pool of converged and federated IT infrastructures for guaranteeing key nonfunctional requirements such as seamless and real-time elasticity, high availability, high performance, and high assurance. Centralized monitoring, which gives sufficient control and deep visibility into systems' operations, is the praiseworthy hallmark of cloud centers. Any individual or company in any part of the world at any point in time can avail this facility for a small fee or sometimes at no cost. Any device with Internet connectivity can connect and make use of personal as well as professional services that are hosted and managed in clouds.

Examples of public cloud providers are Amazon AWS, Microsoft Azure, and Google App Engine. Public cloud providers are offering new services gradually. As an example, Amazon AWS initially offered only Amazon EC2 and S3 but has since then been releasing a new product every few months; some are listed here:

- Amazon Elastic Compute Cloud (EC2)
- Amazon Elastic MapReduce
- Amazon CloudFront
- Amazon SimpleDB
- Amazon Relational Database Service (RDS)
- Amazon ElastiCache
- The AWS Elastic Beanstalk
- The AWS CloudFormation
- Amazon Fulfillment Web Service (FWS)
- Amazon Simple Queue Service (SQS)
- Amazon Simple Notification Service (SNS)
- Amazon Simple E-mail Service (SES)
- Amazon CloudWatch
- Amazon Virtual Private Cloud (VPC)
- The AWS Direct Connect
- The AWS Elastic Load Balancing
- Amazon Flexible Payments Service (FPS)
- Amazon Simple Storage Service (S3)
- Amazon Elastic Block Store (EBS)
- The AWS Import/Export
- Alexa Web Information Service

There are several unique advantages of using public cloud providers as well as a few concerns. Public cloud providers are able to operate at greater economies of scale as all cloud resources are shared by a large number of people; that is, a public cloud is a large yet shared environment for simultaneously meeting the various IT needs of many organizations. In other words, instead of owning and operating a car for travel purposes, people can travel in a bus. A bus, which can accommodate many travelers, is definitely an economic option. Another prime motivator is the grand success of the service paradigm. These aspects of the cloud paradigm collectively lead to cost reduction for cloud consumers. They also give rise to attractive and affordable cost models, such as the pay-per-use pricing model that allows consumers to pay only for their consumption. Ultimately, this transition helps users to negate the need for up-front expenditure in compute and storage infrastructures. There is a gradual shift from personal IT toward shared IT; but this does not mean that the days of dedicated servers for some specific IT needs are over.

A public cloud is inherently not very secure as it allows multiple companies to share a common pool of IT resources. In addition, the open Internet, being the communication infrastructure for clouds, is a temptation for hackers and evildoers. Also, VMs carved out of physical servers are susceptible to security threats and vulnerabilities. There could be at least one or two untrustworthy subscribers in the same cloud facility. For example, virtualized servers operating in a multitenant environment are subject to cartography and side channel attacks, whereby hackers, who can be users of another public cloud, make use of details such as timing information and power consumption to exploit security holes. It is not possible for one person to know another person's profiles and intents; hence, public cloud providers are expected to use a series of advanced security mechanisms and industry-strength standardizations at different levels and layers to boost users' confidence in clouds.

Private Cloud

A private cloud is alternatively referred to as a "local cloud" or an "enterprise cloud." Every corporation has its own cloud in order to ensure that the cloud-based data, services, applications, and processes are accessed and leveraged by its designated owner only (an individual, institution, or innovator). Private cloud offerings are not for public consumption. In a company environment, the employees, executives, partners, retailers, suppliers, and other important stakeholders of the company can access its cloud infrastructures. Private clouds are established and sustained primarily for retaining control and ensuring security, and for deep and real-time visibility. Any company can modernize existing data centers by applying cloud technologies, tools, and best practices or build its own cloud center from the ground up for fulfilling its IT requirements. It is owned by and operated solely for an organization, may be managed by the organization itself or a third party, and may exist on-premises or off-premises. For example, an organization may use Google Apps (public cloud) for corporate e-mail, whereas its human resource and customer applications may be hosted in its internally developed and managed clouds (private clouds). The open source private cloud solutions are as follows:

CloudStack	http://www.cloudstack.org
Eucalyptus	http://open.eucalyptus.com
Nimbus	http://www.nimbusproject.org
OpenNebula	http://opennebula.org
OpenStack	http://www.openstack.org

Community Cloud

A community cloud is a cloud infrastructure shared across several organizations and people with common interests, that is, it supports a specific community of people that has common requirements and shared concerns (e.g., mission and security requirements, and policy and compliance considerations) [1]. The members of the community can access the data and applications made available in the cloud. For example, a community related to health care may have very strict policies toward maintaining the confidentiality of patient records; therefore, such a community cloud may have additional requirements for data security such as encryption of data compliant to certain standards. The key advantage of having a community cloud is that all cloud users can benefit from the technologies established by the community. A community of reasonable size benefits from a vast range of cloud services tailored for that community and is likely to benefit from stricter governance and compliance to standards.

There are a number of potential pitfalls for the community cloud. In particular, managing a community cloud is beset with issues since there is no clarity on the leadership as well as the government body that runs and regulates a community. Who formulates policies, who makes decisions and enforces policies, and who is responsible for any governance paralysis are some pertinent questions as far as the concept of community cloud is concerned. Similar to a public cloud, a community cloud is shared among multiple parties within a community. Therefore, security is a little problematic and users in a community cloud are not as trustworthy as users in a private cloud. However, community cloud users have greater visibility and control over their resources than users of public clouds and, hence, the level of trust for a community cloud is higher than that for a public cloud. A community cloud may be managed by the concerned organizations or a third party, and it may exist on-premises or off-premises. This cloud is also built by networking the underutilized and unutilized computers of its members. Voluntary and virtual computing models are the main motivators for setting up a community cloud.

Hybrid Cloud

A hybrid cloud (Figure 7.1) is a connected and converged cloud infrastructure originated and operated by a composition of two or more clouds (private, community, or public clouds) that remain unique entities, although they are bound together by standardized or proprietary technologies for sharing and synergizing their own capabilities and competencies. Standards-based interactions and resource (data and application) portability are the key advantages of this model. Further, if there is any additional computing power/storage needed, the seamless connectivity between different, distributed, and decentralized clouds comes to the rescue. There are competent techniques that enable such kinds of ad hoc, dynamic, real-time empowerment (e.g., cloud bursting for load balancing between clouds). In this model, users typically outsource non-business-critical information and processing to the public cloud while keeping business-critical services and data under their control. Figure 7.1 describes the utility and usability of hybrid clouds in enriching private and public clouds toward accomplishing better and bigger things for worldwide business establishments.

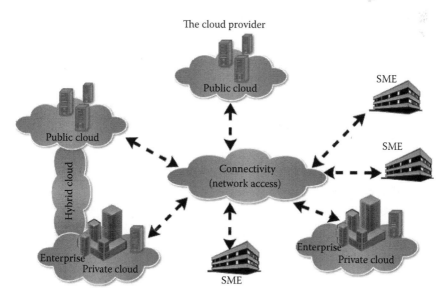

FIGURE 7.1

Formation of hybrid clouds linking private and public clouds.

In summary, we have discussed the most prominent and pertinent cloud structures. Due to some specific requirements, there are many vertical clouds such as service, knowledge, data, storage, science, and high-performance clouds. Due to the convergence of new-generation technologies, there are thought processes, musings, rants, reviews, and blogs on device clouds, mobile clouds, ambient clouds, semantic clouds, and so on. Further, cloud connectivity and portability technologies lead to connected and federated clouds. With semantic and virtualization technologies permeating every type of device, appliance, instrument, and machine, the days of the semantic ambient cloud are fast approaching.

NEXT-GENERATION CONNECTED CLOUDS

Different sets of needs lead to a large number of generic as well as specific clouds being conceived, established, and leveraged over all kinds of networks by an overwhelming array of devices and handsets. As discussed in the previous section, the hybrid cloud is one such grand model for establishing direct connectivity between public and private clouds. Messages can be sent, data can be exchanged, documents can be transmitted, and workload can be shared with the use of the hybrid model (smartly leveraging two or more distinct clouds in real time for a generic or specific reason).

The hybrid model is all set to grow considering the fact that emerging businesses and technical, societal, and ground realities and requirements demand connected, integrated, and extended clouds. Separately, public and private clouds are targeting different sets of businesses, but collectively, these two can do a lot of things in a proactive, preemptive, and simplified fashion. That is, seamless and spontaneous connectivity between clouds guarantees a lot of advantages for innovators, investors, and institutions. In this section, we focus on the differentiating aspects of connected clouds. The key technique for such clouds is cloud bursting, which is the ability of a cloud to leverage computing and storage resources offered by other local or distant clouds when the ones offered by private clouds are not sufficient to meet rising needs or when a sort of pricing arbitrage is exerted. Private cloud users typically leverage cloud bursting for applications or data that have a low degree of confidentiality and sensitivity and do not require the highest QoS levels. The simplicity with which applications and data can migrate back and forth between clouds is the driving force behind connected clouds.

Another popular use case for connected clouds is leveraging its ability to syndicate special contents from public clouds. As a prime example, Google Cloud has stored a huge amount of geographic maps, location and direction details, social networking and exchange information, business data, and so on. Maintaining such a growing and glowing base of decision-enabling and actionable insights in a private cloud is highly prohibitive. Personal as well as professional applications that need such crucial information from public sites must leverage the cloud bursting technique for enabling data and information integration among private as well as public clouds dynamically. Quick creation and crafting of competent mashups, along with composite applications and services, across a wide variety of diverse clouds by even nontechnical people is the principal differentiator for connected clouds. Cloud integration brokers, mashup editors, hubs, and buses are emerging in order to streamline the integration, composition, and collaboration of processes, applications, services, and data available in a wide variety of cloud, enterprise, embedded, and personal systems.

Public clouds that are generally massive in size and have a global outlook can also be used to provide efficient and cost-effective backup for data managed in private clouds. This helps businesses immensely at times to recover quickly from any kind of natural or human-made disasters in order to guarantee the vital aspects of business efficiency, continuity, and resiliency. As we know, any slowdown or breakdown of IT operations comes as a rude shock and costly letdown to providers as well as subscribers. Messages comprising confidential corporate data are subjected to strong encryption not only during their transit but also in their persistence. It is noted that virtual private networks (VPNs) are established among different cloud providers to stop any kind of hacking, peeking, and breaking in by unauthorized individuals. Once the security requirement, which is being projected as the most vital concern and complication for the blooming and booming cloud computing paradigm, is ensured, this hybrid architecture brings to the table many notable benefits by nullifying all identified and unidentified limitations and barriers: First, by using completely separate infrastructures for primary data management and secondary data backup, it enables a neat separation of concerns. Second, the affordability factor becomes important with the emergence of several online low-cost storage providers. Data integrity and availability can be ensured with such hybrid clouds.

Finally, whereas data backup can be done internally, data archival can be done at the location of public storage providers. This ensures a clean division between backup and archival. With petabytes of storage available on-demand from services such as Amazon S3, regular and real-time snapshots of all data managed by private clouds can be archived on public clouds at nominal costs.

In summary, we have discussed a number of mainstream cloud types. We know that there are delivery models (infrastructure cloud, and platform and software clouds) and deployment models (public, private, hybrid, and community clouds). Clouds, being a generic technology, mingle and mix with a number of different domains, whereby newer and nimbler cloud types continue to emerge. Today, the trend is that each domain has its own cloud. In other words, besides generic clouds, there are innumerable specific cloud models gaining momentum in the competing yet calculative marketplace. With the convergence aspect gaining much traction, there are domain-specific clouds (science, mobile, data, device, storage, service, knowledge, and high-performance clouds). Nonfunctional attributes are synonymous and tied with the cloud idea and, hence, we hear more about context-aware, cognitive, instant-on, on-demand, and ambient clouds these days.

CLOUD MIDDLEWARE DEPLOYMENT SCENARIOS

With the faster rollout of cloud infrastructures and buildup of cloud-run services and applications, the next prominent cloud platform is undoubtedly cloud integration, composition, and collaboration middleware. As the trend is toward extreme and deeper connectivity, the functionalities of cloud middleware (CM; Figure 7.2) are steadily going up and several automated and standards-compliant integration solutions are hitting the market. Cloud governance is another mandatory and myopic topic, and cloud middleware is slated to embed governance features. Typically, governance modules contribute to the stricter enforcement of cloud rules/ policies in order to act on incoming feedback for policy upgrades and refinement; rigorous monitoring, maintenance, and management of all participating cloud resources and their interactions with one another; and so on. Governance enhances environment visibility as a result of which any deviation or deficiency can be attended to quickly.

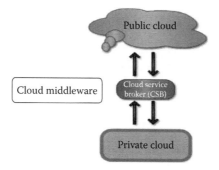

FIGURE 7.2
CSB integrates public and private clouds.

In this section, we visualize how distinctly capable clouds connect, correspond, and collaborate with one another to meet varied expectations. Due to some fundamental issues, enterprises are still hesitating to host and manage their business-critical applications and corporate data in public clouds. However, there is a need for real-time synchronization among applications and data that are spread across public as well as private clouds.

Scenario 1—within a public cloud: Two separate applications are hosted and managed in two different VMs in a single physical server. Alternatively, these applications can be hosted in two different physical servers within a cloud environment. The role of CM is to seamlessly enable these disparate applications to talk to each other by eliminating all the imposed barriers.

Scenario 2—across clouds: These applications can be in two geographically separated clouds. The middleware can be in cloud 1 or 2 or in a third-party cloud (alternatively termed as a cloud brokerage service [CBS] provider). Protocol and content transformations are taken care of by the CM for facilitating their purposeful interactions.

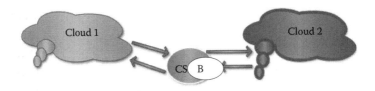

Scenario 3—public versus private clouds: One application is in a public cloud and the other is in a private cloud. There are occasions in which corporate data resides at the private cloud and a customer-facing enterprise application resides in the public cloud. To provide real-time and real-world information, the application must be synchronized with the data at the private cloud. Here too, the role and responsibility of CM are significant. This scenario will become pervasive in the forthcoming cloud-sponsored service era.

In other words, locally hosted and managed applications can be linked with SaaS applications hosted in public clouds and they can interact to deliver integrated systems. Take the following scenario: There is a CRM application in a public cloud; the customer data still persists and is being updated in the company's database system. This soon-to-be-ubiquitous scenario clearly demands well-defined synchronization between the public and the private clouds in order to be proactively productive. Data sharing is the main motto for this example. The major functionalities of the cloud intermediary are explicitly given in Figure 7.3.

The real complication in this case is that the local application or data store in the company server resides behind a firewall, whereas there is no such constraint for SaaS applications hosted in the public cloud. Messages

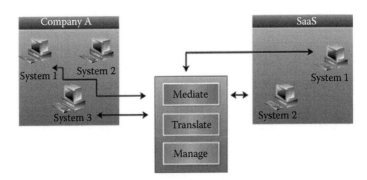

FIGURE 7.3
Enterprise applications accessing cloud-based SaaS applications through a CSB.

from any client can pierce through and reach the cloud server, however, messages originating from a cloud server could not reach cloud clients that sit behind a firewall. This threatening obstacle has induced and inspired researchers worldwide to ponder innovative mechanisms such as http-tunneling so that cloud applications penetrate through the blockade to reach enterprise applications and access data at the private cloud and vice versa.

Cloud Composition and Collaboration

Cloud services are becoming increasingly distributed and, hence, they need to be composed (via orchestration as well as choreography) to create an integrated service environment. In this section, we discuss how cloud composition and collaboration requirements are being met by next-generation CM.

Cloud Orchestration

Figure 7.4 explains how cloud services are orchestrated using a centralized orchestration layer to bring forth composite services [2; http://www .squarehoop.com].

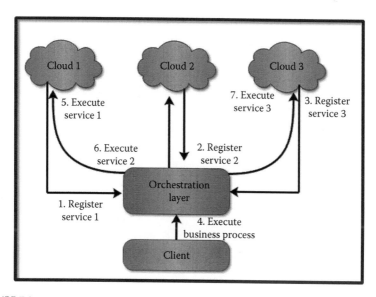

FIGURE 7.4
Working of a cloud orchestration engine.

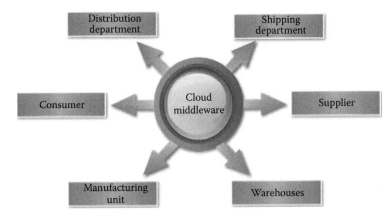

FIGURE 7.5
Cloud collaboration.

Cloud Collaboration

Figure 7.5 vividly illustrates a futuristic scenario in which a wide variety of cloud services syntactically, semantically, and dynamically find, bind, access, leverage, and compose business-aligned and -aware services in real time to meet any kind of business emergencies or exigencies. Purpose-driven interaction without any instruction given and interpretation made by human beings among various participating modules provided by different cloud service providers (CSPs) is the vision behind the introspective and intuitive CM. As companies and corporations are consistently moving their applications to clouds, the constructive and contributive pieces of a sophisticated SCM package are spread across cities, counties, countries, and even continents. Therefore, a brokered architecture is the efficient scheme in such a geographically distributed environment. Based on service-level and operational-level agreements, even a hybrid architecture comprising clustered and federated components is recommended.

For real-time and dynamic processing and notification, CM must be empowered through the incorporation of a business event processing (BEP) engine in order to elegantly capture events emanating from distributed resources; extract all sorts of actionable insights in the form of tips, trends, patterns, associations, alerts, opportunities, and so on; and act on the findings instantly. This way, the soaring expectations of clients, customers, and consumers can be fulfilled. For cloud governance, automated solutions are emerging separately and as additional modules of the cloud broker. Cloud management platforms are being made available by infrastructure software providers. Traditional system management software solutions are being strengthened in order to manage cloud infrastructures and resources effectively.

A business rule management system (BRMS) is another interesting module that helps to segregate business rules from business logic segments of cloud applications. This separation enables application developers to make modifications to the source code easily and quickly. Business managers and analysts make the necessary changes in the rules so that applications behave differently. Business rules can be subjected to any kind of approved changes at runtime. The changes affected have a direct impact on subsequent application behavior. The idea is that all inhibiting dependencies are decimated through a host of proven techniques such as modularity and separation of concerns, whereby complexity can be delegated and displaced to a major extent in order to enhance user satisfaction. The SOA-supported loose-coupling technique is being treated as a pioneering technique of enterprise-grade software design and, hence, architectural innovations are being investigated for salvaging and strengthening the field of software engineering to expectantly welcome the impending knowledge era.

Myriad modules are gradually sneaking into the expanding enterprise stack, such as BI, BAM, PM, user management, IAM, IT and service governance, and process and knowledge engineering. With the regular addition of newer features, facilities, and functionalities to enterprise IT, the relevance of cloud middleware for better and deeper streamlining and synchronization of cloud resources is on the rise, signaling a greater relief for cloud administrators and managers.

Scenarios for Cloud Brokers

Due to the growing diversity of clouds, cloud brokers are given prime importance and are being recognized as the important ingredient in any heterogeneous environment. Brokers are new-generation middleware solutions providing relevant brokerage services (intermediation, aggregation, routing, mapping, arbitration, dissemination, negotiation, etc.) in order that global consumers can peacefully leverage a range of global CSP capabilities. Cloud brokerages are expected to provide a unified, utility-like, enhanced management interface to multiple CSPs for service consumers. A brokerage service extracts, abstracts, and exposes all the common methods, whereas specific capabilities rest with the providers. Cloud consumers interact with the brokerage service directly and the service provider is totally invisible to the client. There are examples (e.g., U.S.

General Services Administration awards) where a broker makes available the resources of a CSP to international cloud consumers.

Scenarios

A cloud consumer may request a service from a cloud broker, instead of contacting a cloud provider directly (Figure 7.6). The cloud broker may combine multiple services into one new service and/or enhance the service by adding value. Here, cloud providers are transparent to cloud consumers.

As per some widely circulated summary reports by market analysts on the prevailing cloud market scene and sentiment, there is a huge market for CBSs. Cloud brokerage firms are emerging and engaging CSPs extensively in order to ensure better services and prices for cloud consumers. Cloud broker is a software suite empowering cloud brokerage firms to plan and provide next-generation CBSs to worldwide cloud users. The cloud ecosystem is steadily growing with the emergence of newer entities such as cloud brokers and auditors.

Cloud Reference Architecture

Brokers are an important part of the growing cloud ecosystem [6–7]. An abstracted view and version of cloud architecture is given in Figure 7.7; it conveys key contributors and participants in the enlarging cloud landscape and how modules interact with one another to accomplish the assigned and articulated tasks.

Scenarios for the Cloud Management Broker

The SAJACC working group has produced a set of technical use cases including a cloud management broker. For the "cloud first" use case analysis,

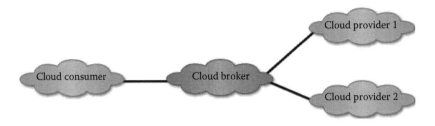

FIGURE 7.6
Cloud broker serving as the intermediary for clients in exposing a common interface by encapsulating all the nitty-gritty of cloud providers [6–7].

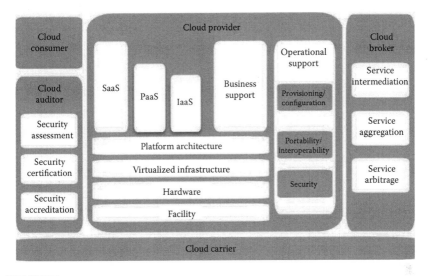

FIGURE 7.7

The reference cloud architecture. Adapted from http://www.nist.gov/itl/cloud/index .cfm.

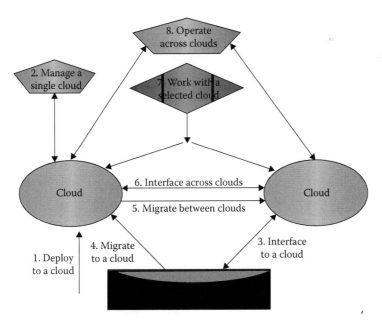

FIGURE 7.8

Scenarios for a cloud management broker.

a set of high-level generic scenarios are defined to clarify the scope of the study. The scenarios are listed as follows and vividly illustrated in Figure 7.8:

Single cloud
  Scenario 1: Deployment on a single cloud
  Scenario 2: Manage resources on a single cloud
  Scenario 3: Interface enterprise systems to a single cloud
  Scenario 4: Enterprise systems migrated or replaced on a single cloud
Multiple clouds
  Scenario 5: Migration between clouds
  Scenario 6: Interface across multiple clouds
  Scenario 7: Work with selected clouds
  Scenario 8: Operate across multiple clouds

The role of a cloud broker in these scenarios is to provide portability across different clouds for applications, data, and tools [3–5]. Specifically, the impact of replacing one cloud infrastructure provider with another should be guaranteed as a way of minimizing any vendor lock-in issue. The next step is to consider scenario 5 (migration between clouds) and scenario 6 (interface across multiple clouds). In future architectures, a cloud broker could support dynamic cloud selection for scenario 7 (work with selected clouds) and interoperability for scenario 8 (operate across multiple clouds). Some more detailed technical use cases for cloud infrastructure deployments are as follows [2]:

1. Creating, accessing, updating, and deleting data objects in clouds
2. Moving VMs and virtual appliances between clouds
3. Selecting the best infrastructure vendor for private externally hosted clouds
4. Tools for monitoring and managing multiple clouds
5. Moving data between clouds
6. Single sign-on access to multiple clouds
7. Orchestrated processes across clouds
8. Discovering cloud resources
9. Evaluating SLAs and penalties
10. Auditing clouds

In summary, CM is the essential intermediary that gives clarity and completeness to the increasingly complicated cloud landscape. Cloud brokers, orchestrators, composers, integrators, routers, mediators, and so on, are being annotated and articulated as CM solutions, and their contributions are enormous and immensely appreciated.

THE CLOUD SERVICE BROKER (CSB) DEPLOYMENT MODELS

The enterprise service bus (ESB) is a very important ingredient for enterprise integration. In a distributed and disparate business environment, the role and relevance of standards-compliant ESB are obvious for numerous business and technical cases. The ESBs are a kind of intermediary for enabling need-based interactions between enterprise services. This special component undertakes enablement, enrichment, and enforcement tasks that are essential in a heterogeneous service environment. This abstract mediator facilitates service reconciliation by providing competent modules for accomplishing protocol binding, data format and type transformation, conciliation of messaging patterns and routing, and so on. Enterprise editions of both open source and commercial-grade ESB vendors have most of the prominent QoS aspects such as security, dependability, high performance, scalability, and availability within their central module. The much sought-after qualities of ESBs include consumability, transparency, resilience, and adaptability. The other attributes to be considered include capabilities for auditing and logging, instrumentation, microorchestration, and collection of metrics. With the strong forecast for cloud brokerages, the veracity, vivacity, and versatility of cloud service bus (CSB), the cloud version of ESB, is rising fast.

This intermediation layer is mainly responsible for wrapping business services and normalizing them for use at the process layer. For example, the different data models used by services may be normalized onto a canonical model, which relieves the process layer from the data format–mapping requirement. The process layer can then focus on composing existing services into chains of events, which further simplifies process definition. The ESB has twin responsibilities; it covers "service enablement" and "policy enforcement":

- Service enablement represents the interoperability aspects that ESB helps to reconcile. Typical examples are different protocol bindings or invocation styles (push vs. pull). Service enablement allows connectivity between heterogeneous service end points that cannot communicate otherwise.
- Policy enforcement is all about applying the right policy guidelines on the right modules and interactions at the right time. It is also the control point for runtime governance. That is, it enforces policies that

were initially planned and agreed upon in all interactions among the various participants and constituents in order to preemptively nip in the bud and nullify any kind of wrong move.

Delegating service enablement and policy enforcement to the intermediation layer (rather than making it the responsibility of services) significantly improves loose coupling in a service environment. An ESB, in essence, is a combination of architectural patterns without any prescriptive details for the physical implementation. It is no surprise, therefore, that modern ESB implementations support a range of deployment models at the instance level as well as at the network topology level. So when it comes to deploying service buses in cloud environments, a host of parameters (architectures, locations, dependencies, business goals, technical capabilities and competencies, etc.) need to be carefully calculated and considered before arriving at the best deployment propositions and potentials. The cloud reference architecture accepted and adopted by an organization plays a critical role in selecting the CSB deployment profiles.

ESB Deployment Styles

Initially, the point-to-point (P2P) integration pattern and phenomenon was more prevalent. As complexity is very high in this case, collaborative efforts were made to do away with this approach. Hubs and buses are the new-generation intermediary infrastructure for establishing seamless and spontaneous connectivity and service-level integration and composition. In this section, we extract and expound hidden insights regarding emerging deployment architectures for the ensuing cloud-enabled service era.

Hub-and-Spoke Style

With the emergence of EAI hubs, enterprises moved away from the inflexible, complicated, and closed P2P model to a more brokered, centrally monitored and managed interaction model named the "hub-and-spoke" (H&S) architecture. A number of traditional ESB platforms are essentially rebranded EAI solutions and, hence, they have inherited the same hub deployment architecture as the EAI solutions. The classic EAI architecture model is characterized by a centralized hub that connects distributed and dissimilar applications at the edges with spokes or connectors. The hub in the middle is the focal point of this architecture; it receives messages from all applications, applies routing rules, bridges communication protocol differences, implements message structure and/or format transformations, and redirects messages to appropriate end points. With this model, the number of connections required to integrate n number of applications gets reduced from $O(n^2)$ to $O(n)$. This significantly simplifies the complexity (development, integration, and modification) and cost of the integration effort. The connectors have intimate knowledge about the communication protocol and data structure and formats of individual applications; they are responsible for mediating a canonical data structure and format and the application-specific data structure and format.

The key benefits of this approach (Figure 7.9) are that the applications at the end points are cleanly insulated from any changes. In other words, when a new application is integrated, only the broker has to support the new rules for routing, which is possibly a new communication protocol and transformation from an individual application-specific data structure/format to a canonical representation, and vice versa. Applications are loosely coupled as all common tasks are moved to the hub at the middle, whereas the application-specific functionalities persist at the end points

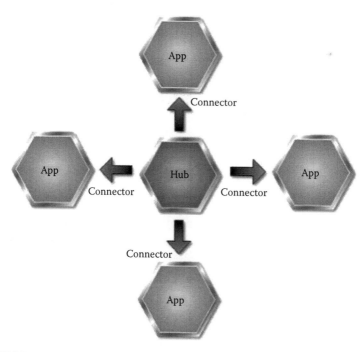

FIGURE 7.9
The EAI hub architecture.

(where each application is situated). That is, the hub is the core and central point in any integrated environment. Centralized administration, monitoring, diagnosis, and management of message traffic is a double benefit and treat for small-to-medium organizations.

However, nothing in life is free and, as it turns out, there are several problems with the hub approach, which are listed as follows:

Single point of failure: A single centralized hub for managing all message traffic between different end points is often a scalability bottleneck. With an increase in the volume of message traffic, the hub gets bogged down leading to poor performance and possible SLA breaches. A single central point of control is also a single point of failure. All applications effectively grind to a halt if the hub suffers a failure.

Otherwise, the rising complexity thickens: Over time, as more and more integration logic around routing and transformation is built into the hub, applications become more tightly coupled with the middleware infrastructure and boundaries between application logic and integration logic become increasingly difficult to enforce.

Extra baggage: When applications use identical data models and/or formats, transformation from and to canonical models and formats is an unnecessary performance penalty to pay for drawing the benefits of centralized mediation infrastructure.

Lack of controllability: In large organizations, centralized administration, management, and monitoring actually turn out to be an impediment as business units no longer have any control over administration of their applications and instead have to coordinate application maintenance, upgrades, and so on, with a centrally managed EAI team.

Technical architects have tried to circumvent the scalability and availability issues of classic EAI solutions and traditional hub-style ESB solutions by deploying multiple instances of hubs by clustering at the software or OS level; but this approach brought its own share of problems because

- Lack of application infrastructure standards meant clustering at the software level was based on proprietary protocols and implementations that only increase the risk of vendor lock-ins.
- Even with a single-instance EAI solution, the licensing costs are exorbitantly high. With multiple EAI instances, organizations have

to incur daunting up-front costs for satisfying common nonfunctional requirements such as scalability and availability.

Distributed Service Bus

For many ESBs, the core service bus is a service-oriented extension of the implementation of the message bus pattern [14–16,20]. A message bus, at its core, is a distributed messaging-channel infrastructure where applications communicate with each other by producing and consuming messages from a common channel (e.g., JMS-compliant queues or MSMQ queue) that forms the integration backbone for the entire application landscape. The service bus pattern embraced the fundamentally distributed nature of the message bus but shifted the focus of integration from message level to service level. In other words, instead of hosting messaging end points, ESBs are containers of standards-based service end points and event subscribers (Figure 7.10). Further, the mediation functionalities of classic EAI solutions are clubbed together in the ESB in the form of support for protocol bridging, service routing, and data structure and format transformation.

There are some noteworthy differences between enterprise hubs and service buses. The key difference originates from the fact that the constituents of a service bus are highly distributed and modular. A service bus, in contrast to a hub, is not a monolithic container deployed on a single physical node. The components of a service bus are able to work together as a logical entity even though they could be physically deployed on separate nodes. This isolated model of separately deployable and scalable service containers and messaging infrastructures in

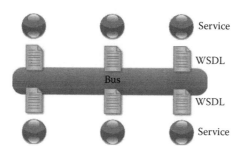

FIGURE 7.10
Conceptual architecture of an ESB.

a service bus is a unique architectural phenomenon and is significantly different from the models of classic EAI middleware solutions (hubs) in the following ways:

Simplicity, sensitivity, and sustainability: The constituents of a service bus can be highly modular and independent, and suitable for stand-alone deployment if necessary. In contrast with the hub model, we can take a data transformation module and deploy it anywhere on the bus without having any impact on the rest of the ESB infrastructure. In addition, if we need to support high-volume data transformations, we can deploy multiple instances of the transformation module and load balance them without incurring the overhead of using a container. Such a loosely coupled, highly cohesive, and independently deployable component architecture (Figure 7.11) neatly promotes a simple yet sagacious deployment model.

Distributed management: A highly distributed infrastructure lends itself well to distributed management. Administrators can selectively and independently manage and monitor ESB modules without having to worry about the rest of the infrastructure, which may be under the administrative control of different teams.

Fault tolerance and high performance: Aspects such as scale-up and scale-out become much easier with the bus-based, distributed deployment architecture. With this architecture, we need to worry about the scaling up and out of only those components that need scaling and not the entire bloated stack.

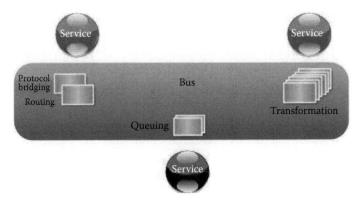

FIGURE 7.11
Modularity of an ESB.

In summary, the service bus is emerging as an important ingredient of the increasingly distributed, decentralized, and diverse cloud environment. In the ensuing and exciting cloud era, cloud-enabled, -deployed, and -managed service buses will become popular and ambient.

Variations in ESB Deployment

Interestingly, ESB deployment architectures can vary significantly among vendors. There are several popular open source and commercial ESBs in the Java world that support running ESB services in stand-alone mode or embedding ESB services in a web container. In the stand-alone mode of deployment, a lightweight daemon Java process runs anywhere on the network; accepts messages; does service invocations; and performs the usual brokering, routing, and integration tasks. Scaling out stand-alone ESB servers usually requires external clustering software and may not be as straightforward or easy to manage as container-level clustering. On the other hand, ESB modules deployed in web containers (as WAR files) can perform the same routing, transformation, and bridging tasks and leverage the container's clustering and failover capabilities while maintaining a lightweight and fairly independent deployment footprint (Figure 7.12).

A more prevalent model of ESB deployment is seen in the ESB offerings from .NET and JEE application server vendors, wherein the ESB is built as an extension of the application server and provides all the necessary intermediary capabilities. The immediate advantage of this model is that service end points can quickly leverage mature and sophisticated container capabilities such as handling concurrency, transaction management, security, clustering, and so on. In other words, incorporation of all nonfunctional requirements (QoS attributes; Figure 7.13) is easier and quicker with this model. One of the main drawbacks of this model is that a few monolithic JEE application server vendors do not offer the flexibility of deploying stand-alone service brokering modules without the

FIGURE 7.12
Different methods of deploying ESBs.

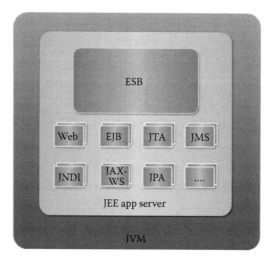

FIGURE 7.13
An ESB sitting on a JEE-compliant application server.

encumbrance of a full-blown application server stack, effectively taking us back to the rejected hub model [4–5]. However, there are some critical differences between the application server–based ESB solutions and the EAI solutions rebranded as ESBs on the deployment front:

- Clustering an ESB for better scalability and availability is quite straightforward as the clustering infrastructure in the Java and .NET application server world is a well-established and well-understood one. This is contrasted with classical EAI solutions in which scaling out horizontally is still a difficult proposition.
- Licensing costs for application server–based ESBs, even for a clustered ESB setup, are orders of magnitude lower than those for an EAI hub, which needs to be installed in multiple locations.

The monolithic nature of Java application server stacks gets mitigated quite a bit in the newer Java EE 6 platform where vendors can choose to implement a profile that is only a subset of the traditional JEE infrastructure, for example, a web profile that includes only the implementations of core web technologies, a lightweight Enterprise JavaBean (EJB) container, and a persistent and transactional API implementation. In the future, a JEE-based ESB platform could be based on the web profile with some add-on capabilities. However, the promise of truly distributed, lightweight, highly modular, and independent component-based ESBs is already being realized by some modern ESBs that are based on a microkernel architecture or modularity standards such as OSGi, which facilitate the deployment of components or subsystems dynamically on a need basis. For example, an OSGi-enabled container (Figure 7.14) can operate with a small footprint of just a few subsystems, for example, a web container, a web service stack, and a persistence infrastructure. The OSGi-enabled ESB platforms extend this model further by allowing administrators to deploy stand-alone mediation modules as OSGi bundles; this brings us much closer to the vision of a highly distributed and optimized bus infrastructure.

Peer-to-Peer ESB Deployment Model

In spite of the differences in deployment architectures between the classic hub model and the bus model, the concept of service brokering through a middleware follows more or less the same pattern in both the models. The peer-to-peer (p2p) interaction model (Figure 7.15), on the other hand, does away with the notion of a middleware altogether and moves the ESB smartly to the service end points. In this model, the smart end points directly communicate with one another, forming what is often referred to as an enterprise service network (ESN). In certain situations, this p2p model is an attractive proposition:

- In an application landscape, not all applications need to be connected to the rest of the applications. In many situations, the intimidating prospect of building $O(n^2)$ connections often turns out to be nothing more than an academic exercise to ponder and the real number of connections ends up in a much more manageable range.

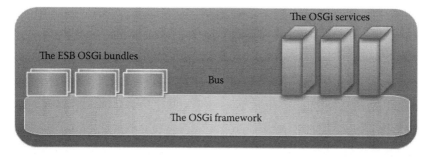

FIGURE 7.14
The OSGi-based modular ESB.

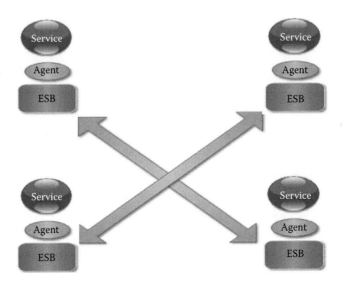

FIGURE 7.15
The p2p ESB.

- As opposed to the hub and bus models where every message flows through a physically separate service broker, thereby incurring a certain performance overhead, the ESB in the end point model eliminates the extra hops and performs well.
- Smart end points can avoid unnecessary protocol bridging or data transformations when there are no or very few differences to mediate. If an application needs to talk to other applications using the same data model and format the messages, it does not have to go through unnecessary transformation to a canonical model or format.

A smart end point is usually implemented through service agents that manage all the routing, brokering, and message-queuing functionalities necessary to hide all the details of service end point locations, mediate the protocol and data differences, and implement reliable messaging at the edges catering to unreliable network connections.

As always, there are trade-offs, and it pays to be aware of the potential pitfalls of the p2p approach:

- Service orchestration with a pure p2p model poses significant challenges because of the lack of a coordinator module, whereas in the hub or bus model service orchestration is usually managed in the hub or in the bus.

- A p2p ESB may work well in the network topology of a single department or division but may not scale very well to span the boundaries of multiple, autonomous divisions where service governance is managed by different teams, and it becomes difficult to agree on the separation of brokering responsibilities between service end points.

Cloud-Ready Mule ESB

Mule ESB (Figure 7.16; http://www.mulesoft.com/mule-esb-open-source-esb) is a lightweight Java-based ESB and integration platform that allows developers to connect applications quickly and easily, enabling them to exchange data. Mule ESB enables easy integration of existing systems regardless of the different technologies used by the applications, including JMS, web services, Java Database Connectivity (JDBC), hypertext transfer protocol (HTTP), and more. Mule ESB includes a set of capabilities called Mule Cloud Connect, enabling the integration of enterprise data and applications seamlessly with SaaS and cloud-based web applications. These capabilities include a set of out-of-the-box cloud connectors for popular cloud, SaaS, and Web 2.0 providers (e.g., Amazon Web Services, Salesforce.com, and Facebook), as well as providing an easy way for users to create their own cloud connectors. In addition, native REST support allows users to publish and consume RESTful services easily and seamlessly using Mule. Finally, AJAX/JavaScript integration enables developers to access enterprise data directly from a browser-based application without requiring heavyweight server-side infrastructure.

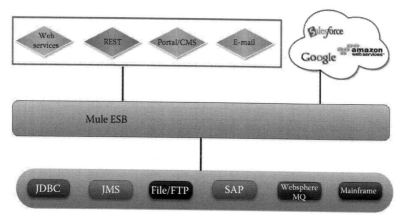

FIGURE 7.16
Mule ESB architecture.

CLOUD APPLIANCES: THE DEPLOYMENT METHOD

Hardware appliances such as web, information, and consumer appliances are becoming tremendously popular across the globe. In the IT world, there are database, network, XML, SOA, and cloud appliances in plenty. In the recent past, cloud integration appliances such as Cast Iron (http://www.castiron.com) are extensively used in applications and data integration across clouds. Appliances are legendary in the IT domain for ensuring high performance and assurance. Due to the surging popularity of virtualization, virtual appliances are now widely available and overwhelmingly used. A virtual appliance is a VM image with a preinstalled and preconfigured application. Deploying the application simply requires copying this VM image to a physical machine, which starts the VM, and performing any required configuration tasks. The cost of installing and configuring the application on the VM is incurred only once, when the appliance is created, and need not be incurred again by users of the appliance. A database appliance is a virtual appliance in which the installed application is a database system. In the future, DBaaS can be provided via such kinds of database appliances. Amazon offers MySQL, Oracle, and Microsoft SQL Server virtual appliances for deployment in its EC2 cloud.

Deployment Challenges

Many issues related to deployment [1] must be addressed before creating a database appliance that can be easily deployed in a cloud and obtaining an easily accessible and usable database instance from this appliance. How to get the best database system performance in this environment is critical. Cloud providers are interested in two related performance objectives: (1) maximizing the utilization of cloud resources and (2) minimizing the resources required to satisfy users' demands. Users are interested in minimizing application response time and maximizing application throughput. Deploying database appliances in a cloud and tuning the database and virtualization parameters to optimize performance introduces some interesting research challenges.

Localization

When we start a VM from a copy of a database appliance, we need to give this new VM and the database system running on it a distinct "identity."

This process is called "localization." For example, we need to give the VM a MAC address, an IP address, and a host name. We also need to adapt the database instance running on this VM to the VM's new identity. For example, some database systems require every database instance to have a unique name, which is sometimes based on the host name or IP address. The VMM and the underlying OS and networking infrastructure may help with issues such as assigning IP addresses, but there is typically little support for localizing a database instance.

Routing

In addition to giving every VM and database instance a distinct identity, we must be able to route application requests to a VM and a database instance. This includes the IP-level routing of packets to the VM; it also includes making sure that database requests are routed to the correct port and not blocked by any firewall, the display is routed back to the client console if needed, I/O requests are routed to the correct virtual storage device if the "compute" machines of the IaaS cloud are different from the storage machines, and so on.

Authentication

The VM must be aware of the credentials of all clients that need to connect to it, independent of where it is run in the cloud.

Cloud computing represents an exciting opportunity to bring on-demand applications to customers in an environment of reduced risk and enhanced reliability. However, it is important to understand that existing applications cannot be unleashed on the cloud as they are. Careful attention to design helps to ensure successful deployment and delivery of applications. In particular, cloud-based applications should be deployed as virtual appliances so that they contain all the components needed to operate, update, and manage the applications.

CLOUD DEPLOYMENT STRATEGY: THE FORMULA

Any visionary idea needs a comprehensive and calculated strategy and a well-planned road map to realize its well-articulated vision [21]. The pulsating and pioneering cloud model is a very recent phenomenon and, hence, a sound strategy must be in place to make the chosen path smooth, risk-free, and devoid of any rough edges. Cloud deployment, being a critical process in any cloud-sponsored transformation and optimization initiative, has to be taken very seriously in order to attain the intended goals. Cloud deployment is a tedious and tough affair; it is beset with a number of tricky concerns and challenges. Feasibility and risk assessment is very much needed before plunging into the cloud deployment process to understand the possible loopholes that must be faced at different levels and layers. Therefore, deployment is a risky as well as rewarding process. This is followed by devising effective mechanisms to combat or mitigate the dangerous and draining effects of any identified and even unidentified risk factors. As a first tangible step, any CSP needs to draw and create a deployment topology, which comes in handy when establishing an implementable and insightful strategy to proceed with the deployment activity.

When organizations move their IT assets to cloud environments (local or remote or both) in order to reap the pronounced advantages of cloud computing, architects and decision makers must consider a number of things for successful cloud adoption. It is all about getting the macro-level picture before deciding on the resources and the subsystems that must be modified and modernized so that they are cloud-ready and can be migrated, deployed, and managed in the chosen cloud environment. Precisely speaking, the people in charge of such a strategic transformation have to first understand (map) the network, classify information assets, identify which deployment models and services align with the company's IT and security strategy, and then vet the solution providers to ensure they can meet the company's particular tactic as well as long-term requirements.

Step 1: Map the Network

This is the critical phase of cloud deployment as network topology includes all the physical and virtual segments that must be migrated so that the most efficient and secure design can be quickly developed and validated. The network-mapping activity comprises not just the mapping of physical network elements but also the identification and classification of all the contributing services, applications, databases, and data flows so that every single component of the network can be properly and precisely mapped and aligned with corporate security policy.

Step 2: Classify Assets

Once the network is properly mapped, data flows must be reviewed to ensure that each of the information assets (source and sink) is properly classified. The International Organization for Standardization (ISO) has come out with an information classification guide (ISO 2701 Information Classification Matrix) that helps immensely in compactly classifying all kinds of information assets. The classification of an asset lists out many precise and decisive details about it, including who owns the asset, who has access to it, and so on. Asset classification is a cornerstone of the information security program and proper implementation of this control surely goes a long way in significantly enhancing an organization's ability to meet its legal and regulatory requirements regarding the safekeeping of consumer data.

Step 3: Map Assets to Cloud Deployment Models

When information assets are being mapped and classified carefully, the bigger roadblock is eliminated. In other words, the accomplished activities clearly help to identify the type of cloud model that is optimally and strategically correct for an organization's short-term as well as long-term needs. The cloud model must be selected based on myriad criteria such as organization, business, technology, operation, and so on. In addition, aspects such as security, compliance, visibility, controllability, and auditability must be weighed before finalizing the cloud deployment model and the particular providers. Table 7.1 provides the security control and compliance model. This table helps to compare cloud deployment models in order to choose the best provider by pinpointing gaps between the services offered and the services desired.

Step 4: Evaluate Potential Cloud Service Models and Providers

This step firms up a flexible and futuristic cloud deployment model and the right providers. The solution architecture and the operational model envisioned in the beginning are the key enablers arriving at the right cloud model. This step involves a number of critical comparisons, verifications, and validations based on SLAs. The vendor lock-in issue must be considered carefully in the beginning stage so that, in the future, if there is any need for migrating data and software from one provider to another, there should not be any major hurdle or hitch. It is also important that a

TABLE 7.1

Identification of Gaps between the Offered and the Desired

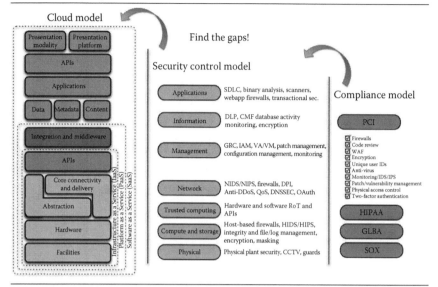

API–Application Programming Interface; CCTV–Closed Circuit Television; CMF–Content Monitoring & Filtering; DDoS–Distributed Denial of Service; DLP–Data Loss Prevention; DNSSEC–The Domain Name System Security Extensions; DPI–Deep Packet Inspection; GLBA–Gramm-Leach-Bliley Act; GRC–Governance, Risk & Compliance; HIDS–Host-based Intrusion Detection System; HIPAA–Health Insurance Portability and Accountability Act; IAM–Identity and Access Management; NIDS–Network Intrusion Detection System; NIPS–Network Intrusion Prevention System; PCI–Payment Card Industry; QoS–Quality of Service; SDLC–Software Development Life Cycle; SOX–Sarbanes-Oxley Act; VA/VM–Vulnerability Assessment/Vulnerability Management; WAF–Web Application Firewall.

financial review of the cloud vendor is conducted prior to deployment as the financial condition of the vendor will be significant at a later point in time. If a provider suddenly goes out of business, then the safety and recoverability of the assets and resources hosted in the respective cloud must be guaranteed. Then the DR factor must be considered so that the goal of business continuity (BC) is ensured. Backing up applications and data in a remote backup cloud is easy and cheap.

Finally, sufficient attention must be given to the security factor. Thus, as it turns out, the deployment strategy being drawn and decided has to consider all kinds of security provisions, measures, and implications at a deeper level. As any security breach by insiders or outsiders can quickly break the hard-earned brand image of CSPs, people at the helm must be stringent and sensitive in incorporating the security risks, threats, and vulnerabilities into the cloud strategy.

THE FUTURE

Cloud computing has created a number of fresh opportunities and possibilities for IT solutions providers. Its impact is exponentially growing across the industry and the market value and mind share are zooming ahead at an astronomical rate. Trendsetting and trailblazing use cases and applications based on the cloud idea are being proposed and publicly presented. There is no doubt in the minds of visionaries and pundits that the cloud is set to become the core of future IT. Not only enterprises, but also the vast and varied embedded space is very enthusiastic and optimistic about cloud infrastructures and cloud-induced deployment and consumption models in creating and sustaining scores of smart environments such as smart homes, offices, hospitals, hotels, and buildings. Not only electronic devices, but also physical objects are being digitally and cognitively empowered to become computational, communicative, connected, analytic, articulative, and sensitive. The stability and success of cloud technologies provides renewed vigor to smart traffic management, supply chain, industry automation, intelligent health care, and smart commerce.

The prevailing trend is that our everyday environments (personal as well as professional) are being stuffed and saturated with a number of disappearing embedded systems such as sensors, actuators, displays, controllers, and robots. Slim and sleek devices are being produced in huge numbers. Device connectivity and integration standards and technologies are emerging to provide extended care, choice, comfort, and convenience to human users. All kinds of events (social, physical, informational, etc.) are being proactively captured, processed, and analyzed thoroughly in real time to extract actionable insights in the form of alerts, tips, trends, patterns, and hidden associations. The resulting intelligence is utilized for intelligent decision making and contemplating appropriate countermeasures. The technology-sponsored convergence of the physical world and cyberspace is gathering momentum. This is the main reason why several multidisciplinary subjects such as AmI, cyber physical systems (CPS), the Internet of Things (IoT), and ubiquitous computing have become the cynosure of many.

Now, every tangible software and hardware component is seamlessly and spontaneously interfaced and integrated with cloud platforms and infrastructures directly or indirectly. Environmental and user data are collectively aggregated and subjected to knowledge extraction and engineering that helps in accurately understanding users' requirements. Clouds are the most appropriate infrastructure for extracting usable and real-time intelligence from data inflows. In short, knowledge engineering, correlation, and corroboration domains will become popular for scientists, scholars, and students. These evolving trends clearly forecast the arrival and acceptance of people, pragmatic, and physical IT.

CONCLUSION

Countless symposiums, workshops, and other confluences are being held these days on cloud computing; debates, discourses, and deliberations are also ongoing as to how cloud computing is going to revolutionize the way we do business. Cloud computing is not exactly a new paradigm; it is the grand result of an amalgamation of several proven technologies. In short, it can be termed as a convergence or cluster of matured and stabilized information technologies. Researchers and practitioners are cooperatively working to make the cloud paradigm pervasive and persuasive. Enabling frameworks, cloud-inspired enterprise-scale architectures, a variety of tool sets and platforms, best practices and strategies, migration and onboarding methodologies, and so on, are being made available in order to take this fast-evolving cloud principle to greater heights.

Deployment models and methods contribute very much to the success of cloud computing. A bevy of deployment scenarios are being explained, deployment strategies are being formulated, and so on. In short, optimized deployment plays a very unique role in shaping the evolution and establishment of clouds and cloud-induced business, operational, aggregation, and consumption models. This chapter is an eye-opener on the relevance of focusing more diligently and decisively on the aspects of cloud deployment.

REFERENCES

1. Henneberger, M., and A. Luhn. 2010. "Community Clouds–Supporting Business Ecosystems with Cloud Computin ," Siemens IT Solutions and Services, http://www.sourcingfocus.com/uploaded/documents/Siemens_Community_Clouds_Whitepaper.pdf.
2. Parameswaran, A. V., and A. Chaddha. 2009. "Cloud Interoperability and Standardization," *SETLabs Briefings* 7 (7): 19–27.
3. Kundra, V. 2011. "Federal Cloud Computing Strategy," U.S. CIO and the Federal CIO Councils, http://www.cio.gov/documents/Federal-Cloud-Computing-Strategy.pdf.

4. SinglePoint Solutions. 2012. "SinglePoint Cloud Service Broker," SinglePoint Solutions, http://singlepoint.ie/sp/solutions/cloud-service-broker.

5. Nair, S. K., P. Pawar, A. Sajjad, M. Kiran, and M. Jiang. 2011. "Requirements and Architecture of a Cloud Broker," Optimis Consortium, http://www.optimis-project .eu/sites/default/files/content-files/document/requirements-and-architecture-cloud-broker_0.pdf.

6. Bohn, R. June 1, 2011. "The Road to Cloud Standards via a Reference Architecture," *MAGIC Meeting*, NCO/NITRD, http://www.ogf.org/SAUCG/materials/2342/The+ Road+to+Cloud+Standards+via+a+Reference+Architecture.pdf.

7. Liu, F., J. Tong, J. Mao, R. Bohn, J. Messina, L. Badger, and D. Leaf. 2011. "NIST Cloud Computing Reference Architecture: Recommendations of the National Institute of Standards and Technology," NIST Special Publication, http://www.nist.gov/customcf/ get_pdf.cfm?pub_id=909505.

8. Louis, A. May 23, 2008. "ESB Topology Alternatives," http://www.infoq.com/articles/ louis-esb-topologies.

9. Nott, C., and M. Stockton. March 15, 2006. "Choose an ESB Topology to Fit Your Business Model," IBM developerWorks, http://www.ibm.com/developerworks/ library/ws-soa-esbtop.

10. MuleSoft. 2012. "Mule ESB," MuleSoft, http://www.mulesoft.com/downloads/ mule-esb.pdf.

11. Imen, F. B. et al. 2010. "ESB Federation for Large-Scale SOA," *SAC'10*, Sierre, Switzerland, March 22–26, 2010, http://www.sti-innsbruck.at/fileadmin/documents/ papers/SAC10-final.pdf.

12. Roy, S. "SOA Implementation," TechTarget Application Development Media, http:// media.techtarget.com/Syndication/STORAGE/Oracle_eGuide_ImplementingSOA .pdf.

13. Paremus Ltd. 2011. "White Papers," Paremus Ltd., http://www.paremus.com/ resources/resources_documents.html.

14. Craggs, S. June 2003. "Best-of-Breed ESBs," Saint Consulting Limited, http://www .sonicsoftware.com/products/whitepapers/docs/best_of_breed_esbs.pdf.

15. Manes, A. T. October 5, 2007. "Enterprise Service Bus: A Definition," Burton Group, Midvale,hUT, http://i.i.com/cnwk.1d/html/itp/burton_ESB.pdf.

16. Andrew W. Mellon Foundation. 2007. "ESB Exploratory Effort Final Report," Andrew W. Mellon Foundation, http://tid.ithaka.org/enterprise-service-bus-project/ esb-narrative-rc-4.pdf.

17. Aboulnaga A. et al. 2009. "Deploying Database Appliances in the Cloud," *Bulletin of the IEEE Computer Society Technical Committee on Data Engineering*, IEEE, http:// sites.computer.org/debull/A09mar/aboulnaga.pdf.

18. Bibles, J. 2011. "Strategies for Secure Cloud Computing: An Introduction to Exploring the Cloud," ComplyGuard Networks, http://www.complyguardnetworks.com/ wp-content/uploads/2011/03/Cloud-Basics.pdf.

19. Marcus, B. 2011. "Cloud First Business Use Case Driven Analysis for IaaS Standards," NIST STDSAHG—003.

20. Keen, M., A. Acharya, S. Bishop, et al. July 2004. "Patterns: Implementing an SOA Using an Enterprise Service Bus," IBM Redbooks, IBM Corporation, http://ck20 .com/MQ/WBIMB/sg246346%20Implementing%20SOA%20using%20ESB.pdf.

21. Aboulnaga, A. et al. 2009. "Deploying Database Appliances in the Cloud," *Bulletin of the IEEE Computer Society Technical Committee on Data Engineering*, IEEE, http:// www.cs.uwaterloo.ca/~kmsalem/pubs/deb09appliance.pdf.

8

Cloud Integration Architecture

INTRODUCTION

The trendsetting cloud paradigm actually represents the cool conglomeration of a number of proven and promising enterprise technologies. Although the cloud idea is not conceptually new, it has caused myriad tectonic shifts for the whole ICT industry. The cloud concepts progressively and perceptibly impact the IT and business domains with respect to several critical aspects. Cloud computing has brought in a series of novelty-packed deployment, delivery, consumption, and pricing models, whereas the service orientation (SO) paradigm prescribes a modular (loosely coupled and highly cohesive) application design mechanism. The noteworthy contribution of the much-discoursed and -deliberated cloud computing paradigm to IT is the fast realization and proliferation of dynamic, converged, adaptive, on-demand, and online computing infrastructure, which is the key requirement for future IT. The delightful distinctions here are that clouds guarantee most of the nonfunctional requirements (QoS attributes) such as availability, high performance, on-demand scalability, elasticity, affordability, global-scale accessibility and usability, and energy efficiency.

Having understood the exceptional properties of cloud infrastructures (hereafter, they will be referred to as just "clouds"), most global enterprises (small, medium, and even large) are steadily moving their IT offerings such as business services and applications, software infrastructure and platform solutions, and IT management systems to clouds. This transition facilitates a higher and deeper reach and richness in application delivery and consumability. Product vendors, having found that the cloud style is a unique proposition and phenomenon, are modifying and moving their platforms, databases, and middleware to clouds to be exposed and delivered as services.

Note: In Chapter 8, the acronym IaaS refers to integration as a service.

Cloud infrastructure providers are establishing advanced cloud centers to host a variety of ICT services and platforms for individuals and companies all over the world. The cloud service providers (CSPs) are quite aggressive in experimenting and embracing cloud ideas and, today, a large number of business and technical services are being loaded in clouds to be delivered to global subscribers over the Internet communication infrastructure. For example, SaaS is a prominent cloud-hosted security service that is subscribed to by a spectrum of users; the users pay for the exact amount or time of use of a particular service. In a nutshell, on-premise and local applications are becoming online, remotely hosted and managed, on-demand, and off-premise applications. With the unprecedented advertisement, articulation, and adoption of cloud concepts, the cloud movement is picking up and peaking as per leading market research reports. Besides modernizing and deploying legacy applications in cloud environments, fresh applications are being implemented and deployed on clouds that are delivered to millions of global users simultaneously and affordably. It is thus clear that a number of strategic and significant things are happening silently and sagaciously in the field of cloud computing.

All these portend and predict a new dimension and direction to the integration scenario. In the past, enterprise data and applications were linked through one or more standards-compliant integration platforms, brokers, and backbones within a corporate intranet. It is noted that B2B integration is facilitated through special data formats, message templates, and networks and even via the Internet. Enterprises consistently expand their operations to different parts of the world as a result of establishing special partnerships with their partners or buying other companies in different geographies for enhancing their product and service portfolios. Business applications are increasingly finding their new residence in clouds. However, most of the confidential and corporate data are still maintained in enterprise (on-premise) servers for security reasons. Thereby, cloud integration challenges and concerns receive the utmost attention today among product vendors, standard agencies and service integrators.

CLOUD INTEGRATION: ORIGIN AND EVOLUTION

The SaaS paradigm is on the fast track due to its innate powers and potential. Executives, entrepreneurs, and end users are ecstatic about the tactical as well as the strategic success of the new SaaS paradigm. A number of positive and progressive developments have started to grip this model. All kinds of IT resources are being readied to be delivered as services. Experts and evangelists are united in their view that the cloud will rock the IT community as the best possible infrastructural solution for effective service deployment, delivery, and management. There are several ways in which clouds can be leveraged for diverse IT problems. Today, there is a small list of services being delivered via clouds; in the future, many more critical and composite applications will be deployed and made available for global users. In short, clouds are set to decimate all kinds of IT inflexibilities and facilitate a variety of beneficial innovations for the IT field.

The Emergence of "IT as a Service"

It is noted that ITaaS is the most recent entrant to the IT landscape; it is an efficient delivery method. With the meteoric and mesmerizing rise of service orientation principles, every single IT element is being viewed and visualized as a service that sets the tone for the service era. These days, systems are engineered as elegant collections of enterprising services. Infrastructures are service-enabled to be actively participative and collaborative. In the same tenor, the much-maligned delivery mechanism has also gone through several spectacular transformations and, today, the whole world has solidly settled for the green and lean paradigm of ITaaS. Clouds are the most value-added and viable infrastructure for effortlessly realizing ITaaS. Another influential and impressive factor is the maturity obtained in the consumption-based metering and billing capability.

Integration as a Service

Integration as a service (IaaS) is a budding and distinctive capability of clouds that helps in fulfilling internal as well as external business integration requirements. Increasingly, business applications are deployed in clouds to reap the manifold business and technical benefits of using clouds. On the other hand, innumerable mission-critical applications and data sources still remain locally stationed and sustained primarily due to the expressed security concerns associated with hosting them in clouds. The question here is how to create seamless data flow between hosted and on-premise applications so that they work together. The IaaS overcomes these challenges by smartly utilizing the time-tested B2B integration technology as the value-added bridge between SaaS solutions and in-house business applications.

The B2B systems are capable of driving this new on-demand integration model because they are traditionally used to automate business processes between manufacturers and their trading partners. This means they provide application-to-application connectivity along with the functionality that is crucial for linking internal and external software securely. Unlike the conventional EAI solutions designed only for internal data sharing, B2B platforms have the ability to encrypt files for safe passage across the public network, manage large data volumes, transfer batch files, convert disparate file formats, and guarantee data delivery across multiple enterprises. The IaaS just imitates this established communication and collaboration model to create reliable and durable linkage for ensuring smooth data passage between traditional and cloud systems over the web infrastructure.

The use of hub-and-spoke (H&S) architecture further simplifies the implementation and avoids placing an excessive processing burden on the customer side. The hub is installed at the SaaS provider's cloud center to do the heavy lifting, such as reformatting of files. A spoke unit at each user site typically acts as a basic data transfer utility. With these pieces in place, SaaS providers can offer integration services under the same subscription/usage-based pricing model as their core offerings. As IT resources are becoming more distributed and decentralized every day, linking and leveraging them for multiple purposes need a multifaceted infrastructure. Clouds, being web-based infrastructures, are the best fit for hosting scores of unified and utility-like platforms to take care of all sorts of brokering needs among connected ICT systems.

APPROACHES FOR CLOUD INTEGRATION

As with any new technology, cloud concepts also suffer from a number of limitations. Cloud technology is being diligently examined for specific situations and scenarios. The prickling and tricky issues in different layers and levels are being vigorously investigated. The overall views are listed here. Loss or lack of the following features deters the massive adoption of cloud technology, especially public clouds:

1. Controllability
2. Visibility and flexibility

3. Security and privacy
4. Dependability
5. Availability
6. Interoperability
7. Standards for seamless cloud service integration, composition, and collaboration

A number of approaches are being investigated for resolving the identified issues and flaws. Private clouds, hybrid clouds and, lately, community clouds are being prescribed as the viable solution for nullifying most of these inefficiencies and deficiencies. As rightly pointed out by someone in his or her weblog, there are miles to traverse before all the originally envisioned and elucidated goals of public clouds are realized. Several companies are currently focusing on this issue. Boomi (http://www.dell .com) is one among them; on its website, there are several well-written white papers elaborating the issues confronted by business executives who are thinking and trying to embrace the public clouds for hosting their customer-facing services and applications.

While cloud applications offer outstanding value in terms of multitenant features and functionalities, they introduce several integration-related challenges. The first issue is that most of the current SaaS applications are point solutions that can service one line of business only. As a result, companies having no means of synchronizing data between multiple lines of businesses are facing serious issues such as lack of data accuracy, inability to make real-time and information-backed decisions, and difficulty in realizing complete business process automation. Real-time sharing of data and functionality becomes difficult in such a heterogeneous environment, whereas in integrated development the task of extraction of actionable insights in time is easier and faster.

Integration Approaches

There are three prominent layers and levels (data, application, and UI) on which the integration process can be initiated and implemented [1]:

1. Data integration: We can reverse engineer the database and the business logic that ties data together; an army of consultants can be employed to do it. However, this process is extremely time consuming and costly. This is not a viable solution in view of the number and

frequency of data integrations needed in a distributed and hybrid world. Further, this approach typically does not work for SaaS applications, for which we have neither the access rights nor the control to manipulate the underlying database. The SaaS providers go to any length to ensure that customer data is secure within the hosted environment. However, transferring data from on-premise systems or applications behind a firewall to SaaS applications hosted outside the client's data center poses new challenges. This is an important change that cannot be sidestepped. It is critical that the integration solution is able to synchronize data bidirectionally from SaaS to on-premise systems and vice versa securely without opening the firewall.

2. API-based integration: This is the approach commonly followed as every enterprise package has its own APIs. Many CSPs have responded to the integration challenge by developing APIs. Unfortunately, accessing and managing data using an API requires a significant amount of coding as well as maintenance due to the need for frequent API modifications. Further, despite the advent of web services, there is little to no standardization or consensus on the structure or format of SaaS APIs. As a result, IT departments of organizations expend a lot of time and resources on developing and maintaining a specific method of communication for the API of each and every SaaS application. Moreover, APIs are rare in proportion to the exploding number of data sources in clouds.

3. Browser-based data integration: Due to the well-known fact that there are more websites without any APIs, browser-based data integration is being viewed as the most practical solution for data integration in the domain of enterprise, Web 1.0, Web 2.0, and cloud servers.

The "Kapow Extraction Browser" (http://www.kapowsoftware.com) is the first web browser to be purposely built for secure and automated data extraction, transformation, integration, and delivery on a massive scale. It brings together the functionality of a presentation browser and that of an extraction browser that automatically and precisely extracts and integrates data from virtually any source on the web, in the cloud, or across an enterprise more quickly, cheaply, and accurately than any other method.

The Kapow Extraction Browser eliminates the need for APIs by leveraging UIs of the applications encountered by it. In the cloud, web-based as it is, all data and business logic is available in the UI, which means we can access and extract any data we need. The Kapow Extraction Browser then automatically transforms the data into meaningful information using business rules, transfers the data to its destination, and integrates it with any existing business systems.

For any relocated application to provide the promised value for businesses and users, the minimum requirement is the interoperability between SaaS applications and on-premise enterprise packages. As SaaS applications were not originally designed keeping in mind the interoperability requirement, the integration process has become a tough assignment. There are other obstructions in the way of smoothly routing messages between on-demand applications and on-premise resources. Message, data, and protocol translations must happen at the end points or at the middleware layer in order to decimate the blockade that inhibits spontaneous sharing and purposeful collaboration among the assorted participants. As applications and data are diverse and distributed, versatile integration technologies and methods are essential for making the integration process smooth. Reflective middleware is an important necessity for generating a real-time and synchronized view of KPIs to brief and benefit executives, decision makers, as well as users. Data integrity, confidentiality, quality, and value need to be carefully maintained as data, services, and applications become increasingly interlinked and saddled to work together.

Pervasive Software, Inc.

Pervasive (http://www.pervasiveintegration.com) uses Pervasive DataCloud as a platform for deploying on-demand integration.

Impacts of the Cloud Paradigm

On the infrastructure front, in the recent past, clouds have entered the scene powerfully and have extended the horizon, access, and boundary of business applications, events, and data. Precisely speaking, increasingly for business, technical, financial, and green reasons, applications and services are being readied for and relocated to highly scalable, affordable, and available clouds.

An immediate motivation is that integration methodologies and middleware solutions have to take the new cloud conundrum very seriously for establishing extended and integrated processes and views. Thus, there is a clarion call for adaptive integration engines that seamlessly and spontaneously connect enterprise and cloud-based applications. Integration is being stretched further to the level of the expanding Internet, and this is really a litmus test for system architects and integrators as days roll by.

The perpetual integration puzzle must be addressed meticulously using out-of-the-box approaches and state-of-the-art products for achieving the originally visualized success of SaaS applications. Interoperability between SaaS and non-SaaS solutions remains the leading demand as integration facilitates the establishment of business-aware and people-centric composite systems. Boundaryless flow of information is necessary for enterprises to strategize effectively to achieve greater successes and value and to deliver on the elusive goal of customer satisfaction. Integration is a big challenge for growing business behemoths, Fortune 500 companies, and system integrators. Now with the availability, affordability, and suitability of cloud-inspired state-of-the-art infrastructures for application deployment and delivery, the scope, size, and scale of business integration is steadily enlarging. However, this beneficial extension has placed worldwide integration architects, specialists, and consultants in deep dilemma and distress as enumerated and enunciated at the beginning of this section.

The Cloud Integration Enigma

As Figure 8.1 indicates, there is a growing array of geographically distributed and divided clouds. Application, service, data, platform, and infrastructure clouds are being set up in several places. There is a new concept of federated clouds that share the distinct capabilities and competencies of distributed clouds to accomplish bigger things. Connectivity and integration among participating clouds are maintained using open and industry-strength standards. The humble and simple beginning of the cloud idea is on a fast track toward the intercloud, or the cloud of clouds.

The IaaS approach is all about the migration of functionality of a typical EAI hub or an ESB into a cloud for smooth data transport between any enterprise and SaaS applications. Users subscribe to IaaS as they would do to any other SaaS application. The cloud middleware is the next logical evolution stage of traditional middleware solutions. In other words, CM is made available as a service. Due to varying integration requirements and

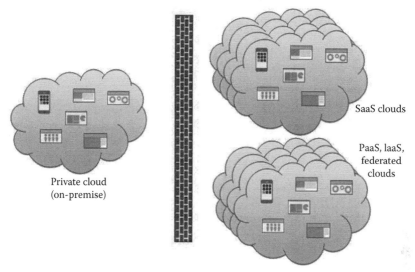

FIGURE 8.1

Connectivity and integration across disparate and distributed clouds.

restrictions, there are a number of middleware technologies and products such as JMS-compliant message queues and integration backbones such as EAI, ESB, EII, and event-processing engines. For the sake of high performance, clusters, fabrics, grids, and federations of hubs, brokers, and buses are being resuscitated and recommended.

For service integration it is ESB all the way, and for data integration there are a few stable approaches such as EII and data composites. Service orchestration and choreography also enable process-level integration. As ESBs are for loosely coupled applications, standards-compliant message oriented middleware and message brokers are used for integrating decoupled applications through message passing and pickup. Events are rapidly becoming the next-generation abstraction and unifying artifact. There are algorithmic event-processing engines that receive a stream of assorted events from distributed sources, process them in real time in a centralized location to extract and figure out the encapsulated knowledge, and accordingly select and activate one or more target applications, resulting in a kind of light connectivity and intelligent integration between source and destination applications. This sort of need-based integration among applications goes a long way in producing people-centric applications. Mashups perform and provide composite services, data, and views. Thus, at every layer or level in the enterprise IT stack, there are competent integration modules and guidelines for emerging and evolving the much-anticipated integration.

With the unprecedented massive adoption of clouds, all these integration software are bound to move to clouds. Amazon Simple Queue Service (SQS) provides a straightforward method for applications to exchange messages using queues in a cloud. The SQS is a classic example for understanding what happens when a well-known on-premise service is recast and repositioned as a cloud service. However, there are some problems with this repositioning. Because SQS replicates messages across multiple queues, it is not guaranteed that an application reading from a queue can see all messages from all queues on a particular read request. Also, SQS does not promise in-order and exactly-once delivery. These simplifications allowed Amazon to make SQS more scalable; but they also mean that developers must use SQS differently compared to an on-premise message-queuing technology.

The unprecedented growth of SaaS means that more and more software components are migrated to reside in off-premise clouds. As widely agreed on, the cloud is the pertinent and perfect infrastructure for hosting, delivering, and managing SaaS applications that are valuable and usable if they have a direct linkage with the corporate data that are typically locked away in various on-site enterprise servers (in cloud parlance, private clouds). So, for cloud applications to offer maximum value to their users, they need to provide a simple mechanism to import or load external data, export or replicate their data for reporting or analysis purposes and, finally, keep their data synchronized with on-premise applications. This mandatory requirement brings out the importance of SaaS integration. Hence, the need for integration between remote clouds with on-premise enterprise systems, in which confidential customer and corporate data are stored for ensuring unbreakable, impeccable, and impenetrable security and privacy, has caught the serious and sincere attention and imagination of product vendors and SaaS providers.

CLOUD INTEGRATION CONCERNS AND CHALLENGES

As per one of David Linthicum's white papers, performing SaaS-to-enterprise integration is really a matter of making informed and intelligent choices. Selection is made mainly on integration approaches to leverage appropriate architectural patterns, location of the integration engine/middleware and, finally, the enabling technology.

For instance, consider a small company that is tied up with the Salesforce .com CRM. The company currently leverages an on-premise custom system that uses an Oracle database to track its inventory and sales. The use of the Salesforce.com system provides the company with significant value in terms of customer and sales management. However, the information that persists within the Salesforce.com system is somewhat redundant with the information stored within the on-premise legacy system (e.g., customer data). Thus, the "as is" state is in a fuzzy state and suffers from all kinds of costly inefficiencies including the need to enter and maintain data in two different locations, which ultimately costs more for the company. Another irritation is the loss of data quality, which is endemic when considering this kind of dual operation. This includes data integrity issues, which are a natural phenomenon when data is being updated using different procedures and there is no active synchronization between the SaaS and on-premise systems.

Once the "to be" state is understood and defined, data synchronization technology is proposed as the best fit between the source system (Salesforce.com) and the target system (the existing legacy system that leverages Oracle). This technology is able to provide automatic mediation of differences between the two systems, including differences in application semantics, security, interfaces, protocols, and native data formats. The end result is that information within the SaaS system and the legacy system is completely and compactly synchronized. In other words, the data entered into the CRM system would also exist in the legacy systems and vice versa along with other operational data such as inventory, items sold, and so on. The "to be" state thereby removes the data quality and integrity issues totally. This directly and indirectly paves the way for saving thousands of dollars per month and for producing a quick ROI from the applied integration technology.

Integration has been a prominent subject of study and research among academic students and scholars for years, as it brings a sense of order to the mess created by heterogeneous compute nodes, network devices, storage servers, and business services. Integration technologies, tools, tips, best practices, guidelines, metrics, patterns, and platforms are varied and vast. Integration is not easy to implement as successful untangling from the knotty situation is riddled with a lot of practical difficulties. The web of application and data silos makes the integration task really difficult and, hence, choosing a best-in-class scheme for flexible and futuristic integration is a frequent demand. First of all, we need to gain insights on the special traits and tenets of SaaS applications in order to arrive at a suitable integration route. The constraining attributes of SaaS applications are as follows:

- Dynamic nature of SaaS interfaces that constantly change
- Dynamic nature of the metadata native to a SaaS provider such as Salesforce.com
- Managing assets that exist outside firewalls
- Massive amounts of information that must move daily between SaaS and on-premise systems and the need to maintain data quality and integrity

As SaaS applications are being deposited in cloud infrastructures vigorously, we need to ponder the obstructions being imposed by clouds and prescribe proven and practical solutions. If we face complications with local integration, then cloud integration, which is of Internet scale, is bound to be more complicated. The most probable reasons for this are as follows:

- Rise of new integration scenarios
- Restricted access
- Dynamic resources
- Performance

Cloud Integration Scenarios

With the emergence of the cloud space, new integration possibilities and opportunities are raising their heads. The CSPs, service developers, application assemblers, and administrators ought to be conversant with cloud-induced novel integration concerns and challenges. Cloud-to-cloud (C2C) and cloud-to-enterprise (C2E) integration styles need to be mandatorily addressed. Before the advent of the cloud model, we were linking local systems together for creating and sustaining integrated applications and views. With the shift to the cloud model in progress, we now have to connect local applications to a cloud and we also have to connect cloud applications with each other, a need that adds new permutations and combinations to the already complex integration channel matrix. It is unlikely that everything will move to a cloud model all at once, so even the simplest scenarios require some form of local/remote integration. It is also likely that we will have applications that never leave the building, due to regulatory constraints such as HIPPA, GLBA, and some general security issues. All this means integration must crisscross firewalls somewhere. We have identified three major integration scenarios, which are discussed in the following subsections. The first two scenarios will become prevalent once there are several commercial clouds and once cloud services become pervasive. Then service integration and composition domains will become important for global computing. Gartner has come out with a note that strongly proclaims there will be more CBS providers across the globe in the future in order to lighten the workloads of cloud consumers in identifying and contracting competent and geographically distributed CSPs.

Integration within a Public Cloud

In this integration scenario, two different applications are hosted in a cloud (Figure 8.2). The role of cloud integration middleware (say, cloud-based ESB or ISB) is to seamlessly enable these applications to talk to each other. A possible subscenario is these applications are owned by two different companies. They may live in a single physical server but run on different VMs.

Homogeneous Clouds

The applications to be integrated are posited in two geographically separated cloud infrastructures. The integration middleware can be in cloud 1 or cloud 2 or in a separate cloud (Figure 8.3).

There is a need for data and protocol transformation and they get done by the ISB. The approach is more or less compatible with the EAI procedure.

Heterogeneous Clouds

One application is in a public cloud and the other application is in a private cloud (Figure 8.4).

FIGURE 8.2
Integration within a public cloud.

FIGURE 8.3
Integration across homogeneous clouds.

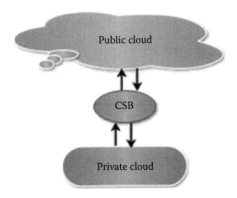

FIGURE 8.4
Integration across heterogeneous clouds.

This is the currently dominating scene for cloud integration. In other words, businesses are subscribing to popular on-demand enterprise packages from established providers such as the CRM of Salesforce.com and Ramco Systems (http://www.ramco.com) and the ERP software of NetSuite (http://www.netsuite.com).

Restricted Access

Access to cloud resources (SaaS, PaaS, and the infrastructures) is definitely more limited than access to local applications. Accessing local applications is quite simple and fast. Embedding integration points in local as well as custom applications is easy. Even with commercial applications, it is always possible to slip in database triggers to raise events and provide hooks for integration access. Applications for cloud deployment should be designed to support integration because there is no longer a low level of access. Enterprises putting their applications in a cloud and subscribers of cloud-based business services depend on the vendor to provide the integration hooks and APIs. For example, the SalesForce.com web services API does not support transactions against multiple records, which means integration code must handle this logic. For PaaS, a platform might support integration for applications on the platform. However, platform-to-platform integration is still an open question. There is an agreement that a limited set of APIs will improve the situation to an extent. But such APIs must be able to handle the integration required. Applications and data can be moved to public clouds, but as a consequence application providers and data owners lose their much-needed visibility, controllability, and flexibility. Most of the CSPs also do not submit their infrastructures to a third-party audit.

Dynamic Resources

Cloud resources are intrinsically virtualized, automated, and service oriented. In other words, everything is expressed and exposed as a service to the outside world for publicly discovering, accessing, and using them for a small fee. Due to the dynamism factor that is sweeping the whole cloud ecosystem, application versioning and platforms are liable to undergo frequent changes. These clearly have an impact on the integration model. That is, in a cloud environment, the tightly coupled integration fails, falls, falters, and fumbles. It is clear that low-level interfaces ought to follow the representational state transfer (REST) route, which is a simple architectural style that subscribes to the standard methods of the ubiquitous HTTP protocol.

Performance

Clouds support application scalability and resource elasticity. However, network distances between elements in a cloud are not under our control. Bandwidth is not a limiting factor in most integration scenarios, although round-trip latency is an issue that cannot be sidestepped. Because of latency aggravation, cloud integration performance is bound to slow down. Thus, cloud-based integration solutions and services need to be chosen carefully.

CLOUD INTEGRATION: METHODOLOGIES AND LIFE CYCLE

Cloud integration has become a strategic advantage for IT departments of all sizes, industries, and geographies. The integration task just gets bigger with the addition of the cloud space, and integration complexity becomes murkier. Hence, it is logical to take the integration middleware to clouds to simplify and streamline the enterprise-to-enterprise (E2E), enterprise-to-cloud (E2C) and cloud-to-cloud (C2C) service integration needs.

Here, we want to walk you through how the cloud paradigm impacts the integration scene, that is, how cloud applications are being integrated with both enterprise as well as other cloud applications. Similarly, the ways in which applications hosted in distributed clouds can find one another and share their functionality is also given its share of attention. We have visualized and written about a few important integration scenarios, wherein cloud-based middleware exceptionally and elegantly contributes to the streamlining of exceedingly complex integration goals. How integration becomes a futuristic cloud-based service is extremely important.

Cloud Integration Methodologies

With the exclusion of custom integration through hand coding, there are three major types of cloud integration:

1. Traditional enterprise integration tools can be empowered with special connectors to access cloud-located applications. This is the most likely approach for IT organizations, which have already invested a lot in integration suites for their application integration needs. With a persistent rise in the necessity of accessing and integrating cloud applications, special drivers, connectors, and adapters are being built and incorporated to existing integration platforms to enable bidirectional connectivity with all participating cloud services. As indicated earlier, there are several popular enterprise integration methods and platforms such as EAI/ESB, which are accordingly empowered, configured, and customized to access and leverage the growing array of cloud applications. For attaining enhanced performance, a variety of integration appliances are available in the market.

2. Traditional enterprise integration tools are hosted in clouds. This approach is similar to the first option except that the integration software suite is now hosted in any third-party cloud infrastructure so that the enterprise need not worry about procuring and managing the hardware or installing the integration software. This is a good fit for IT organizations that outsource integration projects to IT service organizations and systems integrators, who have the

skills and resources to create and deliver integrated systems. The IT divisions of business enterprises need not worry about up-front investment and maintenance of high-end compute machines and integration packages in this approach. Similarly, system integrators can just focus on their core competencies of designing, developing, testing, and deploying integrated systems. It is a good fit for C2C integration but requires a secure virtual private network (VPN) tunnel to access on-premise corporate data. An example of a hosted integration technology is Informatica PowerCenter Cloud Edition on Amazon EC2.

3. The IaaS or on-demand integration offerings are SaaS applications that are designed to deliver the integration service securely over the Internet and are able to integrate cloud applications with on-premise systems. Also, cloud-based applications can be integrated with one another using this service. Even on-premise systems can be integrated with other on-premise applications using this integration service. This approach is a good fit for companies who insist on ease of use, ease of maintenance, quick deployment, and a tight budget. It is appealing to small and mid-sized companies, as well as large enterprises with departmental-level application deployments. It is also a good fit for companies who plan to use their SaaS administrator or business analyst as the primary resource for managing and maintaining their integration efforts. A good example is Informatica On-Demand Integration Services.

In a nutshell, integration requirements can be realized using any one of the following methods and middleware products:

1. Hosted and extended ESB (ISB/cloud integration bus)
2. Online message queues, brokers, and hubs
3. Wizard- and configuration-based integration platforms (niche integration solutions)
4. Integration service portfolio approach
5. Appliance-based integration (stand-alone or hosted integration)

With the emergence and solidification of the cloud space, the integration scope has grown a lot; hence, people are looking for robust and resilient solutions and services that speed up and simplify the whole process of integration.

Characteristics of Cloud Integration Solutions

The key attributes of integration platforms and backbones gleaned and gained from the integration experience are connectivity, semantic mediation, data/message/protocol mediation, data integrity, security, and governance:

- Connectivity refers to the ability of the integration engine to engage both source and target systems using the available native interfaces. This means leveraging the interface outwardly provided by each system, which can vary from standards-based interfaces, such as web services, to older and proprietary interfaces. Systems that are becoming connected are very much responsible for the externalization of correct information and the internalization of information once processed by and received from the integration engine.
- Semantic mediation refers to the ability to account for application semantic differences among the systems being integrated. Semantics refers to how information is understood, interpreted, and represented within information systems. When two different and distributed systems are linked, their semantic differences need to be identified and mapped.
- Data mediation converts data from a source data format to the destination data format. Coupled with semantic mediation, data mediation or data transformation is the process of converting data from the native format of the source system to the data format of the target system. Similarly, messages dispatched from one system to another system must accordingly go through a series of processing steps such as validation, parsing, information extraction, transformation, and enrichment before a decision is made and acted on by the target system to initiate the actions encapsulated in the original message. Similarly, there are several transport and communication protocols that need to be duly and dutifully transformed to empower target applications.
- Data migration is the process of transferring data between storage types, formats, or systems. For example, data warehouses are the main sources for creating actionable insights from data (nonstructured, semistructured, and structured data). The standard steps of BI are data extraction, loading, and transformation.
- Data security is the ability to ensure that information extracted from source systems is securely placed in target systems. The integration

method must leverage the native security systems of the source and target systems, mediate the differences, and provide the ability to transport information safely between connected systems.

- Data integrity means data is complete and consistent. Thus, integrity must be guaranteed when data is mapped and maintained during integration operations, such as data synchronization between on-premise and SaaS-based systems.
- Governance refers to system processes, policies, and technologies that control how a system is accessed and leveraged. Within the integration perspective, governance is all about managing changes to core information resources, including data semantics, structure, and interfaces.

These are the prominent qualities that ought to be carefully and critically analyzed when selecting cloud/SaaS integration providers.

Data Integration Engineering Life Cycle

As business data are still stored and sustained in on-premise servers and storage machines, it is imperative to have a lean data integration life cycle. The pivotal phases, as per David Linthicum, a world-renowned integration expert, are understanding, definition, design, implementation, and testing. The steps are explained as follows:

1. Understanding an existing problem domain means defining the metadata that is native to a source system (say, Salesforce.com) and a target system (say, an on-premise inventory system). By doing this, there is a complete semantic understanding of both source and target systems. If there are more systems for integration, the same practice has to be enacted.
2. Definition refers to the process of taking the information culled during the previous step and defining it at a high level, including what the information represents, its ownership, and its physical attributes. This contributes to a better perspective of the data being dealt with beyond the simple metadata perspective. This ultimately ensures that the integration process proceeds in the right direction.
3. Design the integration solution around the movement of data from one point to another, accounting for the differences in semantics using the underlying data transformation and mediation layer by

mapping one schema from the source to the schema of the target. This defines how the data is to be extracted from one system or systems, transformed to appear native, and updated in the target system or systems. There are visual and simplified data-mapping tools. In addition, there is a need to consider both security and governance concepts within the design of the data integration solution.

4. Implementation refers to actually implementing the data integration solution within the selected technology. This means connecting the source and the target systems, implementing the integration flows as designed in the previous step, and then performing the other steps required for getting the data integration solution up and running.

5. Testing refers to ensuring that the integration solution is properly designed and implemented and that data is synchronized properly between the involved systems. This means looking at known test data within the source system and monitoring how the information flows to the target system. We need to ensure that data mediation mechanisms function correctly. In addition, QoS attributes such as overall performance, durability, security, modifiability, and sustainability of the integrated systems need to be reviewed in order to meet any kind of functional as well as nonfunctional integration needs.

CLOUD INTEGRATION PRODUCTS AND PLATFORMS

Cloud-centric integration solutions are being developed and demonstrated for showcasing their capabilities in integrating enterprise and cloud applications. The integration problem has long been the biggest headache for the IT division of worldwide organizations, due to the heterogeneity and multiplicity-induced complexity of concerned systems. Now with the adoption of the transformative and disruptive paradigm of cloud computing, every ICT product is being service-enabled so that it can be described, discovered, and delivered to users (any personal device) through the open Internet. Along the same lines, standards-compliant, local, and monolithic integration suites are being decomposed and transitioned into autonomous services so that any integration need can be easily, cheaply, and rapidly met. At this point in time, primarily data integration products are highly visible as customer-centric applications hosted in clouds need to interact with enterprise data.

But as days go by, there will be a huge market for application and service integration. Interoperability will become the most fundamental thing. Composition and collaboration will become critical for the mass adoption of clouds, which are being prescribed and proclaimed as the next-generation infrastructure for creating, deploying, managing, and delivering hordes of ambient, artistic, adaptive, and agile services. Cloud interoperability is the prime demand for creating cloud peers, clusters, fabrics, and grids. Realizing federated clouds and the intercloud is the ultimate goal so that the envisioned goals of IoS are completely met (Figure 8.5).

Jitterbit

Force.com is a highly visible and valuable PaaS, enabling developers to create, deploy, and deliver any kind of on-demand business application. Salesforce.com is an on-demand CRM suite that runs on this cloud-based Force.com platform. However, in order to take advantage of this break-through in cloud technology, there is a need for a flexible and robust integration solution to synchronize Salesforce.com with any on-demand or on-premise enterprise applications, databases, and legacy systems. Integration is a daunting task that requires too much time, investment, and expertise.

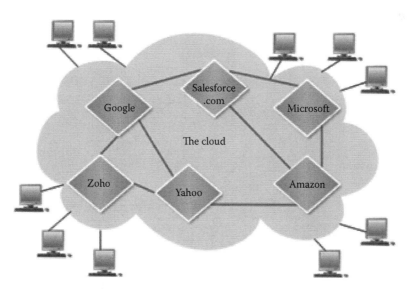

FIGURE 8.5
Smooth and spontaneous cloud interaction using open clouds.

Jitterbit (http://www.jitterbit.com) can be used in the stand-alone mode or synchronized with existing EAI infrastructures. This enables developers to create new integration projects or consume and modify existing ones to enable them to be seamlessly integrated. The Jitterbit solution facilitates integration among corporate data, enterprise applications, web services, XML data sources, legacy systems, and simple and complex flat files. Apart from a scalable and secure server, Jitterbit provides a powerful visual environment to help developers quickly design and develop integration projects. Jitterbit comprises two major components:

1. The Jitterbit Integration Environment is an intuitive point-and-click graphical UI that enables developers to configure, test, deploy, and manage integration projects on the Jitterbit server.
2. The Jitterbit Integration Server is a powerful and scalable runtime engine that executes integration processes.

Figure 8.6 vividly illustrates how Jitterbit links a number of functional and vertical enterprise systems with on-demand applications.

Boomi Software

Boomi Software has come out with an exciting and elegant SaaS integration product. It promises to fulfill the vision of "integration on demand." Although the popularity of SaaS applications is rising dramatically, the integration task is the Achilles' heel of the SaaS mechanism. The integration

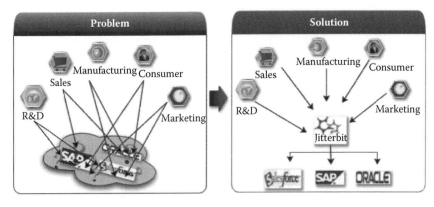

FIGURE 8.6
Linkage of on-premise and cloud-hosted applications using Jitterbit.

challenge is real and is unanimously cited by industry analysts as the leading barrier to the overwhelming adoption of SaaS.

Boomi AtomSphere is an integration service that is completely on-demand and connects any combination of cloud and on-premise applications without requiring the installation and maintenance of expensive and complicated software packages or appliances. Anyone can securely build, deploy, and manage simple-to-complex integration processes using only a web browser. Whether connecting SaaS applications found in various lines of the same business or integrating SaaS applications across geographic boundaries, AtomSphere is a centralized platform that can perform both and deliver integration with all the benefits one would expect from a SaaS solution. As new applications are connected to AtomSphere, they instantly become accessible to the entire community with no adapters being purchased or upgrades installed. Boomi offers the "pure SaaS" integration solution that helps to quickly develop and make connections between diverse and distributed applications.

Bungee Connect

For professional developers, Bungee Connect (http://www.bungeeconnect .com) enables cloud computing by offering an application development and deployment platform that guarantees highly interactive applications integrating multiple data sources and facilitating instant deployment. Built specifically for cloud development, Bungee Connect reduces the efforts required to integrate (mashup) multiple web services into a single application remarkably. Bungee automates the development of rich UI and eases the difficulty of deployment to multiple web browsers. Bungee Connect leverages the cloud paradigm to bring additional value to organizations committed to building applications for the cloud.

OpSource Connect

OpSource Connect expands the functionality of the OpSource Services Bus by providing the pertinent infrastructure for two-way web services interactions, allowing customers to consume and publish applications across a common web services infrastructure. OpSource Connect also addresses the problems of SaaS integration by unifying different SaaS applications in a cloud as well as legacy applications running behind corporate firewalls. By providing a platform to drive web services adoption and integration, OpSource (http://www.opsource.net) helps its customers to craft new SaaS applications to retain them.

SnapLogic

SnapLogic (http://www.snaplogic.com) is a capable, clean, and uncluttered solution for data integration that can be deployed in an enterprise as well as a cloud landscape. The free community edition can be used for the most common point-to-point data integration tasks, giving a huge productivity boost beyond custom code. SnapLogic professional edition is a seamless upgrade that extends the power of this solution with production-management, increased-capacity, and multiuser features at a price that does not drain the budget, which is shrinking owing to the economic slump across the globe. Even the much-expected "V" mode recovery did not happen, and there is a view among economists that the world economy is tending to the "W" mode double-dip recession and recovery. With the shoestring budgetary allocation, the appropriation of SaaS solutions is on the climb. The web, SaaS applications repertoire, mobile devices, and cloud platforms have profoundly changed the requirements imposed on data integration technology.

Windows Azure AppFabric

Windows Azure AppFabric provides prebuilt, higher-level middleware services that raise the level of abstraction and reduce the complexity of cloud development. These services are open and interoperable across languages (.NET, Java, Ruby, PHP, etc.) and give developers a powerful prebuilt "class library" for developing next-generation cloud applications. Developers can use stand-alone services or combine services to provide a composite solution. A few important modules must be discussed here: "Service bus" provides secure messaging and connectivity capabilities that enable the building of distributed and disconnected applications in a cloud, as well as hybrid applications across on-premise systems and the cloud. It enables the use of various communication and messaging protocols and patterns and saves the developer worries regarding delivery assurance, reliable messaging, and scale. BizTalk Server is Microsoft's integration and connectivity server solution. BizTalk Server 2010 provides a solution that allows organizations to more easily connect disparate systems. It includes over 25 multiplatform adapters and a robust messaging infrastructure; BizTalk Server provides connectivity between core systems both inside and outside an organization. In addition to this integration functionality, BizTalk provides strong, durable messaging; a rules engine; EDI connectivity; BAM, RFID capabilities, and IBM host/mainframe connectivity.

The Pervasive DataCloud platform (Figure 8.7) is a unique multitenant platform. It provides dynamic "compute capacity in the sky" for deploying on-demand integration and other data-centric applications. Pervasive DataCloud provides the following capabilities:

1. IaaS for both hosted and on-premises applications and data sources
2. Packaged turnkey integration
3. Integration that supports every integration scenario
4. Connectivity to hundreds of different applications and data sources

Bluewolf

Bluewolf (http://www.bluewolf.com) has announced its expanded IaaS solution; it is the first to offer ongoing support for integration projects guaranteeing successful integration between diverse SaaS solutions, such as Salesforce .com, BigMachines, eAutomate, OpenAir, and back-office systems (e.g., Oracle, SAP, Great Plains, SQL Service, and MySQL). The solution is called the Integrator; it includes proactive monitoring and consulting services to ensure

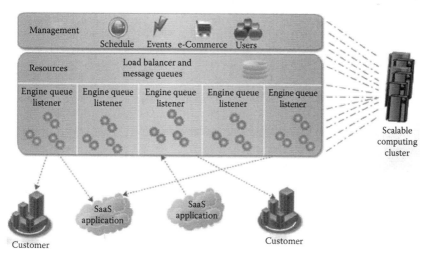

FIGURE 8.7
Pervasive Integrator connecting different resources.

integration success. With remote monitoring of integration jobs using a dashboard included as part of the Integrator solution, Bluewolf proactively alerts its customers of any issues with integration and helps to solve them quickly.

Oracle SOA Suite 11g

Oracle SOA Suite 11g, a prominent member of the Oracle Fusion Middleware (OFM) family, is a powerful suite of products facilitating the painless integration of on-premise applications with applications in cloud environments. At a high level, integrating with an SaaS application might appear just any other integration project. However, SaaS solutions have additional complexity with respect to security and scalability and endless customization options that require proper tooling for the integration to be effective. Brian Sipsey of M&S Consulting has authored a descriptive white paper titled "Bridging the Gap between Internal Systems and Salesforce.com Using Oracle SOA Suite 11g" (http://www.oracle.com). The paper explains how this SOA suite helps to integrate local applications with Salesforce.com applications.

Magic Software's iBOLT

The essence of CRM is to give a 360° view of customer information, and this need simply cannot be achieved without all-round integration. Any CRM solution is supposed to enhance overall customer experience by providing a holistic approach to the business process surrounding that customer. Hence, there is a need for integration with a BPM solution that enhances and extends the capabilities of the CRM solution.

Using iBOLT's (http://www.magicsoftware.com) code-free and hardware-free business integration suite, customer A can supply its sales representatives with a 360° view of customer-facing processes through a comprehensive work environment that enables straightforward work processes. Such a solution enables business analysts and architects to achieve full integration for their users in a matter of days with no need for complex coding and no need to install additional hardware into the server room. Data from the accounting system is easily retrieved and services exposed in the legacy environment are wrapped as services that enable synchronous, easy-to-use integration between Salesforce.com and customer A's internal systems. These services are then easily reused for any future interface with practically zero overhead.

WebSpan

WebSpan (http://www.hubspan.com/webspan) is a single-instance multitenant SaaS integration platform that enables organizations to more cost-effectively integrate their business processes and data flow across internal and external communities. In essence, WebSpan represents a "middleware-in-the-cloud" solution that eliminates the need for costly hardware, software, and staff resources to deploy, maintain, and support cross-entity integration. Companies can utilize the WebSpan integration platform to connect their applications, customers, or suppliers regardless of data models or existing EAI technologies without worrying about compromising the security of systems. WebSpan provides a single and transparent connection to link enterprises internally or externally without forcing them to change their systems or processes as it mediates various data formats, validation methodologies, security protocols, routing systems, and business rules.

Adeptia Salesforce Integration Accelerator

Adeptia Salesforce Integration Accelerator is designed to speed up the implementation of a solution for connecting Salesforce.com with the internal applications and systems of an organization (Figure 8.8). It consists of Adeptia Server (http://www.adeptia.com) process flow templates and services that can be easily and quickly configured to create data flows between Salesforce.com and internal applications and databases.

Online MQ

Online MQ (http://www.onlinemq.com) is an Internet-based queuing system. It is a complete and secure online messaging solution for sending

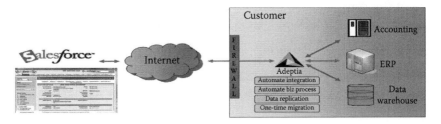

FIGURE 8.8
The linkage between on-premise and off-premise applications.

and receiving messages over any network. It is a cloud message-queuing service. In the integration space, messaging middleware as a service is the emerging trend.

CloudMQ

CloudMQ leverages the power of Amazon Cloud to provide enterprise-grade message-queuing capabilities on demand. Messaging allows breaking up a single process into several parts, which are then executed asynchronously. The parts can be executed within different threads, or even on different machines, and they communicate with each other by exchanging messages. The messaging framework (http://www.cloudmq .com) guarantees that messages get delivered to the right recipient and the appropriate thread wakes up when a message arrives.

Linxter

Linxter is a cloud messaging framework for connecting all kinds of applications, devices, and systems. Linxter is a behind-the-scenes, message-oriented, cloud-based middleware technology. It smoothly automates the complex tasks that developers find difficult when creating communication-based products and services. With the Internet-enablement of personal devices, clothing, toasters, and so on, Linxter's solution (http://linxter.com) securely, easily, and dynamically connects all of them to consolidate, expose, and share their distinct capabilities. Systems connected to the Internet can connect to each other through Linxter's dynamic communication channels. These channels move data between any number of end points and the data can be reconfigured on the fly, simplifying the creation of communication-based products and services.

Online MQ, CloudMQ, and Linxter solutions all accomplish message-based application and service integration. As these suites are hosted in clouds, messaging is provided as a service to hundreds of distributed and enterprise applications using the much-maligned multitenancy property. "Messaging middleware as a service" (MMaaS) is the grand derivative of the SaaS paradigm. It is noted that message-based integration is gaining a lot of ground. Messages are the unifying factor. Data, documents, and events are the prime constituents of messages. In other words, IaaS is being accomplished in the form of "messaging as a service." Data-mapping tools come in handy when linking different applications and databases that are separated by syntactic, structural, symbiotic, schematic, and seman-tic deviations. Templates are another powerful mechanism to minimize integration complexity. A large constellation of protocols and adaptors ensuring seamless connectivity and subsequently fulfilling the integration needs of systems are taking off successfully and swiftly. The integration riddle has become such a big proposition and problem due to the well-known fact that SaaS solutions were designed, developed, and deployed without taking the integration requirements into consideration.

Microsoft ISB

Azure (http://www.microsoft.com/azure/servicebus.mspx) is the cloud OS from Microsoft. It makes developing, depositing, and delivering web and Microsoft Windows applications on cloud centers easier and cost-effective. Developers' productivity shoots up drastically, customers' preferences are looked after, and the enterprise goal of more with less is achieved with Azure. Azure is being projected as the comprehensive yet compact cloud framework that comprises a wide variety of enabling tools for a slew of tasks and a growing library of cloud services. Microsoft ISB is the middle-ware suite for enabling services and applications to link with each other and produce sophisticated applications.

CLOUD INTEGRATION APPLIANCES

Appliances are suitable for high-performance requirements. Clouds too have followed the same path and, as a result, cloud appliances (also known as cloud in a box) are available today. In this section, we discuss a popular integration appliance.

Cast Iron Systems, Inc.

This is quite different from the schemes mentioned in the previous sections. Appliances with relevant software etched inside are being established as a high-performance and hardware-centric solution for several emerging IT needs. Frequently, we read or hear about a variety of integration appli-ances considering the complexities of connectivity, transformation, rout-ing, mediation, and governance for streamlining and simplifying business integration. Even the total cloud infrastructure comprising prefabricated software modules can be produced as an appliance. This facilitates the quicker and easier building of private clouds. Further, the appliance solution is being taken to clouds in order to provide appliance functionality and features as a service. "Appliance as a service" is a major trend sweeping the CSP industry these days.

Cast Iron Systems, Inc., provides preconfigured solutions for every leading enterprise and on-demand application today (http://www.ibm.com). These solutions, built using Cast Iron product offerings, offer out-of-the-box connectivity to specific applications and template integration processes (TIPs) for most of the common integration scenarios. These templates provide a question and answer–based wizard that walks users through a common integration scenario. For example, a TIP might ask all the information needed to transform an opportunity in a CRM system into an order in an ERP system. Hundreds of TIPs are included with a Cast Iron Cloud integration purchase and each one can be customized further to meet individual needs. These cloud integration products reduce the skill levels needed to implement integrations and provide a way to ensure that best practices are followed.

Cast Iron solutions enable customers to rapidly complete application-specific integrations using a "configuration, not the most pervasive coding" approach. Using a preconfigured template, rather than starting from scratch with complex software tools and writing lots of code, enterprises can complete business-critical projects in days rather than months. Cast Iron Cloud integration has everything that is needed to support integrations in a hybrid world in a single integration platform, including data migration capability, process integration capability, and even UI mashups. Connectors, transformations, workflow, management functions, event capture, and event reporting all come in a form that can be run wherever they are needed and completely deployed from a cloud based on the requirements of participating applications.

The Cast Iron Cloud integration solution is a single product with three different deployment options. These cloud integration products can be deployed as an IaaS offering in the cloud or on a VM or as a hardware appliance in an on-premise or managed data center. Deployments can move from one location to another as needed without requiring any redevelopment. The result of this transportability is that one can design an application just once and run it anywhere. If an on-premise application is moved to run on a cloud infrastructure, the cloud integration products can move along with it, from an on-premise virtualized or appliance version to cloud-based deployment. As IBM has bought Cast Iron Systems, Inc., more precise details on the capabilities and competencies of the appliance approach for SaaS integration can be found in IBM's website.

CLOUD INTEROPERATION METHODS

Cloud interoperability is one of the dominant issues hovering over the cloud landscape and professionals are inspired to investigate and install a number of novel solutions to meet this perpetual need, that is, next-generation SOCAs or CBSAs can be realized only if diverse resources on distributed and heterogeneous cloud environments are discovered, picked up and packed dynamically. Similarly, data to be used are also being spread out in multiple clouds across cities, counties, countries, and continents. Thus, it is obvious that clouds need to dynamically and seamlessly interoperate to perceive and perform new tasks. Standardization is one of the overwhelmingly accepted and adopted mechanisms that support distributed computing. Every new CSP has its own mechanism of how a user or cloud application interacts with his or her cloud leading to cloud API propagation. This kills the cloud ecosystem by limiting cloud choice because of vendor lock-in, portability issues, and the inability to use cloud services provided by multiple vendors including the inability to use an organization's own existing data center resources seamlessly. Business applications and data remain in cloud silos.

Unified Cloud Interface/Cloud Broker

The CSPs have formed a consortium (the Cloud Computing Interoperability Forum [CCIF]) to collectively address the problem of cloud interoperability and standardization. The purpose of CCIF is to discuss the issues associated with cloud interoperability and standardization and come up with a common interface. This is a layer of indirection that precisely abstracts all sorts of differences in participating cloud systems. In other words, this layer is all about unifying various cloud APIs exposed by CSPs and abstracting them behind an open and standardized cloud interface. This unified interface is touted as the cloud broker, which is being positioned as the flexible and futuristic solution for enabling seamless and spontaneous interactions among remote and heterogeneous cloud platforms, services, identities, data, applications, and networks. Having a common set of cloud definitions is an important factor that enables vendors to exchange management information between distant cloud providers (CSPs).

Enterprise Cloud Orchestration Platform

The current trend is to express and expose everything as a service. There are myriad cloud services and applications being deployed and delivered through distributed cloud platforms and infrastructures. Hence, the ensuing era is correctly described as the era of federated clouds; the ultimate vision today is to realize the intercloud. All these clouds are full of applications and services. It will not be possible to use them without some type of orchestration. Figure 8.9 illustrates how a client can consume the services offered by more than one CSP using an orchestration layer.

Different CSPs can register the cloud services offered by them with the orchestration layer. The orchestration layer can then dynamically select and bind to services according to criteria/algorithms that determine the best cloud service for a particular job based on factors such as highest performance, lowest cost, or some other requirement specified by the client. The orchestration layer interacts with the cloud services offered by different vendors through different APIs, whereas clients use only a single API offered by the orchestration layer. Figure 8.9 shows an example of how

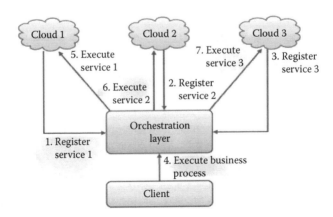

FIGURE 8.9
Cloud service orchestration.

a client request for executing a business process (or workflow) is satisfied by the orchestration layer by invoking a sequence of three different services provided by three different CSPs.

Thus, the cloud ecosystem is expanding with new unification, simplification, composition, decision-enabling, and collaboration platforms, brokers, configuration databases, management consoles, policy bases/rule-books, knowledge repositories, and so on entering the scene. Empowering clouds to talk to each other is the ultimate mission for cloud enthusiasts, evangelists, and exponents. There are more relevant details on this aspect in the study by Parameswaran and Chaddha [5].

Peer-to-Peer Approach for Cloud Integration

A prominent pattern for integration today is one in which ESB/integration middleware hosted within an enterprise (on-premise system) integrates on-premise applications with cloud-based applications. Another emerging pattern is the concept of IaaS in which the integration infrastructure is hosted within the cloud. Applications that expose web services interfaces can be easily integrated using this approach, which also provides the benefits of easy SaaS-to-SaaS integration.

The inherent limitations and problems of traditional on-premise integration and SaaS integration approaches can be overcome using a hybrid of the two based on a peer-to-peer (p2p) ESB platform. This p2p approach of the hybrid model provides the benefits of centralized control while maintaining the inherent efficiency of p2p architectures. Data sources can now be accessed flexibly via web services or via messaging and other APIs. Separate peer servers for SaaS and PaaS clouds ensure that applications within a given cloud are efficiently integrated since there is no need for integration data to leave the cloud. The in-built messaging and queuing capability of the platform ensures that there is global data-flow and event-flow visibility across the entire network including all SaaS applications and applications hosted in the PaaS frameworks. Efficient p2p communications ensure seamless, real-time, flexible integration with no bottlenecks. The platform blends cloud-based integration with general business-process integration since cloud-based applications can now be integrated easily with on-premise applications.

Figure 8.10 illustrates how the hybrid and p2p integration service bus involves both cloud and enterprise users. Management of the distributed bus is fully centralized and control information flows to a central server

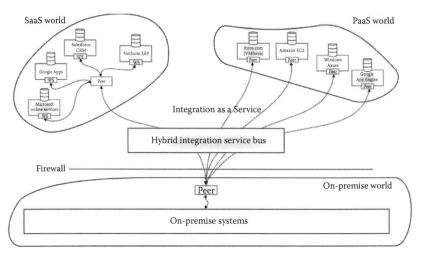

FIGURE 8.10
Involving cloud users via p2p hybrid integration. WS = web services.

hosted within the enterprise, whereas data flows directly between peers. The platform thus incorporates all the administrative benefits of a central-broker architecture while preventing the inefficiencies of the hub from becoming a data bottleneck.

Benefits of Hybrid and p2p Cloud-Based ESB Architecture

A cloud-based ESB is a general-purpose infrastructure platform that lets developers and business analysts create, deploy, manage, and change processes across the private/public cloud; it has the following benefits:

- Distributed and event-enabled architecture
- Flexibility via service-enabled processes
- Support for enterprise standards
- Fault tolerance, reliability, and scalability
- Security in distributed environments
- Develop once and deploy anywhere application architecture
- On-the-fly process changes

With these distinct benefits, a cloud-based ESB allows enterprises to quickly respond to changes and integrate operations efficiently across the cloud regardless of platform, language, database, or application [8].

CLOUD INTEGRATION SERVICES

We have seen state-of-the-art cloud-based data integration platforms for real-time data sharing among enterprise information systems and cloud applications. Another fast-emerging option is to link enterprise and cloud systems through messaging. This has forced vendors and service organizations to take MOM to an all-powerful cloud. Going forward, there are coordinated and calculated efforts for taking the standards-compatible ESB to clouds in order to guarantee message enrichment, mediation, and content- and context-based message routing. Thus, both loosely coupled and decoupled cloud services and applications will soon become a reality with the increase in maturity and durability of message-centric and cloud-based service bus suites. We can still visualize the deployment of CEP engines in clouds in order to capture and capitalize streams of events from diverse sources in different formats and forms in order to infer existing and emerging situations precisely and concisely. Further, all kinds of risks, threats, vulnerabilities, fresh opportunities, possibilities, trends, tips, associations, patterns, and other tactical as well as strategic insights can be deduced quickly and acted upon confidently.

In a highly interoperable environment, seamless and spontaneous composition and collaboration happens in order to dynamically create sophisticated services. Context-aware applications covering all the key constituents and participants (self-, surroundings-, and situation-aware devices such as sensors, stickers, and tags; activation and actuation devices; controllers; media players; utensils; consumer electronics; information appliances; etc.) of a particular environment (home, hotel, hospital, office, station, stadium, etc.) can be built and sustained with enterprise systems, integration middleware, cloud services, and knowledge engines. Fresh endeavors are afoot to achieve service composition in a cloud ecosystem. Existing frameworks such as SCA are being revitalized so that they fit cloud environments. Composite applications, services, data, views, and processes are becoming cloud centric and they can be hosted in order to build next-generation SOCAs. It is noted that SaaS integration is an essential prerequisite for creating flexible and futuristic systems.

Informatica On-Demand

Informatica (http://www.informaticaondemand.com) offers a set of innovative on-demand data integration solutions called Informatica On-Demand services. This is a cluster of easy-to-use SaaS offerings, which facilitate integration of data in SaaS applications securely across the Internet with data in on-premise applications. The Informatica On-Demand service is a subscription-based integration service that provides all relevant features and functions using an on-demand or an as-a-service delivery model. This means the integration service is remotely hosted, thereby providing the benefit of not having to purchase or host the software. There are a few key benefits to leveraging this maturing technology:

- Rapid development and deployment with zero maintenance of the integration technology
- Automatically upgraded and continuously enhanced by vendors
- Proven SaaS integration solutions, such as integration with Salesforce .com, meaning that required connections and metadata understanding are provided
- Proven data transfer and translation technology, meaning that core integration services such as connectivity and semantic mediation are built into the technology

Informatica On-Demand follows the unique approach of moving its industry-leading PowerCenter data integration platform to the hosted model and then configuring it to be a true multitenant solution. This means when developing new features or enhancements, they are immediately made available to all customers of Informatica transparently without requiring any complex software upgrade or additional fee. Fixing, patching, versioning, and so on, are taken care of by providers at no cost to subscribers. Still, the SLAs and OLAs are being fully met. In addition, in a multitenant architecture bandwidth and scalability are shared resources; hence, meeting different capacity demands is smooth and simple.

Business-to-Business Integration Services

Business-to-business integration (B2Bi) is a mainstream activity for connecting geographically distributed businesses for purposeful and mutually beneficial cooperation. Product vendors have come out with competent B2B hubs and suites for enabling smooth data sharing in a standards-compliant manner among participating enterprises. Now, with the surging popularity of clouds, there are serious and sincere efforts to posit these products in clouds in order to deliver B2Bi as a service with very less investment and maintenance costs. The cloud concept and ideals lay a strong and stimulating foundation for cost-effective, highly available, and highly scalable B2Bi.

There are several proven integration solutions in the expanding B2Bi space that can be captured and capitalized for achieving quicker success, better return, and enhanced value in the evolving IaaS landscape. The B2Bi systems are good candidates for IaaS as they are traditionally used to automate business processes among manufacturers and their external trading and channel partners such as retail, distributor, ware-housing, transport, and inventory systems. This means they provide application-to-application (A2A) connectivity along with functionality, which is crucial to linking internal and external software seamlessly. In other words, in ensuring secure data exchange across corporate firewalls without any semantic ambiguity or syntactic differences, the B2Bi back-bone is the key mediator. Unlike pure EAI solutions designed only for internal data sharing, B2Bi platforms have the ability to encrypt files for safe passage across the public network; manage large volumes of data; transfer batch files; convert disparate file formats; and guarantee data accuracy, integrity, confidentiality, and delivery. These abilities not only ensure smooth communication between manufacturers and their exter-nal suppliers or customers but also enable reliable interchange between hosted and installed applications.

The IaaS model also leverages the adapter libraries developed by B2Bi vendors to provide rapid integration with various business systems. Because the B2Bi partners have the necessary expertise and experience, they can supply prebuilt connectors to major ERP, CRM, SCM, and other packaged business applications as well as legacy systems from AS400 to MVS and mainframes. The use of an H&S centralized architecture fur-ther simplifies the implementation and provides good control and grip on system management; finally, it avoids placing an excessive processing bur-den on the customer side. The hub is installed at the SaaS provider's cloud center to perform heavy lifting such as reformatting of files. A spoke unit, typically consisting of a small downloadable Java client, is then deployed at each user site to handle basic tasks such as data transfer. This also elimi-nates the need for an expensive server-based solution and performing data mapping and other tasks at the customer location. As the Internet is the principal communication infrastructure, enterprises can leverage cloud-based integration services to be in sync with their partners across conti-nents to facilitate smart and systematic collaboration.

Cloud-Based Enterprise Mashup Integration Services for B2B Scenarios

There is a growing need for infrequent, situational, and ad hoc B2B applications [7], which are desired and dictated by the majority of business end users. Enterprise mashup and lightweight composition approaches and tools are promising methods that empower end users to develop or assemble aligned and aware composite services in order to overcome the "long-tail" dilemma. Currently available solutions that support B2B collaboration focus on the automation of long-term business relationships. However, such solutions fail to provide their users with intuitive ways to modify or extend them according to ad hoc or situational needs. Conventional methods of development of such applications consume a lot of time and effort due to long development cycles.

Particularly in the area of applications that support B2B collaboration, current offerings are characterized by high richness but low reach, similar to B2B hubs that focus on many features that enable EDI among large industry players. Individuals and small- and medium-scale vendors do not find any distinct value in such high-end B2B solutions.

On the other extreme, there are solutions with high reach but low richness such as websites, portals, and e-mails applications. A lack of standardization and formularization makes these solutions totally inappropriate for next-generation B2Bi needs. Out-of-the-box development approaches are hence demanded to suppress and surmount these hurdles and hitches so that even nontechnical business users can jump into the development process in order to address the long-tail syndrome, realize cost-effectiveness and efficiency gains, and overcome the traditional constrictions between IT department and business units.

Enterprise mashups, a kind of new-generation web-based applications, seem to adequately fulfill the varied and vast requirements of end users and foster the goals of the end-user development (EUD) field. To shorten the traditional time-consuming development process, these new breeds of applications are developed by nonprofessional programmers often in an informal, iterative, and collaborative manner by locating and assembling existing and third-party building blocks through permutations and combinations.

It is noted that SOA is presented as a potent solution for resolving organizational integration dilemmas. The ESBs are used to integrate a variety of services within an SOA-driven company. However, most ESBs are not designated for cross-organizational collaboration and, therefore, problems arise when aiming for extended enterprise collaboration. The SOA simplifies and streamlines integration of new and third-party services. End users usually find it difficult to realize their preferred and prescribed integration scenarios. This leads to, besides high costs for integration projects, unwanted inflexibility because integration projects typically last long. As the market is consumer centric, timely responses to impending requirements are mandated.

Another challenge in B2Bi is the ownership of and responsibility for processes. In many interorganizational settings, business processes are only sparsely structured and formalized, that is, they are loosely coupled and/or based on ad hoc cooperation. Interorganizational collaborations generally involve several participants. More participants mean more diversity and complicity. Also, the participants may act according to their own roles, controls, and priorities. Historically, the focus of collaboration was on purposeful participation within teams, which were managed according to a set of rules previously agreed upon.

Now, in supporting supplier and partner coinnovation and customer cocreation, the focus is veering toward collaboration, which must involve a range of participants who are influenced yet restricted by multiple domains of control and disparate processes and practices. This represents the game-changing shift from static B2B approaches to dynamic B2Bi, which can adaptively act and react to any unexpected disruptions, allow rapid configuration and customization, and manage and moderate the rising complexity through the use of end-to-end business processes.

Both EDI translators and managed file transfer (MFT) have long histories, whereas B2B gateways emerged during the last decade and quickly enlarged their presence and practical responsibilities. However, most of the available solutions aim at supporting medium-scale to large-scale companies as their development life cycles and costs are on the higher side. The high cost makes such solutions unaffordable and unattractive to smaller organizations. Consequently, these offerings are not suitable for short-term collaborations, which need to be set up in an ad hoc manner. Thus, the emergence of infrastructure and platform clouds sends a positive signal to individuals, innovators, and small businesses to jump on the B2Bi bandwagon to enjoy large benefits at a very cheap rate.

Enterprise Mashup Platforms and Tools

Mashups are the adept combination of different and distributed resources including content, data, service, and application components. Resources represent the basic building blocks for constructing and manipulating mashups. Resources can be accessed through APIs, which encapsulate the resources and describe the interface through which they are made available to authorized applications. Widgets or gadgets primarily put a face to the underlying resources by providing a graphical or iconic representation and piping the data received from assorted resources. Piping usually includes operators such as aggregation, merging, and filtering. A mashup platform is a web-based tool that allows the creation of sophisticated mashups by piping resources into gadgets and wiring the gadgets together to create enterprise-class mashups.

Enterprise mashups, which are enterprise-scale mashups, are very advantageous and gorgeous especially in B2Bi scenes. Mashups can resolve many of the intrinsic disadvantages and deficiencies of B2B hubs such as lower reach due to hardwired connections. Mashups enable EUD and lightweight connections of systems. They can also help in adding richness to existing lightweight solutions such as websites and portals by adding a certain level of formalization and standardization. Mashups ease the mixing and transformation of various sources of information internally and from business partners. The growing complexity of B2B operations is often attributed to heterogeneous systems and platforms. The tedious integration process and the perpetual requirements for software support and sustenance form a major hindrance to the target of achieving dynamic B2Bi, especially for small and medium enterprises.

The mashup integration services are implemented as a prototype in the FAST project. The layers of the prototype are illustrated in Figure 8.11, which describes how these services work together. The authors of this framework have given an outlook on the technical realization of the services using cloud infrastructures and services [7].

The prototype architecture in Figure 8.11 shows the services and their relation to each other. Core services are shown within the box in the middle. The external services shown under the box are attached via APIs to allow the use of third-party offerings to reap their functionality. Users access the services through a mashup platform of their choice. The mashup platforms are connected via APIs to the mashup integration services.

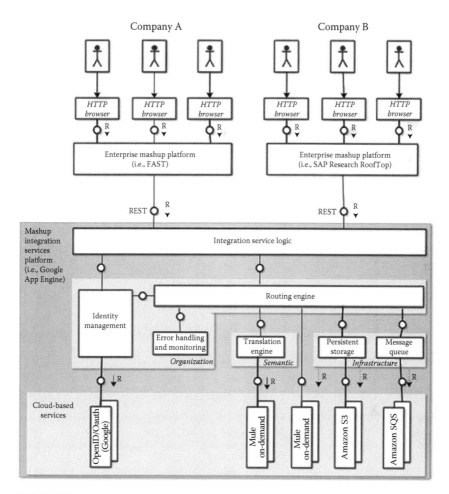

FIGURE 8.11
Cloud-based enterprise mashup integration platform architecture.

To use the services, users have to identify themselves against the user-access control service. This service is connected to a user management service, which controls the users and their settings. The user management service is connected via an API to allow the use of external services, for example, a corporate user database. All data coming from users go through a translation engine that unifies the data objects and protocols, so that different mashup platforms can be integrated. The translation engine has an interface that allows connections to other external translation engines, which adds support for additional protocol and data standards. The translated data is forwarded to the routing engine, which is the core of mashup integration services. The routing engine processes the inputs received from the mashup platforms and forwards them to the right recipient. The routing is based on rules, which can be configured through an API.

To simplify this, a gadget can be provided to the end user. The routing engine is also connected to a message queue via an API. Thus, different message queues are attachable. The message queue is responsible for storing and forwarding the messages controlled by the routing engine. Beneath the message queue, a persistent storage, also connected via an API to allow exchangeability, is available to store large data. The error-handling and -monitoring service allows tracking the message flow to detect errors and collect statistical data. The mashup integration service is hosted as a cloud-based service. Also, other cloud services are made available to provide the functionality required by the integration service. In this way, the mashup integration service can reuse and leverage existing cloud services to speed up the implementation.

Message Queue

The message queue is realized by using Amazon's SQS. The SQS is a web service that provides a queue for messages and stores them until they can be processed. The mashup integration services, especially the routing engine, can put messages into the queue and recall them when they are needed.

Persistent Storage

Amazon Simple Storage Service (S3) is a web service. The routing engine can use this service to store large files.

Translation Engine

This is primarily focused on translating different protocols such as REST or SOAP services.

Interaction between Mashup Services

Figure 8.11 describes the process of messages being delivered and handled by the mashup integration services platform. The precondition for this process is that a user must have already established a route to a recipient. After receiving a message from an enterprise mashup tool via an API, the integration services first check the access rights of the message sender against an external service. An incoming message is processed only if the message sender is authorized, that is, if he or she has the right credentials to deliver the message to the recipient and use the mashup integration services. If he or she is not properly authorized, processing stops and an error message is created and logged. The error log message is written to a log file, which can reside on Amazon's S3. If the message is accepted, it is put in the message queue in Amazon's SQS service. If required, the message is translated into another format, which can be done by an external cloud-based service. After this, the services begin trying to deliver the message to the recipient. Evaluation of recipients of a message is based on rules stored in the routing engine, which are previously configured by a user. Finally, the successful delivery of the message can be logged or an error message appears.

Thus, it is very clear that next-generation services with the massive adoption of clouds will be extremely people centric, composite, and collaborative. Newer service platforms are being built every day to deploy these specialized and sophisticated services in next-generation clouds.

A FRAMEWORK OF SENSOR-CLOUD INTEGRATION

In the past few years, wireless sensor networks (WSNs) have been gaining significant traction because of their potential for enabling very intimate solutions in areas such as smart homes, industrial automation, environmental monitoring, transportation, health care, and vineyard management. If we add a collection of sensor-derived data to various web-based social networks or virtual communities, blogs, and so on, then fabulous transitions will occur in and around us. With the faster adoption of micro- and nanotechnologies, everyday items are becoming digitally empowered and smart in their outlook, operations, and offerings. Thus, the impending goal is to seamlessly link digitalized materials and objects in our environment, including frequently used and handled devices such as consumer electronics; kitchen utensils and containers; household instruments and items; and portable, nomadic, and mobile gadgets and gizmos, with remote cloud-based applications via federated messaging middleware. In other words, cyber systems are being inundated with streams of data and messages from different and distributed physical elements and entities.

Such an extreme and deep connectivity and collaboration will pump up and sustain cool, charismatic, and catalytic situation-aware applications. Clouds have emerged as the centralized, compact, and capable IT infrastructure to deliver people-centric and context-aware services to users with all the desired qualities embedded in them. This long-term vision demands comprehensive connectivity between clouds and these disposable and minuscule systems.

In this section, we discuss a robust and resilient framework that facilitates the integration of sensor networks to clouds [4]. But there are many challenges in realizing this framework. The authors of this framework propose a publish-subscribe (pub-sub)-based model, which simplifies the integration of sensor networks with cloud-based and community-centric applications. Also, there is a need to internetwork CSPs in case of any violations of SLAs with users.

A virtual community consisting of a team of researchers has come together to solve a complex problem and they need huge data storage, computing, and security capabilities. For example, this team is working on the outbreak of a new virus strain in a population. They have deployed biosensors on a patient's body to monitor his or her condition continuously and use this data in large and multi-dimensional simulations to track the origin and spread of the infection as well as study virus mutation and possible cures. This might require large computational resources and a versatile platform for sharing data and results that are not immediately available to the team.

Here, researchers need to register their interest to obtain details of the state of various patients (their blood pressure, temperature, pulse rate, etc.) from the biosensors for large-scale parallel analysis and to share this information with each other to find actionable insights to the problem. So, the sensor data obtained needs to be aggregated, processed, and disseminated based on the subscriptions. On the other hand, as sensor data require much computational power and huge storage capabilities, a single CSP may not be able to handle this requirement. This demands a dynamic collaboration among CSPs. Thus, the formation of virtual organizations (VOs) with cloud integration methods is gaining importance.

Traditional high performance computing (HPC) approaches such as the sensor-grid model can be used in this particular case, although setting up the appropriate infrastructure to deploy and scale the infrastructure quickly is not easy in such an environment. Current CSPs unfortunately do not address this issue of integrating sensor networks with cloud applications. To integrate sensor networks with cloud applications, the authors have proposed a content-based pub-sub model. A pub-sub system encapsulates and transitions sensor data into events and provides the services of event publication and subscription for asynchronous data exchange among system entities. MQTT-S is an open, topic-based pub-sub protocol that hides the topology of the sensor network and allows data to be delivered based on interest rather than individual device addresses. It allows transparent data exchange between WSNs and traditional networks and even between different WSNs.

In this framework, similar to MQTT-S, all the system's complexities reside on the broker's side. But this framework differs from MQTT-S in one aspect: It uses a content-based pub-sub broker rather than the topic-based method. When an event is published, it gets transmitted from a publisher to one or more subscribers without the publisher doing anything to take the message to any specific subscriber. Matching is done by the pub-sub broker outside the WSN environment. In a content-based pub-sub system, sensor data has to be augmented with metadata to identify different data fields. For example, the metadata of a sensor value (also event) can be body temperature, blood pressure, and so on.

To deliver published sensor data (events) to subscribers, an efficient and scalable event-matching algorithm is required by the pub-sub broker. This event-matching algorithm targets a range of predicate cases suitable to various application scenarios and has to be highly efficient and scalable when the number of predicates increases sharply. In this framework (Figure 8.12), sensor data are coming through gateways to a pub-sub broker that is required to deliver information to the consumers of SaaS applications as the entire network is dynamic. On the WSN side, sensor or actuator (SA) devices may change their network addresses at any time. It is quite likely for wireless links to fail. Further, SA nodes can also fail at any time and it is expected that, instead of being repaired, they will be replaced by new ones. Besides, different SaaS applications can be hosted and run on any machine anywhere on the cloud. In such situations, the conventional approach of using a network address as the means of communication between SA devices

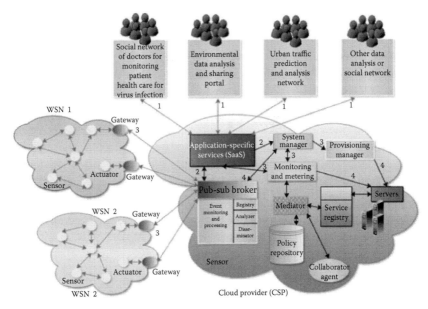

FIGURE 8.12

Framework architecture of sensor-cloud integration.

and applications is fraught with problems because of their dynamic and temporal nature.

Several SaaS applications may have an interest in the same sensor data but for different purposes. In this case, the SA nodes would need to manage and maintain communication with multiple applications in parallel. This might tax the limited capabilities of the simple and low-cost SA devices. So, a pub-sub broker is needed and is located on the cloud side because of its higher performance in terms of bandwidth and capabilities. It has four components, which are described in the following subsections.

Stream Monitoring and Processing Component

The sensor stream comes in different forms. In some cases it is raw data that must be captured, filtered, and analyzed on the fly, and in other cases it is stored or cached data. The style of computation required depends on the nature of the streams. So the stream monitoring and processing component (SMPC) running on a cloud monitors event streams and invokes the correct analysis method. Depending on data rates and the amount of processing required, SMPC manages parallel execution framework on clouds.

Registry Component

Different SaaS applications register to the pub-sub broker for various sensor data required by the community user. For each application, a registry component (RC) stores user subscriptions of that particular application and the sensor data types (temperature, light, pressure, etc.) in which the application is interested in. Also, it sends all user subscriptions along with the application ID to the disseminator component (DC) for event delivery.

Analyzer Component

When sensor data or events come to the pub-sub broker, the analyzer component (AC) determines the applications to which they belong and whether they need periodic or emergency delivery. The events are then passed to the DC, which delivers them to the appropriate users through SaaS applications.

The DC

Each SaaS application disseminates sensor data or events to subscribed users using an event-matching algorithm. It utilizes the cloud's parallel execution framework for faster delivery.

The workflow of pub-sub components in the framework is as follows: Users register their information to get a subscription to various SaaS applications, which transfer all the information to the pub-sub broker registry. When sensor data reaches the system from the gateways, the event monitoring and processing component or SMPC in the pub-sub broker determines whether the just received data need to be processed, stored for a while, or delivered immediately. If sensor data needs periodic and emergency delivery, the analyzer determines to which SaaS applications the events belong and then passes the events to the disseminator along with the application IDs. The disseminator, using the event-matching algorithm, finds appropriate subscribers for each application and delivers the events for use.

Besides the pub-sub broker, the authors propose the inclusion of three other components, mediator, policy repository (PR), and collaborator agent (CA), along with components such as system manager, provisioning manager, monitoring and metering agent, and service registry in the sensor-cloud framework to enable VO-based dynamic collaboration of primary CSPs with other CSPs in case of any SLA violations. These three components collectively act as a gateway for a given CSP in the creation of a new VO.

Mediator

The (resource) mediator is a policy-driven entity within a VO, which ensures that the participating entities are able to adapt to changing circumstances and achieve their objectives in a dynamic and uncertain environment. Once a VO is established, the mediator decides which resources of collaborating CSPs must be used, controls how this decision is made, and determines which policies should be used. When performing automated collaboration, the mediator will also direct any decision making during negotiations, policy management, and scheduling. A mediator holds the initial policies for VO creation and works in conjunction with its local CA to discover external resources and to negotiate with other CSPs.

The PR

The PR virtualizes all the policies within a VO. It includes mediator policies and VO creation policies along with any policies for resources delegated to the VO as a result of a collaborating arrangement. These policies form a set of rules to administer, manage, and control access to VO resources. They provide a way of managing the components when using complicated technologies.

The CA

The CA is a policy-driven resource discovery module for VO creation and it is used as a conduit by the mediator to exchange policy and resource information with other CSPs. It is used by a primary CSP to discover the (external) resources of collaborating CSPs, as well as to let them know about local policies and service requirements prior to the commencement of actual negotiation by the mediator.

In conclusion, to deliver published sensor data or events to appropriate users of cloud applications, an efficient and scalable event-matching algorithm called "statistical group index matching (SGIM)" is leveraged. The authors also evaluated the algorithm's performance and compared it with existing algorithms in a cloud-based ubiquitous health-care application scenario. The authors clearly enunciate that this algorithm in sync with the foundational and fruitful cloud framework enables sensor-cloud connectivity to utilize sensor data for various community-centric sensing and responsive applications on the cloud. It can be seen that the computational tools needed to launch this exploration is more appropriately built from the data center cloud computing model than traditional HPC approaches or grid approaches. Based on this creative work, it is possible for many to visualize new-generation cloud-sensor platforms and applications.

CONCLUSION

The SaaS in sync with cloud computing brings in strategic shifts for businesses as well as IT industries. Increasingly, SaaS applications are being hosted in cloud infrastructures and the open Internet is becoming the primary communication infrastructure. These combinations of game-changing concepts and infrastructures are a blessing especially now that the world is going through an economic slump and instability. The goal of "more with less" is being met with the maturity and stability of the freshly plucked and published advancements emanating out of the cloud technology landscape. Applications are studiously and strategically being moved to clouds and are being exposed as services. In other words, service delivery happens over the Internet to user agents and human beings. Service consumption occurs through a host of browsers (desktop as well as mobile), specific client-side applications, contact and call centers, special instruments put up at public places, and so on.

The unprecedented adoption of cloud technology instigates and instills a number of innovations; already there is a lot of buzz on newer exposition, consumability, modifiability, and accessibility models. Ubiquity and utility will soon become common connotations. Value-added business transformation and optimization along with on-demand IT will be the ultimate output. In the midst of all this enthusiasm and optimism, there are some restricting factors that need to be precisely factored out and comprehensively resolved in order to create an extended ecosystem for intelligent collaboration. Integration is one such issue and hence a number of approaches are being articulated by professionals. Product vendors and consulting and service organizations are mulling over and coming out with integration platforms, patterns, processes, and best practices. There are generic as well as specific (niche) solutions. Pure SaaS middleware as well as stand-alone middleware solutions are being studied and prescribed based on the "as-is" situation and the "to-be" aspiration. Business and technical cases of cloud middleware suites are steadily evolving and expanding; the realization of Internet-scale ESB is being touted the next big thing in the exotic and exciting cloud space. In this chapter, we elaborated upon the need for an on-demand, adaptive, and converging integration backbone that streamlines and simplifies integration among cloud, enterprise, and people environments.

REFERENCES

1. Linthicum, D. S. 2009. *Data Services—The Right Way to Integrate Data for Application Integration.* David S. Linthicum, LLC. http://www.informatica.com/downloads/7041_datasvcs_linthicum_wp_web.pdf.
2. June 2011. *Collaborative Data Integration: Self-Service Bridges the Gap between the Business and IT.* Informatica. http://www.informatica.com/downloads/7066_INFA_Bus_IT_Collab_wp_web.pdf.
3. October 2010. *The Power of the Platform: The Informatica Platform Fuels the Data-Driven Enterprise.* Informatica. http://www.informatica.com/Images/09107_6959-power-of-the-platform.pdf.
4. Hassan, M. M., B. Song, and E.-N. Huh. 2009. "A Framework of Sensor-Cloud Integration Opportunities and Challenges." In *Proceedings of the 3rd International Conference on Ubiquitous Information Management and Communication*, New York: ACM, 618–626. http://dl.acm.org/citation.cfm?id=1516350.
5. 2010. *Rethinking Data Integration in the Cloud: A Revolutionary Approach.* Kapow Software.
6. *Hubspan Business Integration Platform.* Hubspan. http://hubspansitefiles.s3.amazonaws.com/wp-content/uploads/2009/08/hubspan-integration-platform.pdf.
7. Siebeck, R. G. et al. 2009. "Cloud-Based Enterprise Mashup Integration Services for B2B Scenarios," MEM2009 Workshop, Spain.
8. 2010. *Cloud-Based Integration and SOA Architecture: The Benefits of a Peer-to-Peer Approach.* Fiorano Software Ltd. http://www.fiorano.com.
9. Thor, A. and E. Rahm. April 21, 2011. *CloudFuice: A Flexible Cloud-Based Data Integration System.* http://dbs.uni-leipzig.de/file/CloudFuice_techreport.pdf.

9

Cloud Management Architecture

INTRODUCTION

The success of applications solely determines the business value of IT; hence, the effective development, deployment, management, and enhancement of applications are the highest priorities of IT. Further, application performance, availability, scalability, and security are paramount to continue adding to the value of IT. A number of technology-sponsored augmentations, accelerations, and automations are taking place in the IT field. The SOA is one such tidal and tectonic shift that simplifies and streamlines application design and development. Software is built using a dynamic collection of services. Incorporation of service characteristics such as discoverability, reusability, and composability in software came as a big relief to the software engineering community.

Now with the arrival of clouds, there is an unprecedented transition on the service-enablement front. The SOA paradigm introduced software services; with clouds it is possible to have network-accessible hardware services. In other words, every IT resource (virtual and physical IT modules) can be expressed and exposed as a service. The service view has significantly reduced IT complexity (design, development, articulation, management and, finally, use) through the logical separation of interface and implementation. As a result, all kinds of technological heterogeneities are wiped out in one stroke. The restraining and constricting dependencies of software vanish and, thereby, a series of incisive and incredible innovations in the form of service patterns, platforms, practices, prescriptions, and processes flourish in an open and uncontaminated environment. A stream of novel service providers have cropped up across industry segments with the overwhelming adoption and adaption of the venerable service idea.

Clouds are the converged, dynamic, and adaptive infrastructure for next-generation service building, delivery, and consumption. The seamless and spontaneous interrelationships between service and cloud concepts portend better and brighter days for enterprise IT. As expected, most enterprises rely on a mix of physical and virtual servers for hosting their IT applications, services, and data. Besides enterprise-owned clouds, third-party public clouds are also coming up in different parts of the world. As widely known, there are diverse service deployment and delivery models. In addition to these models, purpose-specific cloud environments are being studied and established. All these developments urgently and uniquely demand a stringent and smart cloud management solution for cloud environments. Cloud management involves cloud application, platform, and infrastructure management activities. System infrastructures, application infrastructures, and applications need to be effectively managed to reap all the envisaged benefits of cloud computing. Cloud management is not a simple affair, as a cloud, being a dynamic and heterogeneous environment, is very difficult to manage. Policy-based automation of cloud management responsibilities is gaining much traction.

The path-breaking cloud paradigm has brought an arsenal of noteworthy improvements and improvisations to business enterprises. The IT departments could cut down costs, improve their service delivery level sharply, and achieve business agility. All these improvements are possible through the smart and shared utilization of IT resources across multiple applications and workloads. The cloud idea has brought a series of newer business models, including a promising and potential delivery mechanism. The IT resource utilization has gone up drastically as the adoption of cloud concepts and IT operations are becoming highly flexible.

The cloud space is being positioned as the next-generation service environment to host, manage, deliver, and maintain a variety of IT resources ranging from software to hardware modules. Virtualization, being the key driver for the raging cloud model, facilitates in realizing and retaining virtual IT resources. Thus, apart from the physical entities, virtual elements abound in any decent cloud environment. Due to the continued outpouring of cloud-inspired and novelty-packed solutions, services, and processes, the cloud landscape is fast expanding. Also, the cloud ecosystem is being continuously strengthened with the recent incorporation of cloud brokers, procurers, auditors, governors, and so on, apart from cloud consumers and providers. With the direct fallout of these multidimensional advancements in the cloud field, management complexity is bound to raise its ugly head. In this chapter, we discuss cloud management trends, challenges, standards, technology solutions, and best practices.

CLOUD SERVICE MANAGEMENT

Service science is in the growth trajectory [2]. Aspects such as service engineering, management, governance, delivery, and support are going through a number of metamorphic and mesmerizing changes due to the introduction of cloud computing. The processes and metrics surrounding such services are accordingly getting enhanced. The cloud saga is all set to change the landscape for service consumers, service providers, and the businesses that rely on them. Cloud technology is evolving quickly to deliver pervasive and people-centric services in a secure and reliable fashion. Service value chain management in any cloud enterprise deals with performance issues, consumability, reliability, and scalability of cloud-based services. When there is seamless convergence of service science and cloud infrastructures, the end result is better customer service and improved productivity. Whether it is facilitated through CSPs, managed service providers (MSPs), internal IT departments, or some combination of all or any of these, service consumers need an effective mechanism to contract and modify services and measure their quality, performance, availability, consumption, and costs. Someone within the organization still needs to own the service and ensure that it meets business requirements. Further, IT executives must have deep visibility into what is happening inside the cloud or inside any other provider environments in order to quickly anticipate and resolve issues. Without this sort of sophistication, cloud-provided services expose businesses and their customers to a high degree of risk.

Why Do Cloud Resources Need to Be Managed?

Cloud computing has grown in popularity and become the model of choice for many application and infrastructure services. Applications and services are not tethered to their hardware resources and are usable in an on-demand manner in a cloud environment. Businesses are expectantly embracing and exploiting the family of established cloud services to bring forth disruptive, business-centric IT models and solutions in order to reach out to more people, collaborate on a global scale, reduce operational cost, and grow their bottom lines. In a traditional enterprise environment, IT centralizes procurement, license management, user administration, and security of all applications and infrastructures on behalf of the organization. But the cloud theme is much more accommodative of both centralized and distributed computing styles. In other words, a cloud can be formed through the federation of distributed and decentralized IT resources. The visibility level comes down and, hence, controllability becomes a major issue. This makes it challenging for IT departments to ensure uniform compliance with security and audit requirements, consolidate license management, and ensure a high quality of service and support for their users. The challenges faced are varied; the discovery, deployment, delivery, and management aspects become particularly tough. Therefore, cloud applications need to have the innate capability of adaptation.

Applications being deployed in cloud environments need to be monitored and managed automatically through an autonomy manager module. As a physical machine is segmented into a number of virtual machines, application deployment, administration, security, and governance have to be dynamically accomplished through advanced software solutions.

- Adaptive application monitoring: Cloud applications can now be spread across multiple VMs running on different hardware resources. Also, there are different types of applications, including legacy, packaged, third-party, and homegrown ones, in clouds. This heterogeneity- and multiplicity-induced complexity makes it more intricate to keep track of and monitor cloud applications. Hence, locating and monitoring applications assumes a greater significance in clouds.
- Application SLA guarantee: Measurement precedes management. In a dynamic environment, the service level of applications keeps changing and hence arriving at an accurate measurement is a tough affair. For example, in order to guarantee that an order management application is performing 10,000 orders per minute in a cloud environment, there must be adaptive instrumentation within each VM instance in which the application resides.
- Application change management: Configuration and change management is a difficult process due to the diversity and dynamic nature of cloud resources. Consider this example: To deploy a new secure socket layer (SSL) certificate to web servers, administrators first need to determine which web servers need the new certificate. Due to the employability of different web servers in a cloud setup, the update process is not uniform and is hence a time-consuming and error-prone process.

Increasingly in IT environments, all kinds of automation and adaptation happen through well-intended and defined policies. Policies are the viable and valuable knowledge base empowering applications and machines to work independently without any formal interpretation, instruction, and intervention by human beings. In other words, IT resources need to have the ability to read, understand, and act on policies in time. Business and system events occur in large numbers and emanate from different and distributed sources. In short, cloud infrastructures have to respond insightfully to all kinds of events such as alerts, deficiencies, disturbances, degrades, and insinuations. Consider this example: If a fan in a server fails or a VM needs to be moved to an alternate server, the cloud infrastructure needs to be made aware of this need. It must be able to sense the rise in temperature and apply the right and relevant policies that kick off the migration process smoothly before any irretrievable and irreparable damage occurs.

IT Service Management

As mentioned in the previous section, in the cloud era everything is viewed as an approachable, autidable, and active service. Therefore, the best practices and prescriptions of IT service management (ITSM) can be appropriately refined to elegantly fit the evolving needs of cloud service management (CSM). It is noted that ITSM is mainly concerned with delivering and supporting IT services that are appropriate to the business requirements of an organization [6]. The ITSM is process oriented as opposed to IT management, which is more technology oriented. Due to its process-oriented nature, ITSM shares commonalities with the process improvement frameworks such as total quality management (TQM), Six Sigma, BPM, and capability maturity model integration (CMMI). The key concerns for managers regarding IT services are increasing demands for better returns from IT investments, regulatory requirements for IT control, optimization of costs, and the ability to assess performance against standards.

In order to provide these requirements, ITSM has to have a common vocabulary, a set of management principles, and an approach to ensure the proliferation of best-in-class, portable, and resilient ITSM platforms. Factually, ITIL v2 typically reflects the process-based view of ITSM, whereas the new ITIL v3 focuses on the larger view of the entire life cycle of IT services. The ITSM part of ITIL v2 is divided into two parts: (1) service support and (2) service delivery. In addition, ITIL outlines other operational guidance aspects including ICT infrastructure management, security management, the business perspective, application management, software asset management, and plans to implement service management. However, ITIL v3 has a

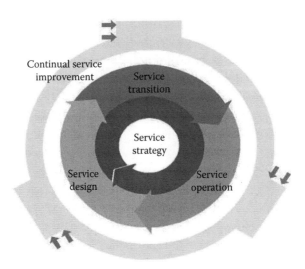

FIGURE 9.1
The ITIL life cycle core stages.

life cycle perspective (Figure 9.1) including service strategy, service design, service transition, service operation, and continual service improvement.

In the service strategy life cycle phase, a number of strategic decisions toward developing a service are made, that is, decisions such as which service should be provided for which customer or what kind of new services a company has to build and supply. In the service design life cycle phase, the trend is to design new services or to design changes in existing services to increase their quality. The processes necessary to transport services from the service design phase to operation are provided by the service transition phase. Within the service operation phase, services run to produce added value for customers. This life cycle phase provides a bevy of processes such as incident management or a process for handling service requests. There is a special life cycle phase that deals with the continuous improvement of services. This phase is responsible for increasing the efficiency of the services provided. Table 9.1 shows which life cycle is primarily responsible for which processes.

Service Assets and Configuration Management

This is one of the processes associated with service transition. A configurable item (CI) is an asset, a service component, or some other item that is under the control of configuration management. All along ITIL, the configuration management process is very effective in keeping track of physical

TABLE 9.1

Service Management Life Cycle Phases [6]

Life Cycle	Processes
Service strategy	Service strategy process, service portfolio management, demand management, and financial management
Service design	Service level management, service catalog management, availability management, information security management, supplier management, capacity management, and IT service continuity management
Service transition	Change management, service asset and configuration management, release and deployment management, knowledge management, transition planning and support, service validation, and testing and evaluation
Service operation	Incident management, problem management, event management, request fulfilment, and access management
Continual service improvement	Seven-step improvement process, service reporting, and service measuring

servers and infrastructure. However, one of the basic attributes of cloud computing is that it supports dynamic infrastructure, which means that the underlying infrastructure in the data center must dynamically cater to changing loads. The much-dissected, discussed, and discoursed virtualization technology facilitates the running of multiple VMs on a single physical server, and these VMs can be started and shut down on-demand. Such unprecedented flexibility and extensibility makes things worse. It is a major challenge to CSPs to flawlessly and fabulously track virtual servers and, hence, there is a demand for highly competent, compact, and catalytic cloud management platforms to effectively manage and govern VMs.

Service Catalog Management and Request Fulfillment

The ITIL itself is designed to be dynamic to provide services on-demand using a well-maintained service catalog. However, for large organizations, the originally designed and developed services are fairly static. Most of the day-to-day needs of users are satisfied with service requests that are actually small changes (low risk, frequently occurring, low cost, etc.). However, service organizations have not fully adopted an automated process to provision new services using a catalog. Clouds are the next-generation service deployment, delivery, and management infrastructure, and there are expectations that service organizations will provide larger service offerings such as a packaged application or a VM as a service.

Financial Management

Financial management is one of the aspects of the service strategy to calculate the return on investment (RoI) of providing services. However, often services are delivered on a fixed-price model, that is, services are measured and charged over a period of time by predicting service levels and number of users. Organizations need to move to the pricing model based on use or subscription. One of the key functionalities of the cloud is to perform complete metering and charging of services that are delivered.

If the goals of self-servicing, flexible access to IT resources, and tighter alignment with business expectations are to be met, then the adoption of cloud computing is inevitable. The paradigm may start small, but it is destined to grow fast to support and sustain mission-critical workloads over time. Whether embarking on the wholesale transformation of IT or on a measured and stepwise approach, forward-thinking IT groups need to craft their plans with the end goals in mind. Some choose to begin with a small pilot project, whereas others jump into architecting the end solution straightaway. However, it has to be noted that architecture and design must deliver against business needs and IT efficiency goals in the years to come.

In cloud environments, it is paramount that services are able to connect and communicate securely with internal IT services and other public services. Service value chain management mandates that resource use and consumption is monitored and managed to support strategically sound decisions. By understanding exactly who is using a service, along with when and how the service is being used, service providers can determine the intrinsic value that the service provides to a business. The IT department can also use this information to compute the RoI and TCO for its cloud initiatives and related services.

CHALLENGES INVOLVED IN CSM

With the cloud idea fast materializing, everything (resource and activity) turns out to be a cool service to be found, bound, and leveraged for bigger and better things. Also, the number of services being deployed and designated for public consumption is steadily growing. Considering this intimidating trend, product vendors have charted out a long-term plan for competent cloud service management solutions. In this section, we dig deeper into the challenges associated with CSM.

A Sample Scenario

To fully comprehend the necessity of holistically managing cloud centers, we can consider the following scenario: An office worker in a remote branch reports a slow application. There could be one or more causes for the slowing down of an application. Is the application really overloading the host, or is the database server not responding fast enough? Is there another application on the same server that is competing for system resources? Is the storage network between the database server and the storage all right? Are the supporting network infrastructure services such as the domain naming service (DNS) servers functioning properly? Did someone recently make a change to network devices, applications, or databases? Is the virtualization server in the process of moving the virtual host containing the application or the database server from one physical machine to another? Are there known unpatched security vulnerabilities in the server? If the application slowdown is caused by one or more security vulnerabilities, the questions to be asked are how did they get into the network, who is the attacker, and who else is affected? Is another user downloading a large file or watching streaming media that is clogging up a shared router interface? The challenge lies in rapidly identifying the exact reason for the sudden slowdown and taking corresponding countermeasures to maintain the agreed on service levels.

Complications of Cloud Centers

With the adoption of cloud technologies, existing data centers get consolidated, optimized, and transformed into lean, adaptive, and dynamic cloud centers. Corporate mergers, acquisitions, and application-specific requirements force IT organizations to own heterogeneous IT centers to run a growing portfolio of web, e-mail, and packaged applications and information assets. Another valid reason to embrace heterogeneity is to avoid the perennial vendor lock-in problem.

By cutting down IT costs and improving IT extensibility immeasurably, virtualization technology contributes immensely to broadening and deepening the complexity of IT. With the wide availability of matured hypervisor (VMM) solutions, IT environments use both physical and virtual infrastructures. The VMs can be easily created and deployed, but monitoring and managing their use and contribution is quite difficult. The IT centers struggle with the VM sprawl and are unable to reclaim all the assigned resources once their roles and responsibilities are over. They find it hard to check if all the assigned VMs are actually needed by the business. They are not sure whether those VM resources should be reassigned to other workloads. This situation results in inefficient use of resources and drives unnecessary purchases of additional physical servers. It also forces IT staff to continue to support VMs and workloads that are no longer contributing copiously.

In addition to virtualization management challenges, multihypervisor environments experience the same issues that affect heterogeneous physical environments. Each vendor's hypervisor has its own set of APIs, performance monitors, and VM provisioning and migration technologies that need to be integrated into consistent, standardized workflows and automated provisioning profiles. This added layer of complexity makes it even more challenging for IT teams to operate effectively. In short, siloed IT management tools are not sufficiently empowered to correlate data effectively and quickly and, hence, the real problem of inferring the root cause is often left to the user. Even after the root cause is identified, getting the true identity and current location of the offending user or host is another tough nut to crack since this information is spread across different management domains, for example, OS logs, router configurations, and VPN logs. This deficiency of real-time visibility affects the organization's capacity to keep an IT infrastructure healthy with minimal service-level disruption and degradation.

Complexity Moderation Techniques and Tips

Having understood the growing complexity of IT environments, professionals and product vendors have produced a plethora of specific automation solutions to dynamically provision and deprovision workloads to augment IT flexibility and productivity substantially. Other time-consuming and error-prone tasks such as job scheduling, brokering, fault tolerance, capacity planning, security, and governance are being completely automated by a host of software solutions. Autonomic computing capabilities such as self-diagnosing, self-healing, self-configuring, self-optimizing, self-managing, and self-protecting capabilities are being incorporated in cloud infrastructures, platforms, and applications to make them autonomic in their dealings and decision-making abilities. In a nutshell, operationally, these heterogeneous environments create a number of operation and management complications, and there are myriad management automation tools catering to both physical and virtual resources.

Other simplifying approaches are being analyzed and articulated widely. Heterogeneous data center management and operations can be easily tackled when processes are standardized and automated. Administrators can work and produce good results if provided with a consistent, accurate, and timely set of information about application and infrastructure performance and availability. If there is any operational problem and information about the root cause is delivered in time, then the desired service level can be quickly restored. It is all about performance engineering and enhancement (PE^2).

In heterogeneous environments, each vendor's server, storage, network, or hypervisor platform is likely to have its own set of provisioning tools and performance-monitoring technologies. Although many provide open APIs that allow third-party tools to collect and analyze the data generated at the system level, it can often be quite time consuming and expensive to deploy and integrate a large number of adapters and agents to provide IT with an accurate, 360-degree, and real-time view of the total environment. To maintain SLAs and keep staffing costs in line, IT teams need to optimize the end-to-end performance of business applications across heterogeneous environments.

Sophisticated management and monitoring tools are used to provide actionable performance and availability insights, facilitate complex root cause analysis, and integrate workflows across teams and technology silos. Tool-based optimization of resource allocation, activation, maneuvering, utilization, and reclamation is very essential for futuristic cloud environments. All participating modules need to individually and collectively perform well and provide their unique capabilities and competencies to guarantee the required business services with all their quality parameters intact.

In conclusion, enterprises rely on enterprise IT infrastructures, processes, platforms, best practices, policies, key guidelines, metrics, and other enabling artifacts and assets for the strict compliance and maintenance of the agreed-on levels of service availability and reliability. Operational complexity is on the rise due to the eruption of newer data center technologies and application categories every day, such as mobile-, cloud-, web-, and browser-based ones. In order to offset the complexity, third-party data center providers and IT organizations respond by facilitating the evolution of processes and building workgroup specialties such as networks, operations, applications, governance, security, and help desks that together lead to effective management. However, this arrangement can be counterproductive too as the aforementioned specialties may produce departmental silos, reduced IT responsiveness, and blurred service capacity. Further, enterprise expansion often drives the procurement of specialized tools designed to manage infrastructure from a component, rather than a service, perspective. The growth in data center and IT complexity, potential blind spots and inefficiencies due to operational silos, and disparate IT management tools, or in some cases the lack of tools in midtier IT organizations, contribute to service delivery risks, outages, and degradation. It consequently eliminates an effective means to monitor and optimize service levels, manage change, and readily resolve the root cause of problems and automate compliance efforts.

CSM PROCESSES

Cloud computing has significantly impacted how companies deploy, deliver, and support applications. On the positive side, the cloud idea increases end-user productivity and reduces infrastructure costs. But on the other hand, IT operation and support teams are forced to manage and maintain increasingly complex application and system infrastructures. A number of factors such as the move from centralized to federated computing styles and the inevitable transition from physical to virtual infrastructures have contributed to the unwanted growth of IT complexity. Traditionally, growth in complexity leads to greater risks and higher costs due to an increase in the number of components that must be taken care of. Because of this, IT infrastructure managers must first determine which IT processes need to be implemented in a cloud environment. The IT best practices and processes have been well documented in ITIL and ITIL version 3 is the most recent version of this widely accepted and used framework.

Earlier, companies mostly relied on change management and problem management to reduce risk and costs. This means that service management was largely reactive as it only scheduled software changes whenever necessary and fixed problems as they occurred. Now with the introduction of the ITIL framework, companies have recognized the need to transcend simple change and problem management to address the growing complexity of its infrastructure. In response to this urgent need, there is a focus on release management to control software releases. With the Internet emerging as the open, public, and cheap medium for data communication, the new and centralized service delivery model "application service provider" (ASP) has become popular. This transition has laid the foundation for formalized capacity management, service level management, and service continuity management concepts. Taken together, the seven systems management processes, detailed in the following seven sections, provide worldwide corporations enough ammunition and immunity with the right and relevant framework to successfully and securely plan and operate in the ensuing cloud era.

Change Management

Change management is a fundamental management aspect in the IT industry. Changes are very common and casual, yet they need to be given prime importance in order to zoom ahead of the competition. Change management deals with changes explicitly and defines what type of changes are required on an application to reach an assigned goal. It also involves executing the right change workflow for the type of change and remedying the change if it does not work out as expected. With the introduction and incorporation of multitier application architectures in IT environments, multiple IT application and infrastructure groups are forced to articulate and apply changes to an application in a production environment and to coordinate changes across geographically distributed teams. The second step is to create a separate quality assurance (QA) environment that parallels the production environment to test the recommended changes. This directly increases the chance that changes get reliably implemented in the application. By tying up an MSP that offers cloud capabilities, the organization is able to implement change management processes much more cost-effectively. Since cloud service provider (CSP) use more advanced and automated systems, the organization squarely depends on the provider to build consistently standardized and identical platforms. In addition, because the provider also uses a configuration database that provides a clear view into infrastructure dependencies, the organization could refocus its developers' attention and competencies on application changes and reallocate the infrastructure support resources to other viable projects.

In summary, the core focus of service management is to support business and IT when it comes to outages and changes. A CSP must ensure that all outages or exceptions to normal operations are resolved as quickly as possible while capturing all relevant details for the actions that were taken. Moreover, change management becomes critical for a CSP whose revenue depends on the delivery of highly impactful, insightful, and intelligent services. Strict change management practices must be adhered to, and all changes implemented during approved maintenance windows must be tracked, monitored, and validated.

Problem Management

The objective of problem management is to minimize the adverse impact of application errors and bugs. The goal is to completely prevent the recurrence of incidents caused by the errors. Problem management encompasses two key processes: (1) addressing one or more incidents as they occur and (2) eliminating recurring errors for which root causes have already been identified. An organization first implements problem management to track the number of bugs in each release of its own software products. It also uses root cause analysis of incidents to identify problem patterns. Fixing the sources of recurring problems empowers the organization to improve its software release process by incorporating tests during QA. However, with the pervasiveness of the Internet, the number and types of problems have increased manifold due to the running of applications by a wider variety of application infrastructures and end-user workstations. To address these problems, the organization takes three steps: (1) It standardizes the types of infrastructure components on which its software is deployed. (2) It increases its control over application and infrastructure changes by bundling all changes into a single packaged release. (3) Finally, it specifies the types of laptops and desktops that can be used as client machines.

Initially, these actions significantly reduce the problems that customers face with the application. By standardizing server builds, the development teams can depend on a well-understood production environment. This in turn enables them to package multiple application changes into fewer and larger releases that are more thoroughly tested in the QA environment. However, the growing variety of available end-user workstations prevents the organization from limiting the ones customers can use. Once this is realized, the organization can change its application's interaction with client hardware to use only standard programming interfaces.

Finally, the organization switches over to a cloud infrastructure and is able to leverage the advertised benefits of configuration automation by taking a just-in-time approach to QA. By creating and operating system integration and production testing QA environments only as needed, the costs can be dramatically reduced. In addition, the provider's use of provisioning automation reduces the number and variety of problems that are caused by manual system and network provisioning. Again, because of automation, the organization is able to reallocate troubleshooting resources to other IT projects comfortably.

A configuration management database (CMDB) provides CSPs with a deep understanding of the relationships between configuration items (CIs). Gaining the details of CI relationships empowers change and incident managers to understand that a modification to one service may impact several other related services and components of those services. This brings more clarity and visibility to the cloud environment, allowing consumers and providers to make more informed decisions not only when preparing for a change but also when diagnosing incidents and problems. As applications and data move to clouds, IT departments of organizations need to support the way in which their employees use these solutions and services. In other words, IT must not only provide the first line of support through the service desk function but also provide detailed training to and arrange knowledge sessions for users on how to address common requests and solve common incidents.

Release Management

Software release is a continuous affair. Release management primarily governs both hardware and software additions and changes to the production environment by having clear-cut deployment plans in place. In other words, release packages can be built, installed, tested, and deployed; subsequently, a knowledge transfer session happens with prospective users and operation teams to optimize service use. Postinstallation technical support is also considered here.

When an organization first creates and releases new products, application development managers only consider bundling all the related changes for major software releases. When the Internet emerged as the principal communication infrastructure for service delivery, additional quality controls were imposed for product redesign and marketing. The organization introduced a formal release management process to govern all hardware and software changes, and developers could no longer view changes in isolation since release management forces development teams to consider what would be impacted by each change.

Within the cloud infrastructure, this well-structured release management process helps to rapidly create standard testing environments that match production infrastructure when needed and release resources when testing has been completed. This cloud feature allows testing each release for completeness and stability before promoting the bundle to its production environment.

Security Management

The perpetual security issue is a prominent topic for deep study, analysis, and research across the globe. The security discipline occupies the top slot in every endeavor these days. Creative security practices, frameworks, and solutions are therefore given due recognition in enterprise IT. Anticipating security threats, vulnerabilities, and risks is necessary to preemptively and proactively provide utmost security and safety for expensive IT infrastructures, platforms, information assets, and applications. Access control through a user ID and a password is one proven mechanism for safeguarding application data. Standards-compliant single sign-on (SSO) solutions are bought and attached to ensure stringent application security while providing easy accessibility to global users. However, when offering a SaaS solution, the organization has to sharply enhance its security level through additional layers such as a perimeter defense to limit general access to its applications. It also introduces a security prescription between each pair of layers in the three-tiered architecture to limit any unauthorized access between layers. Finally, the organization moves its SaaS offering to a third-party CSP and achieves enhanced security for its application assets at a lesser cost. The cloud service provider (CSP) takes the seminal responsibility for patching and protecting system and application infrastructures.

Capacity Management

Capacity planning is a critical and crucial activity in enterprise IT. If capacity is rightly visualized, supplied, and utilized, then a lot of infrastructure costs can be easily saved. It is important to ensure a neat balance between demand and supply. If supply and demand are out of sync, then service delivery is greatly affected. To perform capacity planning and management effectively, organizations need to monitor application infrastructures, end-user experience, and infrastructure utilization over a period of time to correctly judge and gauge the exact requirement that can sufficiently meet SLA requirements.

When an application is reengineered for a three-tiered infrastructure, customers can do a small capacity addition to address user demand.

However, this is problematic with the ASP model since each customer requires his or her own isolated infrastructure and data. The answer is to create a multitenant solution, which isolates customer data in the database and virtualizes the web and application tiers. The fallout is that multiple customers can run on fewer servers. When the application gets migrated into the cloud, cost reduction is enormous. Capacity planning is dynamic and simple in clouds since a host of innovative measures and automated tools are used for this purpose, so that any spike in user base as well as workloads is smartly managed without affecting service delivery. Resource expansion and contraction is completely automated in clouds and, hence, capacity management in clouds is simple and cheap.

Service Continuity Management

It is noted that business continuity (BC) has become a mandatory requirement for businesses. The IT infrastructures and applications are fitted with enough insights in the form of policies to come out of any unplanned and unexpected slowdown or breakdown and continue to serve their customers. Disaster recovery (DR) is planned very comprehensively these days while setting up IT centers, considering the enormity of financial and other losses if applications fail to respond to users' requests. Availability, being the prime nonfunctional requirement, has caught the attention of infrastructure architects and designers. The IT resources are made fault tolerant and they are designed in such a way that any bug or malevolent portion in a component does not spread to other components to bring down the system. In other words, loose coupling is a critical criterion for system resources.

Any security intrusion is also carefully considered as a part of the BC requirement, that is, any security-related incursion should not bring down the entire IT structure, damaging and denigrating the SLA. Recovery solutions are very important for the fulfillment of BC. When applications get modernized and are moved to cloud environments, the BC and DR aspects are taken care of quite comfortably and cost-effectively. The CSP periodically makes a copy of its virtualized system images and replicates them to a secondary location, which could be in a far-off place. It also periodically replicates customer data so that it can be made available in case of any emergency or disaster (human made or natural). Recovery point objectives (RPOs) and recovery time objectives (RTOs) can be thoroughly discussed, defined, and signed with the provider toward the BC mission. Cloud-based deployment, delivery, and management is a real blessing for businesses as the IT spend on IT infrastructures and administration personnel is substantially reduced. Data archiving and backup can be done cheaply through clouds.

Service Level Management

Service level management defines the level of service needed to support customers. Once a company defines the service level for an application, it needs to monitor that application to ensure that its service delivery objectives are fully met. The formal definition of a service level can be documented in an SLA and used to manage all vendors participating in the service delivery process.

In the early days of service level management, corporations set an application availability objective for their product lines. When applications are moved to the ASP delivery model, customers expect to include application availability and transaction response times in the SLA. When applications are reengineered as SaaS solutions, there is a need to buy an end-user experience monitoring package that allows measuring the actual transaction response times of a customer's end users. Finally, when applications move to the cloud infrastructure, the CSP has to offer the monitoring package as a part of the hosted solution. The monitoring product helps problem resolution by pinpointing the root cause of performance-related incidents.

These seven management processes are the leading ones that must be fervently considered when moving applications to cloud environments and for effective CSM. Generally, process-enhancement frameworks are much sought after for significant simplification and streamlining of complex management activities.

CLOUD MANAGEMENT SOLUTIONS

CSM is constantly increasing in complexity. Different means and methods are being contemplated and connected together to elegantly tackle diverse management complications, concerns, and challenges. The adoption of cloud concepts has definitely led to a few noteworthy shifts for both business and IT. At the outset, the pioneering cloud technology is IT centric and evolutionary, but it has initiated a comity of groundbreaking revolutions and revelations on the business front. This is why the cloud paradigm is being hotly debated in industry circles. The transformation in IT is as follows: The cloud idea has accomplished a major breakthrough in IT. The static, siloed, underutilized, closed, and bloated infrastructure is set to become a lean, dynamic, converged, adaptive, extensible, and open infrastructure. This tremendous and tectonic shift in IT has enthused and emancipated businesses to come up with out-of-the-box models to confidently, consciously, coherently, and cognitively take on changing business scenes and sentiments.

A physical server is transformed to a dynamic collection of virtual servers; each server is capable of hosting and delivering heterogeneous applications to global consumers for a small fee. In other words, virtual computing is very much on the horizon due to the indomitable spirit of the cloud paradigm. Computing is set to become the fifth social utility. Other praiseworthy changes include heightened IT resource utilization through optimal and safe sharing; the ease with which IT resources are being created, used, and closed (self-servicing); and a rise in resource elasticity due to hybrid and federated interaction modes. With the number of contributing and participating modules going up significantly, the management part deserves special mention and attention. Anticipating overwhelming support for software-based management solutions, experts and exponents put forward the following core features for any cloud management solution. Cloud management comprises cloud application and infrastructure management goals:

- Dynamically provisions or deprovisions all kinds of infrastructure resources (servers, storage, and networks)
- Ensures provisioned resources can be securely consumed by virtual enterprises and then claimed back once they are no longer needed
- Provides centralized capacity planning, monitoring, reporting, and sometimes even billing of all infrastructure resources used in the cloud

Key Attributes of Cloud Management Solutions

The most efficient system management solutions for cloud environments should have many of the following attributes [5]:

- Scalable architecture that allows standards-based integration with a wide array of platforms and systems
- Out-of-the-box integration with leading server, storage, network, and hypervisor environments

- Extensive automation and orchestration abilities including out-of-the-box templates and best practices to enable IT teams to rapidly improve basic operational activities while providing tools to develop and maintain customer-specific workflows
- Enablement of self-service provisioning based on well-defined and well-standardized service catalogs and SLAs
- Ability to monitor end-to-end performance of applications and systems to provide IT with accurate and real-time information about business impacts and root causes
- Ability to monitor and measure resource consumption and support consumption-based capacity planning for real-time workload performance optimization as well as longer-term capital spending

Cloud Management Software Benefits

One challenge faced by companies as businesses move from pilot projects to a broader adoption of cloud technology is the management of the cloud, including both the physical hardware and the VMs that run on it. Because cloud technologies collectively lead to the transformation of IT, organizations can increase visibility of IT infrastructure, reset IT cost structures, reduce fixed costs, and drastically reduce time to change infrastructure and services.

Very often, effective management of IT resources is the best medicine for reducing IT costs substantially. Clouds, being a complicated environment due to the multiplicity and heterogeneity of services provided by them, demand appropriate management solutions. Leading product and software infrastructure vendors have enhanced their existing management suites to be useful in clouds. A management console (MC) is an important ingredient of any management solution that enables managers and executives to seriously ponder and plan. Any typical cloud management software is capable of positively harnessing the direct and distinct capabilities of both physical and virtual compute machines. A fully functional enterprise-class cloud management software solution is expected to have the following characteristics and competences [4]:

- Adapt IT business processes to provide computing power as a utility.
- Define different levels of computing services with different cost models.

- Manage the computing installations as a multitenant and multiplatform utility with federation both within and outside the firewall.
- Ensure compliance with corporate standards for the use of platforms and middleware.
- Measure use and cost and optimize workload placement based on policies and compliance requirements.
- Migrate workloads transparently across platforms or outside the firewall.

Although cloud infrastructure by itself can deliver cost savings by simplifying the accessibility of hardware resources at a low cost, the resources and applications deployed on them must be actively managed to gain all the promised advantages of infrastructure clouds. In the following section, we discuss state-of-the-art management solutions.

The RightScale cloud management solution offers an on-demand management platform that makes it easier for companies to move their applications to cloud infrastructures and manage them as they evolve. RightScale customers can reduce the time required to initially deploy their applications on cloud infrastructures by up to 85%, save approximately 50% in ongoing maintenance, and decrease the time taken to deploy additional applications by more than 90% by reusing existing cloud assets. These savings reflect significant reduction in the amount of time spent by IT staff on deploying and managing applications on a cloud. For instance, a single systems administrator using RightScale can manage hundreds, even thousands, of cloud servers and this ability fundamentally changes how common tasks are addressed. Many RightScale customers have cited overall IT responsiveness—quick procurement and provisioning of resources to meet demands of all types— as an important benefit of using this management platform. Specific areas of IT productivity improvement include the following:

- Fast onboarding by leveraging proven and cloud-ready solutions
- Less time managing cloud applications through automation
- Defining and reusing system configurations on the cloud

In addition to significant IT productivity gains, there are other notable advantages to using RightScale, including greater IT and business agility. Customers have reported that with RightScale IT resources can be marshalled quickly and at low costs to enable businesses to do things they could not otherwise accomplish. The prominent improvements in IT and business agility that are the result of increased IT productivity include the following:

- Self-service IT
- Faster time to market
- Greater experimentation and discovery
- Access to new business models and markets

The BMC Cloud Management Solution

BMC Software, Houston, Texas, has been in the management domain for a long time. The experience and expertise gained by BMC over many years in the management software field has helped it to come out with an easy-to-use cloud management solution. BMC implicitly brings together the benefits (operational excellence, automation, and service delivery models) of traditional IT management and merges them with the dynamic and decisive potential of cloud architectures.

BMC cloud life cycle management promises to provide a scintillating foundation for a strong, flexible, and valuable cloud infrastructure that supports IT operations and delivers exceptional service quality to businesses. BMC cloud life cycle management delivers a cloud that supports configurable and multitier cloud services as well as intelligent policy-based management for operational efficiency and control. The flexibility built into the solution from open and heterogeneous platform support to secure multitenancy in integration with IT operations ensures a tight alignment with business and IT needs.

Cloud service offerings can be defined by administrators within the BMC cloud life cycle management software. These offerings are stored in a flexible service catalog, which provides options to users according to their role. Each offering is backed by a powerful service blueprint that provides the following facilities:

- A functional description of the single or multitier cloud service including configurations and interconnectivity
- One or more possible deployment models for the service in various sizes including the option of a public cloud deployment
- A set of configurable options that can be selected by the user at the time of the request

These service blueprints ensure that users are getting the right cloud services to meet their specific needs while maintaining tight administrative controls. Administrators are able to design and configure service blueprints and manage the cloud environment within the cloud administrator portal. Similarly, users are presented with their choices through a self-service request and management portal.

To deliver the most flexible service stacks for users, BMC cloud life cycle management supports a very flexible provisioning capability. This is accomplished by marrying the service blueprints with automated full-stack provisioning, which allocates physical resources and an OS in the environment, provisions and configures network containers for multitenant support, and layers middleware and applications into the cloud service. BMC cloud life cycle management can even layer compliance rules and monitoring tools into each service delivered. In other words, it provides users precisely the right stack while maintaining tight control on the complex IT environment. Intelligent placement of the cloud service is driven by the BMC solution's unique service governor functionality, according to the following set of factors:

- Identity of the requestor
- Nature of the workload
- Capacity of different elements in the environment
- The applicable compliance policies
- The required service levels
- Organization-specific policies

Once provisioned, the service enters its operational phase, where BMC solutions manage the normal day-to-day activities of performance and capacity management, as well as patching and configuration management. BMC cloud life cycle management supports a variety of underlying platforms across hypervisors, servers, storage, and networks. Further, BMC works with public CSPs to support the provisioning of those resources in a hybrid model. For ensuring security, a unique feature of BMC cloud life cycle management called the "network container functionality" creates isolated and secure virtualized network zones within the cloud. Network containers are often used by organizations to separate cloud services from one another in a comingled and multitenant environment. The container creates isolated networking environments that can include security zones, firewalls, and load-balancers. Once created, cloud services can be provisioned within their deployment and execution containers.

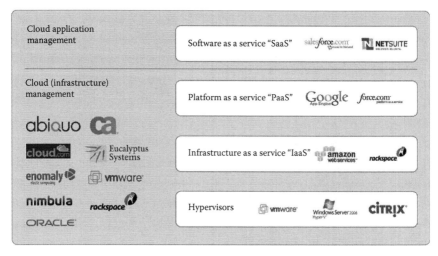

FIGURE 9.2
Cloud application and infrastructure management solutions providers.

Figure 9.2 lists the names of companies focussing on cloud infrastructure management solutions.

vCloud Director is a popular cloud management software suite from VMware, a leading player in the virtualization space. VMware vCloud Director is a software solution that enables enterprises to build secure and multitenant clouds by pooling infrastructure resources into virtual data centers and exposing them to users through web-based portals and programmatic interfaces as fully automated and catalog-based services. The gist of VMware products is to facilitate IT departments of various business organizations to gracefully transform their data centers into secure and cost-effective cloud centers. This sound and strategic optimization in an IT center encourages business innovation and agility significantly while increasing IT efficiency and enhancing security. This cloud onboarding gives businesses the power to reuse existing investments and also flexibility to extend computational capacity on-demand.

The VMware and NetApp Combination

vCloud Director provides the automation and management necessary for internal (private) and external (third-party public) clouds. A vCloud environment requires efficient and highly available storage to deliver an end-to-end infrastructure optimized for clouds. Therefore, VMware has teamed up with NetApp (http://www.netapp.com) for its shared storage

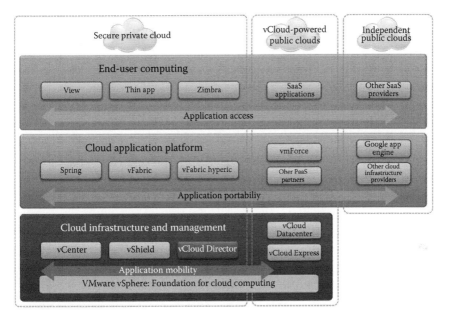

FIGURE 9.3
Cloud infrastructure management stack.

infrastructure. This synchronization assists in moving toward the service model based on vCloud Director while continuing to benefit from the storage efficiency, data protection, and manageability features of NetApp. This joint effort includes beneficial dividends:

- Elastic scalability
- Secure multitenancy
- Rapid provisioning
- Storage efficiency
- Provision of chargeback
- Integrated data protection and high availability
- Unified storage

Figure 9.3 highlights the right products for automating cloud infrastructure management activities.

The BMC and VMware Combination

To address the growing cloud management challenges, BMC Software, with its heritage of producing management and automation software, has teamed up with VMware to provide enterprises with an integrated and end-to-end management solution for cloud infrastructure.

This joint effort between BMC (http://www.bmc.com) and VMware (http://www.vmware.com) has resulted in a solution that substantially reduces operational risk and cost by addressing heterogeneous planning, provisioning, operation, and governance of cloud infrastructure. This solution uses the VMware vSphere and the vCloud API to provide consistent management and performance over the life cycle of cloud infrastructure. The VMware vCloud API is an open and REST-based API that allows scripted access to cloud resources, such as vApp upload/download, catalog management, and other operations. It is noted that BMC can enable business-critical service virtualization for private, public, and hybrid clouds by giving customers control over the full life cycle of virtualization—from service planning to service configuration to automation to service management, service support and, finally, service retirement. Figure 9.4 vividly illustrates how BMC and VMware products talk to each other in order to simplify cloud management tasks.

With this approach, organizations investing in BMC management solutions can deploy more mission-critical workloads on VMware vSphere, thus balancing control and agility to reduce costs and minimize risks. These advanced, integrated solutions enable organizations to leverage existing personnel, processes, and technologies. They perform out-of-the-box integration with other BMC solutions, VMware products, and third-party

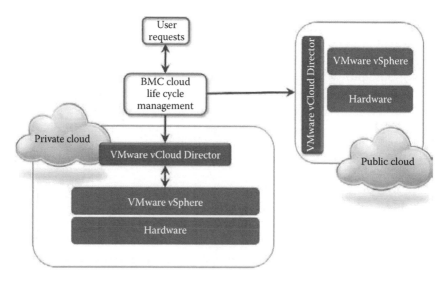

FIGURE 9.4
A cloud management solution.

tools. As a result, IT professionals have a single set of solutions that encompasses physical and virtual assets both inside and outside the data center.

Appirio (http://www.appirio.com) offers a portfolio of cloud management services to help enterprises maintain, enhance, and monitor their cloud applications. These offerings can be customized based on requirements, expected demand, and desired-pricing model. The service offerings are as follows [3]:

Cloud management offerings	salesforce.com force.com Google Apps
Maintain	• Ongoing administration of your environment: user management, profiles, roles, etc.
	• Management of business rules, reports, workflows, or other site or object configuration changes
	• Support: Level 2 tech support, escalations, and knowledge base/FAQs
Enhance	• Enhancements: Cloud application configuation and development updates including new UI pages, Apex triggers, and Google sites and gadgets
	• Release management: Sandbox and regression testing before new platform updates releases
Monitor	• Upkeep and monitoring of integrations across cloud and on-premise applications

AccelOps (http://www.accelops.com) delivers a seamlessly integrated, unified, and service-oriented platform for the collection, monitoring, precise drill down with root cause analysis, and detailed reporting of all IT events/logs and performance metrics that cut across networks, systems, applications, vendors, and technology boundaries. It provides data centers, MSPs, and IT organizations full information (who, what, where, when, why, and how) at their fingertips at any given time, with necessary confidence and control in service delivery. AccelOps brings all the decision-enabling insights to the operator's fingertips so that the operator can monitor and enhance service levels, better optimize resources, and further reduce business risks. AccelOps combines discovery, data aggregation, correlation, out-of-the-box analytics, data management, and reporting to yield a single and synchronized view of data center and IT operations and services. Integrated functionality includes the following [1]:

- Business service management and service mapping
- Performance management/network behavior analysis
- Availability management/SLA
- Security information event management

- Change control/automated CMDB
- Event/log consolidation with cross-correlation
- Identity, access, and location management with directory service integration
- Network visualization and enterprise search
- Compliance and governance automation

Automation of CMDB for Instant Success in Change Management

Figure 9.5 illustrates the various components of an integrated and service-oriented platform for data center and cloud service management. Mapping the infrastructure landscape and relationship in CMDB is a mandatory prerequisite for any data center and IT management solution. AccelOps completely automates the CMDB building process using a bottom-up approach:

- Automatic discovery of resources (networks, servers, applications, and users).
- Automatic resource categorization into specific functional device groups (such as firewalls, storage, virtualized servers, and databases) and into user groups (such as administrators).

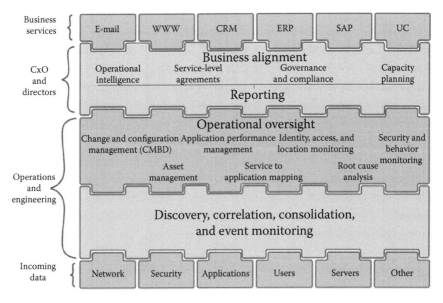

FIGURE 9.5
AccelOps data center and cloud service management platform architecture.

- Automatic identification and maintenance of component relationships: Layer 2 and 3 topology maps, virtual host to physical host mappings, wireless access points (APs) to controller and n-tier application traffic flows, and applications to infrastructure mappings.
- Automatic identity and location mappings: Network identities such as workstation IP and MAC addresses are continuously mapped to user identities such as domain/server/VPN accounts and corresponding locations such as wired switch ports, VLAN IDs, wireless APs, and VPN gateways.
- Automatic configuration and software details mappings: Network device and server configurations. Software details are captured and versioned to detect any worthwhile changes.

Innovations in Analytics and Correlation for Proactive Management and Efficient Root Cause Analysis

Without correlation and analytics capabilities, a CMDB is not complete for any data center and IT management solution. The rich infrastructure relationship information in CMDB needs to be correlated with current events and performance metrics in order to provide proactive measures for identifying exceptions, vulnerabilities, and problems ahead of time and to accurately pinpoint root causes to minimize service disruption.

This is accomplished by the AccelOps' powerful analytics and correlation engine, which is powered with three major innovations: (1) an XML-based language for parsing data, (2) an XML-based search and rule language for mining the parsed data, and (3) a profile and anomaly detection engine that can detect anomalies on any problem dimension. The languages are versatile enough for dealing with a wide range of IT operational data such as events/logs, network flows, and performance metrics from networks, servers, and applications. The XML-based language enables users to rapidly add support for custom applications and share it with the community. The XML files are compiled at runtime to give the same level of performance as handwritten code.

The search and rule language supports a wide range of analytics from simply searching for textual patterns in raw data to complex rules that are triggered when abnormal event patterns are detected. Unified treatment of all data, along with the discovered rich, contextual metadata, allows a user to search and write accurate problem detection rules that span performance, availability, security, and change aspects. Possible scenarios include zero-day malware from unpatched machines, suspicious database log-ons, unusual geographical sources of web server traffic, slow network scans, and sudden increase or decrease of application traffic.

Service Discovery and Impact Analysis to Align IT with Business

Rather than monitoring only the health and security of a data center, network IT infrastructure, and cloud environment separately and on a component-by-component basis, AccelOps allows all kinds of IT organizations to operate, manage, and deliver their offerings in a service mode. This service-centric monitoring and management fulfils the ultimate goal of consistent improvement in IT service delivery. AccelOps defines a business service as a smart container of relevant devices and applications serving a business purpose. This business-centric view enables services to meet business requirements quite effectively. It is possible to track service level metrics, efficiently respond to incidents on a prioritized basis, record business impacts, and provide BI on IT best practices, compliance reporting, and IT service improvement.

AccelOps simplifies the process defining and maintaining business services. Because AccelOps automatically discovers applications running on servers as well as network connectivity and traffic flow, a user can simply choose the applications and their respective servers and be intelligently guided to choose the rest of the components of the business service.

Jamcracker Unified Services Management (USM) enables enterprises to centralize the procurement, delivery, billing, security, administration, and user support of internal and external cloud services (Figure 9.6).

With USM, enterprise IT organizations can consolidate public and private cloud services management by the following mechanisms:

Delivering: Single point of provisioning, billing, use, and user administration across all cloud services

Enforcing: Corporate policies and regulatory compliance across all users, services, verticals, and geographies

Auditing: Visibility and accountability of use in a consistent format for all users and services

Managing: Integrating with existing processes, policies, and infrastructure

Reporting: Quantitative and qualitative data on services usage

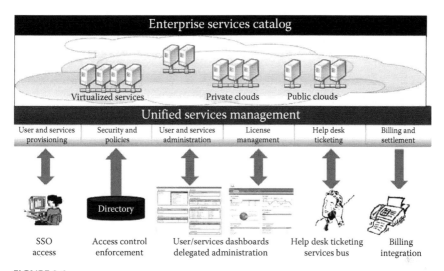

FIGURE 9.6

The Jamcracker unified services management solution architecture.

Other key functionalities include centralized aggregation, integration, and orchestration of internal and external cloud computing services. The services integration tool kit enables enterprises to integrate existing SaaS, PaaS, IaaS, and BPaaS services (e.g., Salesforce.com, WebEx, Microsoft Online Services, and Google Apps) and internal cloud services with USM's centralized access, user and service administration, reporting, billing and settlement, and help desk ticketing functions.

SEMANTIC TECHNOLOGIES FOR CLOUD INFORMATION MANAGEMENT

Peter Haase and his team in their paper titled "Semantic Technologies for Enterprise Cloud Management" have come out with an excellent platform for seamlessly incorporating semantic technologies in realizing completely automated data centers. Achieving automation in data center operations has been an ongoing project for IT professionals. A slew of manual tasks need to be automated through competent software solutions. Visible and perceptible complications arise due to the adoption of myriad technologies, processes, policies, and products in data centers. Load balancing, job scheduling, capacity planning, resource allocation and cancellation, infrastructure management, and so on, are the dominant inflexibilities and inefficiencies that hamper data center operation in fulfilling SLAs. A bunch of software solutions utilizing highly optimized algorithms are therefore essential for realizing the vision of automated data centers. In this section, we discuss the need for intelligent information management solutions and how the semantic technologies are ready to provide this requirement. Related topics of discussion are data integration, documentation and annotation, and intelligent information access and analytics.

Data Integration

Data diversity is a common phenomenon in data centers. The obligatory need for data integration can therefore be achieved through a standards-based integration of data originating from various infrastructure components. This capability is a definite success if integration is able to proceed with the orchestration of subsequent actions as an insightful response to events such as user requests or alarms. Many layers play an important role and, hence, there is a large set of provider APIs ranging from storage to application levels. The situation becomes trickier when products from different vendors coexist in the same data center. The products differ vastly in syntax and semantics from the data supplied and functionality offered through APIs.

Semantic technologies have been acquiring strategic significance in all kinds of heterogeneous scenarios. The authors have used RDF as a data model for semantically integrating heterogeneous information sources in order to get a complete picture across the entire data center, both horizontally across different product versions and vendors and vertically across storage, compute units, network, OSs, and applications. The RDF-based integration offers the flexibility needed to integrate new sources in the presence of heterogeneity in data centers.

Collaborative Documentation and Annotation

Data integration is the key aspect of running data centers and clouds efficiently. For this purpose, cloud management software is fed with data from provider APIs. This data contains technical information about the infrastructure and the software running on a cloud infrastructure. In order to get a complete picture, organizational and business aspects need to be added to the technical data. In order to collaborate efficiently, data center operators need to document procedures and log activities. Proper knowledge management is essential to avoid the repeated resolution of a problem by different staff members. Activities are usually managed using a ticketing system, in which infrastructure alerts and customer complaints are distributed and resolved by operators.

It is absolutely unambiguous that business and organizational information must be addressed in a unified way. When information about systems or customers is stored or documentation about a certain hardware type is written, it should be possible to cross-reference the information collected from the infrastructure providers. Here, the authors have applied semantic wiki technology to satisfy these requirements. Operating on an RDF base that is fed by infrastructure providers, operators can extend this data by documenting and annotating the respective items.

Intelligent Information Access and Analytics

Data center managers need to be supplied with accurate information to make timely and informed decisions. The specific descriptions needed include status reports and utilization information of data center resources over time, visualization of key performance metrics in dashboards, and search for specific resources. These details can be generated through multidimensional queries that span both technical and business aspects.

With an integrated view on the data, it is possible to support queries that overcome the borders of data sources. Apart from predefined queries that drive reports and dashboards, a clear benefit is the ability to perform expressive ad hoc queries. The authors have used schema-agnostic semantic search (a combination of the expressiveness of structured queries with the ease of use of keyword-driven interfaces) to hide the complexity of the underlying data model and query languages from end users. Novel approaches to visualization of structured data as well as visual exploration of resources enable new forms of interaction and provide insights into previously hidden relationships.

The eCloudManager product suite is a Java-based software solution that is targeted at the management of enterprise cloud environments. The macrolevel architecture is depicted in Figure 9.7.

This product has come up with four complementary editions; the most prominent one is the Intelligence Edition, which makes use of semantic technologies to integrate available resources into a semantic data store. At the bottom of the Intelligence Edition lies the data integration layer, which relies on a variety of data providers. A data provider is a component

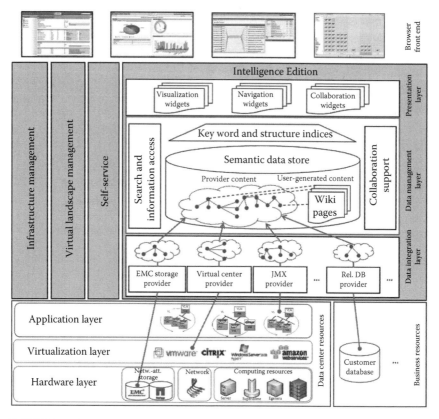

FIGURE 9.7
eCloudManager architecture.

that extracts data from a single physical or logical resource (e.g., an EMC storage device, a VMware Virtual Center, or a relational database), converts it into RDF, and integrates the resulting RDF data into the central repository, which is at the data management layer. Technically, it is realized as a Sesame triple store that adheres to a predefined (yet extendable) web ontology language (OWL) ontology. In addition to the repository, the layer provides components for search- and semantics-based information access. A central component of this layer is a collection of semantic wiki pages that are associated with resources contained in the repository; they offer an entry point to eCloudManager users, allowing one to add new and complement existing information.

The uppermost layer in the Intelligence Edition is the presentation layer. Located on top of the data management layer, it comes with a predefined set of widgets with varying functional focus, for example, offering support to display wiki pages, visualizing the underlying data using charts and diagrams, navigating through the underlying RDF graph, and collaboratively annotating resources in the database using both semantic annotations and free-text documentation.

The eCloudManager Ontology

The authors have introduced a conceptual model for the domain of enterprise cloud management in the form of an ontology that abstracts vendor-specific representations, data sources, and management APIs. The ontology has been modeled as an OWL 2 ontology, consisting primarily of a class hierarchy and of property definitions with domain, range, and cardinality restrictions.

Figure 9.8 surveys the main concepts and relationships of the eCloudManager ontology using the standard UML profile for modeling OWL ontologies. Each concept carries a number of data properties (attributes), which capture information about the properties and status of the respective resource. The four major subareas are storage infrastructure, compute infrastructure, application-level resources, and business-level resources.

In conclusion, the authors have shown that semantic technologies are adept in addressing some of the key challenges in managing enterprise cloud environments. The RDF-based data integration allows one to deal effectively with the highly heterogeneous and changing set of resources

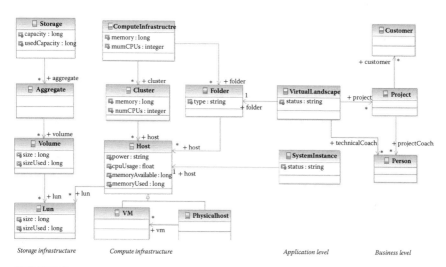

FIGURE 9.8

An overview of the eCloudManager ontology.

encountered in enterprise data centers. Semantic wikis provide an end user with an oriented interface for creating structured and unstructured annotations, support main use cases for documentation and knowledge management, and seamlessly integrate automatically obtained data with user-generated content.

CONCLUSION

Laudable innovations in virtualization and distributed computing methods as well as improved access to high-speed Internet have set the course for cloud computing. As enterprises strategize to move their business-critical and enterprise-class applications, platforms, and infrastructures to the cloud environment, these cloud services have to be taken care of in their new environments. This enforces the view that there must be verified and validated processes, products, and practices in place to effectively measure, manage, and maintain such services. With the surging popularity of the cloud concept, process-compliant, business-aware, model-driven, people-centric, and cloud-based services are emerging and evolving fast to tackle diversifying business needs. As the cloud era steadily unfurls, all the cloud-induced innovation and flexibility factors have to be immaculately recognized and preserved to prosper. Otherwise, there is no point in contemplating this transition, which is being proclaimed the most strategic and significant movement since the advent of the Internet.

Cloud resources require more purposeful, preemptive, and proactive management and maintenance methods and tools. Due to the increasing complicity associated with coexisting and commingling heterogeneous elements, the fast-growing and multidimensional cloud landscape brings in a different set of management challenges. Considering the trendsetting cloud differentiators, processes of dynamically managing, tracking, monitoring, maintaining, substituting, and even cloud services that are being retired have to be fully automated in order to reap all their promised benefits. Myriad cloud management software solutions are available for applications and infrastructures. Some are only enhanced versions of existing solutions, whereas others are being built from scratch with the cloud paradigm in mind. A host of pioneering techniques and algorithms are being recommended by scholars and scientists for constructing next-generation management software suites that would take care of all kinds of cloud resources smartly and successfully so that the cloud concept prevails and proceeds toward its envisaged destination without a hitch.

REFERENCES

1. 2010. *Enabling Datacenter and Cloud Service Management for Mid-Tier Enterprises.* AccelOps, Inc. http://www.accelops.net.cn/pdf/AccelOps_DataCenterITServiceMgmt0110.pdf.
2. June 2011. *The Changing Role of Network Management—Keeping Pace with the New Demands of Virtualization and Cloud.* EMA and EMC. http://www.emc.com/collateral/software/white-papers/changing-role-network-management.pdf.
3. 2011. *Appirio Cloud Management Datasheet.* Appirio Inc. http://www.appirio.com/company/pdf/AppirioCloudMgmt.pdf.
4. Escapa, C. August 6, 2010. *Cloud Management Guide.* http://www.abiquo.com/files/white_paper_cloud_management_guide.pdf.
5. Turner, M. J. April 2011. *Effective Management of Heterogeneous Datacenters and Multi-hypervisor Environments.* IDC. http://i.dell.com/sites/content/shared-content/solutions/en/Documents/managing-datacenters-multiple-hypervisors.pdf.
6. Jansen, M. 2011. "What Does IT Service Management Look Like in the Cloud? An ITIL Based Approach." In *Proceedings of the 2011 International Conference on Applied, Numerical and Computational Mathematics and Proceedings of the 2011 International Conference on Computers, Digital Communications and Computing,* World Scientific and Engineering Academy and Society, Stevens Point, WI, September 15–17, 2011: 87–92. http://www.wseas.us/e-library/conferences/2011/Barcelona/ICICIC/ICICIC-14.pdf.
7. Nothern, D. 2010. *Key Service Management Processes for Cloud Infrastructures.* Savvis, Inc. http://www.savvis.com/en-us/info_center/documents/hos-whitepaper-keyservicemanagementprocessesforcloudinfrastructures.pdf.
8. Turner, M. J. April 2011. *Effective Management of Heterogeneous Data centers and Multi-hypervisor Environments.* IDC.
9. Haase, P. et al. 2010. *Semantic Technologies for Enterprise Cloud Management.* http://www.informatik.uni-freiburg.de/~mschmidt/docs/iswc10.pdf.

10

Cloud Security Architecture (CSA)

INTRODUCTION

According to the U.S. National Institute of Standards and Technology (NIST), "Cloud computing is an enabling model for people to have on-demand network access to a dynamic and shared pool of IT infrastructure, platform, and software assets that can be rapidly and dynamically provisioned and deprovisioned as per changing needs." The much-discussed cloud computing paradigm looks to deliver IT infrastructure and platform services via the Internet to anyone from any corner of the world. Cloud resources can be subscribed to on-the-fly to support specific short-term project needs or they can be leveraged on a long-term basis to add capability to an existing IT infrastructure. Some companies fully team up with one or more third-party cloud providers to fulfill all of their IT requirements.

We have indicated elsewhere that the advent of cloud technology is a definite plus for the ravaged IT industry and this transformative and disruptive paradigm is set to lead the industry on a strategic and successful journey befitting and benefiting every single IT-run business segment immensely in the years to come. In short, the promising cloud technology has the innate wherewithal to unleash a series of decisive innovations and optimizations on all kinds of industries aiming to keep up with the changes (technology, government rules and regulations, social, market, and so on) happening around the world. The proofs, pilots, and prototypes thus far clearly illustrate and illuminate the path toward the originally envisaged cloud-inspired destination.

The cloud paradigm, a relatively new entrant into IT, is growing fast with a number of crucial and critical contributions from different sets of people. The results are in the form of cloud-specific standards, design patterns, assessment, migration and on-boarding strategies, modernization and development methodologies, key guidelines and evaluation metrics, technology solutions for cloud concerns and challenges, and usage scenarios. In this fluctuating situation, it is pertinent for cloud users to diligently weigh and analyze the benefits (tactical as well as strategic), the risks involved, and the costs of operational risk transference from on-site servers to off-site, on-demand, and online cloud servers. The brand value, the willingness for third-party auditability, and the compliance with security and regulatory standards by CSPs are also of prime importance when deciding how and when to migrate resources. There are myriad use, business, and technical cases for cloud enablement. The recessionary and receding world economy and the associated uncertainty have encouraged worldwide corporations and companies to embrace the cloud paradigm enthusiastically to bring in new features and functions on a shoestring budget. In short, with the establishment of interoperable cloud centers across the globe, the long-standing cost center view of IT is to change forever. In this chapter, we would like to present the key technological solutions for efficiently combating the security problem in cloud IT.

The ensuing cloud era represents the overwhelming involvement of a number of different and geographically distributed cloud service providers (CSPs), delivering a variety of IT-enabled resources to consumers as value-added services over the open Internet. There are industry pundits and market analysts claiming that by 2015, the fast-maturing and stabilizing cloud technology will have a solid and stimulating footprint in every kind of business across the world. At the front end are the client devices and user agents looking forward to access to remote and reliable clouds and their distinctive capabilities. At the back end are a pool of consolidated, converged, centralized, and federated servers, network appliances, and storage systems that host, deliver, and manage a growing array of professional as well as personal services. Because every single IT resource is being presented and provided as a network-discoverable and accessible service, the goodwill generated is that users need not have the knowledge or expertise about the underlying technologies, platforms, infrastructures, and connectivity solutions that make up CSPs. That is, cloud accessibility, consumability, maneuverability, and serviceability are made remarkably simpler through a host of software solutions. However, there are some valid concerns and challenges today that are hijacking the massive adoption of the powerful and pioneering cloud concepts. The chief among them is cloud dependability, which in turn includes cloud security, privacy, availability, reliability, performance, and so on. The lack or loss of absolute controllability, auditability, and visibility factors, especially in public clouds, creates consternation in the minds and hearts of many. In this chapter, we describe in detail for our readers the perennial security problem, the most important constriction of the fast-moving cloud idea, and the viable deterrence approaches.

SECURITY IMPLICATIONS OF CLOUD COMPUTING

Business houses across the globe are citing security as one of the chief deterrents for cloud adaption. Financial service providers, governments, and healthcare companies are the leading entities extensively quoting the security risks of the cloud paradigm. However, 70% of companies that have already launched their cloud initiatives plan to move additional applications and data to the cloud. That is, the corporations that have overcome the initial fears are keen to leverage the advantages of the cloud even more. Realistically, there are some real dangers associated with cloud environments, as resources are totally in control of cloud administrators. Data security is definitely a heightened problem in the cloud era. Data integrity and confidentiality are the two major data security aspects garnering enhanced traction these days.

Although the benefits and opportunities offered by the cloud abound incessantly, many recent surveys of potential cloud adopters have pinpointed that security is the number one concern for cloud computing. That is, the plausible risks to data under transmission and in persistence are being well articulated by worldwide security experts and consultants. The cloud, without an iota of doubt, is a dynamic environment in which technologies, processes, and business models continue to evolve. Not only the dynamism, but also the virtualization-induced sharing of computing capabilities as services across different business houses fuels the security fears. As the automation level goes up in a cloud environment, the severity of security rises correspondingly. Several common security threats such as data leakage, insecure APIs, and malicious inside users are applicable to cloud environment as well. Having understood the security insinuations, CSPs are working on a raft of impenetrable and unbreakable security solutions.

Sophisticated malicious attempts aimed at obtaining identities or blocking access to sensitive business data and services come in the way of leveraging the advertised and advanced cloud facilities, functionalities, and features. The massive adoption predicted by visionaries and pundits in the beginning has slowed because of the security conundrum. The cloud-instigated security issues are being attended in different levels. Professors at academic institutions, researchers at labs, and software and hardware engineering professionals in IT organizations have been exploring, experimenting, and espousing a bevy of security and privacy-preserving algorithms and implementations. In short, CSPs have to proactively and preemptively act in order to root out the lingering security concerns expressed more frequently these days so that confidence in the cloud technology can be boosted substantially. CSPs have to stringently evaluate the effectiveness of proven security strategies, technologies, controls, and processes used to mitigate such disruptions and work on bringing forth a set of powerful methods for combating security-related ills. The security knowledge gained in the traditional IT environments can be used to come out with better solutions to curb any kind of unexpected and unwanted incursions in cloud IT environments.

Cloud computing uses various service models such as IaaS and PaaS, and the cloud security scenes vary widely with the models. The decomposition of physical machines into a cluster of VMs raises several serious security issues. The heterogeneity and multiplicity of cloud resources add to cloud complexity. With diminished controllability and visibility, several critical security implications are bound to erupt. Again in a federated environment, which is basically an interworking of cloud systems of various CSPs, there is the possibility of security breaches due to variations in policies and SLAs among CSPs. Another noteworthy cause for security concerns is that the web is the primary communication infrastructure. Modernization and migration to the cloud have to be impeccable in order to run the existing applications in a cloud center flawlessly. The lack of standardization in cloud architecture is another cause for security vulnerabilities.

KEY CLOUD SECURITY ISSUES

A Microsoft author has envisaged the following scenarios that have direct or indirect security implications [1]. It is obvious that well-defined and designed security-centric risk management processes need to be applied to preemptively and productively identify and eliminate any kind of vulnerability or threat.

- Emerging cloud business models create a growing interdependence among public- and private-sector entities and the people they serve.
- Acceleration of adoption of cloud services, including the continuing evolution of technologies and business models, creates a dynamic hosting environment, which is by itself a security challenge.

- Attempts to infiltrate or disrupt online service offerings grow more sophisticated as more commerce and business occurs in this venue.
- Complex compliance requirements must be addressed as new and existing services are delivered globally.

A white paper published by Global Knowledge (http://www.globalknowledge.com) has listed out the top ten security issues to be discussed with CSPs.

1. Where is the data?
2. Who have access to it?
3. What are the regulatory requirements?
4. Does the provider allow third-party audit?
5. What type of training does the provider offer to their employees?
6. What type of data classification system does the provider use?
7. What are the SLA terms?
8. What is the long-term viability of the provider?
9. What happens if there is a security breach?
10. What is the disaster recovery/business continuity plan (DR/BCP)?

There are several obstacles in the way of the unbridled growth of cloud computing. The prominent pains and plagues include availability of cloud services, elasticity, vendor lock-in, data security, data transfer bottlenecks, performance unpredictability, network outage, system malfunctioning, scalable storage, and so on. In public clouds, the lack or loss of controllability and visibility of data is being quoted as the key concern.

Cloud Data Confidentiality

Maintaining confidentiality in the cloud has the same problems as maintaining it within local enterprise servers, plus more. When data are stored in on-premise systems, the administrator knows exactly where it is, the security measures in place on the server and the network, who has access to it, and the legal entities that have jurisdictions over it. However, in a cloud environment, the outsourcing companies do not know where their data are stored, who are accessing them, how long they are being accessed for, any devious and destructive incursions, and so on and hence the security implications are more severe. The data could be stored in a cloud center far from the business operations and they are likely distributed over a number of servers, possibly in different locations to improve performance and fault tolerance. Competent encryption methods could help mitigate many of these risks. During transit or in storage, data can be kept away from any prying and malicious people through stronger encryption processes.

Cloud Data Integrity

Data being transmitted over networks or preserved in cloud storage should be tamperproof. Hackers should not be able to modify the data. Message digest is the common practice of ensuring data integrity when data travels from one system to another. When applications run on cloud servers, they should maintain the correct state of data to avoid introducing any problems. Consider the example of a database transaction involving the transfer of funds between bank accounts. When a person transfers funds from his savings to his checking account, there are two operations that must be completed: funds are deducted from the savings account and the same amount is added to the checking account. If there is some type of failure after deducting funds from the first account, then during the recovery phase, the deduction should be made void or the transaction should be completely done.

The integrity of the account information cannot be maintained in a multistep transaction if some steps complete and other do not. In the cloud, the basic transaction functionality has to be supported. Further, one should assess how distributed copies of data are synchronized. If data are written to redundant servers, how are write operations rolled back if an update cannot complete over all servers?

Cloud System Availability

Servers and networks in the cloud could go down for several reasons. CSPs are using an arsenal of technological advancements in order to guarantee 99.999% availability. Customers, too, contemplate a number of options in order not to be cowed by this availability syndrome. One practice is to maintain minimal amounts of critical data in other locations to allow basic data access during the outage. Backup and disaster recovery mechanisms are the leading propositions to beat down any disruptions. Natural or human-made disasters must be dealt with in an efficient and expedient manner to ensure systems are functioning continuously and consistently.

Typically, businesses team up with CSPs based on a workable contract (SLA) that specify uptime requirements and means for compensating if there is any slowdown or breakdown.

Application layer security insists on vulnerability scanning, application layer firewalls, configuration management, alert monitoring and analysis, and source code analysis. Cloud environments by virtue of their flexibility, transparency, and often public availability challenge many currently held assumptions about application security. Clouds immensely influence security over the lifetime of an application in many ways from conceptualization to concretization, construction, commissioning, and decommisioning. It is vital that all the stakeholders including application architects, security experts, system administrators, and application governance professionals understand how to alleviate impending and invisible risks and effectively provide the required assurance within cloud applications. The application apprehension lies in all the layers of SaaS, PaaS, and IaaS. Cloud-based software applications, therefore, require a rigorous design similar to applications residing in a classic demilitarized zone (DMZ). This includes a deep up-front analysis covering all the standard aspects of managing information reliability.

In any business environment, the IT application portfolio is growing steadily. Any typical enterprise-scale application today has multiple dependencies and descriptions. For example, a dealer management system (DMS) in a manufacturing industry's IT division is integrated with a BI suite, ERP package, back-end database system, and so on. Further, a front-end management console or information visualization tool for corporate executives is mandatory for the DMS. In a connected and extended business landscape, enterprise IT is definitely diversified and distributed. In short, the dependency of business applications on other applications and databases (local and global) is constantly on the rise. Now, with the articulation and adoption of the game-changing cloud landscape, there is one more solid space for applications to live and be leveraged. As business applications and services are systematically modified and moved to cloud zones, configuration management and resource provisioning are becoming more complex when compared with traditional application deployment. The cloud environment drives the need for suitable architectural modifications to reassure the user community and assuage sagging feelings over application security.

The compliance mandate also catches up with cloud applications. For example, regulating how an application implements a particular cryptographic function requires immediate compliance. The vulnerability scene is also not encouraging. Mostly, Web 2.0 social applications are now being delivered from cloud environments. With factors such as maturity and stability being insisted on by end-users and executives, there is a bright possibility for several business applications to move to clouds. There are articles and even books listing a number of unresolved vulnerabilities for social applications. Further, most of the cloud applications are service oriented. That is, there are service oriented cloud applications or cloud-based service applications. As we all know, service-oriented applications support automated interactions among services that are in different machines. This sort of hitherto unknown association encounters and entails a few more vulnerabilities.

VIRTUALIZATION-INDUCED CLOUD SECURITY ISSUES

As widely known, virtualization is the key technological driver for a fair amount of the success of the cloud idea. Although virtualization technology has been around since the mainframe era, the value and power of it in synchronization with other breakthrough technologies are being realized these days. The gist of the virtualization method is to enable the clean separation of software from its hampering dependency on underlying hardware. This segregation ultimately enables the goal of system portability. Virtualization in the context of cloud computing can result in the creation of multiple VMs out of a single physical server. Each VM is itself a virtual server comprising a guest OS, middleware, application, and data. Not only servers but also network, storage, desktop, application, service, and data virtualization techniques are gaining much ground. If virtualization technology is being used at the infrastructure level, then there are concerns about compartmentalization of VMs. The core virtualization technology itself introduces new attack surfaces in the hypervisor and other management components. Another important impact is on network security. VMs now communicate over a hardware backplane rather than a network. As a result, the standard network security controls are blind to this traffic and cannot perform monitoring or in-line blocking. These controls need to take a new form to accomplish their traditional functions in virtualized environments.

Interference and commingling of data in centralized services and repositories is another worry [5–7]. A centralized database provided by clouds should improve the security of data distributed over a vast number of machines. However, the much-written about consolidation and centralization of data leads to the centralization of risks. Risk mitigation is clearly an obligatory need in dynamic, shared, automated, and virtual environments. Another concern is the commingling of VMs having different levels of sensitivity and security. In cloud environments, the lowest common denominator of security will be shared by all tenants in the multitenant environment unless a new security architecture can be achieved that does not "wire in" any network dependency for protection.

Mobile virtualization is on the horizon and hence it is possible to have Android, Apple, BlackBerry, and Windows applications and services coexisting and cooperating with one another in a smartphone. That is, physical computing is transitioning to the promised virtual computing. Every single IT resource is being presented as virtual element to be self-describing, autonomous, collaborative, and cognitive. However, there are some serious security threats due to the virtualization aspect, which are enumerated as follows.

1. *VM hijacking*—During the initiation of a VM, all the information of the VM is stored in the allocated memory. By gaining access to this information, an attacker can launch an attack on the VMs that are hosted on the same server. In the case of multitenancy, a single server would host several VMs on it and thus would have the respective configuration files of all VMs stored on the host. Since each VM is separated by a virtual boundary, an attacker gaining access to one of such files could be able to predict the actual hardware configuration of another VM residing on the same host. The primary configuration file contains all the necessary information of a VM. Gaining access to these files and breaking into a VM is termed "VM hijacking." A malicious user having control of a VM can try to gain control over other VMs' resources or utilize all system resources leading to denial of service (DoS) attack over other VM users. A malicious user can also try to steal the data of other users located on the same server.

2. *VM hopping* is the process of hopping from one VM to another VM. An attacker on one VM can gain access over the other VM. This can be achieved if both the VMs are running on the same host. Because there are several VMs running on the same machine, there would be several victims of the VM hopping attack. An attacker can falsify the SaaS user's data once he gains access to a target VM by VM hopping, endangering the confidentiality and integrity of SaaS.

3. *VM mobility* enables the moving or copying of VMs from one host to another over the network or by using portable storage devices without physically stealing or snatching a hard drive. Although this makes the process of deployment easier, it could lead to security problems such as spread of vulnerable configurations. The severity of the attack ranges from leaking sensitive information to completely compromising the OS. As IaaS lets users create computing platforms by importing a customized VM image into the infrastructure service, the impact on confidentiality, integrity, and availability via the VM mobility feature is quite large.

4. *VM escape* means gaining access over the hypervisor and attacking the rest of the VMs. If an attacker gains access to the host running multiple VMs, the attacker can access the resources shared by the other VMs. The host can monitor the memory being allocated and the CPU utilization. If necessary, an attacker can bring down these resources and turn off the hypervisor. If the hypervisor fails, all the other VMs turn off eventually.

5. *VM diversity* can be a potential security challenge and should be taken care of by well-defined SLAs that mandate that the security management burden has to be shared by both the provider and the user.

Security Threats of the Intercloud

In Chapter 1, we wrote about the intercloud in detail. The concept of interworking can lead to the acceleration of erosion of trust boundaries. In the intercloud environment, a CSP can make use of services of other CSPs. That is, peer-to-peer interactions result in providers acting as consumers as well as providers. CSPs need to know and incorporate the security and other policies of others in order to be seamlessly leveraged by others. Clouds are truly dynamic in nature. But the existing models are designed for static events whereas dynamic agreements are needed to create a cloud federation. When a CSP uses a service of another SP to meet the requirements of his customer, he can act in two ways:

1. He can alter the data for the service connection point accessed by his customers to access another cloud system.

2. The provider can act as a proxy between his customers and the other provider.

The emphasis is on the responsibility of a cloud customer in selecting trustworthy CSPs and cloud systems that meet his or her quality requirements, based on matching the customer's quality requirements with the provider's SLA. Security management functions include methods for authentication, authorization, encryption, and so on.

Michael Kretzschmar, Mario Golling, and Sebastian Hanigk in their research paper titled "Security Management Areas in the Inter-Cloud" detail 10 security management areas in an intercloud environment. One such area is identity management, which defines the ability to confirm and manage the life cycle of a human, device, or process. Federated identity management enables users secure access across multiple external applications through a single sign-on (SSO). Credential management is the ability to manage the life cycle and check the authenticity of digital credentials such as certificates, identity documents, and passwords. Attribute management manages the assigned properties of entities. Digital policy management is the ability to generate, convert, manage, and replace digital policies. The authors have also considered configuration management, privilege management, cryptographic key management, metadata management, audit management, security management, and information management. The paper emphasizes the fact that due to the dynamics on an intercloud-federated infrastructure, a flexible method for building dynamic interactions and enabling the coexistence of different and heterogeneous technologies needs to be provided. To accomplish this, well-established security management approaches have to be considered.

CLOUD SECURITY SOLUTIONS

Crafting a Comprehensive Threat Model

The threat landscape is characterized by increasingly sophisticated attacks and the modern-day attacks typically combine microtargeting, social engineering, technical exploitation of multiple "zero-day" vulnerabilities, and the ability to defeat built-in resilience. Traditional approaches to enterprise security have been based on control of devices, of infrastructure, of information, and of processes inside enterprise firewalls. In the ensuing borderless cloud that vouches for boundaryless information flow, applications, services, and data are being accessed from a variety of users' devices. Traditional physical infrastructure is characterized by single tenancy, physically segmented infrastructure, and static security controls at perimeters. In a virtualized environment of shared infrastructure and mobile workloads, these perimeters are constantly evolving. Security controls must, therefore, be available on demand in the virtual fabric. A well-defined security policy framework has to be in place in order to facilitate the application of right policies to systematically manage privilege isolations and trust zones that dot dynamic workloads and variable perimeter horizons. A comprehensive threat model, therefore, comes in handy in deeply analyzing and articulating security issues and this leads to the design of appropriate mitigation strategies and to evaluation of solutions. The steps include identifying attackers, assets under attack, threats, and other components; ranking the identified threats; choosing the appropriate combating methods; and building solutions based on the knowledge gained.

Security-Enablement Approaches

Robust and resilient security solutions and services are the need of the hour to sustain the continuous penetration of the pioneering cloud model into newer arenas. The security-imposed barriers need to be eliminated totally through a host of technological solutions. Best practices, processes, protocols, products, and patterns need to be collaboratively unearthed to address cloud security needs. In this section, we will see a set of diverse approaches and answers to the pestering security puzzles. Primarily, there are four critical elements: infrastructure, information, devices, and identity (as mentioned in a joint white paper by Symantec and VMware on cloud security).

Cloud Infrastructure Security

Virtualization allows the prominent IT resources (memory, storage, compute, and networking) in cloud centers to be decomposed and composed into a reusable and reclaimable pool of self-describing and autonomous IT resources. The evolution from siloed and monolithic infrastructure to a pool of flexible and functional resources enables dynamic allocation of IT resources to optimally meet the changing requirements. This empowerment thus brings an increased agility and reduced cost through greater sharing. Workloads may be allocated dynamically to different infrastructure components based on scalability, high availability, and DR needs. However, the dynamic ability to relocate a workload's supporting resources according to capacity and availability has to be securely performed [8].

- *Virtualized Security*—Security controls must be available across the virtual infrastructure so that workloads are well-protected as they are being transferred. This security feature must be available in an ad hoc basis to support dynamically constructed relationships among a variety of virtual resources. This requirement can be accomplished through a virtual security appliance, which is made available on demand across the virtual infrastructure. Security appliances are capable of all kinds of access controls, checks, monitoring, filtering, analysis, and decision taking. Appliances come in software form also and are made available as a service and hence appliance as a service (AaaS) is bound to scale up.
- *Automated Provisioning*—These virtual security appliances must be configured on demand when a workload arrives at a host. This requires automated provisioning of these security services that is integrated with cloud management infrastructures.
- *Lifecycle Management*—A new lifecycle context emerges for patching, configuration management, backup, and recovery. Patch management complexity is bound to go up with the addition of a new layer (hypervisor) for configuration and update purposes. There is also the need to patch off-line images and templates. Thus, lifecycle management policies and tools ought to be adjusted accordingly.
- *Logical Security Policies*—With virtualization, workloads are henceforth not tied to any specific devices. Therefore, its security policies too cannot be tied to physical devices such as fixed IPs, Media Access Control (MAC) addresses, and subnets.
- *Dynamic Trust Zones*—A trust zone represents a collection of workloads that share common security and compliance policies. This zone comprises hosts including both private and public clouds as well as physical infrastructure. Attaching policies to workloads is a stepping-stone for addressing security and compliance in the public cloud. Workloads can be migrated to the public infrastructure cloud as long as the same set of policies can be enforced in a consistent and visible manner. It is clear that physical monitoring tools lose the visibility into virtual resources.

Cloud Security Standards

There is no shortage for information security standards and compliance frameworks. ISO27002 ISMS, PCI-DSS, HIPAA, and SOX are some of them. Such industry standards have played a pivotal role in providing organizations and security professionals the ability to measure security in the context of business risks. As the importance of tightly protecting information assets in clouds is on the rise, consortiums and government agencies are again regrouping to fine-tune the existing security frameworks as well as to bring forth new standards to ensure cloud security. As the control of third-party clouds is going away from the data owners, the risk management framework has to take numerous views and factors into consideration. Users need to define the security-specific SLAs beforehand with the cloud providers. Otherwise, the consequences will be very bad.

SAS 70 is an auditing statement being issued by the Auditing Standards Board of the American Institute of Certified Public Accountants (AICPA). Obtaining an SAS 70 report from a trusted auditor can be used by a CSP to demonstrate to customers that the internal controls, related to both technology and personnel, are sufficient to meet the legal requirements. A report such as this may offer some reassurance to cloud customers.

SSL/IPSec

SSL is a very prominent security protocol ensuring encrypted connectivity between users and cloud applications. Because all data are encrypted from the user's machine to the cloud application, there is little chance of data exposure. If hackers did intercept the data, it would be useless for them in its encrypted form. SSL helps solve some of the most crucial and critical security needs of cloud computing. First, SSL encryption keeps prying eyes from reading private data as it is transmitted from server to server and between server and browser. The second benefit is that an SSL certificate can authenticate that a specific server and domain do belong to the person or organization that it claims to represent. This benefit requires that the hosting provider use SSL from a third-party certificate authority.

Another effective means to securely use cloud infrastructures is IPSec connections between the cloud and the user's machine. In essence, IPSec is a virtual private tunnel through the public Internet. It may offer greater security and more flexibility in maintaining segregated access to data. Yet SSL is easier to implement and is more portable than IPSec. Each has their roles to play in public and private cloud infrastructures.

Virtual LAN

Network virtualization is an important advancement in providing a full isolation for shielding and segregating data from other network users. A virtual LAN (VLAN) switching implementation is definitely more secure than a non-VLAN network switch environment. Because administrators can easily restrict network packet broadcasts to specified VLAN segments, the VLAN configuration prevents customers from accessing data from other LANs. That is, each VLAN is a network by itself completely isolated from unauthorized LAN users. Using this strategy, cloud vendors can accommodate a number of customers on one network, yet maintain secure network segmentation between the businesses.

Intrusion Detection and Prevention

Network security is essential for cloud security. There are firewalls, intrusion detection systems (IDS), and intrusion prevention systems (IPS) to stop any kind of network incursion. Intrusion detection and prevention (IDP) shields vulnerabilities in OSs and enterprise applications until they can be patched, to achieve timely protection against known and zero-day attacks. There are hardware appliances as well as software solutions for network security. Recently, powerful and policy-centric IDP firewalls have emerged that can read security policies and act on them quickly. These firewalls are smart due to attached policies and can do much more than traditional firewalls, which are preconfigured to recognize specific incoming (and outgoing) security threats in real time and automate the process to trigger the network telecommunications provider to block or redirect the traffic into a honeypot to quarantine the threat. But these policy-based firewalls are continually and automatically updated so that they can recognize and stop the latest worms, viruses, and DoS attacks before any damage is done.

Firewall

A bidirectional, stateful firewall, deployed on individual VMs, can provide centralized management of server firewall policy. It should include predefined templates for common enterprise server types and enable the following:

- VM isolation
- Fine-grained filtering (source and destination addresses, ports)
- Coverage of all IP-based protocols (TCP, UDP, ICMP, etc.)

- Coverage of all frame types (IP, ARP, etc.)
- Prevention of DoS attacks
- Ability to design policies per network interface
- Detection of reconnaissance scans on cloud computing servers
- Location awareness to enable tightened policy and the flexibility to move the VM from on-premise to cloud resources

Integrity Monitoring

Integrity monitoring of critical OS and application files (files, directories, registry keys and values, etc.) is necessary for detecting malicious and unexpected changes that could signal compromise of cloud computing resources. Integrity monitoring software must be applied at the VM level.

Log inspection collects and analyzes OS and application logs for security events. Log inspection rules optimize the identification of important security events buried in multiple log entries. These events can be sent to a stand-alone security system, but contribute to maximum visibility when forwarded to a security information and event management (SIEM) system or centralized logging server for correlation, reporting, and archiving.

Virtualization-aware malware protection leverages hypervisor introspection APIs to secure both active and dormant VMs. Layered protection uses dedicated scanning VMs coordinated with real-time agents within each VM. This ensures that VMs are secure when dormant and ready to go with the latest pattern updates whenever activated. Virtualization-aware malware protection can also preserve performance profile of virtual servers by running resource-intensive operations such as full system scans from a separate scanning VM.

Information Security

Securing information while at rest in cloud storage or in transit over the Internet is of paramount importance.

Data Encryption and Key Management

Not only is encrypting data during transmission via SSL or IPSec important, but also it is imperative to provide a data encryption facility while residing in cloud storage. This additional layer of protection keeps data safe from potential storage security lapses or even from administrator or management snooping. Encryption has been the most common method for protecting data while in transit and in rest. Governments, too, mandate using high-end encryption algorithms for information security. Both cloud users and providers have the responsibility of protecting against any data loss, leakage, and theft. Cloud customers expect strong data encryption services for their sensitive data from their SPs.

Not only should we have an efficient process for generating keys to encrypt and decrypt data, but we also need robust and resilient key management solutions. Cryptography is a double-edged sword. Strong encryption will prevent anyone from being able to see data including the owner, if the keys are in any way lost or corrupted. Proper key management is critical. If it gets botched, there is a risk that users will not want to activate the cryptography. Keys should also be securely held so that no one can obtain that key to access the data. Key storage, discovery, retrieval, and usage are very vital for unbreakable and impenetrable data security. That is, the encryption provides resource protection while key management enables controlled access to protected resources.

As such, clouds are predominantly shared environments through the much-maligned multitenancy facility and hence SPs often store their customers' data together (in a neatly isolated fashion) in a common database platform. Also for quick DR, discovery, scalability, and fault-tolerance through redundancy and resiliency, data are being stored in various geographical locations. Due to the rapid growth of cloud providers, cloud connectivity, integration, and collaboration schemes are taking shape through a host of industry-strength and open standards. Cloud federation and ultimately the vision of the intercloud are instigating a lot of collaborative activities such as the drafting and deriving of standard specifications for cloud portability and interoperability. In short, the cloud is very dynamic and breeds innovation.

As mentioned earlier, cloud services are shared by many tenants and the SPs have the privileged access to data in their custody. Thus, confidential data hosted in a cloud must be protected using a combination of security methods such as access control, contractual liability, and encryption. Encrypting data on a disk or in a live production database has value, as it can protect against a malicious cloud provider or an unscrupulous cotenant. For long-term archival storage, smart customers encrypt their own data and then send it as cipher text to a cloud data storage vendor. The customer keeps the cryptographic keys on his premises and uses the key to decrypt the cloud data whenever necessary.

Encryption Technologies

The field of cryptography has seen enormous growth due to its unassailable competency and capability in data protection. The RSA algorithm and elliptic curve cryptography (ECC) are the two leading cryptographic mechanisms in usage. There are key generation aspects based on finite ring and field theories too. Security providers are formulating a raft of key strengthening schemes. Security solution vendors consider simplicity and sensitivity as the two prime parameters for gaining market share.

File Encryption

This is by far the most flexible encryption within cloud environments. Encryption is applied at the source and managed by customers or third-party providers that act as reliable "proxies" for key management and encryption policy application. Quality cloud security is actually policy-based encryption for all VMs, with the VMs maintaining their encryption when moved through a cloud provider's environment. All key management and role-based access are defined locally before moving to the cloud. This greatly simplifies the migration of VMs across cloud environments. Cloud security appliances are forthcoming and they provide encryption, key management, tokenization, and user monitoring functionality, among other features.

Tokenization Technology

This is a highly popular method guaranteeing enterprise customers of a cloud provider the distinct ability to store, retrieve, and delete data based on the keys that the enterprise holds. Tokenization is actually the process of substituting original data with randomly generated alphanumeric values (tokens). Although structurally similar to the original data, these tokens have no mathematical relationship with the original data. The mapping between the original data and tokens is stored in a secure token database and access to this database is required to reverse the process and retrieve the original data. By retaining original data within the concerned jurisdiction and storing tokens in cloud applications, data residency challenges can be eliminated. Through this mechanism, neither the cotenant nor the cloud administrator can gain access to that data because the keys are with the concerned customer. Precisely, the data-handling tasks such as storage, retrieval, and deletion can only be accomplished by the keys held by the customer through encryption and decryption.

Identity and Access Management

In an extended enterprise, a growing array of devices (portables such as laptops, nomadic and mobile devices such as tablets, smartphones, etc., and in the future, any consumer electronics in homes, offices, manufacturing floors, etc.) are being empowered to access personal as well as professional cloud-based services. Traditionally, IT has used the enterprise identity concept to control user access and entitlement to a variety of on-premise information and application assets. This principle must be extended to identities at CSPs, controlling what information employees can access in which clouds, from which devices, and in which locations. It is overwhelmingly accepted that the federated identity mechanism is the best way forward for the dynamic cloud environments. This involves the following (from a white paper authored by the Co-Founder and Sr. Security Consultant at DTS Solution).

Extending Enterprise Credentials to Clouds

Existing policy for strong password controls and unique IDs that are consistent with those used by enterprise resources prevents the use of weak or shared passwords and can enforce secure logins for corporate data.

Enabling Single Sign-On to Cloud Applications

In an enterprise setup, there is a clear segregation between identity and SPs for facilitating SSO. The same can be extended to cloud-based applications.

Expanding Access Controls to Clouds

Existing role-based access control should be applicable to the controlled access of cloud resources. Thus, the existing mechanisms that monitor and audit access control are also enlisted in the cloud compliance effort. For example, cloud providers offer their own identity services and entitlement models. For access control purposes, the separate cloud identities must be tied to the respective enterprise identities. Further, policies must ensure that cloud provider entitlements are consistent with on-premise entitlements at all times.

Context-based authorization is critical in securely sharing information across different devices outside the physical infrastructure and augments user identity with attributes such as device location, device identity, and strong authentication credentials. Authorization policies must use such attributes to precisely control information flow between clouds, users, and devices. Beyond user identities, authentication is also an infrastructure and platform consideration—in particular, the authentication of different layers of the infrastructure to one another. Any infrastructure must be able to determine and report its secure and authenticated state before it makes a trust assertion on behalf of the objects and sessions it hosts. Additional considerations for authentication have to do with infrastructure and applications, particularly regarding hybrid cloud implementations. This is particularly true when IaaS is combined with PaaS, because PaaS introduces another abstraction layer that obscures the underlying IaaS details.

Federated Identity and Access Management in the Cloud

Managing identities of users and access control for enterprise applications remains one of the greatest challenges facing IT today. Although an enterprise may be able to leverage several cloud services without a good identity and access management (IAM) strategy, in the long run extending an organization's identity services into the cloud is a necessary precursor toward strategic use of on-demand computing services. Supporting today's aggressive adoption of an admittedly immature cloud ecosystem requires an honest assessment of an organization's readiness to conduct cloud-based IAM, as well as understanding the capabilities of that organization's cloud providers.

Identity Provisioning

One of the major challenges for organizations adopting cloud services is the secure and timely management of on-boarding (provisioning) and off-boarding (deprovisioning) of users in the cloud. Furthermore, the enterprises that have invested in user management processes within an enterprise will seek to extend those processes and practices to cloud services.

Authentication

When organizations start to utilize cloud services, authenticating users in a trustworthy and manageable manner is a vital requirement. Organizations must address authentication-related challenges such as credential management, strong authentication (typically defined as multifactor authentication), delegated authentication, and managing trust across all types of cloud services.

Federation

In a cloud environment, federated identity management plays a vital role in enabling organizations to authenticate the users of their cloud services using the organization's chosen identity provider (IDP). In that context, exchanging identity attributes between the SP and the IDP in a secure way is also an important requirement. Organizations considering federated identity management in the cloud should address the challenges with respect to identity lifecycle management, available authentication methods to protect confidentiality, and integrity, while supporting nonrepudiation.

Authorization and User Profile Management

The requirements for user profiles and access control policy vary depending on whether the user is acting on their own behalf (such as a consumer) or as a member of an organization (such as an employer, university, hospital, or other enterprise). The access control requirements in SP environments include establishing trusted user profile and policy information, using it to control access within the cloud service, and doing this in an auditable way.

Federated Identity

Identity federation builds a trust relationship between the applications that reflect business affiliations so that employees can remotely access applications with an SSO, regardless of whether or not the applications are locally or remotely located. Identity federation also protects an employee's private information. As a first step toward the cloud initiative, it is recommended to use the identity federation solution using an open standard solution, such as Security Assertion Markup Language (SAML), to ensure interoperability in a hybrid cloud environment while extending the internal IAM systems into the cloud. SAML addresses one of the key challenges in how to integrate all cloud resources with internal enterprise resources in order to deliver a unified service to employees and customers anywhere and anytime while still maintaining a secure environment.

Identity federation is based on two important concepts:

- The virtual reunion or assembled identity of a person's user information (or principal), which is stored across multiple distinct identity management systems. Typically, the user's name, being a common token, joins the data.
- A user's authentication process, which is integrated across multiple IT systems or even organizations.

For example, a traveler could be a flight passenger as well as a hotel guest. If the airline and the hotel use a federated identity management system, this means that they have a contracted mutual trust in each other's user authentication. Initially, the traveler can self-identify as a customer for booking the flight and then this identity can be transferred to hotel reservations. The ultimate goal of identity federation is to enable users of one domain to securely access data or systems of another domain seamlessly, without requiring redundant user administration. The goal requires that all participating systems use the same protocol to be interoperable. Public cloud computing SPs such as Google, Amazon, and Salesforce.com offer their own IAM interface, which by default is not capable of SSO. Private cloud computing SPs may recommend different IAM practices than enterprise customers.

To integrate cloud service into an enterprise's access portal with SSO, it is recommended that an identity federation open standard such as SAML is used. The SAML protocol decouples both the SAML identity provider and the SAML SP. This enables the enterprise to have a centralized IDP that can support many other SPs in a distributed fashion. The SAML identity provider focuses on identity management, access policy management, and security token generation, while SAML SPs receive the remote security token, retrieve credential data, and reinforce user access policies locally.

End-User Devices Security

Any discussions of cloud security normally focus on the service itself as well as the provider's security-guaranteeing capabilities. But failure to evaluate the entire service chain from beginning to end can introduce flaws and flops in service design and delivery. Generally, cloud services begin and end on any one of the devices such as a laptop, tablet, or smartphone. In the recent past, there was a plethora of praiseworthy advancements in the device space. Today, there are a variety of simple to smart devices facilitating the access and usage of IT services (local as well as global). Devices vary in size, scope, structure, smartness, and style. They are increasingly wireless and mobile. That is, they could be fixed, portable, wearable, implantable, pocketable, and so on. Web, enterprise, and cloud applications are appropriately enabled so that all kinds of handy and trendy gadgets and gizmos can be able to access them. Mobile enablement is a very fast-paced activity in the IT space. That is, end-users' choice, convenience, and comfort with IT access are progressively enhanced. In other words, anywhere, anytime, any device, and any channel access is being provided. There are scores of embedded system technologies (OSs, mark-up languages, development frameworks, emulators, microvisors, and so on) fueling the massive adoption of handhelds and other digital assistants as convenient and cheap service access instruments. Owing to this unexpected deluge of eye-catching and sophisticated devices, enterprises are forced to formulate workable policies to monitor device usage and to curb such usage in case of any dangerous deviation. That is, policies are required to enable and provision these devices, control access from them, and secure information transmission.

Device identities provisioned by mobile device management systems must be used for authentication, and these become an important attribute for context-aware authorization. The objective is not only to secure the device but also to control the access from that device based on its current security profile. Information and applications reside on devices, on-site servers, and in clouds. Users need to be trained to install natively built apps from app stores. Detecting and blocking installation of harmful third-party apps is another important policy control. Most enterprises today have internal risk management programs with mitigations to protect end points and manage information security. The local and physical infrastructure is well understood and visible to all levels of the environment. However, in a cloud environment, the visibility level is very thin. Cloud services may have dependencies on more than one service provider. Services can be found, bound, composed, and delivered as sophisticated services. Service brokers are very useful in realizing integrated and process-centric applications. Within an organization, there are multiple types of devices and hence end-user device security is very important. Providers cannot be solely dependent on end-device security and hence organizations have to share the burden. In short, the security considerations have to be end-to-end (input/output device to the remote cloud server). This helps to protect users from threats including theft of online identity, web site cross-scripting attacks, phishing attacks, and malicious software downloads.

EMERGING CLOUD SECURITY MECHANISMS

Policy-Based Cloud Security Enforcement (Ulrich Lang, ObjectSecurity, USA)

Automated solutions are being developed to shore up and strengthen the security and privacy attributes of cloud computing. Policies have been a proven mechanism for completely automating several important tasks in the IT field. In enterprise IT, business rule management systems (BRMSs) are a huge value addition. IT service management also depends largely on how policies are created, simulated, attached, accessed, enforced, and refined. It is not an exaggeration to say that policy setting, usage, and management are going to be highly beneficial and impactful in securing and shielding cloud systems. In the recent past, for autonomic and cognition-enabled IT systems, policy bases and a well-defined policy manager module collectively played a very vital role in accomplishing real-time and reliable operations and offerings. Policy-based solutions do not need human involvement in crunch situations. Software agents also sync up with policy services in order to assist IT systems in choosing the best possible routes and decisions in real time to achieve the preferred and prescribed targets. First, Java introduced and invoked the policy route as a viable and valuable method for ensuring the security of Java-based applications and applets.

Conventional security tools tend to work better for more generic security tools that do not require organization-specific policies and target the lower layers of the technology stack (network and OS layers), such as anti-virus, anti-malware, preconfigured network IDS, and generic application vulnerability scanning. Security automation becomes harder when organizational, user, and application behaviors have to be taken into account to enforce and audit security policies. For example, an organization that processes credit card payments will want to implement policies such as "no credit card information must leave the organization unencrypted and credit card information must be deleted when it is not used anymore." Another example would be a healthcare organization that wants to implement policies such as "doctors and nurses should only be able to access their current patients' health records without an alarm audit log being created." Such complex and contextual policies depend on the particular organization's security policies, business processes, applications, application interactions, and so on.

Why Model-Driven Security (MDS)?

MDA is a hot architectural pattern to system-generate workable source code from a variety of UML diagrams such as use case, class, activity, component, state, and sequence diagrams. This kind of shrewd automation at higher levels (model-to-code) goes a long way in streamlining modifiability, maintainability, and portability of code across different technologies. Model-driven software engineering (MDSE) is the latest development method being overwhelmingly evaluated and experimented as several product vendors are redrawing and repositioning their development platforms to be model driven. There is an arsenal of code generators and cartridges that produce code for generic as well as domain-specific applications. There are a number of newer players veering around and venturing passionately into the very challenging arena of MDA-compliant toolsets and platforms to further smoothen and speed up software implementation. Further, enthusiasts, exponents, and evangelists are pitching in with a suite of exemplary methods for suitably mingling the proven agile programming principles with the MDSE approach in order to bring in remarkable and radical enhancements in the software engineering field.

MDA is on a growth trajectory. Not only code generation but also policy generation is becoming automated by adeptly reusing MDA concepts. Especially in the security domain, MDS policy generation is being explored vigorously and rigorously. In other words, MDS intrinsically aids and adds the required level of automation in security policy creation and update by implicitly applying the reasoning behind the MDSE approaches to security and compliance policy management. MDS is a tool-supported process that involves modeling security requirements at a high level of abstraction and using other information sources available within the system, especially the applications' functional models produced by other stakeholders, to automatically generate fine-grained and contextual technical authorization and other security rules. The MDS process can be broken down into the following steps:

1. Policy modeling and automatic policy generation
2. Policy enforcement
3. Policy auditing
4. Automatic policy update

When employed effectively, MDS brings a number of benefits to the table. It reduces manual administration overheads and saves cost/time through automation (policy generation, enforcement, monitoring, and update). It also reduces security risks and increases assurance by minimizing human error potential and by ensuring that the security implementation is always in line with business requirements and with the functional behavior of the system. All these collectively contribute to a significant improvement in assuring and insuring the security and safety aspects of the system. MDS can greatly reduce the cost of protecting the system and improve security and safety compared to traditional, manual policy definition and management.

Policy as a Service

Policies have emerged as the most viable and venerable tool for runtime automation and management of software systems. Policies provide right and relevant insights for enabling adaptive systems dynamically. With the powerful emergence of the SaaS delivery model, the concept of "policy as a service" is slated to grow further decisively for next-generation applications. In particular, policy configurations are provided as a cloud-based service to application development and deployment tools at runtime. That is, cloud application deployment and runtime platforms are empowered to have functionalities and features such as automated policy generation/update, enforcement, monitoring, and so on.

Offering specification, maintenance, and update of policy models as a cloud service to corporations has a number of significant benefits. That is, instead of owning and maintaining the policy models for accomplishing the highly unbreakable MDS solutions, the application developers and security specialists of the corporations can now simply subscribe to the kinds of policy feeds they require without needing to know the inside details of the models. The policy SP takes care of the policy modeling, maintenance, and update activities. All kinds of improvisations in policy models are being taken care of automatically at the cloud front and the corporate executives need not bother about any new releases, patches, editions, and so on. The up-front cost hurdle is also greatly minimized thanks to the cloud-inspired subscription model.

Why Policy-Based Automation at the Cloud?

Business applications and services are being modernized and migrated to cloud environments to achieve a greater reach and to bring out rich enterprise applications (REAs). Cloud service brokers (CSBs) and mashup tools are increasingly finding prominence in the cloud ecosystem. A plethora of business and IT services are finding their new residence in cloud environments. Novel service delivery, subscription, pricing, and consumption models are emerging in order to effectively take care of business changes and challenges. Not only software applications but also platforms (development, deployment, delivery, management, governance, security, etc.) are being taken to clouds. As software development teams are increasingly dispersed in different locations and they are working in a collaborative mode, cloud-based software implementation methods are gaining ground.

Policy formulation, enforcement, and governance tasks are fit to be executed from clouds. Policy development, mashup, deployment, and management platforms are being gradually moved to cloud infrastructures. This enables the automatic generation of policies in the cloud using the fast-maturing model-driven approach. Policy enforcement could be integrated into the application platform so that the generated technical policies are automatically enforced whenever cloud services are accessed. PEPs typically raise security-related runtime alerts, especially about incidents related to invocations that have been blocked. The collection, analysis, and visual representation of those alerts can also be moved into the cloud. This has numerous benefits. That is, incidents can be centrally analyzed for multiple cloud services together with other information (e.g., network intrusion detection). Further, an integrated visual representation of the security posture across multiple cloud services can be provided, integrated incident information can be stored for auditing purposes, and compliance-related decision support tools can be offered as a cloud service.

Information Lifecycle Management in the Cloud

Data is the key component for any IT applications to be successful executing their assignments. Effective data handling, storage, processing, safeguarding, mining, and analysis are paramount for the grand success of IT in its role of precisely and profoundly automating scores of business operations. Data security is all about the pragmatic processes, practices, and tools for efficient preservation of data from any leakage to the wrong hands, pilferage during transmission, misuse, defacement, displacement, and so on. As IT applications and data get readied for cloud environments, the traditional methods of securing data at remote cloud centers are bound to fail. As the revered cloud paradigm rides on a number of unique factors such as elasticity, multitenancy, and virtualization, the security management plan has to be accordingly enhanced. Especially on public clouds, the total loss of controllability and visibility is being prescribed as the prime motivation for security experts and consultants to plunge into unearthing competing techniques and tips for cloud data security. Data security is a prime point and phase in any information life cycle management solution.

Data Dependability

Data confidentiality, integrity and nonrepudiation, data reliability, availability, auditability and access control (authentication and authorization) are the prominent factors and features of data dependability.

Data Location

There must be an explicit assurance that the data, including all of its copies and backups, is stored only in geographic locations permitted by contract, SLA, and/or regulation.

Data Isolation

Data, especially classified, regulated, and sensitive data, must not be commingled with other customer data while in use, storage, or transit. A proven isolation mechanism has to nip any kind of mixing, mingling, and merging with others' data at the budding stage itself.

Data Recovery and Restoration

Data must be available all the time and data backup and recovery methods must be in place in order to prevent any data loss, unwanted data overwrite, and destruction. Data restoration has to be guaranteed.

Data Discovery

For fulfilling various needs including governmental obligations, the data discovery facility has to be a simple task. If there is a need to find and use some important data, the initial discovery process has to be really quick and smooth.

Data Aggregation and Inference

For advanced analytics, data aggregation is a key feature. The data aggregation could become a more complicated affair when data is in the cloud. The data aggregation and its ensuing inferences could result in breaching the confidentiality of classified and customer information. Hence, a strong scheme has to be in place to assure the data owner and data stakeholders that the data is still protected from subtle breach when data is mapped, mingled, and aggregated.

Data Abolition

When users vacate a cloud, all the data have to be completely eliminated and the cloud provider should not keep any remnant data that could be misused or shared at a later point in time. All the data storage (primary as well as secondary) and backups (local as well as distant) have to be double-checked to erase any data that is left over and there has to be an automated mechanism in place to guarantee that what the provider says about data obliteration is absolutely true.

The data security life cycle, which is quite different from the information life cycle, consists of six phases and extra efforts need to be taken as far as data residing in the cloud.

- *Create*—classify and assign rights to data via data labeling techniques, digital rights management and watermarking, and user tagging to classify data.
- *Store*—data access control for DBMSs and document management systems, data encryption and decryption to authorized users, content discovery and data loss prevention.
- *Use*—use of activity monitoring and enforcement using log files, rights management and logical controls using DBMS solutions, real-time alert and notification of any status change to the data owner.
- *Share*—use of encryption for sensitive information and signed documents, activity monitoring for shared information, and integrity preservation for data in transit.
- *Archive*—data residency monitoring within storage environments, asset management, and tracking and encryption on backup archived information and for data at rest; data archived should only be retrieved by the data owner.
- *Destroy*—removal and secure deletion of information by authorized personnel, validate deletion with content discovery tool, crypto-shredding, and content reconstruction should not be possible.

Trusted Cloud Computing

The Trusted Computing Group (TCG) (http://www.trustedcomputinggroup .org) is an industry consortium that has developed standards for using trusted computing techniques in laptop and desktop computers, networking, and storage.

TCG has defined the specification for the Trusted Platform Module (TPM), which will provide stronger security than what software alone can provide. The TPM is a hardware security component that is an international standard and is being built into many computers and computer-based products. The TPM includes capabilities such as machine authentication, hardware encryption, signing, secure key storage, and attestation. Encryption and signing are well-known techniques, but the TPM makes them stronger by storing keys in protected hardware storage. Machine authentication is a core principle that allows clouds to authenticate to a known machine to provide this machine and user a higher level of service as the machine is known and authenticated. When the attestation feature is used, the TPM monitors software as it is loaded and provides secure reports on exactly what is running on the machine. This monitoring and reporting are especially important in the cloud environment where viruses and worms can hide in many places. The TPM provides a strong security foundation for other TCG specifications including Trusted Network Connect (TNC) and Trusted Storage.

The TNC architecture provides an industry standard approach to network security and network access control (NAC). The TNC standards enable administrators to control network access based on user identity and device health while monitoring network behavior and responding immediately to problems as they occur.

The TCG's Trusted Storage specification provides a manageable and enterprise-wide means for implementing full-disk encryption using hardware included right in the drive. These drives, known as self-encrypting drives, simplify the enterprise encryption process for handling sensitive data, since all data, applications, and drivers are encrypted internal to the drive and key management is an integral part of the design. The hardware-based encryption can take advantage of the TPM if desired and does not require user intervention or impact system performance, unlike traditional software-only encryption schemes that require cycle time from the main processor. With a self-encrypting drive, when a drive is removed for any reason (maintenance, end of life, or even theft), the data is completely useless to criminals since they do not know the encryption key.

Hard drive manufacturers are now shipping self-encrypting drives that implement the TCG's Trusted Storage standards. Self-encrypting drives build encryption hardware into the drive, providing automated encryption with minimal cost or performance impact. The TPM can easily provide stronger authentication than username and passwords. TCG's IF-MAP

(Metadata Access Protocol) standard allows for real-time communication between the cloud provider and the customer about authorized users and other security issues. When a user is fired or reassigned, the customer's identity management system can notify the cloud provider in real time so that the user's cloud access can be modified or revoked within seconds. If the fired user is logged into the cloud, they can be immediately disconnected. Typically, a cloud provider would use VMs and a hypervisor to separate customers. TCG technologies can provide significant security improvements for VM and virtual network separation. In addition, the TPM can provide hardware-based verification of hypervisor and VM integrity. The TNC architecture and standards can provide strong network separation and security. In the areas of data retention and deletion, Trusted Storage and TPM access techniques can play a key role in limiting access to data. TCG's IF-MAP specification enables the integration of different security systems and provides real-time notification of incidents and of user misbehavior.

CLOUD SECURITY PATTERNS

Gunnar Peterson, from Arctec Group, insists that security must extend beyond infrastructure and into the infostructure (applications and data) and metastructure (policy). Infostructure concerns include the following:

- Service bindings: service protocols and message formats
- Service mediation: services that mediate access to applications and data
- Message and communication encryption: confidentiality services at the data and transport level
- Message and data integrity: tamperproofing messages and data
- Malicious usage: dealing with asset abuse

Metastructure concerns include the following:

- Security token exchanges: the ability to validate and issue security tokens
- Security policy management: policy definition, enforcement, and lifecycle management

- PEPs: mapping name spaces, resources, uniform resource identifiers, channels, and objects
- Policy decision points (PDPs): the workflow for determining access
- Message exchange patterns: defining claims and schemas
- Detection services: logging and monitoring (recording and publishing events)
- Key management processes: key generation, distribution, and lifecycle management

There are four technology patterns: security gateways, monitoring (and logging), security token services (STSs), and PEPs. Each pattern lets security architects address security policy concerns in the metastructure and improve the runtime capabilities in the infostructure. Such a stack of security architecture services enables the following:

- Visibility into security events
- Attack surface reduction
- Context-specific security tokens
- Fine-grained access control

Security Gateways

The gateway manages the attack surface for the cloud's entry and exit points. The attack surface comprises the data, methods, and channels that are integrated via the cloud. So, the gateway must have visibility across these layers, including data and application methods, and not merely into the communication channel, as network firewalls do. The gateway acts as a proxy for communication between the enterprise and the cloud. Gateways mediate all communication to and from cloud services, enabling more granular control of cloud use. A service gateway lets an enterprise gracefully lose some but not all of its control over its security policy when it moves to the cloud. The gateway security architecture responsibilities fall into five main categories:

- Communication channel security services include transport encryption, transport authentication, transport integrity, proxy services, and protocol bridging.
- Message security services include authentication (signing and verifying a message using XML Signature), integrity (hash messages

using XML), and encryption (message-level encryption using XML Encryption).

- Message processing includes message transformation and content validation.
- Systems management includes systems logging, administrative interfaces, and testing. Threat protection includes input validation, protection against escaping data, XML denial of service (XDoS) protection, output encoding, and virus protection.

Monitoring and Logging

Monitoring implements network security monitoring, wiretaps, audit logs, and other tools to provide sensors for detecting security events. Because these systems are mainly passive, they can be incorporated into cloud system design without making any heady impacts on SLAs. Implementing this technology poses several questions. Where do sensors have to be placed? Who are in control of those sensors? What events are important? How should they be published? And who reviews the logs created?

Security Token Services

An STS has two main interfaces: it can issue a security token and validate a security token. The ability to first validate and then issue security tokens means an STS can exchange tokens. Cloud providers implement SAML assertions and proprietary token types. A policy-based way to exchange tokens that ensures the secure exchange of attributes and session data is becoming obligatory. An STS can be deployed mainly in two ways: on the IDP and SP side. The location of an STS dictates its function. The responsibilities of an IDP STS include the following:

- Subject-claim mapping
- Policy-based map requests and responses to tokens
- Policy-based route and transform requests and responses
- Policy-based payload access

In addition, the IDP must communicate with authentication systems, user stores, and directories such as those following the Lightweight Directory Access Protocol (LDAP). The IDP might also be required to support any number of multifactor authentication systems. So, the STS can dynamically gather attributes and session data required by the relying party on the SP side. The responsibilities of an SP STS include the following:

- Mapping of objects or resources to claims
- Policy-based mapping requests and responses to tokens
- Policy-based route and transform requests and responses
- Policy-based payload access

In this case, the SP STS must know about the managed objects such as Java Naming and Directory Interface (JNDI) trees, JDBC, databases, and Web service methods. In cloud scenarios, either deployment type is appropriate. On the SP-initiated side, the capabilities are similar to access management—defining and enforcing access control policies. On the IDP-initiated side, the capabilities are similar to an identity management suite. To enable the STS trust fabric, a federated identity has to be agreed upon. The role of STS is to support, validate, issue, and exchange tokens. But the enterprise gains a composite security protocol.

Policy Enforcement Points

In the security policy life cycle, the security architect must create, enforce, and manage policy. But in cloud architectures, these policy decisions are often dynamic. PEPs enable fine-grained and decentralized security policy decisions through languages such as Extensible Access Control Markup Language (XACML). These languages associate subject and object policy targets with rules specifying authorized conditions and actions. The security policy manager bundles these decisions into standards-based XML documents that can be transported and consumed across many disparate parts in the system. This lets a PEP query PDPs to make authorization decisions in a highly distributed way.

In summary, in a cloud environment, the infrastructure is outsourced and inherently not trustable. The infostructure is responsible for verifying what it receives, and the metastructure defines where and how to perform the verification.

CLOUD SECURITY BEST PRACTICES

The *Cloud Trust Protocol* (CTP) (http://www.csc.com) is positioned and prescribed as an effective mechanism by which cloud users ask for and receive information about the elements of transparency (the compliance, security, privacy, integrity, and operational security history of service elements) from cloud providers. These elements bear testimony about the essential security configuration and operational characteristics for systems that are deployed in the cloud. The elements of transparency embolden cloud consumers to make the right decisions about what applications and data need to be moved to the cloud and to decide which cloud is best suited to satisfy the identified processing needs. The primary purpose behind the CTP and the elements of transparency is to generate an evidence-based proof that everything that is declared by cloud providers is indeed true. With this immutable assurance, cloud users become completely liberated to bring in more sensitive and valuable business functions to the cloud and reap even larger payoffs in due course of time.

The CTP is a down-to-earth asynchronous protocol and follows a "question and response" pattern. The CTP is intended to be presented to all cloud providers and is ultimately controlled by cloud users themselves. The CTP solves two parallel needs for security and trust in clouds with one simple and straightforward mechanism. First, it provides a way for cloud users to specify and ask about the configuration, vulnerability, access, authorization, policy, accountability, anchoring, and operating status conditions. This puts the control and decision making back in the hands of the users. Second, the CTP provides a standard and low-impact technique for cloud providers to prepare and deliver information in response to requests about elements of transparency in the best possible way for them.

Assessment and Reliability Audits

Cloud providers need to be more open in revealing rather than concealing the facts about their daily operations to their current and perspective clients. There are a few incidents and instances widely published in the worldwide media that cloud vendors have not adequately divulged their security and reliability audit findings/report. This does not mean that the cloud installations are insecure or unreliable, but openness goes a long way in convincing the users about the capacities and capabilities of the cloud installations. There are specific standards being prescribed for data centers. Users always like to know about the well-being of their data, the standards which are complied with, the security strategy in place, the DR mechanism, any information about any kind of outages, and so on. That is, vendors need to be more accommodative for assuaging clients' concerns. Third-party auditability has to be allowed to boost the clients' confidence. Cloud providers have to be very proactive and prompt in implementing the right and relevant security solutions and best practices in order to guarantee utmost security for customers' data.

Security Compliance

Managing and maintaining compliance status within our own environment is by far simpler and sustainable than ensuring that the compliance is satisfactorily met in cloud environments. When IT resources are under the control of the organization, ensuring compliance through governance is pretty straightforward. Roles and responsibilities are clearly defined, and compliance controls are designed and implemented with management approval while the audit of compliance status can easily be tracked and measured. The moment services are migrated to cloud, an organization effectively loses control on how compliance has to be implemented and maintained at the cloud site. There has to be a thorough investigation and a detailed gap analysis before moving mission-critical assets to the cloud if there is a slight fear of an asset being dismantled and deprived.

Hypervisor security is the process of ensuring the hypervisor (alternatively termed as VMM) is secure throughout its life cycle. The hypervisor is the core software for creating, provisioning, deprovisioning, and management of VMs. It is also responsible for the security of all the VM assets that are functioning in the physical server. The VM-to-VM communication is also enabled by the hypervisor. Similarly, any communication between a VM and one or more external entities is facilitated by the VMM. In short, the hypervisor is the most crucial component for providing security in virtual zones. As indicated earlier, the VM-to-VM communication does not traverse the network infrastructure and everything happens inside the physical server and hence the traditional network security firewalls cannot be a right answer for traffic inspection. It is highly recommended to go for a virtual security appliance to strengthen hypervisor security. A virtual firewall that operates at the hypervisor level provides ample security for functional VMs and sharply enhances the required visibility of VMs and their interactions.

Cloud Risk Management Framework

The following focus areas of risk management should be at the forefront when considering cloud deployment.

1. Identify the information assets for cloud migration, deployment, and delivery.
2. Evaluate the assets and measure both technical and business risks associated with each of the assets.
3. Correlate the asset to the type of proposed cloud service and deployment model.
4. Identify the potential data flow, the information asset, and the users.
5. Develop audit controls that can be delivered to the data owner as a self-service or on-demand by the cloud provider.
6. Validate the information life cycle for the asset—data encryption and decryption, data residency, retention, and deletion.
7. Verify the consistency of authorized use of assets by users between existing in-house and cloud provider services.
8. Ensure there is no lock-in clause for the cloud provider and confirm that assets are portable between cloud providers.
9. Insure data protection from leakage during data transit and storage and malicious cloud administrators.
10. Understand the legal risks associated with the transnational data flow across countries with differing legal jurisdictions.
11. Create a security SLA with the cloud provider with financial penalty clauses for any violations.

WHY THE SAAS-BASED "SECURITY AS A SERVICE" MODEL?

Security as a Service

A comprehensive security strategy with a sound risk, threat, and vulnerability management plan is mandatory for organizations considering the emerging security scenario. The perpetual vigilance against any kind of attack is not something to be taken lightly. More often, business organizations face a number of changes and challenges on the business and technology fronts. The financial instability, peer pressure, shifting and soaring expectations of marketplace, and so on combine to create a big headache for people in charge of security assurance. As IT is being recognized as the best enabler of business operations, IT security is a very critical component for any organization to move forward successfully. It involves both physical and logical security. In the recent past, there has been a paradigm shift from on-premise to off-premise computing styles. A kind of consolidation and centralization is gripping the entire IT industry. This transition brings in significant and strategic benefits for business houses. Instead of committing a large amount of money upfront for buying, installing, and administering a suite of security solutions, current and future security needs could be easily accomplished through the formal subscription of SLA-driven security solutions and services from competent cloud-based security providers. Also, the expenditure on expensive security experts can be avoided through this game-changing transition.

The SaaS model has grown phenomenally and this has laid the successful foundation for IT platforms and infrastructures also being provided as services over the web to global users. The trend, without an iota of doubt is "everything as a service." Thus, the model of "security as a service" is gaining a lot of traction these days. The new service delivery model guarantees the rapid deployment of security solutions and they can be instantly retracted when the need slides down.

Security Compliance as a Service

The strict compliance to rules and regulations is very critical for any organization. Corporations have to be very demanding to sternly measure and transparently report how their security policies are being followed by each entity within. Being complacent or getting it wrong in this area can have devastating and irreparable consequences. Hence, many organizations willingly invest huge amounts of resources in auditing and assurance services to fully ensure the required compliance. As far as physical security is concerned, the compliance failures can easily result in data breaches, exposure to financial losses, DoS, and bodily injury to employees and visitors. The use of traditional physical security architecture exposes company assets and personal information to constant threats. Further, effective compliance management entails huge costs. The SaaS model greatly simplifies the enforcement of policy compliance and audits by providing centralized capabilities to establish standards. Also, SaaS providers install and involve a family of tools to track and report on compliance. Since a SaaS solution database is centralized, the cost for performing compliance audits is significantly small. Many SaaS providers are also able to provide evidence of internal controls certified by independent auditors, thus eliminating the need for a subscriber to incur these costs.

Affordability

The survival of every organization hinges on its ability to deliver value for its customers at lesser costs. Due to the uncertainty prevailing in the world economy, IT budgets are being pruned down. This forces the IT divisions of business behemoths to look out for new models that involve less cost and risks for the solid IT enablement of their business operations, outlooks, and offerings. In other words, the current IT model is very capital intensive and hence executives and experts are moving toward a pragmatic strategy of employing the utility-like, subscription-based, and usage-centric cost model for IT services. The hot "as a service" model provides an excellent alternative. That is, apart from cutting down the costs, it enables organizations to focus on their core and competency areas. Thus, instead of wasting their money on IT maintenance, this new SaaS model helps them to insightfully spend their hard-earned money on springing forth a series of innovations (Figure 10.1).

Business Continuity

Disasters can strike anywhere and can be nature induced and human-made. Fires, floods, hurricanes, earthquakes, terrorism, and so on can be the prime cause for massive disasters. Power and network outages can knock down IT centers totally. Hence, it is essential to plan ahead to ensure quick DR and BC. This highlights the need for redundancy and resiliency in IT systems. Having backups is absolutely mandatory. DR facility for strengthening BC cannot be compromised.

Fortunately, the SaaS model is the perfect solution. Multitenant SaaS services are normally hosted in highly reliable data centers with built-in redundancy. DR centers come to the rescue if there is damage in the primary cloud center. Redundancy in the communication path is built into this model due to the Internet's capability to send information via a large

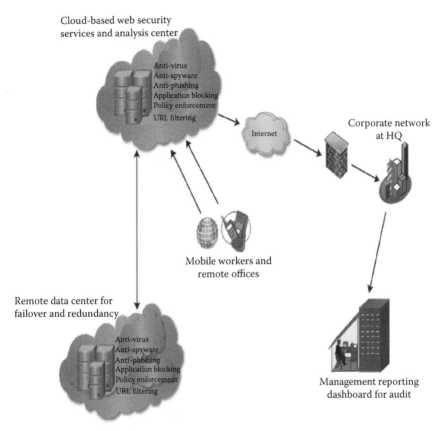

FIGURE 10.1
Security as a service model.

number of routes. Even if a wired network fails, there are wireless options. In the SaaS model, there is no need of any special computing machines or software to operate a physical security application. That is, any thin client device with Internet connectivity is more than enough to plunge into action in case of any emergency.

Global Coverage

Reach and richness are two important parameters for industries to grow and glow in their specialties. Organizations often put their branch and sales offices in new territories in order to capture and retain greater market and mind share. However, any expansion comes with significant challenges, risks, and expenses. Solutions that provide good results in one location or at a small place can become troublesome or insufficient when extended for many geographically dispersed sites. Typically, such installations expose the vulnerabilities, complexities, and hidden expenses of traditional client/server solutions.

The "security as a service" solutions provide tangible benefits for organizations with geographically dispersed offices. The online, on-demand, and off-site SaaS-based solutions are inherently scalable to wider areas across the globe instantly at very minimal costs. The centralized resource provisioning and security management go a long way in revitalizing the pervasive and penetrative SaaS model. In this model, IT facilities can be quickly deployed and availed.

In conclusion, as widely known, IT is the best fit for business augmentation, automation, and acceleration. The recent yet potent SaaS IT model brings in a slew of fresh and practical improvisations for businesses to be substantially empowered. Everything expressed and exposed as a service through this paradigm ensures business agility, autonomy, adaptability, and extensibility along with affordability.

CLOUD SECURITY PROPRIETARY SOLUTIONS

Joyent SmartOS: Hardened Kernel

Traditional applications and VMs are executed almost literally on sand. The porous nature of the OS allows security breaches and the direct access to hardware leads to the introduction of new vulnerabilities and holes. The Joyent SmartOS, on the other hand, is a solid, hardened foundation for applications, with a tightly secured layer between applications and the underlying hardware and OS. The Joyent SmartOS is an integral part of the Joyent Smart Technologies architecture, integrating with its Smart DataCenter management and SmartPlatform development environment.

SmartMachine Security

Like other virtual OSs, the Joyent SmartOS allocates CPU, memory, disk, and network I/O for customers to run their applications with SmartMachines. However, Joyent SmartMachines offer virtual computing resources within individual containers so that the virtual memory and disk are completely isolated. This allows Joyent to better customize and scale virtual resources for customers, and to provide greater control and security than the existing approaches to virtualization. Most importantly, Joyent's SmartMachine virtual resources are a part of the Joyent SmartOS rather than a VM application running on top of an OS. This inclusive virtualization eliminates potential application OS interface vulnerabilities at the outset, reduces the risk of hyperjacking, and reduces overall attack surface within the VM. Each of the SmartMachine resource containers is isolated from the rest. Storage, memory, and network I/O remain in separate containers in the system, while only CPU cycles are shared across SmartMachines to offer the economies of CPU bursting using a fair share algorithm to allocate idle CPU resources to containers as needed. By capping the memory and storage space, Joyent is able to control costs while passing the savings on to clients with variable demands for CPU cycles with no financial burden to consume idle CPU resources that would otherwise go unused.

Security Gateways

Because of the co-location of multiple VMs in a cloud, it is important to combat the threat of malicious activities spreading fast into the VMs. Segmentation in a physical environment prevents this; but in a virtualized environment, there is no such facility. Policy enactment and enforcement is the most desired mechanism as it helps to apply the same critical rules, logins, and access privileges. A Virtual Security Gateway of the type developed by Clavister (http://www.clavister.com) is a firewall that runs inside virtual infrastructure and ensures that security policies are enforced for all communications inside the virtual environment. VMs are not allowed to talk to each other unless they go through the security gateway. The Gateway uses VPN encryption (as illustrated in Figure 10.2) to secure communication between VMs. Since the Virtual Security Gateway can be run inside the virtual infrastructure, security auditing can be achieved and thus regulatory compliance requirements can be met. Users have the scalability to simply deploy new security gateways as they expand their environment. Also, since the virtual security gateway is part of the virtual infrastructure, it becomes easier to create lab/test environments, which decreases the complexity of security tests and, in turn, improves the overall security.

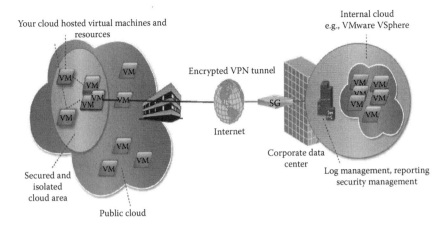

Your cloud hosted virtual machines and resources

Internal cloud e.g., VMware VSphere

Encrypted VPN tunnel

Internet

Corporate data center

Secured and isolated cloud area

Public cloud

Log management, reporting security management

FIGURE 10.2
Security gateway.

Navajo Systems Virtual Private SaaS

Virtual Private SaaS (VPS) (http://www.navajosystems.com) is a revolutionary concept in SaaS application data security. VPS transparently encrypts all SaaS application data deemed sensitive by the enterprise before it is transmitted to the SaaS provider. Thus, all sensitive data are stored in encrypted form when stored in the SaaS provider's databases. When the data are returned to the client, the process is reversed (encrypted data elements are automatically decrypted by VPS). End users remain completely unaware of this background process, yet their data are completely unreadable (and therefore meaningless) when stored on the SaaS provider's servers.

- When VPS is used, database theft, whether by a dishonest employee of the SaaS provider or by an outside hacker, becomes harmless because the stolen data is completely undecipherable without decryption by VPS. Likewise, identity theft outside the borders of the organization becomes harmless, and regulatory compliance is ensured, as all sensitive data remain undecipherable, stored encrypted on the SaaS provider's servers.
- With VPS, the enterprise has full control over its sensitive data since it holds all the encryption keys and is solely responsible for its data security. All encryption/decryption operations are performed by VPS, which can be located inside the corporate firewall or in the cloud (with exclusive VPN access). The security officer of the

enterprise can use VPS to modify security policies to ensure that all sensitive data are protected to the extent required by the company's needs and by regulatory mandate.

- The uniqueness of VPS encryption is that even while sensitive company data is undecipherable when stored in the SaaS provider's database, full application functionality is retained. Supported functionality includes searching, sorting, report generation, and field validation. This is accomplished through a unique set of patent-pending encryption methods, based on NIST-standard encryption algorithms. All VPS operations are completely transparent to both the end users and the SaaS application itself.
- VPS is a "universal on-ramp" to the cloud, allowing enterprises to safely use one or more SaaS applications with a single device. VPS can be configured to apply the desired levels of security/encryption to individual data fields in each SaaS application independently.
- VPS is shipped with preconfigured encryption policies for selected SaaS applications, allowing easy and out-of-the-box implementation. The enterprise may further customize the types of encryption applied to each data field of each SaaS application.

Vormetric Data Security

Vormetric Data Security (http://www.vormetric.com) provides a single manageable and scalable solution to encrypt any file, any database, any application, anywhere it resides—without sacrificing application performance or creating key management complexity. Vormetric Data Security helps to alleviate security and data governance concerns surrounding cloud computing using the same encryption, policy and key management, and reporting that enterprises use today for securing on-premise data. By securing data with encryption and controlling the security policies around data usage, Vormetric allows organizations to overcome the cloud security challenges of multitenancy, data privacy, data remanence, separation of duties (SOD), and reporting. Vormetric protects data and controls access irrespective of whether the data is located in private, public, or hybrid clouds.

- *Rapid Deployment*—Vormetric Data Security transparently encrypts data without requiring application or database redesign or recoding. Enterprises can rapidly deploy cloud applications with encryption of specific files in place.

- *Centralized Key and Policy Management*—While data is protected in the cloud, Vormetric Data Security allows enterprises to directly maintain control over key and policy management through an FIPS-validated system that can ensure the custody and security of encryption keys needed for regulated data.

- *Enforcing SOD*—Vormetric Data Security enforces SOD by allowing developers to do their work in developing and deploying applications in private cloud or Infrastructure-as-a-Service environments while IT Security establishes and enforces policies around data access via the Vormetric Data Security console. This approach ensures that policies are enforced and avoids the possibility that operational or cloud staff accidentally "turn off" policies.

- *Precise, Granular Encryption*—Vormetric operates at a granular file level to enforce encryption, enable access control policies, and audit usage at the server, process, and user layers. This approach extends the security value of encryption beyond simple media theft protection and allows enterprises to address insider threats and SOD, and gain insight into access activity for data in the cloud. IT administrators can mount storage volumes, but cannot access data unless the policy established via the Vormetric console permits such access.

- *Portability from Physical to Virtual to Cloud Environments*—Evolving business requirements are causing enterprises to consider moving data between private and public clouds, driving a need for data-centric controls that travel with data. Vormetric addresses this need through an encryption and access control policy model that can automatically follow data. This capability eliminates redundant policy stores for on-premise/private cloud and public cloud infrastructures, while ensuring consistent enforcement of security standards and adherence to compliance requirements wherever the data resides.

Intel Service Gateway

This is a new class of platform (http://www.intel.com) designed for massive scalability and control for mediating service interactions from enterprise to the cloud. As a control agent, the gateway sits at the edge of the physical network and provides runtime enforcement of security policies, threat prevention, quality of service enforcement, and the mediation of identities and credentials for cloud services. The service gateway is also able to enforce persistent security properties on enterprise data (Figure 10.3).

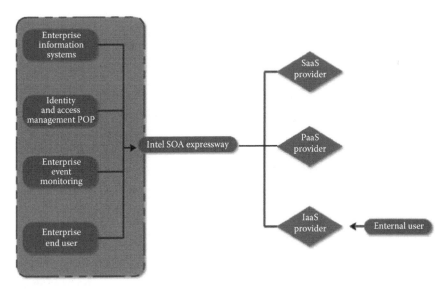

FIGURE 10.3
Intel service gateway.

This is an important point and refers to message-level data protection such as encryption and digital signature operations. This capability extends the perimeter of the enterprise directly into the cloud provider itself by protecting the data even while it is outside the enterprise control. The service gateway also has additional properties such as compatibility with any enterprise and cloud service. The service gateway is itself scalable through virtualization in the private cloud, and has the unrivaled capability to run on low cost, commodity server hardware already deployed throughout the enterprise.

CONCLUSION

It is a fact that the much-published security problem stands in the way of widespread adoption of cloud infrastructures, platforms, and services by worldwide users as envisaged and expounded originally. Security professionals and university professors have come out with a series of cloud-specific security risks. Cloud computing is being presented and projected by many as the flexible and futuristic computing model. It is capable of strategically and significantly empowering and enhancing the sagging and sliding value and verve of web, enterprise, and embedded systems. Having understood the various cloud-induced security concerns, CSPs are striving hard and stretching forward to come out with dependable and foolproof security solutions in order to enable global consumers, clients, and customers to accept and adopt the powerful and potential clouds instantly and to retain them.

Especially as public clouds leverage the pervasive, public, open, and cheap Internet as the communication infrastructure, new security and privacy threats at various levels (system, network, application, and data) have emerged and solidified. Further, as physical servers are being segmented into a number of virtual servers for enhanced utilization of expensive IT resources through optimal sharing (i.e., via the newly introduced multitenancy concept), the security risks at the VM image level also have to be closely monitored and measured for any kind of unwanted and unexpected deviations. Individuals and innovators find the cloud handy and trendy in taking their innovations and inventions to market quickly without spending anything substantially on the relevant IT infrastructures. Visionaries and consultants are therefore working overtime on guaranteeing application security. As described previously, the hard-to-crack automation of application security is being approached via setting and sustaining effective policies.

REFERENCES

1. Microsoft Global Foundation Services. May 2009. "Securing Microsoft's Cloud Infrastructure," Microsoft Global Foundation Services, https://cloudsecurityalliance.org/securing-the-MS-Cloud.pdf.
2. Sheikh, S. 2011. "A Holistic Security Approach to Cloud Computing," DTS Solution, http://www.dts-solution.com/wp-content/uploads/2011/10/A-Holistic-Security-Approach-to-Cloud-Computing-v1.0.pdf.
3. Cattedu, D., and G. Hoben, eds. November 2009. "Benefits, Risks and Recommendations for Information Security," The European Network and Information Security Agency (ENISA).
4. Securosis. 2012. "Welcome to Securosis Research," Securosis, https://securosis.com/research.
5. Tsai, H., M. Siebenhaar, A. Miede, Y. Huang, and R. Steinmetz. 2012. "Threat as a Service? Virtualization's Impact on Cloud Security." *IT Professional Magazine* 14 (1): 32–37.
6. Owens, K. 2009. "Securing Virtual Compute Infrastructure in the Cloud," Savvis, Inc., http://www.savvis.com/en-us/info_center/documents/hos-whitepaper-securingvirutalcomputeinfrastructureinthecloud.pdf.
7. Cloud Security Alliance. 2012. Cloud Security Alliance, https://cloudsecurityalliance.org.
8. Trend Micro, Inc. August 2009. "Making Virtual Machines Cloud-Ready," Trend Micro, Inc., http://www.trendmicro.com/cloud-content/us/pdfs/business/white-papers/wp_cloud-computing-security.pdf.

9. Jasti, A., P. Shah, R. Nagaraj, and R. Pendse. 2010. "Security in Multi-Tenancy Cloud." *2010 IEEE International Carnahan Conference on Security Technology (ICCST)*, Wichita, KS, October 5–8, 2010, http://ieeexplore.ieee.org/xpl/articleDetails.jsp?arnumber=5678682.

10. Kretzschmar, M., M. Golling, and S. Hanigk. 2011. "Security Management Areas in the Inter-Cloud," *IEEE 4th International Conference on Cloud Computing*, Munchen, Germany, July 4–9, 2011.

11. Subashini, S., and V. Kavitha. 2010. "A Survey on Security Issues in Service Delivery Models of Cloud Computing." *Journal of Network and Computer Applications* 34 (1): 15–11.

12. Takabi, H., J. B. D. Joshi, and G.-J. Ahn. 2010. "SecureCloud: Towards a Comprehensive Security Framework for Cloud Computing Environments." *IEEE 34th Annual Computer Software and Application Conference Workshops*, Pittsburgh, PA, July 19–23, 2010.

11

Cloud Governance Architecture

![rule]

INTRODUCTION

The cloud paradigm has brought several innovations and improvements to IT, which is at the forefront of successfully fulfilling the fast-changing needs of global business. Several enterprise-scale and empowered technologies gel well to create and sustain the cloud paradigm, which is turning out to be strategically and significantly transformative and disruptive not only for technocrats but also for business executives. There have been some fabulous ideas such as "separation of concerns," abstraction, and encapsulation, which have been contributing consistently and immensely to moderating and minimizing the growing complexity of IT. In a way, IT can be subtly and succinctly touted as the adroit usage of two pervasive and persuasive mechanisms: (1) decomposition and (2) composition. Further, componentization and modularization using coupling, granularity, and cohesiveness techniques could resolve diverse IT challenges. Cloud computing is being viewed as the complexity-mitigation technique for overhauling and overcoming several IT issues and ills and fulfilling the unique goals behind the elastic IT.

The much-hyped cloud computing concept is reaching greater heights due to the maturity of virtualization technology, which mainly deals with completely decoupling hardware and software components. This loose-coupling facility has done a lot of good for IT in bringing much-needed suppleness and maneuverability to the table. In other words, the inhibiting dependencies, rigidity, and stickiness of various IT modules are eliminated completely to bring in fresh possibilities and newer opportunities in easily tracking and tackling existing and emerging IT challenges. Another noteworthy factor is transparency. Location, technology, platform, and language transparency goals are being achieved with cloud computing.

With cloud computing in place, any future changes and challenges could be inherently taken care of in next-generation IT infrastructures.

The cloud, being an enterprise-scale technology, must guarantee several quality attributes in its offerings. Simplistically, a cloud is an advanced IT infrastructure comprised of a server, and storage and networking systems, and hence, the service and operation-level parameters are of the utmost importance. Incidentally, several enterprise-level qualities are being realized with the adept leverage and use of flourishing cloud technologies. Newer deployment and delivery models are being developed and rendered comfortably and conveniently with the adroit adoption of clouds. Further, the potential of clouds to cut capital expenditure and rein in operating costs is so compelling that chief information officers (CIOs) are pushing and pitching aggressively for cloud adoption. However, good managers understand that cost savings is not the only variable to consider when evaluating whether to go for cloud IT. Cloud computing enables a tremendous amount of flexibility and scalability in deploying and managing IT services and applications. With this flexibility comes a list of items that have to be managed more closely compared to traditional systems. Availability, security, serviceability, and controllability of cloud services and strict compliance to local and governmental rules and regulations need to be guaranteed by cloud infrastructures. These expectations have to be effectively monitored and managed.

As far as service providers are concerned, they always want to have highly optimized, dynamic, converged, and on-demand cloud infrastructures. To achieve the goal of a lean and open cloud, they seek to optimize the use and management of resources and assets in their IT environment, from servers to storage to software licenses. Service providers are also required to strictly comply with security and governance policies. For this reason, the final activity to consider in a mature and stabilized cloud infrastructure is cloud governance. With cloud governance in place, cloud service providers are in a position to not only deliver superior value through cloud infrastructures and cloud-instigated business models, but also prove that their use of resources is responsible, reasonable, and aligned with the requirements of the business.

Information Technology (IT) is trekking steadily and safely toward much-envisaged agility and autonomy. As IT and business domains become tightly intertwined, all kinds of advancements and advantages of IT are being expediently and elegantly replicated for business augmentation, transformation, and optimization. In the recent past, service oriented architecture (SOA) came along and laid the strategic and sustainable foundation for achieving a host of complete and compact automation in service composition, enterprise modernization, and business integration. That is, services dynamically find one another, bind, and compose to generate smart and sophisticated services that in turn lead to adaptive processes and applications. Mashups, in the form of integrated user interfaces, are fast gaining momentum with the emergence of mashup editors. Other aspects and agents also contribute immeasurably to the much-anticipated and articulated self-adaptation in personal as well as professional applications. Autonomic computing is a strategic initiative for bringing tangible and perceptible autonomy (self-management) to enterprise-scale compute infrastructures.

Therefore, every noteworthy aspect in IT is becoming automated with competent and catalytic technologies and their solutions. The recent and the most resilient paradigm is nonetheless the cloud, which is being positioned as the prominent and dominant contributor and contender in the ongoing battle for IT accessibility, availability, and affordability. The cloud paradigm brings several value-added qualities to IT, such as elasticity/scalability, performance, flexibility, agility, adaptability, and so on. However, in the fast emerging and evolving cloud environment, issues such as the lack of controllability, accountability, auditability, security, privacy, and visibility have emerged as a barrier and dampener for massive-scale adoption of the brewing cloud idea. Therefore, in an increasingly automated, active, malleable, and production environment, there is an insatiable need for automated monitoring and governability/oversight through policy enablement and enforcement, in order to guarantee service and operational level agreements to retain the loyalty of and the earned brand value among clients, customers, and consumers. In this chapter, we explain exactly what cloud governance is and its various types, the need for governing the expanding array of cloud infrastructures and resources, the short- and long-term consequences of governance mechanisms and platforms, and finally, how policies play a vital role in effective and runtime governance of clouds.

EMERGENCE OF CLOUD SERVICES AND APPLICATIONS

The cloud is being established as a strategic, spectacular, and sustainable paradigm for the forthcoming service-centric knowledge era. Clouds have have had a tremendous impact on a wide variety of business houses, ICT service organizations, telecommunication service providers, consulting companies, hardware, and enterprise IT infrastructure vendors. Further, individuals, innovators, investors, and institutions are gaining much ground and traction through this novelty-packed concept. In a nutshell, the shift being rendered and readied is phenomenally huge. Not only small and medium enterprises but also business behemoths and IT powerhouses are fast adopting this highly successful and proven phenomenon. There is no doubt that the hugely popular cloud landscape and ecosystem is accelerating steadily toward the envisioned goal.

The real beauty and key differentiator is that this stabilizing and trailblazing concept has created a new buzzword: "cloud space." We are already familiar with enterprise and embedded spaces and their enabling technologies. The cloud space, the recent and resounding result of cloud computing, is growing at a much faster pace than enterprise and embedded spaces and is simultaneously synchronizing and synergizing with the enterprise space. Efforts are afoot to achieve device-cloud-device integration; this will result in seamless and spontaneous connectivity among cloud, enterprise, and embedded spaces in the days to come. This crucial and critical linkage and assemblage will lead to a cornucopia of intelligent services, networks, systems, and environments in the near future.

According to a Gartner research report, the worldwide cloud computing and related services market is expected to touch US$150 billion in 2013. There is another positive indication that around 65% of worldwide enterprises will have their presence in clouds by 2015. Different sets of people passionately and pragmatically work in myriad ways to advance the unique concepts and capabilities of this new computing paradigm to different sections of society. Besides established market researchers, academic researchers across the globe are frantically and fervently pondering the practical drawbacks and limitations of clouds in order to propose and provide versatile technology-based solutions. Corporate professionals are keenly looking for streams of use and business cases in order to convince their managers and decision makers to plunge into the vast and varied opportunities promised by the new paradigm to instigate fresh possibilities. The chief executive officers (CEOs), chief technology officers (CTOs), CIOs, and COOs of companies are also extremely upbeat and optimistic about this cool paradigm. Visionaries chip in with their valuable contributions for the fast growth of cloud technologies for rooting out some of the perpetual ills of business industries. No doubt, there will be widespread and vociferous support for the enticing and endearing cloud concepts to mature and materialize soon.

Clouds: The Robust and Resilient Platform for Business Services

The much-proclaimed service era has already dawned with service engineering, science, management, and modeling principles attaining maturity. With decisive advancements being achieved in knowledge engineering, the knowledge era will soon be upon us. Knowledge-packed services, applications, networks, systems, and environments will emerge and be sustained. The long-drawn transition from data and information to knowledge and, finally, wisdom is very much on track. There are already discussions among technical wizards, IT pundits, and visionaries on how to realize the goal of the smart planet. We are hearing and reading extensively about smart cities, classrooms, hospitals, homes, hotels, and so on these days. Pervasive computing, autonomic communication, ubiquitous sensing and actuation, calm technologies, disappearing computers, ad hoc networking, sentient materials, composite services, self- and surroundings-aware objects, and so on, for AmI and IoT are trendsetting and tantalizing buzzwords today. The vision of establishing a connected world is steadily progressing toward realization, and the cloud is being touted as the core and critical infrastructure.

The ultimate fallout is that everything is being announced, articulated, and accessed as a service. Every tangible artifact is being perceived as a service-providing, -consuming, or -brokering entity. This is the power and potential of the service orientation concept. Thus, it is not an exaggeration when one says that cloud as a powerful and pragmatic service deployment and delivery platform has a magnificent role to play in the ensuing knowledge era. Besides service orientation and SaaS approaches, clouds are being empowered through a combination of technologies such as virtualization, automation, convergence, federation, and multitenancy. Various types of services (as per a Gartner report on cloud computing) that benefit from clouds are as follows:

- "Business process services" are any business processes (e.g., e-business, payroll, printing, and e-commerce) delivered as services using web interfaces by exploiting the emerging WOA. Process services are typically analogous to composite services and applications. In short, process services are element services that directly or collaboratively implement processes.
- "Application services" are cloud-based reusable services that directly engineer and enable enterprise-scale software. Applications across domains can be built through these cloud services. A variety of

EAs can find and use these application-level services over the web, which is the open, public, and cheap communication infrastructure to build sophisticated systems. Not only business applications but also RIAs, B2B, and even multienterprise applications can be realized quickly and easily by smartly utilizing such services over the web. The EDA, which is being touted as the next-generation scheme to arrive at dynamic, real-time, and adaptive systems, will benefit immensely and immeasurably from these application services.

- As cloud applications are typically multitenant ones in order to enable access and use by many concurrent users, these contributive and constructive services are also made compliant with and compatible to the "multitenancy" tenet. Customization and configuration features are the leading ingredients of multitenant systems. Cloud services can be composed manually or programmatically to craft highly consumable and usable mashups and business-aware composites. Finally, these services assist in creating and sustaining cloud brokerage services by establishing smart connectivity across services that are posted in geographically distributed, diverse, and decentralized clouds.

- "Information services" offer search services or other mechanisms to provide access to external data or content. Unlike other cloud service categories, information services do not require the consumer to move any of their data or business process logic into the cloud. The information service simply delivers information that already exists in the cloud. Information services are most typically accessed using a simple web-based API or delivered as feeds using really simple syndication (RSS)/Atom.

- "Application infrastructure services" represent application design, development, testing, and execution platform services. There are also other infrastructure services such as connectivity, access, security, identity, directory, intermediation, and concierge services and several IDEs and rapid application development (RAD) tools in the enterprise space that speed up and streamline application conceptualization, concretization, compilation, and correction. For different services to interact with one another, middleware is classified as the most sought-after software. These days, with the unprecedented adoption of the cloud paradigm, cloud middleware, brokers, service buses, and orchestration engines are being implemented for integration, composition, and collaboration of services and applications across different cloud environments. All kinds of infrastructure and platform services are accordingly modernized and migrated to clouds for global subscription and use.

- "System infrastructure services" include virtualized system-level capabilities such as server, server OS, client OS, storage, or network on which the consumer can run a variety of applications. Web-based provisioning—via a browser form, programmatic calls, or automated response to an application load—is used to provide dynamic access to these resources.

- "Brokerage, governance, and management services" provide operational management of access, consumption, monitoring, delivery, and SLAs associated with cloud-based services. Although these have some similarities to operations management tools used inside an enterprise, global-class, cloud-based applications require additional capabilities.

In conclusion, all kinds of personal as well as professional services are being modified and moved to clouds. On-site and local services are being delivered as off-premise, on-demand, online, hosted, managed, and remote services. Service deployment, delivery, management, and maintenance are taken care of effectively by well-educated and experienced professionals using versatile cloud infrastructures and platforms.

EVOLUTION OF GOVERNANCE PRINCIPLES, POLICIES, PRACTICES, AND PRODUCTS

In the recent past, governance acquired special significance in the IT world. Corporate, IT, SOA and now cloud governance methods are evolving fast. Having understood its strategic importance, consortiums, vendors, and practitioners are actively collaborating with one another in taking forward the crucial governance concept to resolve some of the key challenges of IT.

Governance is the art and discipline of managing outcomes through structured relationships, procedures, and policies. Policy formulation; effective monitoring, management, execution, and enforcement of such policies; and an overseeing authority form the vital ingredients of any governance process.

The concept of IT governance in particular describes how people entrusted with authority over some aspects of a business consider IT in supervising, monitoring, controlling, and directing the concerned business entity and how the various lines of business applying IT will have an impact on whether the company is able to attain the vision, mission, and strategic goals set by the management of the company. IT governance clearly specifies who has the right to make decisions regarding IT, what decisions they can make, and an accountability framework that encourages the use of IT. It is not about making specific IT decisions (the company's management does that), rather it determines which individuals and roles within the company can systematically make and contribute to these decisions.

With IT becoming the core enabler of business offerings and operations, IT governance is becoming an essential element within business. Another noteworthy point is that alignment between business and IT must be very tight in order to make any business successful and sustainable. The prevailing trend indicates that the success of any business squarely and solely depends on the smart adoption of IT. However, as IT is a cost center for any business, it has to be correctly and cognitively handled so as not to affect the profit margin. As business dynamics and sentiments undergo frequent changes and chops, the IT governance aspect is gaining momentum as a business empowerment strategy. Business executives are also expected to learn the tricks of the trade very fast these days so that they can play a proactive, preemptive, and prompt role in putting in place an effective governance process. IT governance involves four basic capabilities:

1. The ability of an organization to define IT-focused business practices, technical standards, and repeatable processes for accomplishing organizational goals
2. A governing body that provides compliance tools to individuals responsible for complying with IT requirements and policies
3. Tracking, monitoring, and enforcement capabilities enabling the organization's management to ensure compliance with or take action if the company is not in compliance with stated requirements and policies
4. Making all activities within the enterprise available for analysis and ensuring their active involvement in the evolution of policies as well as conformance processes

Thus, IT governance refers to the allocation and supervision of a company's IT assets. IT governance controls how authorized people utilize IT within their business entities to supervise, monitor, and perform the tasks of these business entities [1]. Some disciplines that make up IT governance include change management, problem management, release management, availability management, and service-level management. How IT is applied in an organization has a tremendous impact on the organization's productivity and profitability. It is noted that IT governance deals with who is authorized to make decisions on IT matters and what decisions they are authorized to make. It does not provide answers to IT problems; IT governance simply determines which individuals, roles, or organizational units typically deal with certain IT decisions. It is noteworthy that IT governance encompasses nearly the entire organization because almost all departments and virtually all people in an organization utilize IT in their day-to-day operations. As time progresses, IT is further ingrained into the organization as more and more uses for IT are found and implemented.

As the need for IT grows, many organizations operate using a governance system by default—simply solving problems one at a time to address a particular need. This defensive tactic leads to limited opportunities to extract strategic benefits from IT. Instead, management should actively design IT governance around the enterprise's objectives and performance goals. There are many established IT governance models available today that help organizations to manage their IT assets better. The most popular one is ITIL. ITIL has widespread support in Europe and has recently gained support in North America. ITIL defines a set of best practices in 24 disciplines.

Another established IT governance framework is Control Objectives for Information and Related Technologies (COBIT). COBIT was established with the objective of aligning IT resources and processes with business objectives, quality standards, monetary controls, and security needs. It is composed of four domains:

1. Planning and organization
2. Acquisition and implementation
3. Delivery and support
4. Monitoring

SOA Governance

SOA is a very distinct design paradigm, principle, and pattern that is gaining significant traction these days. It is being touted as the most elegant architectural style with substance for the struggling software engineering field. Architects and designers are wearing the service cap while articulating their designs and architectures. The service concept has expanded fervently and furiously among IT professionals and pundits. Having understood the tactic and strategic advantages of the service concept, many organizations are aggressively pursuing SOA to transform their creaky and chaotic IT infrastructures and monolithic application silos to process-centric, loosely-coupled, on-demand, and service-enabled infrastructures and applications. This transition is supposed to bring a number of improvements and improvisations that enable service reuse and sharing across applications. In this tightly coupled world, business functionality is often buried deep within applications, whereas interfaces to other systems are proprietary, making it complex and costly to access data and business functionality.

SOA makes data integration and reuse of functionality cost-effective and widely accessible. This has a profound impact on organizations and makes them more agile and adaptive. SOA can also contribute to simplifying and streamlining application development and maintenance, business integration, legacy modernization, and service composition, which clearly brings down the complexity and costs associated with IT. There is no doubt that SOA facilitates shared and supple IT environments for businesses to grow and glow. Reusability, which has been a dream so far, will become common and casual in any service ecosystem. Enterprises are scurrying to adopt SOA as their flagship IT strategy in the hope of gaining competitive advantage and being perceived as innovative leaders.

Today, all architecture is somehow positioned and proclaimed as service architecture; the definition of a service has been muddled to the extent that almost any piece of software can be termed a service. The net result is that there are many services available with little differentiation, which ultimately adds to the confusion and chaos. Such kinds of ad hoc and casual service engineering do more harm than any real good. In short, the much-dreamt capabilities of service reuse and IT agility are once again eluding us. We now know that the uncontrolled and carefree production and proliferation of services have not done any good for IT. Of course, the problem is not with SOA. The pathbreaking service paradigm is definitely a novel one, with a promising architectural style, strategy, and science. Researchers are developing scores of SOA principles, practices, procedures, and platforms that are really creative and contributive. The reality is that any technology can survive with an efficient methodology in place.

An overseeing and overarching mechanism has to be in place to closely monitor and profile each service interaction. Without such supervision, there is a high possibility that any rogue service may emerge and eradicate the very purpose of its design, implementation, and deployment. An unauthorized service transaction is also equally culpable and capable of spoiling the whole environment. The situation is similar to one in which a herd of sheep is left to graze on its own. Without the oversight of a shepherd, each sheep wanders off in its own direction and is lost from the herd. It is noted that SOA governance is the shepherd in the world of SOA.

SOA governance is a mandatory process and cannot be purchased and installed as a packaged product [2]. Of course, there are SOA governance platforms and engines available in the market. Still, these tools need to be appropriately strengthened with a set of well-defined procedures, practices, and policies. Specific life cycle steps are formulated for simplifying and streamlining obligatory SOA governance. In a nutshell, the very foundation of SOA governance is the ability to enforce and automate defined policies across the SOA life cycle.

Any SOA governance methodology has to be applied across the entire service life cycle from development and operation to retirement and replacement. The service development life cycle involves modeling and identifying business services, designing interfaces and QoS requirements for these services, implementing new services, assembling services, and deploying the services in production. Once services are deployed, as additional requirements are developed and operational information is made available, the services undergo change management and mature through iterative development. As services are deployed, the infrastructure is configured to provide QoS factors such as security, scalability, and sustainability. Services are very frequently monitored to measure how they are meeting the SLAs, for performance and capacity information, and for problem detection [3].

Strong and Sustainable Governance for Agility

Due to the extreme agility and autonomy provided by SOA to businesses, there is an extra caution to be heeded for SOA adoption. If unattended, SOA can and does introduce more chaos into the application development process. This is especially true if agile development methods are adopted in conjunction with the service-centric architecture. Applications using SOA are inherently more complex than conventional applications built using traditional and monolithic application architectures. Interactions among networked services may go awry and sometimes induce unwanted and unexpected transactions and troubles, which nullify the envisioned goal of SOA. A bunch of local as well as remote services discovering, connecting, communicating, and collaborating with one another in an uncontrolled manner makes it very difficult to perform maintenance tasks. If any third-party services are involved and invoked, then there is a possibility for greater risk as the control of those services does not remain with users, clients, and requesters.

The IT divisions prominently leverage runtime SOA governance solutions for effectively managing the performance and consumption of services during production. However, this is not enough to fully utilize the benefits promised by SOA. Governance must start in the design phase, continue through development, and carry on through production. Context, constraints, and control need to be in place for safe and sound service interactions. Otherwise, business problems cannot be solved by SOA and P2P services are not reusable, which negates all the positives of SOA.

This can wreak havoc within IT development organizations, too. Recent studies clearly show that the cost of building an EA using SOA is often greater than the cost of building the same application without SOA. Only through service reuse do these development costs pay off. Because SOA-based applications have more moving parts and may depend on services not under the control of IT, ensuring the quality of a running application is extremely difficult [4]. The promise of agility and the cost savings resulting from reuse will come to nothing without there being strong governance policies and procedures in place.

Implementing an SOA governance strategy requires the definition of enterprise policies and establishment of strong auditing and conformance mechanisms to ensure that enterprise policies are strictly adhered to throughout the life cycle, as illustrated in Figure 11.1 [5].

In conclusion, with the pervasiveness of SOA across industrial domains, SOA governance is an essential task that must be meticulously planned and executed. There are plenty of resilient software solutions as well as best practices that can govern each and every interaction and transaction and that can, in case of any palpable deviation, immediately halt the transaction or chalk out and implement competent countermeasures in real time. As automation levels and scales go up continuously, scrupulous monitoring and management mechanisms and schemes are being mandated. Policies are the best instruments for governance as they can be tweaked by

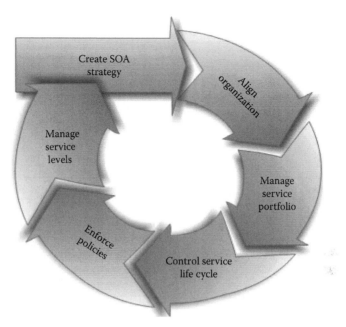

FIGURE 11.1
The SOA governance life cycle.

business executives and managers also. As policies and services are loosely coupled, policy changes can be done without impacting the service under production. Policy creation, representation, and persistence languages are emerging, and policy engines are the latest addition to the growing software infrastructure family. When the subject of knowledge engineering gets sufficiently stabilized, knowledge bases too can be attached with the service system and, thus, not only agility and autonomy but also adaptability is supported in service environments. Figure 11.2 indicates the growing importance of SOA governance within IT and corporate governance modules.

Data Governance

Data is always essential for any enterprise; there is a need for an enterprise to innovate in order to surge ahead of its competitors by extracting all the right and relevant insights and intelligence from its data heap. BI is an important component in any growing business. For any business to be ready for the future, data-driven intelligence is very much required. For setting a financial target, the past data of an enterprise is vital for

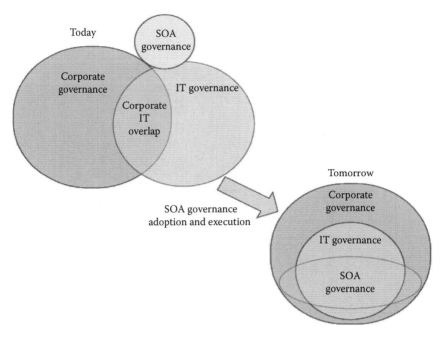

FIGURE 11.2
The growing importance of SOA governance in service-oriented enterprises.

effective estimation and forecast. Predictability is an emerging nonfunctional requirement. Company data that is gathered, cleaned, polished, processed, prioritized, and persisted is the critical component for any kind of strategic data analysis and predictive modeling. Data is the principal item for implementing and sustaining decision-support systems (DSSs). Databases, data marts, data cubes, and data warehouses are the different entities for storing data in different schema and structures, facilitating easy and quick search, retrieval, mining, management, and governance of data.

Data governance is touted as an important enterprise function that is focused on protecting and managing data as a corporate asset. The prime mission of governance is to serve as a link between an enterprise's corporate and strategic initiatives and its business and technology teams. Within this context, governance becomes an integral part of enterprise line management. Executed properly, the governance function can actively and effectively direct an organization's resources to maximize the value obtained from it. Two action steps for successful data governance are discussed in the following subsections [6].

Define What Data Governance Means to an Organization

Defining data governance in any organization means understanding the specific objectives to be achieved through governance, setting the appropriate scope, and recognizing the risks and limitations that might come with the finalized approach. The initial thrust to embark on a data governance engagement is to find a suitable motivator (or business driver) that will serve as a rallying point for governance.

Determine Which Data Management Functions to Include

Some of the data management functions that are included by any governance program are as follows:

- "Data quality/certification" addresses the accuracy, integrity, cleanliness, correctness, completeness, and consistency of data in an organization.
- "Metadata, master data, and reference data management" refers to the ability to create, store, maintain, exchange, and synchronize a "system of record" for core business entities.
- "Data stewardship" assigns ownership of data assets to enable consistent data usage, maximize data quality, and ensure the integrity of business-critical information.
- "Program management/prioritization" refers to the ability to manage multiple data-centric projects and the data environment to achieve defined objectives.
- "Data security/access" addresses issues such as network security, physical control, systems logs, incident response, and security audits.
- "Data standards and architecture" provides the high-level design of the data environment and ensures that individual data-centric projects work together as a whole.
- "Resource management" establishes and manages project and program budgets and accountability.
- "Reporting tools and support" establishes and manages the process of adding new reports, retiring old ones, measuring progress against objectives, and defining metrics that support the governance initiative.
- "Change management" evaluates and approves proposals for change, implements business changes as needed, and monitors data usage and quality metrics. Although the choice of which data management

functions to include depends on data governance objectives, there are a few functions that should be at or near the top of the priority list: data quality; metadata, master data and reference data management; data stewardship; and program management/prioritization.

In summary, a data governance program is being recognized as an important enterprise function focused on protecting and managing data as a corporate asset. As data directly or indirectly contributes to BI, the preservation of data is gaining good traction these days.

OVERVIEW OF CLOUD GOVERNANCE

The concept of governance is vague, and there is no fixed definition of governance. Different people prescribe different definitions. However, no matter how we slice and segment it, the overwhelming consensus is that governance is bound to play a crucial role in the actuation and ascension of cloud computing. All sorts of cloud offerings are encapsulated within services and are delivered to worldwide users over the web in the emerging ITaaS format. The services are self-provisioned and delivered from highly elastic and scalable infrastructures according to the proven pay-per-use model. The SOA governance concepts can be replicated in clouds.

Governance in the cloud is all about defining right, realistic, and relevant policies around managing and overseeing cloud resources and tracking/enforcing the policies at runtime when applications are running. Different cloud vendors have varying degrees of flexibility when it comes to giving their clients access to the underlying infrastructure. It becomes imperative for businesses to understand these capabilities and define policies that mirror their needs. One noteworthy point is that SOA primarily deals with the design of flexible and adaptive service-based systems. Services are the discrete and decisive constructs for service systems. Using this design approach, the developmental complexity of enterprise systems can be substantially reduced. In short, the service orientation paradigm has turned out to be a superb method for designing new-generation process-centric, service-oriented, enterprise-scale, multienterprise, and dynamic applications. On the other hand, clouds are being positioned as the cost-effective and compact IT infrastructures for developing, deploying, configuring, tuning, and delivering services (designed using the SOA approach) for global users utilizing the SaaS format. As governance is a key factor in the full service life cycle ranging from creation to replacement stages, both SOA and IT governance aspects are anticipated to play a major role in shaping the ensuing cloud era. Hence, cloud governance represents a smart convergence of service and infrastructure governance aspects.

Governance is not about just technology. It is all about the vision, oversight, and control of actions and reactions within a system. Much of governance is about people working within the defined governance process. It leans more toward behavioral aspects. However, technology plays a momentous role as an enablement tool that controls, monitors, and adapts, which are the three pillars of any governance program. As the cloud inspires a more autonomic IT environment, there is a need to develop a dedicated and disciplined governance program for the cloud space too. As a cloud is mainly about establishing and maintaining elastic and centrally managed IT infrastructures, newer service delivery and consumption styles could become a reality through the adoption of cloud computing. Therefore, it is clear that cloud governance banks on both service and IT governance concepts.

Cloud governance substantially extends SOA governance in several ways. Policies need to be formed formally to address the extraordinary challenges and changes posed by cloud adoption. Service design and development remain the same even in the forthcoming cloud era. However, the deployment and delivery scenarios totally change as cloud platforms and infrastructures represent a tectonic shift in the credentials, capacities, and capabilities of applications compared to the traditional servers utilized for hosting and managing SOA-compliant applications. The amazing cloud concept has inspired many to emerge and establish themselves as CSPs and, hence, myriad infrastructures, platforms, software, and even business process providers are available today. In other words, the cloud ecosystem and landscape are consistently on a growth trajectory. On the other side, there are millions of cloud service subscribers tending toward the cloud model. Not only individuals, innovators, and investors but also institutions are showing extraordinary interest in cloud prospects. In other words, small, medium, and large enterprises are deliberating modernizing their existing assets and artifacts and smoothly moving the updated and upgraded ones to cloud centers.

Thus, besides some new entrants to the cloud space, scores of existing hosted and managed services providers on hearing and reading about the potential of clouds are repositioning themselves as cloud providers. With globally distributed subscribers, providers need to sign SLAs that primarily deal with service consumability, availability, scalability and infallibility, infrastructure elasticity, performance, dependability, and accessibility. Providers have to toe the line in terms of meeting changing rules, regulations, and guidelines on cloud centers made by governments very cautiously. They need to take the security and privacy requirements of corporate and confidential data very seriously and work on viable and veritable mechanisms sincerely. Vendor lock-in problems and lock-out threats loom large on the consumer's mind. Regional and cultural differences need to be taken into account. Legal issues need to be sorted out. The cloud, being a shared and virtual environment, may be liable to hacking, spamming, and attack by viruses, adware, malware, and contagious bugs. As the open Internet is the dominant communication infrastructure for clouds, breaking into network connectivity products, servers, and VMs is easier compared to traditional data centers and server farms. This clearly portrays the gravity and complexity of cloud governance.

The advantage of SOA governance is that there are versatile technologies and robust solutions that take care of SOA asset life cycle management, service deployment and security, and policy enforcement across service inception, elaboration, and execution stages. However, there are some severe challenges to be faced while moving traditionally deployed services to clouds. Cloud services could be encapsulated in different VMs, in diverse physical servers, or even in geographically and globally distributed and decentralized clouds. Some corporate services might still reside in enterprise servers. Creating a resilient cloud governance solution capable of elegantly handling these possibilities is a tough affair. Service governance engines and platforms must be appropriately modified to become cloud-centric systems in order to be easily applied and deployed in the widening cloud space. Deployment must be simple, dependable, and rapid across the wide variety of cloud infrastructures. They must operate independently under all conditions, including circumstances in which they are disconnected from any centralized asset stores or monitoring consoles. In addition, they must operate seamlessly across on-premise and off-premise environments, including legacy enterprise SOA deployments. Cloud governance systems must also of course monitor any completely new applications deployed in cloud centers.

In most SOA governance engagements, effective management of assets for simplifying reusability is the first-order problem, with enforcement and monitoring of such assets being the second. This often leads to early purchases of registry/repository solutions that have little practical use because they never integrate well with enforcement and monitoring systems. In contrast, in the cloud space, enforcement and monitoring tasks come first, whereas asset management is a secondary affair. Service deployment, delivery, consumption, monitoring, tracking, and billing are the most important assignments in a cloud. Also, users and customers lose their controllability and visibility in a cloud. Therefore, cloud governance primarily focuses more on the latter part of the service life cycle.

Design-Time Cloud Governance

As indicated in the previous section, there is no major difference between design-time governance of SOA and that of clouds. Service and application development platforms are hosted in cloud infrastructures these days. This trend is increasingly to take even developmental tasks to cloud platforms. In other words, the idea of development as a service is being realized using PaaS, and cloud-based development is being hailed as affordable, simple, and quick.

When we own and use an IDE for service development and an SOA registry repository for depositing and managing service metadata and implementation, respectively, service visibility, version and change management, and governance become a little easier. However, the much-needed visibility goes down sharply if service assets are developed by unknown developers. Thereby, the synchronization among services is affected and subsequently the service life cycle governance falters and fumbles. The ultimate fallout is that a bunch of services is left behind and all the SOA advantages fall flat. In the cloud case as well, a development environment and editor can be distinctly shared for producing application-specific and common services. Developers from different departments and divisions create and consume cloud services, and this distribution and disintegration does a lot of harm in the form of visibility, controllability, and changeability. This goes against the originally envisioned service design principles and practices and clearly reflects the importance of having effective design-time cloud governance in place to safeguard service interactions.

In other words, providers need to put SOA governance tools and policies in the cloud environment. There has to be a central place to look up and use these resources by cloud developers, assemblers, and consumers.

Further, design-time policies are easily enforceable when we have control over the development and QA process, but the cloud-specific design-time policies are notoriously lacking in the cloud environment. The result is that design-time policies are not consistently enforced on the client side, if at all.

Runtime Cloud Governance

A collection of runtime and policy issues that are complicated by the fog of cloud infrastructure make matters worse. Data reside on systems over which we do not have any control, which may be physically in other countries or legal jurisdictions. Further, systems are unlikely to have the same security standards as we have internally. This means that our security policies need to be much more granular. We cannot count on using perimeter-based approaches to secure our data or service access. Every message needs to be scrutinized and we need to separate service and data policy definition from enforcement. The cloud does not simplify security issues; in fact, it complicates and exacerbates them. Strong SOA security approaches have always pushed the "trust no one" approach and the cloud is simply another infrastructure for enforcing these already stringent security policies.

Cloud reliability is pretty much out of our hands. What happens if the cloud service is not available? What happens if the whole cloud goes out of business or is made unavailable by any spike, outage, disaster, or terrorist act? In other words, there is more than just service failure. The cloud system may slow down and even undergo total breakdown. How to make clouds more reliable is the key question. An effective cloud governance approach must provide the means to control, monitor, and adapt services for both on-premise and cloud-based implementations and provide consistency across internal SOA and cloud SOA. Consumers should not be made to guess whether the services being consumed are inside the network or in the remote cloud. The whole point of loose coupling and adoption of the cloud is location independence. To make this concept a reality, we need management and governance that spans SOA infrastructure boundaries.

Yet, there is more to the runtime cloud governance picture than management and policy enforcement. Data and compliance issues can be the most perplexing and problematic obstacles. Most third-party cloud providers provide little means to do the sort of auditing and logging that is demanded from most compliance and regulatory requirements.

Companies need to intentionally provide all cloud services with internal auditing and logging services that are deployed on the cloud or preferably local network, negotiate better access to logging data with the cloud provider, and implement policies for cloud service use to control leakage of private information to the cloud. Furthermore, companies need to implement usage policies to control excessive, and potentially expensive, use of cloud services in unauthorized ways.

One way to solve this problem is through the use of network intermediaries and gateways that keep a close eye on traffic between the corporate network and the cloud. Intermediaries can scan cloud-bound data for leakage of private or company-sensitive data, filter traffic sent to cloud platforms, apply access policies to cloud services, provide visibility into authorized and unauthorized use of cloud services, and prevent unsanctioned use of cloud services by internal staff, among other things. Of course, these benefits do not extend to intracloud service consumption, but they can provide a lowest common denominator of runtime governance required by the organization.

POLICIES FOR RUNTIME CLOUD GOVERNANCE

Policies are the building blocks and fundamental pieces of runtime cloud governance. Policies have to be aptly defined, refined, and posited in order to be accessed at runtime. Policies delegate the decision-making powers to services, thus automating the whole process of governance. Policy representation languages are coming up, and policy managers are the key interlocutors who inject policies to the right resources dynamically. Policy managers thus have a crucial role to play in administering autonomy and agility for clouds.

Policy Engineering

During the design and development stage, it is important to establish rules and policies that clearly specify how the various participating services in a cloud are going to be monitored and managed. The attributes (QoS) of the underlying cloud infrastructure must be ensured, whereas SLAs of both the platforms and the applications must be monitored and tracked. Additionally, defining a variety of policies for authorizing and empowering different sets of people with special power to access and control applications and make decisions is important. Policies, which specify who is going to do what, are the key components of policy engineering. For example, governance policies should be defined for the following [7]:

- Role-based access to establish control over who has access to deploy and manage cloud assets
- Metrics for monitoring an application's performance and other business-critical KPIs
- Rules for defining critical levels of the aforementioned metrics
- Service levels of both the application and the underlying infrastructure
- The QoS levels

Policy Enforcement

One of the main attractive features of the cloud is its ability to reduce the "time to market" significantly. Cloud gives businesses the ability to roll out changes to applications almost instantaneously compared to the traditional onsite models. This distinct capability comes with its own set of issues around versioning, upgrades, and compatibilities of services. Well-defined and well-enforced policies are a must to ensure robustness and trustworthiness of cloud-based applications. Policies can be enforced through the following mechanisms:

1. Change management reports track and log the changes happening to cloud assets.
2. Alerts and notifications ensure that changes are captured and bubbled up to the decision makers in a timely fashion.
3. Threshold-based actions are based on predefined rules, for example, automatically increasing the footprint (i.e., the number of load-balanced cloud instances) if the performance of a system is below a certain threshold level.

Thus, cloud computing introduces new security risks and compromises the traditional control of IT. Therefore, it is imperative that IT management establishes firm control and oversight over cloud initiatives. Cloud governance, which is a logical evolution of SOA governance strategies, offers a viable and veritable means to assert control over both internal and external applications and data.

Virtual Policy Enforcement Point

Policy enforcement and monitoring is fundamental to SOA and cloud governance (Figure 11.3). IT can deploy a single entity, the virtual policy enforcement point (vPEP), to accomplish both tasks. The idea of a stand-alone policy enforcement point (PEP) is not new; indeed, its use is widespread in most SOA environments [9]. In traditional SOA, the PEP acts as a gatekeeper and monitors all service traffic. Common functionalities of PEP are listed in Table 11.1.

These devices were traditionally hardware-based devices and deployed in an enterprise network DMZ to manage all XML-based streams flowing in or out of an organization. New technological developments now allow virtualization of all PEP functionality so that it can be deployed easily either on-premise in the traditional data center or externally in the cloud. The new virtual PEP offers a lightweight deployment model that allows a closer binding to services, following them through cloud deployment and making localized services governance practical.

Policy Enforcement on Outgoing Traffic

This involves applying policy enforcement to all outgoing traffic in the organization (Figure 11.4). This helps us to discover who is attempting to use cloud services, and to manage this we need to know when an employee

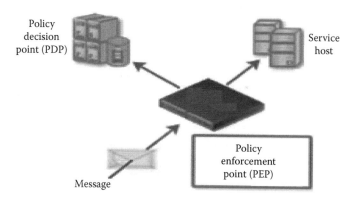

FIGURE 11.3
Policy enforcement and monitoring services.

TABLE 11.1

The Common Functional Features of PEPs

Authentication: Interfacing with most identity and access management systems.	Audit: Collection of information related to events and transaction processing on the PEP.
Authorization: Fine-grained authorization management including attribute- and role-based authorization models.	Alerts or events: Synchronous or asynchronous events that are raised as a result of conditions being met on the PEP, such as reaching a transaction threshold or exceeding a memory consumption threshold.
Confidentiality: Acting as an encryptor/decryptor for all information streams (i.e., data and services).	SLA: Enforcement and/or alerting of various thresholds relevant to business. An example might be to redirect traffic to a secondary service cluster when the primary is overloaded.
Integrity: Ensuring communications are not altered in transit.	Monitoring: Collecting rich data sets describing both individual transaction data and aggregate counters, and generation of graphs and reports to summarize these.
Routing: Directing messages to different destinations based on policy decisions.	Adaptation/transformation: Alteration of the physical data stream in flight. Can be used to provide interface versioning or to produce entirely new aggregate services that combine results from several individual service calls.

accesses a new SaaS service using their credit card. Further, we need to stop an unsanctioned use of PaaS components by well-meaning developers and we need to regulate the use of IaaS technology. Policy access profiles allow continuous monitoring of authorized cloud service activity and provide a customer view of use that is critical to discovering vendor billing discrepancies or identifying SLA violations. Outgoing policy enforcement allows us to measure the value we are deriving from each of our partners and suppliers and every third-party organization with whom we engage electronically.

Policy Enforcement on Incoming Traffic

The same deployment model is equally appropriate for managing traffic entering the corporate network. Application of policy enforcement and monitoring across all incoming traffic (Figure 11.5) provides a secure, managed gateway layer that enables safe publication of internal services. Consider the following use case: A third-party SaaS application requires access to data locked on a mainframe, which is clearly a system that is

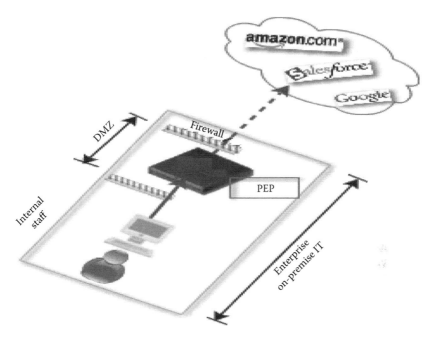

FIGURE 11.4
Policy enforcement on outgoing traffic.

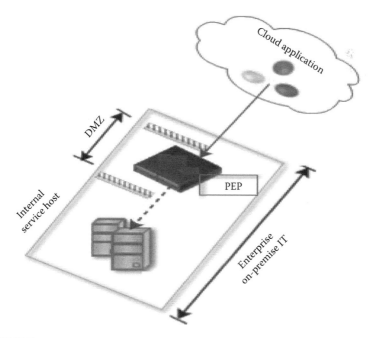

FIGURE 11.5
Policy enforcement on incoming traffic.

not moving into the cloud soon. How can IT publish an interface to the mainframe that ensures only authorized cloud services can access it, that protects the mainframe from attacks originating in the Internet, and that audits all access for chargeback purposes and forensic investigation? A PEP installed in the DMZ can offer all these functions and even more. Policy is not just a way of articulating and enforcing security requirements; it is the integration glue between systems. A rich policy language meets the demands of business and IT, offering both high-level contracts such as SLAs and billing and low-level details such as dynamic routing, failover, and data transformation.

Policy Enforcement on Cloud Services

Deploying distributed vPEPs in front of cloud applications allows owners to protect and manage their services. Application-level policy enforcement gives fine-grained access control and in-depth understanding of use patterns of actual services, instead of VMs.

Application-level policy enforcement not only protects data and applications from unauthorized use but also allows managing the distribution of requests to virtualized application instances and providing balancing or failover within or between different vendors. This provides the necessary abstraction layer that discourages single-vendor lock-in. Finally, the fusion of all three of these components enables the hybrid on-premise, in-cloud deployment model, which is the likely future for most organizations. Policy enforcement technology for clouds can create secure and managed communications between legacy applications in the enterprise and new applications residing in the cloud (Figure 11.6).

In conclusion, SOA is an architectural approach that philosophically guides and guards the development and management of service systems. The cloud is the potential and promising extension to the SOA paradigm significantly simplifying and streamlining the tasks of deploying and delivering hordes of SOA services. The cloud concept within the SOA context represents service infrastructure, implementation, composition, and consumption. The SOA concept within the cloud context is the application-level abstraction of cloud resources. Abstraction, encapsulation, and transparency collectively eliminate all sorts of restraining dependencies. Therefore, it is not an exaggeration to say that cloud governance has evolved from the very matured and stabilized SOA governance in order to

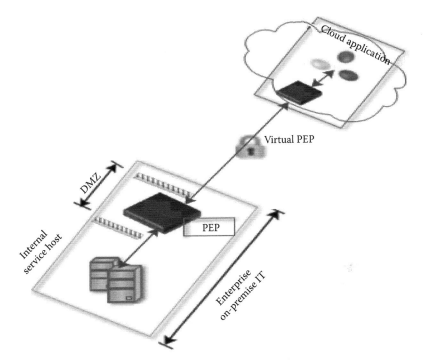

FIGURE 11.6
Policy enforcement on cloud services.

take care of unique obstacles faced in achieving secure, safe, reliable, and smart clouds. A well-defined cloud governance strategy that can factor out possible and probable risks and eliminate them in the commencement period must be framed to build and sustain dependable cloud systems.

A METHODOLOGY FOR CLOUD GOVERNANCE

The journey toward obligatory cloud governance begins with the solid fundamentals of traditional SOA governance [9]. This is essential for all CSPs, cloud brokerage firms, and cloud service consumers (CSCs). SOA governance provides a firm yet flexible foundation for the evolution of cloud governance. Just embracing the cloud is not enough in the long run to take advantage of all the eulogized benefits. The human elements of SOA governance are transferred cleanly to the cloud. However, the real challenge is to have a process and policy in place so that it is readily evolving to meet the additional vendor challenges that come with any cloud deployment.

All the phases of the cloud governance methodology play a vital role in revitalizing and safeguarding cloud environments for all the transformations guaranteed by cloud IT.

Cloud Evaluation Phase

As usual, the initiation activity belongs to the evaluation phase. We need to painstakingly and purposefully evaluate business goals and strategy, and the planned approach in order to initiate the cloud adoption process successfully. This will go a long way in straightening and strengthening the rough and tough path toward the grand target. In this phase, cloud providers need to actively and astutely reuse the knowledge gleaned and gained during the SOA governance activity while formulating the scheme for putting forward a sound cloud governance solution and strategy. Providers have to set transparent, unambiguous, and measurable goals up front; otherwise, there is a possibility for failure down the road. They need to ask themselves several questions in order to extract the applicable and appropriate details to plunge into establishing cloud governance mechanisms.

Cloud Governance Definition Phase

The cloud evaluation phase is followed by the most important phase, that is, the definition phase. Providers need to leverage the knowledge gained in the previous phase to come up with a good definition. This phase includes the following:

Assess people and culture: The cloud paradigm challenges traditional roles and responsibilities. People who are really motivated to take up such challenges are important for an organization to successfully meet this impending transition. The culture is another important factor that must be reckoned with.

Assess process: Processes are critical and crucial to the ultimate success of any initiative, especially for realizing the goal of cloud governance. Existing processes have to go through a rigorous grind so that they are usable and implementable in clouds. Process innovation is another objective when processes are subjected to detailed analysis and empowerment. Newer processes have to be created, simulated, verified, and refined.

Assess data: Take an inventory of all the data assets in the organization. Categorize these data into the following governance groupings:

- Data resides in an existing data center. This may be for security or compliance reasons. Take note of special challenges such as the data being locked up in a legacy mainframe application.
- Data resides in a private cloud. Companies that have acquired a good amount of cloud knowledge have started having their own private clouds in order to safely and securely stock their applications and data, which may be highly confidential; their integrity has to be preserved at any cost.
- Data resides in a public cloud. The data could be deposited in a public cloud; but this option is not taking off as desired due to the lack of security and privacy, noncompliance to third-party auditing, reduced controllability and visibility, and so on.

Assess applications and services: Increasingly, a whole lot of on-premise applications and services are calculatedly being moved to private, public, hybrid, and even community clouds in order to realize the professed benefits. Thus, it is mandatory for CSPs to access each of the services and applications very carefully. Services may have some dodging loopholes, bottlenecks, or even security holes. Services may also have some special restrictions that mandate that they be hosted on-premise due to a variety of reasons. Analysis of these implicit or even explicit reasons in order to get an idea of the overall service ecosystem is vital.

Develop Relationship with Providers

Cloud users have to establish a kind of relationship with providers and vendors in order to know the capabilities and value additions of their offerings. This gives a good grasp and understanding about the provider and, ultimately, consumers develop a sort of trust and confidence about the providers. Vendor lock-in is an undesirable phenomenon and hence users need to get the platform and technology details of providers through the established relationship. It is important to create lists ranking all relevant providers by the following criteria:

By SLA: This is often about uptime and response time, but there are other factors to consider. What is their backup policy, and how fast can they recover from a catastrophic data loss? Can one request the retrieval of old copies of data? How far back, and how often, are snapshots taken? What is the data retention policy? Does the data stay on their backup media after the relationship gets terminated? How about their BC and DR capabilities?

By security capability: Cloud clients have to carefully take note of the security and privacy capabilities of cloud providers. Security is the number one issue with clouds as of now. Enterprises are reluctant to transfer their confidential and corporate data to public clouds considering the extreme gravity of security implications. As clouds turn to virtualization technology extensively, a fresh security hole arises, as per a recent research report: The VMs can be easily pierced so that the integrity and confidentiality of resources are in grave danger. These looming threats must be considered, and any provider has to be weighed accordingly.

By trust: Trust is the most plausible concept for ensuring complete and compact security. Trust is considered a viable and valuable aspect for cloud security and privacy. How a trust mechanism is implemented by cloud providers must be analyzed before formulating the migration scheme.

Cloud Governance Execution Phase

Once the system is defined, the execution phase starts. Start with a primitive and basic policy and check whether the system abides by that. This provides some control and confidence without discouraging innovation or compromising agility.

Build Management and Monitoring Layer

This is the single most important piece of infrastructure for cloud governance. Traditional SOA governance advocates starting with the heavyweight registry and repository infrastructure. In contrast, the current cloud and modern SOA governance schemes start with effective enforcement and monitoring tools. This technology layer of management and monitoring remains the cornerstone of futuristic cloud governance. An additional layer of indirection enables flexibility so that all kinds of future governance needs can be easily inserted.

Set Up PEPs in DMZ

Start by protecting the resources that are already in place. Placing PEPs in the DMZ allows strict management of access to internal resources.

Deploy Virtual PEPs in the Cloud

Begin the deployment of vPEPs. Providers can optionally begin by deploying these throughout their organization, creating a robust defense-in-depth strategy in the application network. As applications and services are moved to the cloud, bind them to vPEPs that also reside in the cloud, giving them policy-driven control over security and the monitoring of every service being hosted.

Integrate Heavy Components Later

Modern PEPs provide all the functionality a provider needs for a governance story, including local persistence and life cycle management of all-important assets such as policy and service descriptions. As the usage scope expands, providers have to look for centralized management products that integrate seamlessly with PEPs. This might also be a good cloud service.

Operational and Review Phase

This is the last phase of the cloud governance life cycle. The system must be cross-checked for its operational performance and compliance. Once the cloud governance system is ready, it has to be subjected to a host of checks in order to evaluate its performance and compliance. Whether the system fulfills the originally agreed-on goals or not has to be verified and validated. In other words, whether it is a success or an abject failure has to be comprehensively investigated. Further, if any lacuna or limitation is found or if there is any room for improvement or improvisation, the system has to be accordingly and astutely remedied, refined, and subjected to repeated checks for verifying its operational goals. This is a continuous process and, hence, a dedicated team has to be assigned to continuously monitor, profile, maintain, and enhance the functional as well as the non-functional qualities of the system.

WHY IS CLOUD GOVERNANCE IMPERATIVE?

Different modules participate in and contribute to the unprecedented success of the cloud paradigm. Cloud infrastructures, storage, connectivity solutions, development and deployment platforms, middleware suites, applications, processes, services and data, research test beds, tools and utilities, and so on, enable the realization of the goals of cloud computing. Virtualization, automated management, resource provisioning, load balancing, and job scheduling software are the dominant and prominent components vouching for the success of cloud computing. In this section, we dig deeper in order to understand why governance solutions are essential for the transformative, augmentative and disruptive cloud technology.

As per worldwide press reports and online blogs, there are many success stories in the exploding cloud space that one can be proud of. Both small and big cloud infrastructure, platform, and service providers are jumping on the cloud bandwagon and, hence, press coverage about this trendsetting IT paradigm is steadily on the climb. Both IT professionals and university professors are consciously concentrating on understanding the inhibiting drawbacks, bottlenecks, and challenges of the pioneering cloud technology in order to come out with robust and resilient solutions for identified issues and limitations. Explorations, experimentations, and expositions are very much visible in this new field.

Yet the usage of the cloud is still in its nascent stage on the enterprise side because of an increasing number of concerns being voiced about the appropriate and accurate use of cloud resources. Cloud availability, performance, and controllability; erosion of security, confidentiality and integrity of cloud resources; and data replication and consistency are the most prevalent problems putting barriers on leveraging the promising cloud approach. There is no cloud interoperability method, which is mandatory for achieving open, smart, and interoperable clouds. The irresistible intercloud idea is hence becoming more popular and the delta cloud is one such initiative aimed at overcoming cloud diversity.

It is being proclaimed and projected in the industry arena that we need to have fertile and futuristic cloud governance solutions and systems in place to support the adoption of cloud technology and to identify and arrest any kind of risk, which is unfortunately and unexpectedly sagging due to colossal misunderstandings. The success of clouds solely depends on the success of cloud governance practices, processes, products, platforms, and patterns. In short, cloud governance is for the massive cloud adoption across industry segments. Other factors underlining the need for elegant governance solutions are discussed in the following subsections.

Guaranteeing Reliability

People have started to realize the necessity of effective governance, because they know what the penalty is when IT fails. People do not want to consume stuff from a cloud or put stuff into a cloud and risk the fact that the cloud may not be available or the service of the cloud may not be available. They need to have contingency plans, but IT contingency plans are a form of governance. Clouds have to be made more dependable and trustworthy. Governance is undoubtedly the key for realizing the goal of cloud dependability.

Managing Cloud Services

Centrally managed and maintained ICT services and applications are being modernized and migrated to cloud infrastructures and platforms. In other words, a large variety of local and on-premises services are being transitioned to remotely managed on-demand, off-premises, and online services in clouds. Personal as well as professional application modules are increasingly finding consolidated, virtualized, automated, and shared residence on clouds. Governance therefore involves the efficient management of cloud services and their life cycles in a meticulous and methodological manner. In other words, everything from the definition of services, through the deployment and management of services to the performance analysis of services and the replacement and retirement of services is smartly accomplished in clouds. As those services get aggregated into larger business processes, there arises a different set of governance characteristics and capabilities. Every existing and new service asset has to be carefully managed to make it available, usable, and consumable all the time and to deliver the promised services with all the guarantees intact to the subscribers.

Managing Scale

With the deeper acceptance and adoption of cloud concepts, a number of innovations and inventions are happening in this field. Newer business, pricing, delivery, and operational models in IT are emerging and being leveraged extensively across the globe. Clouds clearly enable wider recognition and result in a bevy of ramifications. That is, the total business and IT ecosystems are bound to grow further and farther toward the greater mandate of articulating and accommodating more IT resources, user bases, and business entities. Business-to-consumer (B2C), B2B, business-to-employee (B2E), and consumer-to-consumer (C2C) models will become more pervasive and persuasive with the increase in maturity and stability of cloud infrastructures. All these portend higher-scale computing, networking, and communication compared to current trends. Governance is currently the decisive factor and feature for managing the mounting scale being visualized for future ICT.

Managing Cloud Ecosystems

Service science and engineering are on the rampage. With a large number of diverse, distributed, and decentralized services looming on the cloud horizon, it becomes imperative for multifaceted and reflective middleware such as cloud integrators, brokers, connectors, orchestrators, and mediators to bring a semblance of control and solidity to the vast and varied cloud systems. Companies specifically focusing on CBSs have emerged in the recent past to pick, polish, negotiate, intermediate, and aggregate cloud services from partners and third-party developers to provide polished, people-centric, composite, and adaptive cloud applications. Brokerage service providers need to know what services are available in order to discover and identify the assets to build customer-specific applications or complete a business process. The much-improved service governance concepts and controls come in handy when doling out competent and compact cloud governance solutions.

In short, for any agile and autonomous environment, a strong governance system must be put in place in order to nullify and notify any kind of reversal, deviation, misappropriation, or mismanagement of applications.

CLOUD GOVERNANCE: BEST PRACTICES

Cloud computing presents us with a novel paradigm for offering and managing IT services that are delivered through a converged, consolidated, shared, and virtualized infrastructure. It allows individuals as well as enterprises to leverage centralized and distributed IT systems and applications in a consistent and compact way through a host of CSPs. Clouds deliver high-quality and high-value IT services to businesses while lowering overall costs, reducing complexity, facilitating newer consumption styles, and increasing productivity, which in turn enables businesses to better focus on their core competencies and leave IT capabilities to cloud servers. Cloud computing, even with its significant and strategic benefits, introduces new risks and dangers if there is no sound management and governance in place to set them right; this is where best practices and key guidelines are critical and gladly welcome to continuously support and sustain the cloud journey. To correctly manage distributed, hosted, on-demand, off-premises, and online cloud-connected services, IT must focus on the QoS attributes being delivered, the veracity and validity of transactions, the privacy of the information being handled, and the agreed-on basis for calculating cost. This is where service management plays a critical role.

Service Value Chain Enablement

Robert Stroud, vice president at Computer Associates, insists on effectively managing IT service value chain in order to derive more decisive insights and visible impacts on all stakeholders. Services have the special feature of combining, clustering, composing, and even clouding to create smart services. Service chaining is the umbrella term to represent all kinds of merging, mingling, and mashup processes, and it empowers services to forge ahead. The service chain has to be empowered to add business and technical values. The user community too has to secure a measurable value out of the service chain paradigm.

Imagine that a complaint is expressed by a consumer that the mortgage application is not processing applications online. The mortgage application is a hybrid service consisting of multiple internal components, and the approval process is dependent on the outsourced credit check with a third-party service in the cloud. The SLA calls for all applications to be processed within 2 minutes, which allows the credit check result to be returned and an analysis to be performed on internal customer information records. Further, there may be an agreement in place as part of the SLA to have additional capacity available at a third party, which kicks in when certain thresholds are exceeded.

All this becomes part of the service value chain. The service value chain might have many key stakeholders including the internal IT department, end users, and business application owners, along with external service providers, that is, all individuals who have a stake in the right QoS being delivered at the right price at the right time. Ultimately business is about serving and satisfying customers, so service value chain management must not only manage and optimize customer experience but also ensure maximum business value. The enterprise cannot afford to have customers abandoning their mortgage applications because IT could not get credit checks processed on time. In delivering services to end customers, IT managers must remain focused on maximizing the service consumption experience and meeting expected service levels in terms of quality, performance, and availability. In this new paradigm, the view is total alignment from the first link of the chain to the last, with every link contributing value-driven capabilities. The meeting of these expectations requires that service providers leverage their investment in best practices, especially in processes such as supplier management, service level management, availability and financial management, and so on.

Process Innovation

Cloud governance can be a potent weapon and pivotal element only if an organization is entitled and empowered to be governed. This empowerment cannot be realized just because organizational structures such as steering committees and review boards are in place. Competent and composite processes, besides the structures, have to be modeled, developed, simulated, validated, and refined. Processes need to be analyzed and altered accordingly to suit the underlying behavior and culture of the organization. A cloud strategy and road map have to be taken into consideration when bringing into effect the relevant and right changes in cloud processes. Cloud migration is no joke. Processes need to go through a lot of renovation and innovation to keep up the momentum of moving to the cloud. The cloud model establishes a tactical as well as strategic relationship between IT users and service providers, thereby prescribing a collaborative linkage. A service management strategy enables every single organization to attain success in sync with the progressive and path-breaking cloud technology. The secret of delivering services within a cloud environment can be summarized as follows: "Develop the processes first, measure the throughput, and fine-tune based on the learning and understanding gained." Process engineering, control, integration, management, and enhancement are the important stages toward process innovation.

Risks Identification and Control

Having identified most of the emerging and emanating risks and threats (internal as well as external) of the much-hyped cloud computing paradigm, professionals and pundits are of the view that a strong cloud governance strategy comes in handy when convincing executives and entrepreneurs to embark on the long and arduous cloud journey. As traditional data centers are in a transition phase toward the cloud center for reaping all the expressed cloud benefits, governance function promises a painless transition for the initiated, as well as those planning to plunge into cloud-induced IT transformation. Cloud adoption is strengthened and solidified through IT governance mechanisms. Cloud governance provides a unified and application-centric view of the total cloud environment and ecosystem. Governance sharply enhances cloud visibility and flexibility. It clears the way for secure, managed, and incremental cloud adoption. But cloud governance can go awry if it is implemented too hastily or as an afterthought. K. Scott Morrison, the Vice President of Engineering and Chief Architect of Layer 7 Technologies, has come up with 10 implementable tips for successful cloud governance (http://www.eweek.com).

Entities considering a move to the cloud would do well to examine closely both their technology and processes to gain the cloud's advantages rather than suffer its perils. The moral of the story is that without proper planning and oversight (i.e., governance), the state of cloud computing will inevitably be the same. As in the case of SOA, each department and business unit of an enterprise will have its own cloud or its own version of a cloud. Further, the business partners and retailers of the enterprise will also do the same. Ultimately, cloud proliferation may end up creating its own set of problems that could be more painful than the set of problems we face today. If the IT community does not learn from its historical blunders, the cloud evolution that started out as a blessing may become a curse, resulting in chaos.

Tarak Modi, vice president and CTO, CALIBRE Systems, Alexandria, Virginia, has thus elucidated the ways and means of avoiding the storm and becoming successful in the cloud journey. He lists a series of governance-centric best practices. Thus, identification of risks and controlling them at the budding stage go a long way in garnering the envisioned benefits of cloud technology.

Building Trust

A critical success factor for addressing the need for trust and thereby enabling effective cloud governance is how well an organization can bring about a shift along two key dimensions: (1) trust and (2) pride. Trust is a complex interpersonal and organizational construct. Trust occurs when parties holding certain favorable perceptions of each other reach expected outcomes without worry and without the need to monitor each other's behavior. Trust is a serious business for dependable systems and is being prescribed as the most effective weapon for sharply enhancing the reliability and security of cloud services and infrastructures.

The PKI X.509 architecture, the basis for Internet commerce today, states that when two entities trust each other, the first entity makes the assumption that the second entity will behave exactly as the first entity expects and vice versa. Numerous studies have clearly substantiated that "the relationship between trust and good governance is circular." Establishing this trust relationship in the context of cloud governance requires two fundamental things [2]:

Standardization: Standardization has been an important factor in facilitating several things including interoperability and portability in the heterogeneous and propriety world of IT. Trust may also be established if cloud providers sincerely implement industry-strength standards. Standards give the right confidence and cue to worldwide users to jumpstart the cloud bandwagon. Switching from one provider to another is also automated if cloud systems are completely based on standards. If standards are given primary importance, the perpetual problem of vendor lock-in is destined to become history. Consortiums and government agencies have to come up with open and implementable standards for any technology to gain the much-needed critical mass. The overarching goal for standardization should be to provide a minimalistic framework that guides implementation rather than attempting to formalize every conceivable situation as attempted with the myriad WS-* family of standards.

Regulations: Cloud computing presents a compelling case with the promise of providing a shared, yet secure, platform that allows fast access to the best-of-breed business applications and services, compute resources, storage, and other infrastructures at a low cost. In order to ensure that this promise will not be broken, a regulatory environment that allows shared platforms to be certified is required. In a certified environment, any number or kind of applications can be run without being certified independently. This means the cloud will bear the responsibility of providing not only a secure platform but also accountability.

Best practices as usual give some valuable tips for attaining quick success with any new initiative. Here too, you can find some vital practices for effective and elegant cloud governance.

CLOUD GOVERNANCE SOLUTIONS

All of a sudden, there are numerous CSPs in the market. Both small and large providers are articulating and augmenting their special cloud capabilities in order to attract and retain loyal customers. Single as well as multiple CSPs are setting up their shops these days, promising a lot for their prospective clients and consumers. Small and big businesses are steadily moving their customer-facing applications to one or more clouds. However, due to the implicit and inhibiting security problem, customer and confidential data are still being kept in their own on-premises data centers. Thus, the enterprise scenario is becoming expansive. Enterprises are more and more considering the use of cloud facilities. Connectivity is being established and expanded between local servers and cloud infrastructures, asserting a kind of hybrid model to reap the distinct cloud benefits and to guarantee utmost safety, security, integrity, and privacy of customer data. The point to be noted here is that interactions happen over the web. The participants and constituents of this new and expanded computing paradigm are quite diverse, distributed, and decentralized. This has propelled and compelled the development of a fresh set of governance solutions. To be the first in this fiercely competitive scene, leading global infrastructure software vendors are busy preparing and producing platform-/middleware-/container-/engine-based governance solutions for effectively governing clouds, which look to be the core and critical infrastructure for future IT. The pioneering cloud idea gives rise to a number of transformations and, hence, the current complex, expensive, and stagnant IT is set to become green, clean, catalytic, elastic, and affordable.

Things to Look for in a Cloud Governance Solution

This is taken from a white paper published by the company Layer7 Technologies. The following are the 10 important factors to be considered as CSPs begin to look for a complete and compact governance solution:

1. Policy enforcement scheme: Cloud environments are turning out to be sophisticated and distributed environments and, hence, there is a need for distributed enforcement of policies in order to comprehensively govern the expanding cloud scene. So when a CSP looks for a features-packed governance solution, he or she has to first look

for a policy enforcement module that stringently enforces right and relevant policies in real time. This offers immediate stand-alone value and the ability to integrate with heavyweight registries/repositories.

2. The vPEP: Enforcement and monitoring must scale in and out without impacting its functional and nonfunctional obligations. Hardware appliances will always hold their place for their speed and performance quality, but vPEP appliances are nowadays preferred over hardware appliances as they are cheaper options and can be rapidly deployed in the cloud.

3. Distributed and virtualized management: Management systems for policy monitoring and enforcement, whether in traditional SOA systems or in clouds, need to be distributed so that there is no single point of failure. These consoles are expected to manage mission-critical applications. If a local network becomes segmented or a cloud provider is inaccessible, the management components should be locally available on every enforcement point.

4. A central system of record for critical assets: There must be a central and authoritative system of record for assets such as policies. Think of this as a library storing the laws of the land.

5. Loose coupling between enforcement points and repository: Following factor number 4, enforcement points must not be tightly bound to central repositories because of the latency and reliability issues associated with the cloud.

6. Policies are centrally authored and globally deployed: Policy will move with the applications in the cloud. Localized differences (time zones, IP addresses, SLAs, etc.) must be mapped automatically during provisioning. This is a difficult problem, because policy itself is often riddled with unanticipated dependencies.

7. A global view of the application network: A critical need exists for an application-centric management and monitoring system. It must accommodate the subtleties of application protocols so that it can provide an actionable view of problems as they occur.

8. Flexibility in policy languages: The need of the hour is flexible policy languages, considering the growing variety of policies. It is through one or more policies that all correspondences between cloud services

are managed, adapted, and controlled. Therefore, a richly expressive and formal policy language will give the necessary tools to manage any situation easily and quickly.

9. Cloud governance is the subtle extension of SOA governance: Any cloud governance solution should be as applicable to traditional SOA as it is to a cloud.

10. Utilization of the cloud in the solution: If a vendor is serious about a cloud, a cloud governance solution has to make use of cloud-based services.

These are all the most prevalent features to be deeply and diligently contemplated before choosing an appropriate cloud governance solution. In the near future, there may be additions to this list and fresh guidelines will emerge for enabling decision making before committing to a governance solution from a particular vendor. With the fast proliferation and utilization of cloud services and applications, a governance solution will soon become a mandatory asset. As users and service developers lose control and visibility, cloud governance solutions come as a solace for deprived souls.

VORDEL CSB

Besides formulating and firming up processes and policies (business, management, usage, cultural, and technical), there is a need for automated tools such as a policy manager and a runtime container. The Vordel CSB is a kind of middleware for proactively managing the perfect and preferred usage of all kinds of cloud resources and for moderating and mediating interactions among the resources. In a nutshell, this CSB from Vordel allows organizations to add and apply a layer of trust into their cloud services and applications. It adaptively brokers the connection to the cloud infrastructure by applying governance controls for service usage and service uptime. The broker sits between the organization and the CSP. It can be deployed as software or as an edge device for brokering connections to the distant cloud. Additionally, it may also be deployed in a cloud as an Amazon EC2 instance.

Elements of Cloud Governance

The Vordel CSB provides a set of value-added services for establishing connections to clouds (Figure 11.7). These services allow an organization to link cloud services with their existing infrastructure, without compromising throughput and security.

Analytics of Cloud Usage

Organizations require a record of how they are using external cloud services. Analytics of cloud usage includes information about service quality, patterns of usage over time, and identity of users. In this way, an organization can understand how they leverage the cloud services. Developers could use or misuse services for application development and maintenance without worrying about the impact. Similarly, cloud services can also be subjected to misappropriation. Thus, a broker with analytic capability is very much needed in order to stop such kinds of improper usage. This CSB is capable of detecting new cloud service usage and bringing it to the attention of IT staff; the IT staff can then apply policies to it and bring it under an umbrella of governance.

The CSB records cloud service usage by service type, time of day, and the identity of a user. In this way, an organization can ensure that it knows who is using cloud services, as well as understand the pattern of usage. This means that the organization will not be surprised by bills for excessive cloud usage, as the broker reports keep them abreast of usage as it happens.

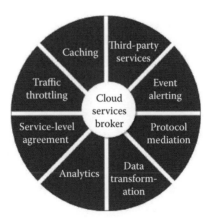

FIGURE 11.7
Cloud service broker capabilities.

Content Analysis

Data sent to third-party cloud providers should not contain sensitive data, such as data that would identify a customer or, in the case of health care, a patient. All content sent to cloud services must be analyzed for leaked data in order to enable data loss prevention (DLP). In addition, content-level threats must be detected and blocked. This includes application-level attacks at the API and payload levels. Content analysis is also important so that organizations can meet compliance regulations.

Caching

The broker provides caching for two broad reasons: (1) Caching protects the enterprise from the latency associated with connecting to a cloud service. When the response is fetched from the broker's cache, this is significantly faster than connecting to the cloud service itself. (2) The broker cache saves an organization's money by allowing some requests to be serviced by the broker itself, removing the need for a billed connection to the cloud provider.

Monitoring SLA

Cloud infrastructure is often a mission-critical factor, and organizations must ensure that if a cloud connection is not responding as required, then an alert is raised. The broker includes comprehensive SLA monitoring, which monitors not only the response time of a cloud service but also the entire transaction throughput time. In this way, the user of a cloud service can understand exactly where a slowdown is happening and take remedial action. This augments the monitoring provided by cloud providers themselves, by providing a trusted internal solution for cloud service monitoring.

Traffic Throttling

Throttling is the surge protector of clouds. If an application makes a high number of calls to a cloud service, then this broker can deflect a portion of the calls to a newly provisioned application instance. In this way, elasticity is provided. This broker makes use of proven traffic management functionality. Throttling also allows different levels of service to be guaranteed to different customers. In this way, the premium model is enabled: Nonpaying users receive one level of service, whereas paying users receive another.

Event Alerting

There must be alerts for events such as cloud outages so that corrective measures can be taken. For example, if a connection to a CSP is lost due to a local ISP problem, then the CSP will not raise an alert since its service is still running as normal. However, this ISP outage affects local users of the cloud service. A local broker will detect the outage and raise an alert.

Besides the governance-related features, more traditional broker services are also enabled by this broker.

Identity as the Key

Cloud services are typically accessed using an API key. This is the model used by Amazon web services, Salesforce.com, Google, and others. However, rather than using API keys, local applications make use of identity technologies such as Kerberos for Windows networks or access control products such as CA SiteMinder and Oracle Access Manager. This broker bridges the connection from an on-premise identity management infrastructure to cloud services. This enables users, who access applications locally or simply sign on to their PCs, to access various cloud services all the time, governed under the umbrella of an identity management infrastructure. Rules applied to internal applications, governing who can access which applications and how they can use the applications, can now be applied in the same way to cloud-based applications.

Connecting an Enterprise to a Cloud

The broker enables the hybrid model of multidomain integration connecting locally hosted EAs and the cloud. For example, the broker allows local applications, linked by an ESB, to leverage Amazon S3 for external storage. The broker allows external cloud-provided services to be leveraged just like local services, in conjunction with local applications on the network. The broker uses its extensive range of enterprise computing connectors in order to seamlessly link cloud services to local EAs.

Composition of Cloud Services

The broker links together local applications with cloud-hosted applications. The local applications may be accessed using service interfaces, database calls, message schemes such as MQ or JMS, or simply the file system. This allows a developer to compose an application that combines local resources with cloud-based resources. By expanding this simple enterprise domain example to a cloud domain example, one can envisage a multidomain scenario in which services are composed across several CSPs and the enterprise.

Enabling the CSP

CSPs such as Amazon and Google provide code examples for organizations who wish to connect to their systems. However, not all organizations wish to code connections to a cloud. The broker allows an out-of-the-box approach for enterprises to connect to a cloud.

Enabling Cloud Service Brokerages

As per a Gartner report, there is a huge market for cloud service brokerages. This broker enables organizations to act as brokerages between cloud services. Brokerages can be defined as businesses that act as intermediaries to negotiate the interactions between service providers and consumers. These brokerages are charged with enabling trust and governance between the contracting parties.

Policies are very important for runtime governance of cloud infrastructures, platforms, services, and applications. Therefore, any governance solution must be capable of policy engineering, utilization, management, maintenance, and refinement. Further, there will be multiple types of clouds in the near future. Hence, proactive and preemptive monitoring, management, and rule-/policy-based overseeing of communication, composition, and cooperation among clouds form a crucial differentiator for any future governance solution.

CONCLUSION

Once in a while, a truly disruptive technology comes along with the potential of changing completely the way we do business. Cloud computing is such a technology that has already started and will continue to create massive and memorable shifts for end users, employees, executives, and entrepreneurs. As the cloud environment is becoming highly distributed, federated, decentralized, and dynamic, a strong governance/oversight solution has to be installed and integrated in order to optimally utilize all sorts of cloud resources to face business changes and challenges. In other words, in order to continuously utilize the distinct benefits of clouds, an efficient governance procedure, practice, and platform need to be in place. Governance ensures a tighter control on and proactive monitoring of cloud resources and their interactions, ensures accurate countermeasures are taken to nullify any deviation, and also brings to the table innovative and integrated cloud processes. Further, operational requirements and agreements can be met only if there is an efficient governance solution in place. As discussed in previous sections, new technologies may bring in some hitherto unexplored risks and incompatibilities that have to be resolved using a host of technological solutions. Policy engineering, representation, management, and enforcement have to be automated in order to promote and provide runtime/dynamic cloud governance for guaranteeing that all runtime transactions and interactions happen as defined and desired.

REFERENCES

1. Oltsik, J. January 20, 2003. "IT Governance Allows You to Do More IT with Less Money," TechRepublic, http://www.techrepublic.com/article/it-governance-allows-you-to-do-more-it-with-less-money/1054749.
2. Modi, T. November 23, 2009. "Avoiding the Storms: Why We Need Cloud Governance," ebizQ, http://www.ebizq.net/topics/cloud_computing/features/11934.html?page=2.
3. Dodani, M. H. 2006. "Change Happens!." *Journal of Object Technology* 5 (1): 39–44, http://www.jot.fm/issues/issue_2006_01/column4/.
4. Shaw, K. A. and B. Carlson. August 8, 2006. "Change Governance for the Agile Enterprise—a Service Oriented Architecture (SOA) Perspective," Serena Software, Inc., http://www.serena.com/docs/repository/solutions/soa%20and%20agility.pdf.
5. Potter, D. June 28, 2007. "The Truth about SOA Governance," WebLayers, Inc., http://www.weblayers.com/wl2/rc/collateral/WebLayers_Truth_About_SOA_Governance.pdf
6. April 2007. "Managing Data as a Corporate Asset: Three Action Steps toward Successful Data Governance," Hewlett-Packard Development Company, L.P., http://www.safekidsnystate.org/My%20Downloads/Data-Governance-White-Paper-HP-standard-April-2007.pdf.
7. Walker, G. May 31, 2012. "Inside the Hybrid Cloud, Part 4: Implementation Considerations," IBM developerWorks, http://www.ibm.com/developerworks/cloud/library/cl-hybridcloud4/cl-hybridcloud4-pdf.pdf.
8. Layer 7 Technologies, Inc. 2010. Steer Safely into the Clouds: Why You Must Have Cloud Governance Before You Move Your Apps, Layer 7 Technologies, Inc., http://www.layer7tech.com/main/images/Steer%20Safely%20into%20the%20Clouds%20v3.0.pdf.

Cloud Governance Solutions and Resources
9. http://www.oracle.com/us/technologies/soa/soa-governance/index.html

10. http://www-01.ibm.com/software/solutions/soa/gov/
11. http://web.progress.com/en/Product-Capabilities/soa-governance.html
12. http://petalsmaster.ow2.org
13. http://www.weblayers.com
14. http://www.layer7tech.com
15. http://www.vodel.com
16. http://www.boozallen.com/consulting-services/information-technology/cloud-computing
17. http://www.opstera.com

12

Cloud Onboarding Best Practices

INTRODUCTION

Clouds are emerging as the consolidated, virtualized, automated, and shared IT environment for efficiently hosting, managing, and delivering scores of service-centric and enterprise-scale applications, platforms, and infrastructures as services to worldwide users through the pervasive and public Internet, which is being touted as a cheap communication infrastructure. In other words, as the knowledge-driven service era sets in and stabilizes, the utility and ubiquity of the cloud as the pathbreaking service deployment and delivery container will increase further.

The main benefit of adopting the pioneering cloud concept is that clouds enable IT agility, affordability, and autonomy. The goals of making IT simple and sensitive are realized with the adoption of novelty-packed cloud concepts. As a result, IT resource utilization goes up significantly; IT resource elasticity and application scalability are all set to soar with the emergence of lean, green, and optimal infrastructures; and the goal of self-servicing of clouds is nearing realization due to numerous enhancements, such as enhancements in the extensibility, malleability, usability, and consumability of IT module at different layers and levels of the enterprise IT stack. The increase in IT efficiency translates to overall business efficiency and has the potential to result in new innovations and opportunities. On the operational side, an increase in the manageability, performance, maintainability, and simplicity of IT modules through the separation of concerns is the prominent reason why businesses are very optimistic about cloud computing. By delegating the management of infrastructure and software platforms to a team of skilled professionals employed by CSPs, customers can offload operational responsibilities to CSPs.

A cloud environment gives an illusion of the existence of infinite processing, storage, and networking resources. This empowerment does a lot of good for some specific enterprise applications. Applications that are designed to spread their workload across multiple servers will benefit immensely from the automated scaling of resources to match current demand. This is quite appealing for applications with unpredictable or cyclical usage patterns, because a cloud orchestrator/broker can monitor usage and dynamically scale resources up or down on a need basis. This behavior, in sync with the pay-by-use characteristic of clouds, can lead to significant financial savings.

With a better understanding of the business, technical, and use cases of clouds, organizations across the world are preparing strategies and road maps to enter the cloud space, which is steadily expanding through a host of innovations and improvisations. However, cloud onboarding has to be articulated and accomplished very carefully and calculatedly as there are several constrictions and challenges associated with onboarding. This chapter gives an overview of why, when, how, and what for cloud onboarding and a lean migration methodology for smartly and successfully embarking on the long and arduous process of cloud onboarding.

A PERSPECTIVE ON CLOUD ONBOARDING

There are several kinds of cloud delivery and deployment models. Moving applications, services, and data stores to cloud infrastructures and platforms is beset with a number of critical challenges and concerns. This movement involves a lot of up-front planning and facilitation of migration tools, best practices, and pragmatic experiences. Many factors must be considered when moving an application to the cloud, including applications components, the network stack, management, security, dependency, and orchestration.

Benefits of Cloud Onboarding

Cloud onboarding is the deployment or migration of data, applications, or integrated solutions of compute, storage, and network resources to a public, private, or hybrid cloud [4]. Onboarding addresses business needs such as spikes in demand, BC, backup and archival, and capacity optimization.

Enterprises can use onboarding to address capacity demands without needing to deploy additional infrastructure. Cloud onboarding should be considered in the design of overarching and enterprise-wide cloud infrastructure that supports internal, external, and federated clouds. It provides a compelling use for enterprises who want to maximize the elastic capabilities of cloud computing.

Cloud onboarding allows a cloud to act as an additional resource or extension of the data center for the following reasons:

- Occasions when the data center becomes overloaded by demand spikes
- Cost-effective capacity management and seamless load balancing
- Disaster recovery and failure mitigation

Application Migration: A Case Study

Company C is a small oil and gas company that owns some offshore assets in the North Sea oil fields [3]. Company C needs a data acquisition system to allow it to manage its offshore operations by monitoring data from its assets on a minute-by-minute basis. Company C's assets rely on the production facilities of company A (a major oil company); therefore, the data comes onshore through company A's communication links. Company C does not have the capabilities to develop its own IT systems; hence, they outsource the development and management of its system to company B, which is an IT solutions company with a small data center. Figure 12.1 provides an overview of the system, which consists of two servers:

1. A database server that logs and archives the data coming in from the offshore assets into a database. A tape drive is used to take daily backups of the database, and the tapes are stored off-site.
2. An application server that hosts a number of data-reporting and -monitoring applications. The end users at company C access these applications using a remote desktop client over the Internet.

The system infrastructure was deployed in company B's data center some years back. Since then company B's support department has been maintaining the system and solving any problems that may have arisen. This case study investigates how the same system can be deployed using the cloud offerings of Amazon Web Services. Figure 12.2 provides an

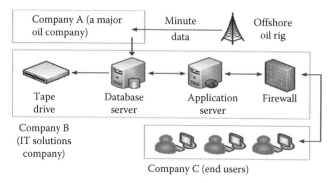

FIGURE 12.1

Overview of a system having two servers, a database server and an application server.

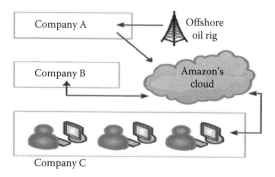

FIGURE 12.2

System deployed in a cloud.

overview of this scenario, in which company B deploys and maintains the same system in the cloud.

Application modernization and migration to the cloud bring a number of advantages. There are empirical studies by researchers in public and private organizations all over the world for understanding and articulating the financial advantages of developing, deploying, delivering, and managing applications in cloud environments. The results clearly show that there are long-term capital as well as operational benefits.

Cloud Onboarding Use Cases

The Intel Cloud Builders Guide (http://www.intel.com/content/dam/www/public/us/en/documents/guides/cloud-builders-xeon-5500-5600-citrix-netscaler-guide.pdf) has detailed the following types of use cases for cloud onboarding:

Use case 1—onboarding simple, self-contained applications or VMs: The migration and instantiation of a single, integrated, virtualized application such as a static web application and simple, self-contained applications into an external or public cloud.

Use case 2—onboarding multiple VM workloads with storage and services residing in the enterprise: The instantiation of a multi-VM workload with interconnections to storage and other enterprise applications. One or more VMs of the workload are migrated to the cloud, whereas storage and other services (infrastructure, database, and so on) reside in the enterprise. Network transparency between the two clouds enables seamless execution.

Top Considerations for Cloud Onboarding

Cloud onboarding is complicated; it can require the redesign or rearchitecture of application components, the network stack, management, security, or orchestration, which are all dependent on the application and infrastructure intricacies and complexities. Before an application is successfully onboarded to the cloud, some key aspects must be considered.

The application will likely consist of more components and infrastructure dependencies than what initially appears in the cloud environment. Some of these components, such as directory services, DNS, and dynamic host configuration protocol (DHCP), are shared by other applications cannot simply be moved to the cloud, and cloud applications that require them must integrate back into the enterprise implementation.

Enterprises want to run applications across multiple CSPs in an integrated, secure manner with an integrated management solution. Enterprises must also consider the way in which applications run in the enterprise versus the way they run within the cloud. Cloud onboarding may involve a conversion from physical to virtual (P2V) or virtual to virtual (V2V) environments. Corporations still want to keep their customer, corporate, and confidential data locally in their own enterprise servers or private clouds. Even mission-critical applications are still kept in local and on-premise servers. Customer-facing applications can be moved to public clouds. This sort of distributed and decentralized application landscape is bound to create much management complexity. Integration becomes an issue, controllability and visibility go down, and security and privacy pose problems.

Applications need to go through a series of optimizations before being exported to cloud environments. Sometimes existing applications may require re-architecture to facilitate the migration. To exploit the flexibility of a cloud environment, we need to understand which application architectures are properly structured to operate in a cloud, the kinds of applications and data that run well in cloud environments, and data backup needs and system workloads in a cloud environment. The key is to architect applications that reduce or eliminate the number of difficult-to-resolve dependencies between the application stack and the capabilities provided by a CSP. There are at least three cloud application architectures on the scene today [7]:

1. "Traditional application architectures" such as three-tier architectures are designed for stable demand rather than large variations in load. They do not require an architecture that can scale up or down.
2. "Synchronous application architectures" are those in which end-user interaction is the primary focus. Typically, large numbers of users may be using a web application in a short time period and may overwhelm the application and the system.
3. "Asynchronous application architectures" are all essentially batch applications that do not support end-user interaction. They work on sets of data, extracting and inserting data into databases. Cloud computing offers scalability of server resources, allowing an otherwise long-running asynchronous job to be dispersed over several servers to share the processing load.

There are legacy (siloed, massive, and monolithic), web, enterprise, and embedded applications that are prime candidates to be carefully considered for cloud-enablement so that they can be ported to cloud environments without any compatibility issues and provided as a publicly discoverable, accessible, and leveraged service over the web for subscription and a usage-based fee.

A CLOUD ONBOARDING PROCESS

This section discusses a process that helps in rediscovering the optimal balance of performance, agility, sustainability, and cost. There are five steps to this process:

1. Evaluate
2. Select
3. Migrate

4. Optimize

5. Operate

The Evaluate Step

Every cloud migration has to begin with a deeper analysis of the existing infrastructure. There is a need to identify the technical, business, legal, dependency, and usability constraints of the applications designated for migration. The nonfunctional aspects of the applications to be migrated (QoS attributes such as performance, scalability, mission criticality, availability, and security) ought to be evaluated. Finally, a business-centric evaluation must be performed according to the business architecture. The major focus is on the business advantages, challenges, potential revenue, and so on of the migration.

The Select Step

Once the applications are evaluated for their suitability to cloud environments, cloud deployment and delivery models and platforms need to be selected to get as much flexibility as possible through this migration. Each application must be considered according to costs, burstiness, proximity to end users, security, and many other factors. A broad range of deployment options are available today [5]:

Bare metal: Traditional "down to the concrete" machines in which you control every aspect of the environment and there is no overhead for virtualization or management. Although this requires up-front investment, it is the most powerful option for applications with known and relatively consistent resource profiles.

VMs: Virtualization can turn a physical server into many virtual servers. It is a great option for workloads that play well with others, but it still needs custom environments and nonstandard configurations.

Private cloud: This option includes consolidation of underutilized and unutilized computing machines; creation of VMs out of them using hypervisors; and incorporation of several types of automation software for self-service, workload management, job scheduling, system management, capacity prediction, and service governance. Private clouds are very safe and provide high controllability and visibility.

Virtual private cloud: A virtual private cloud is not a private cloud; it is siphoned from a public cloud with enhanced and foolproof security via a dedicated IP address.

Infrastructure cloud: An infrastructure cloud, the common and widely talked about public cloud, provides virtual infrastructure boxes such as servers, load-balancers, and firewalls on-demand, which are charged on an hourly or usage basis. It is a dynamic pool of commodity servers for creating and shutting down VMs as per changing needs. This is by far the cheapest option with resource elasticity and application scalability (horizontal).

Platform cloud: There are a stream of platforms for application design, development, debugging, deployment, and delivery on cloud infrastructures. Cloud infrastructure management solutions take care of platform management requirements. But this option has lock-in risks and limits the choice of languages and tools.

Mashups, SaaS, and RESTful APIs: Due to the extremely simple nature of RESTful services, CSPs are giving out RESTful APIs for their resources to application developers and user agents. There are mashup editors for composing business-aligned mashups, which are crafted quickly and delivered to business users. Service composition is sharply simplified with the use of RESTful APIs.

The Migrate Step

Once we understand what belongs where, it is time to migrate applications and data to a cloud environment. This requires careful planning to avoid any unanticipated surprises and downtime. For systems that are migrating from on-premise to on-demand environments, this often begins with virtualization and making the applications portable. On the other hand, for cloud-based systems that will benefit from dedicated hardware, this may involve performing architectural changes and server farm configuration. There are myriad supporting services such as DNS, authentication, monitoring, metering and billing, and backup services, which must also be migrated in order to streamline cloud-based application delivery.

APPLICATION EVALUATION CRITERIA

Candidate applications need to be further evaluated to make sure that it is feasible to migrate; they must also be readied for the migration process itself [6].

As clouds are being positioned as the next-generation IT infrastructure, scores of business and IT applications are being systematically readied to be easily and quickly deployable and executable in clouds. There are several things to be considered for applications to run smoothly and securely on cloud systems. These days, monolithic legacy applications and packages are being replaced with distributed applications. Service oriented architecture specifies that enterprise-scale applications need to be built as a dynamic collection of interoperable, replaceable, and portable services. That is, increasingly, application components and their associated databases are deployed in different and distributed systems. Therefore, it is critical and crucial for cloud application architects to clearly identify application dependencies. Just redeploying existing applications in a cloud does not make it effective and efficient. Modernizing traditional applications in order to be useful and usable in a new environment involves a number of carefully defined steps. Multi-tenancy is one important factor for cloud applications. Applications and services taken to clouds need to precisely and perfectly discover and use other applications (cloud, enterprise, embedded, etc.). The following list casts some light on these cloud modernization and migration aspects.

Application architectures: The application architecture affects how an application can be migrated to cloud environments. Sometimes, it also determines whether an application is suitable for migration.

Multitiered applications: The majority of enterprise applications are built using multiple tiers to decouple the major functions and modules in the system. One such approach is to organize the application using three tiers as follows:
- A data management tier, which consists of relational or other database components
- A business logic tier, which uses application platform or containers, such as JEE or Microsoft's .NET
- A presentation tier, which is responsible for interfacing with the user interfaces or other external systems, including managing state and data for presentation to the external systems

Applications that use a layered architecture approach have well-defined interfaces between the aforementioned layers. Based on application usage patterns, it might be possible to have migrating application tiers or modules within a tier, separately. For example, in a web application, static content can be migrated to a content delivery network provider so that parts of a website can load more quickly. In other cases, WAN bandwidth restrictions might prevent tiers from being separated, and all layers of an application will be migrated to a cloud. In either case, each layer and its major distributed components and modules should be evaluated separately to determine how that layer should be sized and migrated to a cloud. Application tiers might also have varying security and zoning requirements. For example, some application data might have to be secured behind a firewall.

Scale-up and scale-out architectures: A scale-up architecture is one in which an application can benefit from more resources, such as CPU and memory, added to a single server or node. In contrast, a scale-out architecture is one in which an application scales by additional nodes being made available for the workload, that is, it scales horizontally. Scale-out applications can take advantage of the pay-by-use cost model of the cloud. When there are increased requests for an application, more nodes can be deployed to handle the increased load. When requests slow down, the additional nodes can be powered off to reduce costs. Today, it is not possible to dynamically scale up an application running on a single machine instance. This might change in the future, because virtualization systems are starting to support hot-plug features, which means more memory and CPU can be added dynamically.

Multitenancy is a vital factor that is given utmost consideration when transitioning applications from on-premise to cloud environments. Sharing is a foremost feature of clouds and there would be several concurrent users for an application. Multitenancy is all about leveraging just one instance of the application for meeting the requirements of multiple users. There are different mechanisms for enabling multitenancy in cloud applications at different levels (infrastructures, applications, databases, etc.).

APPLICATION DEPENDENCY MAPPING

This activity identifies dependencies among applications on a shared data center infrastructure. Data collection can be done in multiple passes or phases, initially to identify all of an application's immediate dependencies and then to identify what other applications are dependent on the application's dependencies. For example, if both application A and application B are using the same database server, this needs to be identified so that the migration plan can include a combined move or can include steps to split the dependencies.

Application profiling is used to measure and collect real usage data of an application before it is migrated. This data can help to size application deployment in a cloud. Ideally, application data should be collected for at least 10–15 days to allow capture of variances in daily and weekly usage patterns. For each node on which the application runs, the following data should be collected:

- The CPU usage
- Memory usage
- Storage data such as throughput, latency, and input/output operations per second (IOPS)
- Network data such as throughput, connections per second, and dropped connections

The node-level data can be used to estimate how many and what type of machines will be necessary when the application is migrated.

In addition to node-level statistics, it is also important to profile user activity, such as the total number of connected users, request and transaction rates, and request latencies. The usage data can also be used to build automated tests for the application to ensure the same or an improved level of service after the application is migrated.

The node data, along with application usage data, can also provide an initial estimate of the costs of cloud resources.

The Optimize Step

Once applications find a new residence, they need fine-tuning. Cloud-based systems need to grow and shrink automatically, that is, autoscaling to meet demand and shrinking when not needed (to save money). Systems running on dedicated infrastructure may need tuning to squeeze the most out of the platforms on which they run and can often benefit from acceleration and optimization techniques that simply are not available in a cloud environment. The optimization activities ultimately result in high performance, flexibility, dependability, lower costs, and so on.

The Operate Step

To simplify and streamline cloud IT operations, there are several software-based automated solutions. All kinds of virtual resources that are created are smartly closed once their role and responsibility come to an end. There are cloud service brokers, cloud service governance engines, service gateways, system management solutions, and so on. All these assist administrators in guaranteeing high performance and assurance.

CLOUD ONBOARDING SERVICES

The recent recessionary trend in the world economy has made company executives and decision makers across the world rethink and refine their priorities and business directions. The number-one priority is to derive maximum value from all the IT investments made so far. As there is a growing disconnect between business and IT, the envisioned advantages of IT cannot be fully leveraged by businesses and hence expectations for IT are consistently on the rise. As IT is being overwhelmingly recognized as the best business enabler, there will be constant insistence on finding ways and means of simplifying and streamlining IT-sponsored business acceleration, automation, and augmentation. There are a few pioneering business-impacting technologies such as SOA and cloud computing. The seamless convergence of these two and EA methods results in service-driven and cloud-centric enterprises.

Emergence of Cloud Enterprises

The cloud rage is definitely on. Worldwide corporations are seriously strategizing their businesses to embark on the cloud journey. The ultimate goal for global organizations is to reposition and rebrand themselves as cloud enterprises. A dazzling array of cloud concepts, technologies, platforms, products, processes, and practices are being recognized and utilized overwhelmingly by companies of all sizes across the globe so that they can benefit immensely from all the remarkable achievements and accomplishments in the cloud arena. Although appropriating the pathbreaking cloud paradigm presents new opportunities and fresh possibilities, the cloud journey is by no means free from obstacles and stumbling blocks. Here, cloud technology consultants can chip in with their cloud experience, education, and expertise-spurred insights to articulate workable and specific schemes to facilitate business transformation.

CLOUD ADVISORY AND ADVOCACY SERVICES

Cloud advisory services help organizations to arrive at the right cloud architecture that fits their current and future computing, communication, storage, and analytic needs. Through a comprehensive and closer engagement with corporate decision-makers, it is possible to come out with a pragmatic cloud strategy that helps to craft a specific cloud adoption road map with time lines and a migration plan. The engagement comprises several phases utilizing a structured delivery approach. The major activities in this engagement are as follows:

The CEA services: The cloud, being the most pioneering and penetrating idea in the enterprise space, will seamlessly link with EA to result in the emergence and establishment of CEA. The prominent architectural modules of CEA are as follows:

1. Cloud business architecture
2. Cloud application architecture
3. Cloud information architecture
4. Cloud technology architecture
5. Cloud integration architecture/CBSs
6. Cloud security architecture
7. Cloud management architecture
8. Cloud governance architecture

The other noteworthy developments in the cloud space include the following:

1. Cloud databases (the hybrid of transactional and analytical databases)
2. Big-data computing (Hadoop, HDFS, and NoSQL databases)
3. Cloud backup and archival
4. Cloud analytics
5. Next-generation clouds (mobile, device, sensor, high-performance, service, social, science, data, and knowledge clouds)

Cloud Adoption Assessment Service

This is the foremost step toward embarking on the cloud journey. Assessing, analyzing, and articulating actionable insights about the IT landscape go a long way in facilitating the adoption of the cloud paradigm. In other words, analyzing currently running IT infrastructures, platforms, databases, applications, and support systems diligently in order to come out with a comprehensive report is the key, and such a report details which systems are good for the cloud and which are not. Consultants can also identify and analyze workloads to get a deeper understanding of the IT landscape. They can provide the right and relevant details about how cloud-enablement of some systems creates fresh opportunities and new possibilities. They can identify the positive as well as the negative implications of this transition and provide cost-benefit insights regarding embracing the cloud model. The challenges, risks, and security threats in adopting an identified and agreed-on cloud model can be expressed in detail. Best practices, tools, and frameworks with a detailed map of migration opportunities can also be shared. The predominant questions to be answered when plunging into the cloud readiness evaluation phase include the following:

- How is the new cloud model helpful for your organization?
- What systems and subsystems are suitable for cloud-enablement?
- What kind of cloud delivery and deployment models are suitable for your organization?
- How is modernization of selected systems and their migration to cloud going to happen?
- Should you go to a public cloud provider, set up a private cloud, or transition the existing data center to a private cloud?
- What are the business, technical, and user benefits of adopting the cloud concept?
- What would be the TCO and RoI of cloud embarkation?
- How can you enable tighter cloud security?
- How can you manage and govern the cloud service portfolio?
- How can you explore new avenues for fresh revenues?
- What are the pros and cons of the proposed cloud model?

Cloud Design Service

Consultants can design futuristic cloud infrastructure by leveraging the open and industry-strength standards, design patterns, and best practices gained through empirical evidence and practical experience. They can develop private clouds quickly using a cloud appliance/cloud-in-a-box and prefabricated hardware, software, and service modules.

There are some real concerns for organizations about moving their IT assets and artifacts to a public cloud due to the persisting security and privacy challenges. There are other worries such as the lack of accountability, auditability, controllability, and visibility. Corporations are working toward building a private cloud due to the aforementioned reasons. The primary factors behind developing private clouds are that they are completely secure; are accessible only to your employees; and have heightened flexibility, controllability, and visibility. All the underutilized and unutilized computing machines are consolidated, centralized, virtualized, and automated to establish private clouds. The availability, scalability, and performance of IT resources can be quickly fine-tuned by your own administrators, and utilization of resources through resource consolidation, management, and sharing can rise significantly. Regulatory compliance can be achieved without much effort. An existing data center can be fully analyzed to recommend a series of plausible and pragmatic measures toward operational and cost optimizations. The prime focus will be on defining the maturity of and gaps in the following:

- Virtualization; server, storage, network, desktop, application, service, and information
- Capacity planning, workload distribution and management
- Management and monitoring of virtual resources
- Infrastructure elasticity and application scalability
- Auditing and security compliance

As part of this service, consultants can do a kind of "pilot application migration to the cloud." The consulting team would want to undertake a pilot exercise with a handful of applications to uncover any hidden risk or any need for process changes and to also help justify the business case for migration to the cloud. It is beneficial to perform the first migration properly, thereby forming a baseline process that can be evolved before undertaking further application migrations to the cloud. Consultants can provide experienced cloud consulting services to plan, oversee, and implement your pilot or phased migration. The purpose of any pilot is to ensure a seamless shift of operations to cloud services.

Cloud Development Service

This is about designing, developing, debugging, deploying, and delivering enterprise-class, mission-critical, service-oriented cloud-based applications for both public as well as private consumption.

Cloud Management and Operations

On the one hand, there is a growing portfolio of services and applications and, on the other hand, virtualization facilitates the dynamic formation of a number of VMs from physical machines. Thus, besides managing such virtual resources, there is a need to effectively manage physical resources too. Hence, the topic of cloud service and infrastructure management is getting hotter by the day. Cloud management solutions, cloud service brokers, cloud governance engines, SDPs, and so on are fast emerging for sustaining the adoption of clouds. This is about understanding the challenge and criticality of managing business applications and infrastructure in a cloud environment and pondering viable and value-added solutions. Consultants can empower companies to reap maximum RoIs, ensuring QoS requirements as per the SLA, guaranteed uptime, and zero disruption. System integrators and independent service vendors are investing heavily on building intellectual capital in this potential space. Through purpose-specific partnerships with different cloud product vendors, they can fulfill the industry expectations of setting up and sustaining cloud application and infrastructure management solutions.

Cloud Implementation and Migration Services

This is all about leveraging hard-earned expertise and experience in areas such as application rationalization and reengineering, infrastructure virtualization, data center consolidation and optimization, and migration services to provide quicker and quality implementation and the migration of customers from traditional data centers to flexible and futuristic computing environments such as public, private, or even hybrid clouds.

For building private clouds, one must leverage standards-compliant infrastructure cloud solutions such as Eucalyptus, Nebula, OpenStack, and CloudStack. Then the process of application modernization to make applications ready for clouds must be initiated to deploy SaaS-enabled IT solutions and products in clouds.

Cloud Protection Service

This is all about understanding, analyzing, and approaching all sorts of security needs at different levels and layers: physical security, network security, application security, and data security.

Cloud Support Services

This is a support service for ensuring continual service improvement and application life cycle management (ALM) services.

CLOUD CENTER TRANSFORMATION IMPLEMENTATION SERVICES

Cloud technology brings a number of pioneering transformations to the IT infrastructure front. Existing data centers are being modernized into cloud centers. IT networking, storage, and server disciplines are bound to go through a litany of desirable and delectable shifts with the adoption of cloud technologies. This cloud-enabled instigation will help IT service organizations explore fresh avenues for additional revenues. A representative list of cloud-centric consulting and implementation service is given below.

1. Cloud infrastructure design, integration, and planning
2. Cloud center network architecture and engineering
3. Cloud center storage architecture and engineering
4. Cloud center optimization for lean and green centers
5. Enabling hybrid and connected cloud centers

The Roles of the Cloud in Structuring and Sustaining Next-Generation Business Enterprises

The cloud primarily represents infrastructure transformation [1]. As it is widely and overwhelmingly accepted, infrastructure optimization plays a very important role in realizing enterprise/business transformation. Thus, cloud technology is being received as a transformative and augmentative method by business executives as well as infrastructure architects. Apart from a lot of cost savings, especially capital cost, the much-discussed, dissected, and discoursed cloud paradigm brings to the table a litany of benefits as enumerated below for the benefit of our readers. Corporations mandate their own IT divisions to jump-start the cloud journey whereas others tie up with IT service organizations. Jain [1] says companies benefit by using an outsourcing service provider for their IT transformation because suppliers can

1. Better Manage Cost and Risks – Outsourcing allows buyers to do the job with the least possible risk and at the most optimized cost through their service provider's global delivery model. IT service organizations and system integrators, through their long years of service delivery experience, are capable of overcoming all kinds of impediments to bringing the designated success to their esteemed customers.
2. Support Business Innovation – Due to the repeatable and reusable expertise gained over the years, service providers understand their customers' current and future needs precisely. Accordingly, the right innovation can be quickly incorporated into the solution being supplied. All kinds of architectural, technical, and infrastructure complexities can be taken care of by service providers by simplifying IT through application rationalization and infrastructure consolidation. The IT agility being derived out of this transition leads to business agility.
3. Increase the Market and Mind Shares – Service providers help their clients increase their touch points with their customers, reduce their time to market, and help them deliver more efficient and premium services to their customers. The brand value and competency of business are bound to instantly reach greater heights.
4. Enhance the End-User Experience – Today, the end-user experience of business services is essential for determining the success and survival of a business. There are several nonfunctional (quality of service (QoS)) attributes, such as performance, scalability, availability, security, simplicity, accessibility, usability, and so on. How easy and fast a business transaction is accomplished by business users matters most in this competitive environment.

CONCLUSION

With the adoption of clouds, promising novel business models that include next-generation delivery, pricing, subscription, deployment, and consumption models have come to the forefront; hence, there is an unprecedented rush for cloud adoption. Businesses are seriously evaluating the irresistible cloud option. Professionals are working overtime to identify the constraints (internal as well as external) involved in the adoption process and collaborating with one another toward developing competent technology solutions to overcome the identified limitations. It has been made clear by leading market watchers and analysts that every single company and corporation will have a substantial and strategic presence in clouds in the days to come. Cloud migration strategy is one core requirement for efficiently utilizing the emerging and expanding cloud landscape for the betterment of tomorrow's enterprises.

REFERENCES

1. Rosenthal, B. E., ed. 2010. "How Outsourcing Service Providers Enable Business Growth through IT Infrastructure Transformation," Outsourcing Center, http://www.outsourcing-center.com/2010-09-how-outsourcing-service-providers-enable-business-growth-through-it-infrastructure-transformation-article-39870.html.
2. Hiller, A. September 13, 2011. "The Importance of Policy in Cloud Migration," Data Center Knowledge, http://www.datacenterknowledge.com/archives/2011/09/13/the-importance-of-policy-in-cloud-migration/.
3. Khajeh-Hosseini, A., D. Greenwood, and I. Sommerville. 2010. "Cloud Migration: A Case Study of Migrating an Enterprise IT System to IaaS," *2010 IEEE 3rd International Conference on Cloud Computing (CLOUD)*, St. Andrews, UK, July 5–10, 2010, http://arxiv.org/ftp/arxiv/papers/1002/1002.3492.pdf.
4. Holland, R. March 2011. "Ten Steps to Successful Cloud Migration," Eagle Genomics Ltd., Cambridge, UK, http://www.eaglegenomics.com/download-files/whitepaper/CloudWhitePaper.pdf.
5. CloudOps. 2012. "Step Two: Balancing On-Premise and On-Demand," CloudOps, http://www.cloudops.com/cloud-migration-services/balancing-on-premise-and-on-demand/.
6. Cisco Systems. 2010. "Planning the Migration of Enterprise Applications to the Cloud," Cisco Systems, Inc., http://www.cisco.com/en/US/services/ps2961/ps10364/ps10370/ps11104/Migration_of_Enterprise_Apps_to_Cloud_White_Paper.pdf.
7. Claybrook, B. June 2011. "Resolving Cloud Application Migration Issues," TechTarget, http://searchcloudcomputing.techtarget.com/tutorial/Resolving-cloud-application-migration-issues.

Index

A

ABBs, *see* Architecture building blocks
ABC, *see* Activity-based computing
AC, *see* Analyzer component
AccelOps, 343–346
ACF, *see* Architecture content framework
ACID transactions, 192
Across clouds scenario, 239
Actionable enterprise architecture, IBM, 126–127
Activity-based computing (ABC), 173
Actuation services, 173
Adaptive enterprises, 12, 180
Adeptia Salesforce Integration Accelerator, 293
ADM, *see* Architecture development method
Agent-driven SOA, 154–155
Agile principles, 63
Amazon AWS, 232
Amazon Dynamo, 190, 193
Amazon EC2, 443
Amazon S3, 238
Amazon Simple Queue Service (SQS), 276, 308, 309
Ambient cloud, 26–27, 80–82
American Institute of Certified Public Accountants (AICPA), 368
Analytics-attached business processes, 59
Analyzer component (AC), 313
Apache Cassandra, 194
Apache Hadoop, 196–198
APIs, *see* Application programming interfaces
Appirio, 343
Application architectures, 109, 116, 459, 460
  asynchronous, 456
  components of OEAF, 122
Application domains, 51

Application infrastructure services, 408–409
Application layer, 130
  security, 361
Application-level policy enforcement, 428
Application network, global view of, 442
Application profiling, 461
Application programming interfaces (APIs), 218, 281, 299, 306, 308, 348
  based integration, 272
  cloud, 297, 298
  implementation, 254
  key, 446
  RESTful, 342, 458
  VMware vCloud, 342
Application server, 453, 454
Application service provider (ASP), 328–329
Application services, cloud computing, 407–408
Application-to-application (A2A), 303
AR, *see* Architecture repository
ArchiMate, 128–131
Architectural analysis, FEA process, 119
Architectural definition, FEA process, 119
Architectural development processes, 124
Architectural stack of enterprise cloud, 95–96
Architecture building blocks (ABBs), 113
Architecture content framework (ACF), 112–113
Architecture development method (ADM), 110, 114
  AR, 115
  basic structure of, 111
  guidelines for using, 112
Architecture repository (AR), 115–116
Architecture space in information technology, 3
ARIS Business Architect, 131–132
ARIS platform tools, 131

Printed and bound by CPI Group (UK) Ltd, Croydon, CR0 4YY

23/10/2024

01777673-0019